THE CRY FOR FREEDOM

THE CRY FOR FREEDOM

*An Anthology of the Best That Has Been
Said and Written on Civil Rights Since
1954*

Compiled and Edited by

Frank W. Hale, Jr., *President*

Oakwood College, Huntsville, Alabama

South Brunswick and New York: A. S. Barnes and Company
London: Thomas Yoseloff Ltd

A. S. Barnes and Co., Inc.
Cranbury, New Jersey 08512

Thomas Yoseloff Ltd
108 New Bond Street
London W1Y OQX, England

SBN 498 06709 2
Printed in the United States of America

TO MY WIFE, CHILDREN, AND PARENTS,
and to those students who have helped direct my course
with the inspiration of nearly two decades.

Preface

The Cry for Freedom is an anthology of representative speeches on the urgent issue of civil rights. The collection includes speeches of preachers, educators, Congressmen, lawyers, literary figures, labor leaders, government officials, a diplomat, and civil-rights leaders.

It is the aim of this volume to focus on some of the most important civil-rights speeches given since the famous 1954 Supreme Court Decision, which reflect in some degree America's contribution to a critical issue.

The collection embraces various forms of oratory—deliberative, forensic, philosophic—aflame with the same theme. Our choices of speeches were determined by merit, availability, space, and scope.

One of the features of this collection is the biracial character of the speakers. On a subject so given to swords and stirrings, it is refreshing to see leadership—black and white—use creative means to provide enlightenment in these troubled times.

This book should be useful as a source book for students of the humanities and social sciences. It will provide excellent models and materials for criticism to students of public speaking.

A brief biographical sketch identifies each of the speakers. In addition, I have attempted to give the reader some insight into the occasion and the audience.

In the preparation of this volume I have incurred numerous obligations. It is a pleasure to express gratitude to all of those persons who so graciously contributed their manuscripts, and in doing so, made this anthology possible.

Expressions of appreciation are due to Mrs. Maxine Crump for editorial assistance and for typing the final manuscript and to Mrs. Evelyn Rockhold for her correction of the manuscript and proofreading. Finally, I wish to express appreciation to Pioneer Publishers for permission to reproduce "The Black Revolution" by Malcolm X; to the National Association for the Advancement of Colored People for permission to reproduce the March on Washington speeches of Martin Luther King, Jr., A. Philip Randolph, Walter Reuther, and Roy Wilkins; to the *Journal of Human Relations* for permission to reproduce the speeches of Berl Bernhard and George L. P. Weaver; and to Alfred A. Knopf, Inc., for permission to use six of the poems of Langston Hughes on our division pages.

Frank W. Hale, Jr.

Huntsville, Alabama
1968

Contents

Contents

Contents   11

PART SIX   CIVIL RIGHTS ACTIVISTS

Introduction

When the Supreme Court "manifesto" of 1954 concluded that "the doctrine of 'separate but equal' has no place" in the field of public education, it accelerated the struggle against the traditional forms of racial and religious discrimination in the United States. In affirming the truth that law lends support to our highest ideals, the decision provided civil-rights champions with a "new birth," thus creating the dramatic surge that made possible the series of Civil Rights Acts which followed in 1957, 1959, 1964, and 1965.

Though men have, with tongue and pen, protested conditions like *de facto* segregation, poverty, inadequate housing, and the disparity of income between whites and nonwhites, efforts to implement the new legislation will require agitation and protest to be effective.

It is in this vein that the task of the orator and the writer take on new meaning. This anthology will present some of the significant speeches that have treated selected issues or aspects of the civil-rights controversy. Some few articles have also been included in this volume because of their stimulating and helpful contribution to the progress of the cause. Speakers and writers were chosen on the basis of their ability, effectiveness, and concern in seeking to resolve the great American problem of our century.

Speechmaking has always flourished in enlightened society. The distinguishing characteristic of the Greek and Roman mind is its intrinsic and intimate relation with oratory. No Greek prose presents us with a more vivid or instructive picture of Greek life and thought than Greek oratory. Ehninger reminds us that in the Hellenic world of the fifth century B.C., "a demand for excellence in speaking and an environment congenial to the study of rhetoric converged to produce the first organized works on the subject."[1]

---

[1] Douglass Ehninger, "History of Rhetoric and Public Address," *Introduction to the Field of Speech* (Chicago: Scott, Foresman and Company, 1965), p. 165.

Politics is made more real and society more animated as we study the oratory of a civilization. Public speaking is an instrument of power and persuasion. The competition for public approval and acceptance is the very heart of a democracy. Such a credo was implied in Aristotle's definition of oratory as "the faculty of discovering all of the available means of persuasion." Persuasion, consequently, aims at influencing human opinion and conduct.

The credibility of oratory as a source for history has on occasion been in question. It would be a pity to disregard the world of ideas, brought so vividly into focus by the great orators of the past and present, as insignificant. Issues become practical and personal, and events are illuminated when the dead facts are resurrected to the imaginative expressions of those who have insight and invention.

For at times, it appeared that oratory was a lost art. As the newspapers, radio, and television gained in ascendency as a means of providing information to the public, it is apparent that in some quarters speech became less conspicuous as an instrument of persuasion. However, the crises which produced two world wars also spawned orators of the caliber of Winston Churchill and Franklin Delano Roosevelt.

The ancients categorized oratory into three classes: deliberative, forensic, and epideictic. In our day we have contributed pulpit speaking, the lecture, business speaking, and the technical presentation as additional types. Deliberative speaking concerned itself with political speeches delivered as a part of political campaigns or before legislative bodies. The forensic speech was designed to protest the rights of citizens in the early courts. In epideictic oratory the ancients aimed to please their hearers by delivering commemorative addresses. The great position of influence which the Christian Church has held since the fourth century helped to introduce pulpit oratory as a new type, with substantial influence after this period. Reformation and Counter-Reformation preachers established once and for all the reality of the religious platform as a special oratorical type.

It is in the category of pulpit speaking that the Negro as a spokesman in the American community has made his mark. This, of course, results from the fact that generally he has not been an active participant in legislative halls or in courts. When Rosa Parks refused to move to the back of a city bus in Montgomery, Alabama, on December 1, 1955, she not only produced a new form of Negro protest in the famous bus boycott, but she also triggered the beginning of a new type of leadership in the Negro ministry, as evidenced by the sudden spiraling prominence of Dr. Martin Luther King, Jr., as a dynamic leader in the civil rights crusade. He recognized full well that religion was an outlet for the Negro's deepest feelings of an environment that is overwhelmingly against him. His leadership was not based on exploitation for personal gain, but rather on the needs of the Negro masses whose everyday problems he shared.

Fortunately the burden of the civil-rights effort has not rested upon the shoulders of the Negro alone. The Negro's "cry for freedom" has carried with it a "humanizing theme" that has appealed to the ethical sense in men of goodwill from every station of life. Although there are discordant elements in our society that would expand the chasm that exists between black and white America, there is reason to be hopeful; for blacks and whites with direct-action effectiveness often march, demonstrate, walk-in, sit-in, lie-in, and sleep-in to dramatize their concern for the worth and dignity of the human individual.

The biracial character of this volume further attests to the concern that binds brothers, black and white, in bridging the gap that has separated Americans into black and white camps. Leaders in religion, government, education, jurisprudence, and the service fields recognize the alternatives which rest before us. They, as leaders, are concerned with the shaping of public opinion. They are dedicated to the proposition that opportunities must be provided for the Negro and other minorities to enter the mainstream of American life. They know full well that whether out of altruism or simply out of the desire to survive, the United States, competitor that she is in the international arena, cannot afford to make any individual in her society expendable. They know, too, that our future may very well be determined by the extent to which they can influence others to believe as they believe and to respond to the Negro's "cry for freedom." The sliding scale of imponderables, which may result if we do otherwise, has left us with little choice.

F. W. H.

THE CRY FOR FREEDOM

PART ONE

Men of Letters

Democracy is a way of life that recognizes the dignity of the human spirit. It values the individual above the state, and makes government the servant of the people. In the humanist tradition of Western civilization, the Greeks provide us with some of the earliest literary support for the doctrine of equality for all men.

The writers of the Declaration of Independence suggested that all men have a right to "pursue" happiness unimpeded by unreasonable obstacles. And so, James Baldwin, Harry Golden, Langston Hughes, and a host of others share a concern over the black man's fate in America by daring to challenge "the system" that would thwart his progress.

Baldwin, like no other writer, is insulting and demanding in his dramatization of the black-white conflict. He blatantly accuses the white man of being the instrument of the Negro's oppression; yet he seems less preoccupied with the results of inequalities than have some other writers.

But now that some writers have dared to assert that no state is any stronger than the value which it gives to each individual within it, America is alerted to her role as never before as leader, teacher, and servant of all of her people.

THE NEGRO MOTHER
—Langston Hughes

Children, I come back today
To tell you a story of the long dark way
That I had to climb, that I had to know
In order that the race might live and grow.
Look at my face—dark as the night—
Yet shining like the sun with love's true light.
I am the child they stole from the sand
Three hundred years ago in Africa's land.
I am the dark girl who crossed the wide sea
Carrying in my body the seed of the free.
I am the woman who worked in the field
Bringing the cotton and the corn to yield.
I am the one who labored as a slave,
Beaten and mistreated for the work that I gave—
Children sold away from me, husband sold, too.
No safety, no love, no respect was I due.
Three hundred years in the deepest South:
But God put a song and a prayer in my mouth.
God put a dream like steel in my soul.
Now, through my children, I'm reaching the goal.
Now, through my children, young and free,
I realize the blessings denied to me.
I couldn't read then. I couldn't write.
I had nothing, back there in the night.
Sometimes, the valley filled with tears,
But I kept trudging on through the lonely years.
Sometimes, the road was hot with sun,
But I had to keep on till my work was done:
I *had* to keep on! No stopping for me—
I was the seed of the coming Free.
I nourished the dream that nothing could smother
Deep in my breast—the Negro mother.
I had only hope then, but now through you,
Dark ones of today, my dreams must come true:
All you dark children in the world out there,
Remember my sweat, my pain, my despair.
Remember my years, heavy with sorrow—
And make of those years a torch for tomorrow.

Make of my past a road to the light
Out of the darkness, the ignorance, the night.
Life high my banner out of the dust.
Stand like free men supporting my trust.
Believe in the right, let none push you back.
Remember the whip and the slaver's track.
Remember how the strong in struggle and strife
Still bar you the way, and deny you life—
But march ever forward, breaking down bars.
Look ever upward at the sun and the stars.
Oh, my dark children, may my dreams and my prayers
Impel you forever up the great stairs—
For I will be with you till no white brother
Dares keep down the children of the Negro mother.

The Negro Child—His Self-Image
JAMES BALDWIN

James Baldwin, the son of David and Berdis Emma (Jones) Baldwin, was born in New York City in 1924 and educated there. He is the recipient of the Rosenwald (1948), Guggenheim (1954), and Partisan Review (1956) Fellowships, the National Institute of Arts and Letters Award (1956), and the Ford Foundation Grant-In-Aid (1959). After being named a Guggenheim Fellow, he spent some time in Europe before returning to America to broaden his literary career. James Baldwin is a member of the National Advisory Board of the Congress of Racial Equality (CORE) and the National Committee for Sane Nuclear Policy. He is an avid lecturer on civil rights. His best-known writings include *Go Tell It on the Mountain* (1953); *Notes of a Native Son* (1955); *Giovanni's Room* (1958); *Nobody Knows My Name* (1960); *Another Country* (1962); *The Fire Next Time* (1963); and *Blues for Mr. Charlie* (1964).

The speech printed here was given by Mr. Baldwin on October 16, 1963, in New York City's Harlem as part of a special in-service course taken by about two hundred of the city's public school teachers. The course was called "The Negro: His Role in the Culture and Life of the United States," and James Baldwin, born and brought up in Harlem, again "faced facts" as he talked to the teachers about "The Negro Child—His Self-Image."

* * *

Let's begin by saying that we are living through a very dangerous time. Everyone in this room is in one way or another aware of that. We are in a revolutionary situation, no matter how unpopular that word has become in this country. The society in which we live is desperately menaced, not by Khrushchev, but from within. So any citizen of this country who figures himself as responsible—and particularly those of you who deal with the minds and hearts of young people—must be prepared to "go for broke." Or to put it another way, you must understand that in the attempt to correct so many generations of bad faith and cruelty, when it is operating not only in the classroom but in society, you will meet the most fantastic, the most brutal, and the most determined resistance. There is no point in pretending that this won't happen.

Now, since I am talking to schoolteachers and I am not a teacher myself, and in some ways am fairly easily intimidated, I beg you to let me leave that and go back to what I think to be the entire purpose of education in the first place. It would seem to me that when a child is born, if I'm the child's parent, it is my oblgiation and my high duty to civilize that child. Man is a social animal. He cannot exist without a society. A society, in turn, depends on certain things which everyone within that society takes for granted. Now, the crucial paradox which confronts us here is that the whole process of education occurs within a social framework and is designed to perpetuate the aims of society. Thus, for example, the boys and girls who were born during the era of the Third Reich, when educated to the purposes of the Third Reich, became barbarians. The paradox of education is precisely this—that as one begins to become conscious one begins to examine the society in which he is being educated. The purpose of education, finally, is to create in a person the ability to look at the world for himself, to make his own decisions, to say to himself this is black or this is white, to decide for himself whether there is a God in heaven or not. To ask questions of the universe, and then learn to live with those questions, is the way he achieves his own identity. But no society is really anxious to have that kind of person around. What societies really, ideally, want is a citizenry which will simply obey the rules of society. If a society succeeds in this, that society is about to perish. The obligation of anyone who thinks of himself as responsible is to examine society and try to change it and to fight it—at no matter what risk. This is the only hope society has. This is the only way societies change.

Now, if what I have tried to sketch has any validity, it becomes thoroughly clear, at least to me, that any Negro who is born in this country and undergoes the American educational system runs the risk of becoming schizophrenic. On the one hand he is born in the shadow of the stars and stripes and he is assured it represents a nation which has never lost a war. He pledges allegiance to that flag which guarantees "liberty and justice for all." He is part of a country in which anyone can become President, and so forth. But on the other hand he is also assured by his country and his countrymen that he has never contributed anything to civilization—that his past is nothing more than a record of humiliations gladly endured. He is assured by the republic that he, his father, his mother, and his ancestors were happy, shiftless, watermelon-eating darkies who loved Mr. Charlie and Miss Ann, that the value he has as a black man is proven by one thing only—his devotion to white people. If you think I am exaggerating, examine the myths which proliferate in this country about Negroes.

Now all this enters the child's consciousness much sooner than we as adults would like to think it does. As adults, we are easily fooled because we are so anxious to be fooled. But children are very different. Children, not yet aware that it is dangerous to look too deeply at anything, look at everything, look at each other, and draw their own conclusions. They don't have the vocabulary to express what they see, and we, their elders, know how to intimidate them very easily and very soon. But a black child, looking at the world around him, though he cannot know quite what to make of it, is aware that there is a reason why his mother works so hard, why his father is always on edge. He is aware that there is some reason why, if he sits down in the front of the bus, his father or mother slaps him and drags him to the back of the bus. He is aware that there is some terrible weight on his parents' shoulders which menaces him. And it isn't long—in fact it begins when he is in school—before he discovers the shape of his oppression.

Let us say that the child is seven years old and I am his father, and I decide to take him to the zoo, or to Madison Square Garden, or to the UN Buildings, or to any of the tremendous monuments we find all over New York. We get into a bus and we go from where I live on 121st Street and Seventh Avenue downtown through the park and we get into New York City, which is not Harlem. Now, where the boy lives—even if it is a housing project—is in an undesirable neighborhood. If he lives in one of those housing projects of which everyone in New York is so proud, he has at the front door, if not closer, the pimps, the whores, the junkies—in a word, the danger of life in the ghetto. And the child knows this, though he doesn't know why.

I still remember my first sight of New York. It was really another

city when I was born—where I was born. We looked down over the
Park Avenue streetcar tracks. It was Park Avenue, but I didn't know
what Park Avenue meant *downtown*. The Park Avenue I grew up on,
which is still standing, is dark and dirty. No one would dream of
opening a Tiffany's on that Park Avenue, and when you go downtown
you discover that you are literally in the white world. It is rich—or at
least it looks rich. It is clean—because they collect garbage downtown.
There are doormen. People walk about as though they owned where
they are—and indeed they do. And it's a great shock. It's very hard
to relate yourself to this. You don't know what it means. You know—
you know instinctively—that none of this is for you. You know this
before you are told. And who is it for and who is paying for it? And
why isn't it for you?

Later on when you become a grocery boy or messenger and you
try to enter one of those buildings a man says, "Go to the back door."
Still later, if you happen by some odd chance to have a friend in one
of those buildings, the man says, "Where's your package?" Now this
by no means is the core of the matter. What I'm trying to get at is
that by this time the Negro child has had, effectively, almost all the
doors of opportunity slammed in his face, and there are very few
things he can do about it. He can more or less accept it with an absolutely inarticulate and dangerous rage inside—all the more dangerous
because it is never expressed. It is precisely those silent people whom
white people see every day of their lives—I mean your porter and
your maid, who never say anything more than "Yes Sir" and "No
Ma'am." They will tell you it's raining if that is what you want to
hear, and they will tell you the sun is shining if *that* is what you want
to hear. They really hate you—really hate you because in their eyes
(and they're right) you stand between them and life. I want to come
back to that in a moment. It is the most sinister of the facts, I think,
which we now face.

There is something else the Negro child can do, too. Every street
boy—and I was a street boy, so I know—looking at the society which
has produced him, looking at the standards of that society which are
not honored by anybody, looking at your churches and the government and the politicians, understands that this structure is operated
for someone else's benefit—not for his. And there's no room in it for
him. If he is really cunning, really ruthless, really strong—and many
of us are—he becomes a kind of criminal. He becomes a kind of
criminal because that's the only way he can live. Harlem and every
ghetto in this city—every ghetto in this country—is full of people who
live outside the law. They wouldn't dream of calling a policeman.

They wouldn't, for a moment, listen to any of those professions of which we are so proud on the Fourth of July. They have turned away from this country forever and totally. They live by their wits and really long to see the day when the entire structure comes down.

The point of all this is that black men were brought here as a source of cheap labor. They were indispensable to the economy. In order to justify the fact that men were treated as though they were animals, the white republic had to brainwash itself into believing that they were, indeed, animals and *deserved* to be treated like animals. Therefore it is almost impossible for any Negro child to discover anything about his actual history. The reason is that this "animal," once he suspects his own worth, once he starts believing that he is a man, has begun to attack the entire power structure. This is why America has spent such a long time keeping the Negro in his place. What I am trying to suggest to you is that it was not an accident, it was not an act of God, it was not done by well-meaning people meddling into something which they didn't understand. It was a deliberate policy hammered into place in order to make money from black flesh. And now, in 1963, because we have never faced this fact, we are in intolerable trouble.

The Reconstruction, as I read the evidence, was a bargain between the North and South to this effect: "We've liberated them from the land—and delivered them to the bosses." When we left Mississippi to come North we did not come to freedom. We came to the bottom of the labor market, and we are still there. Even the Depression of the 1930's failed to make a dent in Negroes' relationship to white workers in the labor unions. Even today, so brainwashed is this republic that people seriously ask in what they suppose to be good faith, "What does the Negro want?" I've heard a great many asinine questions in my life, but that is perhaps the most asinine and perhaps the most insulting. But the point here is that people who ask that question, thinking that they ask it in good faith, are really the victims of this conspiracy to make Negroes believe they are less than human.

In order for me to live, I decided very early that some mistake had been made somewhere. I was not a "nigger" even though you called me one. But if I was a "nigger" in your eyes, there was something about *you*—there was something *you* needed. I had to realize when I was very young that I was none of those things I was told I was. I was not, for example, happy. I never touched a watermelon for all kinds of reasons. I had been invented by white people, and I knew enough about life by this time to understand that whatever you invent, whatever you project, is you! So where we are now is that a whole country of people believe I'm a "nigger," and I *don't*, and the battle's on! Because if I am not what I've been told I am, then it means that *you're* not what you thought *you* were *either*! And that is the crisis.

It is not really a "Negro revolution" that is upsetting this country. What is upsetting the country is a sense of its own identity. If, for example, one managed to change the curriculum in all the schools so that Negroes learned more about themselves and their real contributions to this culture, you would be liberating not only Negroes, you'd be liberating white people who know nothing about their own history. And the reason is that if you are compelled to lie about one aspect of anybody's history, you must lie about it all. If you have to lie about my real role here, if you have to pretend that I hoed all that cotton just because I loved you, then you have done something to yourself. You are mad.

Now let's go back a minute. I talked earlier about those silent people—the porter and the maid—who, as I said, don't look up at the sky if you ask them if it is raining, but look into your face. My ancestors and I were very well trained. We understood very early that this was not a Christian nation. It didn't matter what you said or how often you went to church. My father and my mother and my grandfather and my grandmother knew that Christians didn't act this way. It was as simple as that. And if that was so there was no point in dealing with whtite people in terms of their own moral professions, for they were not going to honor them. What one did was to turn away, smiling all the time, and tell white people what they wanted to hear. But people always accuse you of reckless talk when you say this.

All this means that there are in this country tremendous reservoirs of bitterness which have never been able to find an outlet, but may find an outlet soon. It means that well-meaning white liberals place themselves in great danger when they try to deal with Negroes as though they were missionaries. It means, in brief, that a great price is demanded to liberate all those silent people so that they can breathe for the first time and *tell* you what they think of you. And a price is demanded to liberate all those white children—some of them near forty—who have never grown up, and who never will grow up, because they have no sense of their identity.

What passes for identity in America is a series of myths about one's heroic ancestors. It's astounding to me, for example, that so many people really appear to believe that the country was founded by a band of heroes who wanted to be free. That happens not to be true. What happened was that some people left Europe because they couldn't stay there any longer and had to go someplace else to make it. That's all. They were hungry, they were poor, they were convicts. Those who were making it in England, for example, did not get on the *Mayflower*. That's how the country was settled. Not by Gary Cooper. Yet we have a whole race of people, a whole republic, who believe the myths to the point where even today they select political representatives, as far as I can tell, by how closely they resemble Gary Cooper. Now this is dangerously infantile, and it shows in every level of national life. When I was living in Europe, for example, one of the worst revelations to me was the way Americans walked around Europe buying this and buying that and insulting everybody—not even out of malice, just because they didn't know any better. Well, that is the way they have always treated me. They weren't cruel, they just didn't know you were alive. They didn't know you had any feelings.

What I am trying to suggest here is that in the doing of all this for 100 years or more, it is the American white man who has long since lost his grip on reality. In some peculiar way, having created this myth about Negroes, and the myth about his own history, he created myths about the world so that, for example, he was astounded that some people could prefer Castro, astounded that there are people in the world who don't go into hiding when they hear the word "communism," astounded that communism is one of the realities of the twentieth century which we will not overcome by pretending that it does not exist. The political level in this country now, on the part of people who should know better, is abysmal.

The Bible says somewhere that where there is no vision the people perish. I don't think anyone can doubt that in this country today we are menaced—intolerably menaced—by a lack of vision.

It is inconceivable that a sovereign people should continue, as we do so abjectly, to say, "I can't do anything about it. It's the government." The government is the creation of the people. It is responsible to the people. And the people are responsible for it. No American has the right to allow the present government to say, when Negro children are being bombed and hosed and shot and beaten all over the Deep South, that there is nothing we can do about it. There must have been a day in this country's life when the bombing of four children in Sunday School would have created a public uproar and endangered the life of a Governor Wallace. It happened here and there was no public uproar.

I began by saying that one of the paradoxes of education was that precisely at the point when you begin to develop a conscience, you must find yourself at war with your society. It is your responsibility to change society if you think of yourself as an educated person. And on the basis of the evidence—the moral and political evidence—one is compelled to say that this is a backward society. Now if I were a teacher in this school, or any Negro school, and I was dealing with Negro children, who were in my care only a few hours of every day and would then return to their homes and to the streets, children who have an apprehension of their future which with every hour grows grimmer and darker, I would try to teach them—I would try to make them know—that those streets, those houses, those dangers, those agonies by which they are surrounded, are criminal. I would try to make each child know that these things are the results of a criminal conspiracy to destroy him. I would teach him that if he intends to get to be a man, he must at once decide that he is stronger than this conspiracy and that he must never make his peace with it. And that one of his weapons for refusing to make his peace with it and for destroying it depends on what he decides he is worth. I would teach him that there are currently very few standards in this country which are worth a man's respect. That it is up to him to begin to change these standards for the sake of the life and the health of the country. I would suggest to him that the popular culture—as represented, for example, on television and in comic books and in movies—is based on fantasies created by very ill people, and he must be aware that these are fantasies that have nothing to do with reality. I would teach him that the press he reads is not as free as it says it is—and that he can do something about that, too. I would try to make him know that just as American history is longer, larger, more various, more beautiful, and more terrible than anything anyone has ever said about it, so is the world larger, more daring, more beautiful and more terrible, but principally larger—and that it belongs to him. I would teach him that he doesn't have to be bound by the expediencies of any given Administration, any given policy, any given time—that he has the right and the necessity to examine everything. I would try to show him that one has not learned anything about Castro when one says, "He is a Communist." This is a way of *not* learning something about Castro, something about Cuba, something, in fact, about the world. I would suggest to him that he is living, at the moment, in an enormous province. America is not the world and if America is going to become a nation, she must find a way—and this child must help her to find a way—to use the tremendous potential and tremendous energy which this child represents. If this country does not find a way to use that energy, it will be destroyed by that energy.

Some Mob

KENNETH G. CRAWFORD

Kenneth Gale Crawford was born in Spartan, Wisconsin, on May 27, 1902, the son of Robert Levy and Madge (Gale) Crawford. Having earned degrees from the Bachelor of Arts (Beloit College, 1924) to Doctor of Letters (1954) and then awarded the honorary degree of Doctor of Laws (Olivet College), he has been active in journalism since 1924.

Beginning his career as a United Press reporter in the Midwest, Kenneth Crawford has worked as a news bureau manager, Washington correspondent, war correspondent (North Africa, Italy, the Middle East, England, France, 1943–44), and is currently a contributing editor for *Newsweek*, writing under the Washington by-line.

He has been decorated with the United States Navy Commendation and the French Liberation Medal; he is past president (1939–40) of the American Newspaper Guild, and is a member of the National Press Club, Overseas Writers (Washington); City Tavern (Georgetown); Players (New York). He has been married to Elisabeth Bartholomew since 1928, and is the father of a son and a daughter. He is the author of *The Pressure Boys* (1939) and *Report on North Africa* (1943).

"Some Mob," which first appeared in Crawford's *Newsweek* column September 9, 1963, "accounts" and "discounts" the March on Washington of August 28, 1963.

*   *   *

Now that it is over, it would be unnecessarily cruel to recall some of the forebodings about the March on Washington for civil rights and jobs if the foreboders were identified. Several Congressmen instructed their female employes to stay at home with doors securely locked because the streets would not be safe. Some closed their offices and talked as though they thought barricades were indicated. Others could hardly wait for a chance to defy the mob—to strike poses and announce that they would not be coerced. Indeed, some didn't wait. They struck poses and announced that they wouldn't be coerced if anybody tried to coerce them.

A police detail large enough for President de Gaulle was assigned to the Capitol to guard the lawmakers from their constituents. Contingents of troops stood by at nearby Army posts to reinforce the police in case the constituents won.

Many business establishments closed down and a large proportion of government workers sacrificed a day of annual leave to stay away from their offices. Washington citizens were officially advised to avoid the downtown section unless participating in the march.

BIG AND GENTLE

As it turned out, the 210,000 marchers were the best mannered, best disciplined, and most engaging, as well as the biggest delegation of petitioners for the redress of grievances this city has received within the memory of its oldest demonstration fans. The Capitol was freer of lobbyists, including masters of the craft of subtle coercion, than it has been on any working day this year. Congressmen's female assistants were safer on the streets than they would have been indoors with Congressmen's male assistants, or in some cases, with the Congressmen themselves. Police reported fewer crimes than usual—and none by the marchers.

Nobody got a chance to defy anybody. One white policeman, stationed at Lincoln Memorial and resigned to inactivity, was observed clapping in time to Mahalia Jackson's gospel. Some of the few Washingtonians who ignored official advice in order to have a look at the Hollywood contingent, stayed to cheer Dr. Martin Luther King, Jr., whose dream of a just tomorrow proved that the art of oratory is not yet dead in America, the evidence in Congress to the contrary notwithstanding.

FALSE PROPHETS

The imposing dignity and patience of A. Philip Randolph, who conceived the march as a display of the Negro's determination to share first-class citizenship 100 years after Lincoln's Emancipation Proclamation, toned the whole affair. The only embarrassing moments of the day were provided by the Senators picked by television interviewers to "balance" their coverage. Russell Long, telling television watchers that what they were seeing was a mob scene, must have made them wonder whether his deficiency was of eyesight or of heart.

And his wasn't the only, or the worst, betrayal of poverty of spirit. David Lawrence could write, even with the evidence all in, that "the March will go down in history as marking a day of public disgrace."

As a result, he lamented, tens of thousands of Washingtonians "remained secluded in their homes lest they become injured or subjected to unwarranted delays in moving to and from their residences." Lawrence in recent newspaper columns also has warned against miscegenation, quoted Lincoln against race equality, and suggested that rape victims march on Washington. He of course agreed with Long that Washington had been menaced by a mob on August 28.

Some mob. If you bumped into a marcher, he smiled and said: "Sorry. Excuse me." Maybe Lawrence and Long have led such sheltered lives that they've never seen a mob or a gathering of pleasant people with a serious purpose and so can't tell the difference between them. Or perhaps devotion to the cause of inequality obscures the distinction for both of them. If lack of experience has left a blank spot in their education, it may yet be filled in. For if the Negro can't join America Randolph's way and King's way, he'll try somebody else's way. And it won't be Lawrence's way.

The Conscience of the North

TRUMAN NELSON

John Truman Nelson was born February 18, 1912, in Lynn, Massachusetts, the son of John Wilson and Ida (Seymour) Nelson. A former stagehand and spearbearer with a repertory theater company, he worked at General Electric Company in Lynn, Massachusetts, as a machinist for ten years. Now a full-time writer and lecturer, Nelson has devoted his literary career to bringing the lonely rebels of American history to the attention of the public. He writes what he calls "the novel of the organic event." He believes that by reconstructing the actual history, the places, the personalities and the physical and ideological motion of some turning and breaking point in history, deep psychological truth may be achieved. His writings include *The Sin of the Prophet* (1952), *Passion by the Brook* (1953), *The Surveyor* (1960), and *John Brown Reader, Anthology* (1959). Currently he is completing the novel, *Man's Blood*, a work on John Brown at Harper's Ferry. He has also contributed to *Nation, New York Times Sunday Magazine, Saturday Review*, and other magazines.

As a self-educated man, author Nelson says, "I have no diplomas, no passports whatsoever to the academic world. I am a graduate of the public library."

"The Conscience of the North" was delivered before the Community Church of Boston in the Boston Conservatory Auditorium on March 12, 1961. It is another striking position presentation pinpointing Nelson's great concern for the freedom of all men.

* * *

The first thoughts, the first words that come to me on occupying this desk must be in praise, in thanksgiving to, and in memory of, the great prophet who gathered this congregation over a hundred years ago. At every occasion at which the human condition, its plight, and its potential becomes the question of the hour, the enduring presence of Theodore Parker is evoked in my mind and in the mind of your present preacher, the carrier of the Parker tradition.

It is Theodore Parker who makes it possible for me to stand here and bear witness against the wrong that I perceive. It is Theodore Parker who brings all of you here, week after week, to one of the few places in the country where public crime, official crimes, acts of repression and sickness against the people of the country and the world are dealt with rationally, intelligently, and in earnest, and whenever necessary, the public punishment of denunciation is meted out. Without this there are many of us who would feel that humanity has fallen into cureless ruin, who would suspect our own unspoken revulsions and dissents and sour ourselves forever out of that faith in man and his perfectibility which saves us from melancholy and malignity . . . and even madness and self-doom.

The reason why Parker could do this and why he could maintain the continuity of his purpose and his strength in the personalities and the purposes of those hundreds of scholars, dissenters, radicals, and truthtellers who have followed him here, is because he founded this pulpit as a place where a man was obliged to deal out to you his life, passed through the fire of his thought . . . still roughly fused by this fire, with all the underground edges of his effort, his confusion, and his agony. The example Parker laid down here for others to follow was that conscience was a primary function of man and should be listened to above every other voice.

We used to believe that we could be told that our conscience should accept or reject. It used to have much to do with whether we prayed enough, whether we were obedient, or sexless, or dutiful to our betters or our employers or to a wrathful God who crushed erring man like a worm beneath his enormous boot. Even Parker, who more than any other theologian destroyed this notion that conscience was a kind of invisible concentration camp, put it that conscience disclosed the moral law of God . . . and that God, in turn, was absolute perfection. I don't want to offend anyone here but I must say that anyone who waits for the voice of God to tell him what to do will never hear it.

He may hear some irresistible command that to follow out may bring him trouble and woe, particularly if it enjoins him to attack the vested power of the community or state. It will come lunging out of his deepest consciousness with a divine imperative and it does not really matter who put it there. It is my belief that it is our social existence that determines the consciousness from which these compelling calls to action arise. This is not new, but was stated by another great prophet of Parker's time.

What is or is not the "Conscience of the North" is a big and actually indefinable subject. But we do know, by observation and sensation, the quality of the world around us and we do know that there are certain ideological forms existing in the placenta of time and place in which we grow that can make us conscious of vast moral problems and contradictions and which arouse in us compulsion to act on them on one side or the other.

This is what I mean then when I talk about the conscience of the North; its reflection of the life around us. I know that it exists: society demands it . . . there is no real escape from our consciousness of the real world. Wendell Phillips had a very good definition of conscience. He called it the common sense of the mass. But in order to create this conscience so that it will be mature, active, and mutually effective, it must be confronted with realities day by day, so that the whole complex of events and contradictions which stir men into action from principle is given concrete expression before our eyes. You cannot get it by listening to Jack Paar, Mort Sahl records, or joining the Book-of-the-Month Club. You have to really know the way things are.

One majestic moment of human advance which has penetrated the whole American consciousness, I believe, is the emergence of the new African nations and the evidence it presents that the brutal colonial conquest by the white man of the darker people has come almost to an end. The two great power blocks of the world are frantically courting the Africans; the red carpet is out in Washington and Moscow.

This is all to the good and I applaud it but I still find it somewhat sickening that with all this adulation, all these fervent promises of cooperation, of defense to the death of the liberty, fraternity, and equality of the black man ten thousand miles off, a black man trying to buy a modest home in Danvers, Massachusetts, has to go to the courts and invoke the law before he can get the liberty, fraternity, and equality which has been his birthright and privilege since 1776, right here at home.

I find it equally sickening to hear all these pious disclaimers of any sympathy with segregation in the South, without any concern for the fact that there are segregated schools in Boston . . . schools in which over ninety percent of the pupils are Negroes . . . not by law, but by the unwritten commandment of our business civilization which has forced the Negro citizens to live almost exclusively in the ninth and twelfth wards of Roxbury.

You may feel that it is sensationalism for me to call these schools segregated. But there has been a recent court fight in New Rochelle over this very situation, segregation by school district. There it was legally decided that the Supreme Court in finding that segregated education is injurious to children, laid down the constitutional principle that segregated education violates the constitutional rights of the children of minority groups.

It is a fact of life that in Boston the Negro people have made three migrations and in every one of them have been compelled to live together in restriction. They have moved from the West End to the South End to Roxbury, intact from first to last as an unwanted minority group, while every other ethnic minority has passed into integration with the whole community. It is also a fact of life that the Negro population is increasing, and the problem is becoming more intense, while other minorities are decreasing. By 1940 the increase was 23,000 plus, in 1950, 42,000 plus, in 1960, approximately 55,000.

We all know why these people come here and where they come from. The hope that they had of their children being educated in equality in their Southern homeplace because of a decision of the highest court in the land has been answered there by the integration of about 74 children in the first five years, a rate of acquiescence in which it would take nearly eighty thousand years for the two million five hundred thousand children to receive what has always been one of their inalienable rights.

So they come here and find more of the same . . . schools crowded with other Negroes, apartments and houses as unavailable to them outside the Negro district as if they were back in Dixie. The segregation is neither open or lawful here . . . it is a kind of sneaky, underhanded experience in which they are met face to face with smiles and agreement and cut to the quick when their back is turned . . . somehow never being able to prove that they are being kept out of schools, jobs, or residential districts but never getting there either. But all the same, they are infinitely better here, for anyone who discriminates against them is not only befouling his conscience, he is breaking the law of his state and should and can be punished.

Nevertheless the glaring discrepancy between what official America is saying to black Africa and what it is doing to black Americans is so shocking, so profoundly evil, so indicative of a split in our national consciousness that I begin to wonder if the whole nation is not insane . . . or at least so out of touch with reality, with rational thinking, that some terrible doom is awaiting us, some awful day of reckoning. In April of 1960, the best reporter of *The New York Times* described the conditions which are driving these fellow Americans to tear up their roots of generations and come to us as wanderers, as political refugees, for us to accept with love and compassion.

> Every channel of communication, every medium of mutual interest, every reasoned approach, every inch of middle ground has been fragmented by the emotional dynamite of racism, enforced by the whip, the razor, the gun, the bomb, the torch, the club, the knife, the mob, the police and many branches of the state's apparatus. The difference between Johannesburg and Birmingham, said a Negro who came South recently from the Middle West . . . is that here they have not opened fire yet with the tanks and the big guns.

When I read this or think about it, I wonder how in good conscience the American people can think of anything else . . . why they worry about the Soviet or Cuba with this awful cancer eating at our inside! I marvel that we can face the men of color anywhere, in the United Nations or elsewhere in the world, where they are the majority of this earth's people. There is no place in this planet where they have not suffered from the bloody advance and triumph of our white business civilization. W. E. B. DuBois, the great Negro prophet, said this about it:

> This is the modern paradox of sin before which the Puritan stands open-mouthed and mute. A group, a nation or a race, commits murder, and rape, steals and destroys, yet no individual is guilty, no one is to blame, no one can be punished. The black world squirms beneath the feet of the white in impotent fury or sullen hate.

There are many Americans pondering this . . . some fearfully. Some dreading that when the day of reckoning comes and the sleeping giant

of color rises in his might and sets things to right, that he will follow
our path and mete out justice and rewards according to the pigmenta-
tion of the skin.

There are others, and Theodore Parker was one of them, who find
a racial defect in the circumstance that the darker people have not
risen long before to defend their rights. The answer to that is, they
have, but they were suppressed and the history of their uprisings
suppressed along with them. When the white man rises up to claim
gloriously his inalienable rights under natural law, he is universally
applauded by other white men as a liberator, as a saint. The black
man's revolution is a bestial, servile insurrection when the white man
tells the tale.

When Garrison, here in Boston, was being mobbed by gentlemen
of property and standing for saying to the black men, cast off your
chains, your masters are thieves, kidnappers, and murdering scoundrels
with no moral right to enslave you, these same gentlemen were holding enthusiastic meetings in Faneuil Hall to acclaim the glorious
revolution in France, the glorious revolution in Greece, in Hungary,
in Poland.

Tiny Boston school children were taught to read by the revolutionary texts of Adams, Otis, and Hancock, but when the Negro David
Walker published his revolutionary tract known as "Walker's Appeal,"
it was instantly and hysterically denounced and suppressed and a year
afterward, its author was dead, under mysterious circumstances. David
Walker had assured his brethren that they would be free, if not
peaceably, then by the crushing arm of power. If they were treated
as men, they would use power as men; if as brutes, their triumph
would be as brutish as the slaveholders, who had already piled up a
debt of unspeakable wrongs against them, wrongs that came back to
haunt him in the terrors of the night. As long as the Declaration of
Independence remained a living creed in this country, David Walker
said,

> My color will root some of them off the face of the earth. They
> shall have enough of making slaves. This country is more ours than
> theirs, we have enriched it more with our blood and tears.

David Walker in his day felt the recoil of those well-meaning senti-
mentalists to whom any expression of hate for a vulgar abomination
and who said then, and are saying today, that any violence by the
Negro in the South will "lose him all his friends." But this did not
bother him. "Some will accuse us of a bad spirit," he said, "but I

do not care. You should not be astonished that we hate you, for we are men and we cannot help but hate you while you are treating us as dogs."

It is a pity that the insidious evil of racism has stained so deeply into our national consciousness that this revolutionary tract, written in 1839, of such noble intensity, such fierce pride, such consummate powers of eloquence and intellect, is missing from almost all historical indexes and bibliographies. Otherwise, it is thought highly desirable, in fact it is demanded that our historians remind every other white that this country was founded on the moral concept that resistance to dictators, large or small, or to oppressive laws which stop short of the full scope of dispassionate justice is our most honored tradition. But the Negro is another matter . . . when he states it he is stirring up racial hatred and reopening wounds which have not bled since the merciful stillness at Appomattox.

Then there is another class of whites, and these include many people of honesty and perception, who charge the Negro masses of the Deep South with apathy toward voting and claiming full citizenship. This may be true; such apathy does exist. But they are apathetic because we are apathetic. We poison them with our lassitude and disclaimer for we have the vote already and the implied power over rulers and yet we have let almost as many of our acknowledged liberties slip away by default and indifference as those they never had.

We have been silent when we should have been heard, tolerant and objective when we should have been fighting, frightened and secretive when we should have been rising in righteous power to rebuke and punish those who subvert the rights of man for profit and privilege, and so swiftly and totally that they will see that no one who is trying this again will have the slightest chance of escape.

The past few days have provided shocking evidence of the inability of the liberal whites to protect themselves and maintain a legal resistance to usurpations of the Bill of Rights. The Un-American Activities Committee, whose years of steady harassment of dissenters has now been openly denounced by most of the big newspapers and all of the liberal organizations of this country, has just received a smashing victory over its critics. The Congressman of every person in this audience voted to maintain and endorse it. The six Congressmen resisting it were called Communist sympathizers on the floor of the House.

Coevil with this, two distinguished white men who have devoted their lives to fighting segregation were summarily ruled against by the Supreme Court on contempt charges and will now have to serve jail sentences for their efforts. The case of Carl Braden was directly related to the problem now under discussion. In the noble dissent of Justice Black it was baldly stated that from now on, "no legislative committee, state or Federal, will have trouble finding cause to subpoena all persons anywhere who take a public stand against segregation. . . ." Furthermore, the decision, says Justice Black, "May well strip the Negro of the aid of the white people who have been willing to speak on his behalf."

There are many well-intentioned Northerners who feel that the white South should not be pushed too rapidly into social change. This is based on the notion that they have a secret gnawing guilt and that this should arouse our compassion . . . that somehow this guilt feeling explains away and absolves them of the constant wrong they are doing their colored brethren. I do not believe this guilt exists to a significant degree. The crime of the white South springs from their racist units of loyalty which, to my mind, places them beyond redemption until they take an honest look at their society and its discontents.

First of all they must wake up to the brute fact that the golden age they hark back to was a slave-holding, slave-breeding, slave-driving hell on earth. They might realize that its image and all the so-called heroes who sustained it with fire and blood, Robert E. Lee, Stonewall Jackson, Jefferson Davis, and all the other traitors, are anathema to at least one-third of their fellow citizens at home and the overwhelming majority of the citizens of the world.

Secondly, they must be told that most of us know that when they talk about states' rights they mean white rights. Their continuing horror over John Brown's raid on Harper's Ferry . . . all the present acts of Negro resistance, the sit-downs, the pray-ins, the trespasses, would be swallowed not as a sacrament if performed to protect the purity of the white race. If the Negroes rode as the Ku Klux Klan has, in the night and on an errand of lynching, murder, and human degradation, and against their own people, they would be hailed as saviours. There was never a time when the white South did not put racism above every other form of loyalty.

There was very little talk of states' rights whenever they were able to compromise Congress and the Supreme Court into bringing the power of the Federal Government against the Negro and not for him. Is it states' rights which tells a man that he cannot send his children to those common schools to which they are entitled to by the law of the land of their birth because he is colored? What is the political system that prevents colored men and women from voting for the agents that represent them in the government and there form policies to which the disenfranchised peoples are supposed to give their unquestioning loyalty . . . and when called upon, in wartime, their heart's blood? The John Brown that is in me, and there is a little John Brown in all of us, once we have been exposed to the greatest Yankee of them all, tells me that this is white rights, it is a form of slavery, and that it will never be anything else until everyone in the South can vote and attend common schools.

As for time taking care of the problem, we have all seen the fallacy of this answer; seen with our own eyes Southern mothers of New Orleans, typical young matrons such as we encounter in the supermarkets, solemnly telling their helpless children before the astonished eyes of the world, "You don't want to go to school with niggers . . . you don't ever want to go to school with the black niggers." It is not hard to imagine these children telling their children . . . that is the exact way it has been carried on since the Emancipation Proclamation . . . these cherished customs of the Old South.

While in the North there is the glaring sin of omission. Look at your children's schoolbooks sometime. You will find that the history of the slave and the abolitionist is never told . . . your children may never know of them unless you tell them. The grand names of Garrison, Phillips, Frederick Douglass, Theodore Parker, are barely mentioned; and if they are, it is as raving fanatics who started the Civil War as a demented incendiary starts a fire. And so the towering personalities whose lives could give a child the manliest examples of the courage and breadth of intellect so desperately needed today are withheld from their consciousness. All the values these men thought out and implanted in the living tissue of the republic have been lopped off, and in their place we are offered, as patriots to be venerated, traitors like Lee and Davis, bigots nike Andrew Johnson, drunken hirelings of the rich like Daniel Webster, racists, all of them who have spread filth on the garment of the American dream of the brotherhood of all.

You will find by your indifference that your children are being taught a false and vilely corrupt version of history, one that deliberately distorts the role of the Negro and feeds the obscene myth of white supremacy and keeps it unnaturally alive in the face of supreme Negro achievement on every side. When they ask the historian why the colored race has slipped back so far after a war was fought to free them so long ago, they will be told that when the Negroes were given full equality after the Civil War, they abused it in an unpardonable way, selling their votes and wandering lazily about, stealing and frolicking in a saturnalia of corruption and bestiality. Furthermore, the men who made this possible, Charles Sumner and Thaddeus Stevens, were not themselves interested in the Negro but were merely fanatic and vindictive Yankee radicals drunk with power and determined to grind a noble, defeated adversary into the dust. The historian Du Bois names dozens of historians who believe the Negro to be subhuman and congenitally unfitted for citizenship and the suffrage. Authority after authority has made it part of our historical canon that the South was right in Reconstruction, the North vengeful or deceived, and the Negro stupid. This is not *Mein Kampf* I am speaking of, it is mine history, the texts our children are reading every day.

And so the strong fabric of the American past is torn apart, the threads are snapped that lead back to the best hope man ever had. A whole race is slandered by separation from the continuity of truth.

There might be some slight excuse for these omissions if the actual historical struggle between the sections was being played down to present a united nation to a disorderly world. But the opposite is true. The Centennial of the Civil War is coming in, loud and clear. The best place to read about this is in the *Wall Street Journal*. A whole new industry has been born. The blue-chip possibilities of yield are said to be enormous. Disney's Law of Proliferating Profits will come into play: the Civil War Book becomes the TV spectacular, then the movie, then breaks up into an unceasing downpour of golden fragments . . . the toys, the hats, the uniforms, the facsimile and hardware and the new brand names . . . we may see, for instance, the Jefferson Davis Freedom Fighter's Plastic Cannon . . . an exact copy of the one designed for shelling the capital of the United States. The largesse never stops raining on restaurants, gift shops, motels, gas stations, and above all on the cars and roads which will carry the celebrants of the worshipful rights of this American passion play to the shrines that embody them.

As in every successful industry every effort will be made to remove from the product every abrasive element . . . anything that might give offense to the least possible consumer by casting aspersions on his region, his religion, his politics, his home life, or his day-to-day assurance that every act of his government or his employer is solely for the purpose of producing the very best state of well-being in the very best of nations. The battle soil of the South will be sterilized to the depth of three generations to remove any suspicions that there was a racial conflict going on there. Everybody will be told that it was really just an exercise of great gallantry between four noble men, Lee and Davis, Lincoln and Grant . . . and that they were, all of them, all-

American-Americans laboring under a slight, and still unresolved, constitutional misunderstanding. Thus the pageantry will not be half safe, but a completely dependable national product . . . both sides separately, but equally righteous in their own Cause.

This is the way it is supposed to be set up, but as in all separate and equal formulations, one side is always a little bit more separate and equal than the other. The scenes reprised so far have been largely Confederate. Not long ago we were treated to a backward glimpse of Jefferson Davis taking office as President of a government based on a wild and tragic fantasy that slavery was to be the perpetual condition of the majority of its citizens. We saw the Southern whites in their broadcloth and crinolines re-enacting this obscenity, while passing by in the streets of Montgomery and looking at them as if they were raving mad were the colored descendents of the American men and women whom they were struggling to keep enslaved. As usual, the resurrected Confederate heroes acted as if their fellow citizens were not there . . . as if they were utterly invisible.

The next momentous public scene to be revived will be a full-scale reenactment of the battle of First Manassas, a Confederate victory. The resurgence of Confederate interest and ardor in these rites has become so intense that *The New York Times* complained bitterly to the court in Montgomery that it was impossible for them to get a fair verdict in their libel suit in the atmosphere of this passionate reawakening of the Lost Cause. The irony is that *The Times* has been one of the most avid publicizers of this fumigated and deprincipled Centennial. Furthermore, they have joined with most of the other mass media in the obvious attempt to rescue the white South from the embarrassment of its resistance to desegregation, playing hard attitudes down wherever possible, and making it seem that the white South had excuses for causing delays in treating Americans as Americans.

Neither the *New York Times* nor any other agency has called for counterevents to be dramatized as an offset to this triumph of Southern Arms. No one has called for a re-enactment of the Nat Turner Insurrection in Virginia, really the first scene of the war, although these Negroes were only carrying out the forefather's injunction that "Resistance to tyranny is obedience to God." No one has requested the restaging of the rescue of Shadrack, the Fugitive Slave of Lewis Hayden, and other Negroes from the Boston Courthouse, although this is another beginning of the beginning. And it is absolutely unthinkable that the parade of the Fifty-fourth Massachusetts Negro Regiment marching off to South Carolina in 1863, passing the house

of Wendell Phillips on Essex Street in Boston, saluting William Lloyd
Garrison as he stood there on a balcony with his hand resting on a
bust of John Brown, and with the massed bands playing "John
Brown's Body" be added to this pageant of dusty death . . . of death
and dust made futile by the continued oppression of the Negro.

Many people feel that these ceremonies are harmless and a little
ridiculous, but I do not agree. Their flagrantly one-sided direction
makes me suspect that they are part and parcel of the resistance movement the white South has been carrying on against human rights for
a hundred years. These nostalgic mummeries are entered into with
such devotion that I agree with what Garrison wrote long after
Appomattox.

They are under the Union but not of the Union. They are under
the Constitution but not for the Constitution, except as a matter
of duress. They are nominally Americans but really Southerners in
feeling and purpose. If they could see their way clear to throw off
the authority of the federal government and to resuscitate their
defunct confederacy, they would instantly rise again in rebellion
and expel every loyal Northerner from their territorial domains.

There is not much danger of this, but there is a very real danger
that these tides of bogus sentimentalism engulfing us with tributes paid
the old South for its honor, integrity, and heroism are being used to
bedazzle the rest of the nation out of thinking about and having a
concern over the shameful foot-dragging going on in respect to desegregation and all the other overdue demands of the American Negro.

But there is another element here far more offensive and degrading
than the broadcloth and crinoline glorification of a society of enslavers.
This symbol is the flag under which they fought and which will be
carried proudly on these synthetic battlefields and entwined in honor
with the Stars and Stripes as the hallmark of these festivities. This is
the same flag which the world has seen flying in every shameful
and demeaning crisis in this country for the last five years . . . from
the march of the White Citizens Council members in force to besiege
a public school and spit in the faces of some small, helpless, and
vulnerable Negro children to the latest orgy of moronic white racist
students on the campus of the University of Georgia. It is inevitably
paired with "Nigger Go Home" signs and other national obscenities.
Before this, the Confederate flag has a long unbroken tradition of
appearing at the time and place of every gross offense against Negro

citizens, in the hands of night riders, hooded bigots, floggers, lynchers, and burners alive.

Most people seem to be unstirred by such a connection and I cannot figure why. This nation has lately been convulsed with horror over the outbreak of Nazi symbols in many places, but surely the brash persistence of the Confederate flag is as deep a symbol of insult to the Negro as the swastika is to the Jew, both being standards of a political system which had written their code of laws that one sort of human was to forever be the prey and slave of another. I can never be made to understand why racism in Berlin is a crime against humanity and racism in Berlin is a crime against tolerable local custom so honored that to defend it, all the libertarian aphorisms of the founding fathers can be brought into play. Nor can I understand why the Confederate struggle for the right of individual states to enslave people because of their color is somehow noble, while there is universal agreement that a German Reich founded on the bleached bones of millions of Jews was manifestly obscene.

Granted that nothing in the world so far can equal the impacted horror of the Nazi racial onslaughts, there still exists the slow horror of the bitter, no-exit life of the Negro in the concentration camp of his skin; without the larger anguish of the deep physical pain and unspeakable death, but full of the day-to-day degradation so eloquently put by John Hope Franklin:

> The degradation of finding human advance and achievement negated by a black skin, of finding himself mobbed or shot at if he tries to vote, of being shunted into ghettos to be exploited by landlords, of being insulted and driven out of every community of whites, North and South, where he seeks eating, sleeping, or even toilet facilities.

And now I have a very practical suggestion. It is a little more than a century since John Quincy Adams preserved for us the right of petitioning Congress, while he was brilliantly carrying out the political phase of the abolitionist struggle. It is still not too late to commemorate this with a new abolitionist petition which will arouse the same howls of bigot rage from the same quarters that wanted to lynch Adams for his abolitionist petitions. This will focus the awareness of the nation on the sad and significant truth that many members of Congress have a set of loyalties indistinguishable from those who trained the enemy guns at Gettysburg on the Stars and Stripes on Cemetery Ridge. We have been too long and too forgetfully a country under two flags.

Therefore, Whereas the flag of the defeated and defunct Southern Confederacy is today the most prominent and consistent symbol of forcible attempts to deny citizens their rights; and as it was, and is, the battle emblem of a Negro-whipping, Negro-enslaving, and Negro-degrading Society, in flagrant opposition to a democratic form of government, we, the undersigned citizens of the United States demand that it shall not be displayed on any occasion, partially or completely under the sponsorship of the United States.

I am speaking to you from a lacerated conscience in the hope that I can lacerate yours. The purpose of this pulpit is to arouse and organize conscience and to deal with the relationship between man and man and the duties that grow out of this in a completely honest way. At its best such duties are a labor of love, but there are times when hate is evoked.

In the quickening and deepening of the desegregation of the South, a new leader of the Negro people has arisen. He is young and vigorous. He has been tested and found among the bravest of the brave. He is eloquent, his personal life is stainless, and he sheds credit on his people wherever he goes. As a reconstructed abolitionist, this should be an event of the greatest joy to me. . . . I should celebrate his arrival and glorify his name. But, contrariwise, I find his personality and his policy among the saddest stories of this long and heart-rending struggle.

The leadership of Martin Luther King, Jr., was achieved by his developing a position which would be acceptable to large masses of people North and South. He feels that it is an honest and attainable one . . . and it is, indeed, an exact reflection of the limits to which he feels the conscience of the North will support him. But it is unbearably tragic. . . .

His position, as he states it, is this,

> The American Negroes must say to their white brothers we will match your capacity to inflict suffering with our capacity to endure suffering. We will meet your physical force with soul force. We will note hate you, but in good conscience we cannot obey your unjust laws. Do to us what you will and we will still love you. Bomb our homes and threaten our children; send your hooded perpetuators of violence into our communities and drag us out on some wayside, beating us and leaving us half dead and we will still love you. But we will soon wear you down by our capacity to suffer. And in winning our freedom we will so appeal to your heart and conscience that we will win you in the process.

People of the North . . . you people out there . . . is that what you want the Negro to go through in order to regain the rights which he had already in 1776? He was here then, you know, and he fought alongside of us. He always had this freedom; it was only taken from him by force and fraud. And do you want him to suffer another hundred years of fraud and force, of beating, bombing, and degradation until the heart and conscience of the South gets round to accepting him . . . to loving him? That is a lunatic society down there: they willl never stop beating until we make them stop!

There has been enough of this . . . two hundred years of it is enough, enough, enough. Today I cannot look at my colored brother but what I see the ancestral welts upon his back and feel the anguish in his heart! The Negro is a citizen, he has no right to endure this for any reason other than his own survival. As a citizen he has a clear duty to resist tyranny and dictatorship, legally and peacefully if he can, forcibly if he must. He is the birthright possessor of inalienable rights . . . he cannot give them away if he wants to. He is not born to be a punching bag to test the longevity of the Southern whites' desire to beat him!

My friends, I am not afraid of hate . . . or to be hated. Theodore Parker has taught me that any physical violation of the rights of man or of his person . . . which is a sacred thing; the body of a man and woman is a sacred vessel and should not be violated . . . is a crime against all humanity. He who spits in the face of a Negro child spits in my face. Therefore, I hate the Southern racists and all their works. I hate them for clapping me into a prison of my white skin as inescapable as that of my darker neighbor. What they do to others in the South makes me want to secede from the white race . . . and what the white-skinned racist does in the North is just as abhorrent. I hate them because they have stolen my own birthright of human brotherhood, alienating me from my blood brothers by their cruelty to them in my image . . . setting up impassable barriers of suspicion between me and the people I want to clasp hands with in loving admiration of the dignity, patience, and restraint they have shown in struggling upward to a level of liberation and privilege which my kind accept as due them by birth alone. I hate them because they have blocked out of the culture of my time the full expression of the wisdom of a people to whom the meaning of life has had to be privation, suffering, and alienation but who have lived with quiet confidence, and far more than we have, with infectious and inexplicable joy. I hate the white South because they have made me ashamed of my own country

... which not only presents to a vibrant world grappling with problems we ignore the complacent surface of a sluttish society whose mass ideal is the unlimited consumption of all possible goods and services ... but which has lost all of its revolutionary virtues in an hour when the darker people are finally climbing into the light and are forced to seek elsewhere the encouragement which our Revolutionary fathers meant for us to bestow on mankind.

Thus I have revealed to you without restraint my own conscience, formed and activated, I hope, by a long study of the lives and words of our great American prophets. It does not come from the great beyond, from mystic voices or vision, but from men like myself, only infinitely more gifted and courageous. If reading their words and the brave promises of my country's founders I ignore the contradictions between them and the ground rules of our national life, day by day, I would be committing a sin against my own senses, against the light that is in me. If I accepted these gross disparities between man and man all around me with complacency, I would be committing the greatest sin, that of hyprocrisy, which blinds man to his own failures and gives him a false idea of his position and purpose in the world. If I should deny the Negro any form of resistance for which white men have been applauded and venerated, I am acting as a racist. To me they are citizens and men in the old sense, in the revolutionary sense. We have no right to deny them the truths that only upheavals and outbreaks can tell . . . the terrible judgments which prove without any doubt that the future and the fate of black and white in this country are indivisible forever.

Humbly I say this, no amount of invited suffering, of passive resistance, will restore to the Negro his inalienable rights. Only the united conscience of the North can do it, standing beside him and supporting him under any circumstances. Now this conscience lies inert, confused and deprincipled. That is why we need the Negro almost as much as he needs us. We must travel the road to perfectibility together . . . to our fulfillment as persons, as citizens, and the road goes in only one direction . . . into the life of principle, under the guidance of ideas, in response to the great and accursed questions of personal independence, the citizen's relation to the state, the right to resistance, the wrong of poverty, racism, and bigotry, and the quickening vision of the brotherhood of man all over the world.

Let us begin our regeneration right now . . . in standing together against the segregationists North and South and crying out . . .

Verily Thou Art Guilty Concerning Thy Brother.

Are Negroes Inferior?
and
Answering Eric Hoffer

HARRY GOLDEN

Harry Golden was born in New York City on May 6, 1920, the son of Leib and Anna (Klein) Goldhirsch. He was married to Genevieve Gallagher in 1926 and is the father of four sons. He attended the College of the City of New York from 1919 to 1922, and was awarded the Doctor of Humane Letters degree from Belmont Abbey College in 1962.

A self-styled editor, publisher, and writer, Harry Golden has edited and published *The Carolina Israelite* since 1942. He was named "man-of-the-year" on three separate occasions—in 1957 by Carver College and in 1958 by Johnson C. Smith College and by Temple Emanu-El, New York City. Golden is a member of the American Jewish Congress and serves on its Board; he holds a lifetime membership in the National Association for the Advancement of Colored People. He is a member of the Shakespeare Society of America, the Catholic Inter-racial Council, and B'nai Brith.

He is author of *Only in America* (1958), *For 2¢ Plain* (1959), *Enjoy, Enjoy!* (1951), *Carl Sandburg* (1961), *You're Entitled* (1962) and *Forgotten Pioneer* (1963). He is active in the civil-rights movement and has delivered a few hundred speeches since 1948.

His two contributions following appeared in the January-February 1965 issue of *The Carolina Israelite.*

* * *

Arthur Krock of *The New York Times* devoted his attention on December 8th to the recent Supreme Court action on the Florida statutes which defined Negro-white sexual intercourse as criminal. Mr. Krock's account was fair, but in one particular he completely misrepresented the situation.

Explaining the basis of disapproval of interbreeding between Negroes and whites, he said, "It is partly conceived in theory, which has considerable support among anthropologists, that Negro-white fusion in particular has a deteriorating effect on both races."

Mr. Krock is a highly articulate man. If he meant the offspring of a Negro and white marriage of cohabitation would find it sociologically hard to achieve the good life he would have said so. Mr. Krock unmistakably meant there was a biological deterioration. And the danger of Mr. Krock's thinking is that, without mentioning names, he suggests there is considerable support for this view among anthropologists. Arthur Krock is a man of reputation but he is wrong and we must hasten to prove him wrong. No anthropologists lends this theory of biological deterioration and support whatsoever. To the credit of the South, indeed, one of the facts to make us all proud of being Southerners, is its denial of Mr. Krock's speculation. There are 624 professors in the "Confederate" South, professors of medicine and anthropology and of the allied studies and sciences, biology, genetics, and the like. And no more than two such scientists, no more than two men who have made their reputation, have expressed the view that the Negro is inferior in intelligence because of his race. Only two men with any standing at all have walked out of their universities and stated that racial segregation is justified on genetic grounds. This is a remarkable record considering this tremendous controversy tthat has raged throughout the South for the last ten years.

Intelligence based on race is a subject which has been widely treated in our generation by the great anthropologists and scientists of the world. Unlike Mr. Krock, who mentioned no names when he said that his view has wide anthropological support, I can mention the names of the great scientists who have studied this problem across the years. For example, Professor Ralph H. Turner, sociologist:

> Intelligence is an individual rather than a group characteristic . . . to the extent that it has an inherited basis, it is influenced by the individual's immediate antecedents and not by the total race to which he belongs. By the time an individual's antecedents have been traced back a few generations, their number becomes so large that the contribution of any single one of them is trivial.
>
> So long as Negroes are socially set apart they are bound to maintain a subculture somewhat at variance from that of whites. Hence, there is every reason to expect that on social and cultural grounds that any group differences in scores on IQ tests between Negroes and whites would persist over generations.

Professor Sherwood A. Washburn, one of America's great anthropologists:

> With the tests as known, there is no way to tell whether the

differences are determined by heredity or environment. . . . When environmental factors change, the results go up and down.

Dr. Henry C. Dyer, an authority on educational testing:

There is no sense I can think of in which it is legitimate to speak of Negro intelligence vs. white intelligence. An intelligence test samples a variety of mental functions that are, to some extent, predictive of performance in schools, in college, and in the vocations. . . . Both Negroes and whites have scored both at the top and the bottom of our tests. . . . If a group of Negro children were given cultural opportunities superior to those available to their parents, the mean score of the Negro children would be higher than the mean score of their parents.

And Dr. Harry L. Shapiro, chairman of the Department of Anthropology, the American Museum of Natural History:

There is a very considerable, indeed an overwhelming agreement among anthropologists that no sound scientific evidence exists for such statements as Mr. Krock's.

Now, the sociological objection to Negro-white offspring is different. Marriage under the most favorable conditions is a great gamble. All we need do is consider our divorce rate. And when I say under the most favorable conditions I mean a boy and girl from the same economic level, the same religion, the same race, same family attitudes, interest in sports, hobbies, politics, etc. Under such most favorable conditions, marriage is still a gamble. Thus when the conditions are less favorable, different religions, rich-poor, differing political attitudes, social attitudes, and at the furthest extreme, different races, the prospect of a happy marriage grows dimmer and dimmer. This has nothing whatsoever to do with "inheritance" or intelligence by race, or character by race; it has to do only with the attitudes of the surrounding society.

Eric Hoffer's article, "The Negro Is Prejudiced Against Himself" appeared in *The New York Times Magazine* on November 29, 1964, and was reprinted in *U.S. News and World Report* on December 8. The article is a center of controversy. Mr. Hoffer, a social philosopher, has spent years as a longshoreman on the West Coast. His first book, *The True Believer*, was universally received with deep respect and enthusiasm.

His important observations on the current social revolution of the American Negro are:

1. Even when it tries to be gentle, the voice of the Negro revolution grates on us and fills us with scorn. The Negro seems to say: "Lift me up in your arms. I am an abandoned and abused child. Adopt me as your favorite son. Feed me, clothe me, educate me, love and baby me. You must do it right away or I shall set your house on fire, or rot at your doorsteps and poison the air you breathe.

   To sum up: The Negro revolution is a fraud. It has no faith in the character and potentialities of the Negro masses. It has no taste for real enemies, real battlegrounds, and desperate situations. It wants cheap victories and the easy way.

2. The simple fact is that the people I have lived and worked with all my life, and who make up 60 percent of the population outside the South, have not the least feeling of guilt toward the Negro. The majority of us started to work for a living in our teens, and we have been poor all our lives. Most of us had only a rudimentary education. Our white skin has brought us no privileges and no favors. For more than twenty years, I worked in the fields of California with Negroes, and now and then for Negro contractors. On the San Francisco waterfront, where I spent the next twenty years, there are as many black longshoremen as white.

   My kind of people do not feel that the world owes us anything, or that we owe anybody—white, black or yellow—a damn thing. We have: the right to vote, the right to join any union open to us, the right to live, work, study, and play anywhere he pleases. But he can have no special claims on us, and no valid grievances against us. He has certainly not done our work for us. Our hands are more gnarled and work-broken than his, and our faces more lined and worn.

To all of which, we say, "Of course." There has been no parallel in either past American or European experience for the social revolution of the Negro in the United States. The Negro is a revolutionary who does not want to destroy or change existing institutions. The Negro does not throw tea over the side, he does not storm the Bastille, or behead the King, he does not want to tear up a Constitution, dismiss a Parliament, he simply wants that which everyone else is guaranteed.

He does not want to set our house afire; on the contrary we have put his house to the flames. If indeed he is rotting on our doorstep, it is because since 1940 he has had to present writ after writ to the same judge who keeps telling him he hasn't exhausted all the remedies available to him. If he rots on our doorsteps it is because certain segments of our judiciary and voting registrars, and police, and juries, are themselves rotten.

And as far as feeding and clothing go, it was the white merchant who encouraged this by coaxing the Negro out of his ghetto. "Come uptown. Only a dollar down. Cheaper and better goods than you can get from your slum merchant." And the Negro answered the summons. He found his money eagerly sought at nine counters but not at the tenth where they sold hot dogs and orange drinks. To go downtown, the Negro found he had to sit in the back of the bus. He found no public facilities available.

It is hardly a coincidence that Negroes pitched one of the battles of their revolution in front of the store itself and won.

To discuss the Negro revolution and not to discuss the materialistic cast to American life is to blot out probability. The Negro represents one-tenth of the buying power in America and one-fourth of the total credit purchasing power in the South. Admittedly, this is no reason why anyone should be free, but it is one reason why the Negro's revolution succeeds. The mercenary white man is involved. Because merchants all over America want the Negro dollar makes them in a way victims, too. The sooner the Negro wins, the sooner this merchant, used-car dealer, corporation executive will breathe easier about his profit spiral.

If Martin Luther King did nothing else for America, he proved to whites and Negroes that Christianity still has its uses. In the hands of authentic Christians, as no one doubts some Negroes are, Christianity has become a unifying and cohesive force for social reform, an instrument for justice and spiritual inspiration. Were it not for the Negroes of America, would Christianity here be anything more than a simple Sunday adventure?

Nor is Mr. Hoffer original when he remarks that disfranchisement should have borne the brunt of the Negro attack.

Mr. Hoffer comes up with an idea in 1964–65 which I heard discussed back and forth in 1950–52. The struggle in the courts and in Congress against Negro disfranchisement has been going on since 1926 with few dramatic results. The struggle against disfranchisement remained dramatically futile even after the passage of the Civil Rights Act of 1957 which directly concerned itself with voting rights. For two-and-a-half years after this bill was law, the Eisenhower Administration through its Justice Department initiated ten cases where Negroes had been deprived of their voting rights and two of these were filed on the last day of Eisenhower's second term of office and none of them in Alabama or Mississippi. Had the NAACP asked me in 1948, I would have made health the target of the revolution. I once pointed out to Judge Thurgood Marshall, then head of the NAACP Legal Defense, that there could be little resistance to an assault on hospital facilities once the American people knew the facts, one of which was that the South's second biggest killer was not cancer or stroke, but pregnancy—Negro pregnancy. Negro deaths in birth were four times that of whites and Negro infant mortality five-and-a-half that of white infant mortality. But even if Negro women won the privilege of service in white hospitals, Marshall pointed out, the pattern of racial segregation would remain. (In 1964 in desegregated hospitals in the South, the bed linen used by Negro women is never mixed with the laundry used by white women, but washed separately.)

The Negroes judged correctly that we are a school-oriented society and if segregation were eliminated in the schools the pattern would receive a crippling blow. The wisdom of such an attack is evident. Ask a white mill worker in Greensboro, North Carolina, how he feels about having to work beside a colored man in order that his mill may bid for government contracts and he will say, "Hell, they're already going to school with my kids."

I have heard another of Mr. Hoffer's arguments a thousand times. All of us have to work for a living. Why should the Negro get any special favors? The Irish immigrants did not stage sit-ins, the Jews did not need an FEPC, the Italians embarked on no freedom rides, why can't the Negroes pull themselves up by their bootstraps? The reason is that the Negro cannot move from one place to another with any degree of anonymity. He cannot change his name, hide his religion, or disguise his origin. He is black and his very presence triggers an emotion in all of us, ranging from affection to fear, from condescension to contempt, from sympathy to hate. Because of this, John F. Kennedy, an American politician-philosopher, who also occupied the White House, told me, "This fellow *must* have legislation every step of the way."

Mr. Hoffer should not worry too much about his Negro fellow-workers in San Francisco who are indifferent to the current Negro movement. These Negro longshoremen are no different from the fifty-year-old Jews who warned us against leaving the "security" of the ghetto. And when the Jews took over the New York ghetto at the end of the nineteenth century they found some Irishmen who had apparently refused to move on, and there were even a few Germans left from a full generation before. Mr. Hoffer should visit more with Negro students around the country. It is there he will find his story.

I agree with Mr. Hoffer that the fight for Negro equality starts in Mississippi and Alabama and that the Negroes in the North who claim there is no difference one side or the other of the Mason-Dixon line are wrong. I think the attack by the Negro intellectual upon the white liberal is shameful.

I don't worry about such attacks. James Baldwin, LeRoi Jones, and Adam Clayton Powell have vilified some brave men and women. But these are precisely the Negro intellectuals who have had no participation in the revolution and perhaps it is participation for which they long. They have "opposite numbers" among white intellectuals who have not participated either and are at pains to condemn the sit-ins, the freedom rides, and the court fights, and perhaps the Negro is undeserving after all. When the folks are in the street, there is no time for thoughtful neutrality. A man falls behind the first barricade he finds.

If the Negro is prejudiced against himself, I say "So what?" Every unpopular minority sooner or later begins to believe some of the propaganda used against it. The Jewish vaudevillians created the stage Jew and it was the Irish who gave our language the differentiation between "lace-curtain" and "shanty" Irish.

The best answer to Mr. Hoffer's charges comes from a paragraph he himself wrote in *The True Believer*: "The discarded and rejected are often the raw material of a nation's future."

PART TWO

Educators

The man of learning is a skeptic, for he seeks to determine truth by questioning and argument; in his impatience with conventional answers he is an adversary of any brand of authoritarianism. No true educator isolates himself from society; rather he helps society in remedying its ills. The extent to which numerous educators have enlisted in the civil-rights struggle has given strength, meaning, and creativity to America's struggle to guarantee and protect the rights of all of her citizens.

America has come to learn that the task of reconciling our practice in human relations with the Judeo-Christian tradition and with the highest values of our democratic ideal to which our nation is committed is not the exclusive concern of civil-rights leaders and crusaders. This is a pursuit that should engage the attention and creative effort of all citizens.

The educator, however, has had special reason to be distressed. For nearly two centuries he has been party to a pattern of exclusion that has denied certain Americans full participation in the educational framework of our nation.

The quest for a solution to the problem must continue to take into consideration all forms of segregation and discrimination in education, *de facto* segregation, and impact on educational opportunities, racial barriers which have created systematic exclusion of Negroes and other minorities in many areas of our educational community, the role of the predominantly Negro college, the welfare of the Negro teacher who is caught in the crossfire of the integration struggle, and many other problems.

THE NEGRO SPEAKS OF RIVERS
—Langston Hughes

I've known rivers:
I've known rivers ancient as the world and older than the
flow of human blood in human veins.

My soul has grown deep like the rivers.

I bathed in the Euphrates when dawns were young.
I built my hut near the Congo and it lulled me to sleep.
I looked upon the Nile and raised the pyramids above it.
I heard the singing of the Mississippi when Abe Lincoln
went down to New Orleans, and I've seen its muddy
bosom turn all golden in the sunset.

I've known rivers:
Ancient, dusky rivers.

My soul has grown deep like the rivers.

The Crisis of American Democracy and the Negro

DR. KENNETH CLARK

Kenneth Bancroft Clark, an educator and psychologist, received
the Bachelor of Arts (1935) and the Master of Arts (1936) degrees
from Howard University, and the Doctor of Philosophy degree from
Columbia University (1940). He has been on the staff of the Psychology Department, College of the City of New York, since 1942
and a Professor in that department since 1960. In addition, he is Research Director of the Northside Center for Child Development, a
post he has held since 1946; he is Social Science Consultant of the
Legal and Educational Division of the National Association for the
Advancement of Colored People, and he served from 1961 to 1962
as Consultant in the Personnel Division of the U.S. Department of
State.

He was with the Commission on Integration, Board of Education,

New York City, from 1954 to 1958, and has served with the New York State Youth Commission since 1956. He has also served on the Advisory Committee of the Division of Intercultural Relations in Education, New York State Department of Education, since 1957. Dr. Clark also serves as Director of the National Child Labor Committee, National Scholarship Service and Fund for Negro Students, and is Director of the New Lincoln School. He is a member of the Board of Trustees of Howard University and Antioch College.

A recipient of the Spingarn Medal, Dr. Clark is also a Fellow of the American Psychology Association. He is a past president (1959–1960) of the Social Psychology Studies Social Issues and has been a member of the Council of that organization since 1954. His publications include *Desegregation: An Appraisal of the Evidence,* (1953) and *Prejudice and Your Child* (1955); *Dark Ghetto,* (1965).

"The Crises of American Democracy and the Negro" is the title of a speech delivered by Kenneth Clark at the Annual Luncheon of the National Committee for Rural Schools on November 19, 1955, in New York City. Dr. Clark stresses the Gandhian principle of nonviolence and says of his speech that he presented the ideas and suggestions for consideration because

> . . . I would not have been honest with my audience or myself if I had said anything less. Probably more relevant is the fact that I would accept the opportunity to play a part in a nonviolent action program designed to reaffirm and strengthen the equality and citizenship rights of Americans in any community of our nation where these rights are being threatened.

*   *   *

This, the middle of the twentieth century, the beginning of the atomic age, may well become known as the period of paradox.

This is a period in which man may achieve either peace or the ultimate social psychosis of mass suicide.

This is a period in which the fruits of human intelligence will either provide the leisure, comforts, and challenge for creative living or will increase intolerably the tensions, fears, and conflicts of life.

In this period of world history the promises of the democratic ideal will be fulfilled for all men everywhere—in Mississippi, New York, South Carolina, or South Africa—or human beings everywhere will be doomed to an Orwellian existence of social and spiritual stagnation.

In short, this is a period of hope or despair, social progress or retrogression. Sometimes one or the other of these dominates. Sometimes they alternate and vary in severity. It is difficult to predict which will prevail. Those of us who are optimistic and have accepted the moral ideals taught us in our youth believe that social progress is inevitable—that reason will in the long run control the irrational—that knowledge will banish ignorance—that truth and justice will conquer untruths, hypocrisy, and barbarity.

But can we be sure? How do we know that we are not indulging in the seductive habits of wishful thinking? Even a superficial look at human history reveals that there is no inevitable law that right and human progress must prevail. Rather, it seems clear that each step that man took toward the goals of social justice and humanity required sacrifices, pain, and turmoil. Social progress has never been attained by default. It must be planned for, worked for, and be the passionate meaning of the lives of dedicated individuals, who for various motives and reasons cannot tolerate social injustice.

Without these counterforces, time itself is an ally of the powerful and primitive forces of irrationality and social barbarity. What is more, those men whose lives are constricted by ignorance and inhumanity are not infrequently aided by a general social apathy, hypocrisy, and amorality. This diseased social condition can easily be exploited by seemingly respectable men of power and prestige.

There then develops a vested interest in the perpetuation and extension of ignorance, cruelty, and other subtle or flagrant forms of social injustice. Such a society might well be efficient; might even be rich and powerful in material and technological grandeur—but only at the tremendous cost of the stagnation and degradation of the human spirit. Such a society might even become free of social tensions, turmoils, and conflicts—but only because the human conscience has become calloused and corroded to the point of insensitivity to the aspirations for freedom and dignity which men possess but may all too easily lose.

But this is no time to chant a dirge of despair. Those who would seek to destroy our humanity would be encouraged by any sign that we had lost hope and confidence in the future. If they succeed in intimidating us they gain courage and become more pompous. If we cringe in fear and defeat they strut in empty arrogance and become more cruel. This, then, is a time of challenge—a time for courage —and a time for cold, hard, intelligent, and realistic appraisal of our assets and liabilities, and an assessment of the task which confronts us. And, above all, this is a time for bold and effective action.

THE UNITED STATES SUPREME COURT—
A SYMBOL OF HOPE

The period between May 17, 1954, and May 31, 1955, was a period of rejoicing for all men throughout the world who believed deeply in democracy and human equality. The United States Supreme Court had announced to the world that the American concept of democracy and freedom was no longer to be qualified by the color of a man's skin. In simple, clear, and eloquent language the nine men who constituted that Court cut through the complicated doubletalk of the segregationists and gave hope to the millions of people—black, white, yellow, and brown people—throughout the world who had dared only to dream of freedom. This decision made it clear that the masses of mankind in their quest for a better life need not substitute one tyranny for another. It reflected the inherent vitality of the American concept of democracy. It indicated that equality could be fought for and approached—within this framework—with the weapons of reason and law, and that it was not necessary to resort to the irrational weapons of force and violence.

This decision confounded the primitive racists and segregationists. They retreated temporarily in confusion and desperation. They questioned the authority and integrity of the United States Supreme Court. Publicly, they counseled evasion, subterfuge, secession, or anarchy. Privately, however, they knew that they were defending a lost and dying cause. They burlesqued indignation by exaggeration. Like us, they knew that it was just a matter of time before the plantation structure of the old order would collapse and engulf its defenders in its rubble. They had to play for time—the longer the time the better. They hoped that the United States Supreme Court would give them an infinite amount of time within which they could continue to impair the hearts and minds of Negro children and brutalize the souls of white children. Frantically they dusted off all of the old excuses and created some new ones in their attempt to justify injustice.

On May 31, 1955, the United States Supreme Court handed down a decree outlining the details by which the public schools would be desegregated. This decree could be considered an extension of the decision of the previous year. It contains a number of safeguards which the Court believed would assure effective desegregation in the public schools. While the Court did not state a definite deadline for the termination of the processes of desegregation, it did contain a deadline for the beginning of desegregation. It was clear that the nine justices of the Supreme Court who handed down this thoughtful and reasonable implementation decree expected that attempts would be made to implement it immediately and that these attempts would be made in good faith. In the language of this decree the Court stated:

> The courts will require that the defendants make a prompt and reasonable start toward full compliance with our May 17, 1954, ruling. Once such a start has been made, the courts may find that additional time is necessary to carry out the ruling in an effective manner.

What is more the Court stated that "The burden rests upon the defendants to establish that such time is necessary. . . ." This language is clear and on the face of it does not give aid and comfort to those who would desire indefinite or infinite time to begin to desegregate the schools. The Court also emphasized the fact that "The vitality of these constitutional principles cannot be allowed to yield simply because of disagreement with them."

REACTIONS TO A MISINTERPRETATION

In spite of the clear and reasonable language of this implementation decree of the United States Supreme Court, a number of the segregationists have taken the position that this implementation decree represents a retreat on the part of the Court from the ideals and constitutional principles which were clearly enunciated in the May 17, 1954, decision. Some of them were even brazen enough to suggest that they had been successful in intimidating the Court by their threats of violence and that the Court was forced to make this strategic retreat. It now has become clear that on the basis of this mininterpretation these segregationists are now operating as if they have been given extreme latitude by the Court to continue racial segregation indefinitely. On their assumption that this implementation decree is ambiguous they have now seized the initiative and have developed various types of devices and organizations for the purpose of intimidating whites and Negroes and attempting to terrorize them to the point where they will voluntarily give up the quest for their constitutional rights.

The modern versions of the Ku Klux Klan in the form of so-called respectable White Citizens Councils and the ironically named Southern Gentlemen have become bolder and more powerful since last May. Their methods are the methods of open and covert terror: undercurrent, brutal intimidation, economic boycott, and threats of starvation of Negro men, women, and children. They openly bully and bulldose whites who dare to protest their inhumanity. They demand absolute and complete conformity from whites and abject submission from Negroes. Theirs are the methods of desperate men. They publicly claim that they abjure violence. They state in pious mockery that they are respectable people who are concerned with preserving their way of life. They even insist that they are protecting good Negroes from the dastardly contaminating influence of Northern troublemakers. Their hypocrisy is transparent. They are, in fact, if not the actual murderers of men and children, the accessories to these murders. They incite the less respectable masses and the dehumanized to such murders. These are the apostles of racism. They are advocates of open and covert cruelty and violence under the proud banner of white supremacy.

THE ISSUES AS NOW FOCUSED

But these men could not get away with this reign of terror if it were not tolerated by those of us who consider ourselves respectable and law-abiding.

It apparently has not yet become perfectly clear to the American people that the citizenship rights of Negroes cannot be destroyed or flouted without weakening the citizenship rights of every other American. It has not yet become clear that a cynical miscarriage of justice where a Negro victim is involved weakens the structure and protection of our laws and our courts for all. Subtle or overt anarchy in Mississippi weakens the very foundation of lawful government in the other forty-seven states. Denying Negroes their citizenship rights and equality before the law makes a mockery of these protections for every American. It is pathetic to observe the apathy of the average white person as he views the chaos in Mississippi, South Carolina, and Georgia and believes that this is only the same old problem of whites oppressing Negroes. As important as this problem is in itself, this is not the only problem. It is equally a problem of whites destroying the foundations of their own government and blindly pulling down the temple of their own legal protection. There is no clearer example of the tragic words of Puck: "What fools these mortals be."

The price which America must pay for the continued oppression of the Negro is the price of its own destruction—not because the Negro has the power to bring about this destruction by military or economic means; and certainly not because the Negro could or would conspire with the enemies of American democracy, but because the treatment of the Negro in America is the index of the essential strength and stability of the American concept of democratic government. This observation is trite; it was stated with much greater scholarship and eloquence by Gunnar Myrdal and his associates. It remains, however, an unavoidable fact. It is a fact which the murdering of Negro children will not obscure but make ever more clear.

These are the basic issues as I see them. This is the social problem which reasonable men, moral men, men of clarity and vision must solve. These problems cannot be solved by chance or time alone. The solution of them cannot be on the terms of the racists and the gradualists. To postpone justice perpetuates and reinforces injustice. The diehard supporters of racial segregation in America have made it clear that they are not above full and complete defiance of the United States Supreme Court and they will not only risk anarchy, but will stoop to the depths of murdering children. This is their concept of what it means to be civilized and superior. These individuals can no longer be dealt with as if they were reasonable or humane men. They are desperate men, they are fanatical men, and they believe that no crime is too cruel or too brutal to obtain their ends. Only when this fact, this painful fact, is clearly recognized and accepted by the American people will we demand that our federal government mobilize its constitutional powers to enforce our laws. The choice which these men have forced is the choice between anarchy and stable democratic government.

The fact that Emmett Till and others like him can be murdered with impunity matters little to these victims, but will be seen to matter a great deal to those who now believe themselves secure, privileged, and propertied members of our society. Disregard of human values makes easy the disregard of property values. Were I a member of the propertied and privileged classes of America, I would be terrified at what is happening to Negroes in Mississippi. Even if I had no humanitarian basis for my concern, it would seem clear to me that in a social climate in which this could happen to Negroes today, it could happen to my industrial plant, my home, my property, my child, and my person tomorrow. Mass cruelty, once unleashed, is difficult, if not impossible, to control. It is the crucial sign of a stable, democratic government that such anarchy is not tolerated in any segment of society lest it destroy the whole structure of society.

WORDS AND ACTION

Given this appraisal of the situation, what is now being done? The picture at present is unclear. On the one hand it appears that within

the past few months there have been some setbacks in the whole
area of race relations in America. For example, in a suit brought by
a Negro for admission to a state university a federal court based its
decision on its interpretation of the meaning of the May 31 implementation decree of the United States Supreme Court. This lower
court, instead of ordering the immediate admission of the Negro to
the state university, provided a period of time within which the state
could make the necessary arrangement. This would seem to be a
step backward from the earlier graduate school and college decisions
which were based upon the legal assumption that the right of a Negro to admission to a state-supported university was personal and immediate. It is quite possible that subsequent decisions from the
United States Supreme Court will rectify this apparent loss.

In some recent decisions, the United States Supreme Court has
extended the legal principle of its May 17, 1954, decision to other
areas of life. It is now clear that separate facilities cannot be equal
in such areas as public recreational facilities and parks. This is a
definite gain. There is no doubt that the fight for racial justice has
gone almost as far as possible on the legal and judicial front. If the
legislative and executive branches of our government were as concerned with the protection of our citizenship rights without regard
to race, color, creed, or political expediency as our federal courts
have been, then the task which confronts the American people in general and Negroes in particular would be infinitely easier.

In spite of the crucial role of the federal courts and the United
States Supreme Court in clarifying constitutional principles and removing the legal support to the maintenance of segregation in our
society, it would be a serious mistake to believe that the courts themselves can actually change social conditions. The courts can take away
the legal basis for segregation and other conditions of injustice. They
cannot in and of themselves enforce their decisions on the community
level. The matter of enforcement remains the responsibility of the
executive branch of the government, which is in turn responsive to
and reflective of the vigilance and social morality of the people.

How have the people responded to the new legal climate created
by the United States Supreme Court? Immediately after the May 17,
1954, decision of the Supreme Court, leading churchmen, educators,
labor leaders, and leaders in social welfare organizations expressed general agreement and satisfaction with the spirit and content of that decision. Many of these groups passed resolutions expressing their support
of this decision and their desire to work for a nonsegregated society.
Some of these resolutions were conspicuous by their mildness or am-

biguity. They were, however, clearly against the sin of racial segregation. It was not clear, however, how these verbal protestations against sin would be translated into action for virtue. Up to the present it seems safe to say that not one single church group, educational organization, labor union, or social welfare agency has published and implemented an action program or the type of program wherein their members can actively work to bring about a change from segregation to nonsegregation in the public schools of a single Southern community. What is more, to my knowledge, they have not developed a program or a plan whereby individuals in these communities, who are against segregation and who desire to work as individuals, can receive organizational support and protection in the face of economic, psychological, or physical violence. Such specific and concrete programs for the implementation of the previous righteous resolutions are now mandatory. Such action programs can be developed; and if they are not developed, pious words are useless in the present social realities.

A ROLE FOR LIBERALS

What has been the role of white Northern liberals in the struggle for racial justice and equality which is now taking place in America? Many of these people plaintively ask: "What can we do?" A reasonable reply to this general question is: "What would you do if these problems confronted you or your children personally?" Sometimes the answer is: "I would get the government to take strong action. I would talk to my Congressman: I would make him understand that this could not be tolerated." Certainly this could also be done if we felt the same sense of urgency about the present situation in Mississippi, South Carolina, and similar Southern states.

Realism impels us to recognize the limitations of a political approach to a solution of this problem at this time. Politicians and public officials in both parties seem to have an endless reservoir of good reasons why the unpleasant topic of race relations should not now be opened up for public discussion, and certainly should not be the basis for splitting party harmony. Always there appear to be good political reasons why some other problem or issue should take precedence over the human and civil rights of Negroes. In this regard there is precious little to choose from between the two major parties. The fact remains, however, that the issue of racial justice in America is and will remain a paramount political issue. It cannot be successfully evaded nor will it disappear with doubletalk. The rationalizations for avoiding meeting these issues squarely have now become transparent. These issues must be faced and resolved in terms of the contemporary facts.

A PROGRAM OF AFFIRMATION—
THE NEGRO'S CONTRIBUTION

In the final analysis, the problem of obtaining full and equal citizenship rights for the Negro is a problem for which the Negro himself must assume the primary responsibility. It may well be unrealistic for him to expect that others, no matter how liberal, no matter how religious, no matter how clear in their concern for moral justice, will bring to the solution of this problem the same intensity of feeling and fervor of the soul which he himself must have. It may well be that one of the most insidious, damaging effects of past segregation on the personality of the Negro is that many Negroes may have become conditioned not only to the acceptance of their oppression, but have become possessed with the delusion that if they are to be freed of oppression it will be through the efforts and sacrifices of others.

If the 300 years of oppression have caused Negroes to accommodate to injustice or merely to seek a hollow imitation of the spiritual emptiness of Western materialistic civilization, then they have been wasted, tragic years of meaningless suffering. If, on the other hand, these years of oppression have forced the Negro to recognize that in order to be free and in order to be human he must work for his freedom, he must sacrifice for the future of his children, and, if necessary, he must be willing to die as an affirmation of his humanity, then those years of oppression have not been in vain.

The Negro in America cannot permit himself even to flirt with the idea of retaliatory violence. Violence appears to have become the inseparable twin of Western materialism. It has even become the hallmark of its grandeur. It, nonetheless, solves no social problem. It merely creates new and more complicated ones. Furthermore, the American Negro, fortunately, does not have the techniques, resources, or methods by which he could hope to be successful through the use of retaliatory violence. He must fight his battles for freedom not with the weapons of arms, anger, or corroding hatred, but with the power inherent in the dignity of the human personality. He must refuse to be intimidated; he must stand proudly before those who reveal their own inhumanity by their need to deny him his. He must accept their challenge unflinchingly. He cannot flee like a slave in the night from his home. He cannot listen to the glib suggestions that he migrate to other regions of the country. In seeking escape he can make no contribution to the moral strength of our nation, nor does he set an example of courage for himself and his children.

But what if these acts of violence continue and increase? When then can be his defense? His only defense is to meet every act of barbarity, illegality, cruelty, and injustice toward an individual Negro with the fact that 100 more Negroes will present themselves in his place as potential victims. The weakness of the Negro can be his strength.

The only specific proposal which my limited vision and intelligence make possible for me to present is that the Negro must stand before his oppressors with head unbowed as he demands full and unqualified equality for his children and himself no matter what the personal cost. Specifically, this means that if he is threatened with economic ruin and violent reprisals because he petitions a school board to admit his children to a nonsegregated school, then he must accept these risks with the full knowledge that physical death may be more merciful than to doom himself and his children to a life of permanent psychological death. If these are the only alternatives, he has no choice. He will either die like an animal or will be permitted to live a despicable life on the sufferance of others. Or he will die as an affirmation of his humanity so that his children may live with pride and dignity.

If his oppressors burn the home of one Negro for his courage, then this must be met by the fact that they will be required to burn the homes of hundreds and thousands of Negroes. If they deny bread and milk to Negro children whose parents want them to be free, then they must be required to deny these children every necessity of life—water and air itself. They must be glutted with their own barbarity. They must be forced to stand before the world and their God splattered with the blood and reeking with the stench of those they consider their inferiors. Let this be the pyrrhic symbol of their superiority.

The Negro cannot win the respect of his cowardly oppressors by groveling. To grovel in the mud merely increases the oppressors' arrogance and contempt for their victims and is seen as proof of the Negro's inferiority. The Negro cannot maintain self-respect or win the respect of the peoples of the world if he is willing to settle for the crumbs of citizenship and if he is willing to sell the future lives of his children for his personal and immediate comfort and safety. It is now clear that equality is indivisible and uncompromisable.

The Negro in America is fortunate in that he has little to lose by way of material wealth. He need not compromise away his soul for silver. It requires no great effort on his part to be heroic. He has only his life. And to be treated as a subhuman is to die a thousand deaths.

I, therefore, conclude that the Negro's contribution to the effective desegregation of the public schools and other areas of American life can be made by his insistence upon his democratic rights in the community in which he lives; by his petitioning his school board and other public officials that these rights be granted without regard to their attitudes toward him, but because they are constitutionally guaranteed. If his petitions are ignored, then he is obligated to present himself in mass on the steps of their churches, in the vestibules of the schools, in legislative halls and in the courts of justice.

Candor requires us to recognize that not all Negroes will have the strength and courage to engage in this type of mass demonstration of positive and firm insistence upon being treated as human beings— —in this affirmation of their humanity. While there is no substitute for personal courage in bringing about social progress, the success of this plan is not dependent upon its being unanimous. It will require only 5 to 10 percent of the Negroes of any community in order that it be effective. Even this small number will demonstrate to the world the fact that America is afflicted with a cancerous disease which it must cure if it is to be taken seriously as one of the leaders of democratic civilization. I do not know how many Negroes would be willing to be a part of this type of program. It might mean death for many of them. All I know is that the possibility for success in this struggle for equality will be determined and limited by the number of people who are willing to give their lives for the future of their children. Only when sufficient numbers of Negroes have reached this stage in their reaction to racial oppression will they earn that dignity and equality which is essential to their humanity.

This suggested program is not without successful precedent. We have the magnificent example of Gandhi who challenged the might of the British Empire and won with only the weapons of dedication, courage, dignity, morality, and the power of his own contagious humanity. In our own history, we have examples of men and women who fought against the overwhelming odds of slavery and by their courage awakened the conscience of others. Through their past sacrifices we are now able to join the battle at its present level of complexity. Today we have examples of the effectiveness of courage in the daily lives of those individuals who continue to live and fight for freedom in the South—and in the North; in the work of the lawyers and the field staff of the NAACP who are in personal jeopardy each time they enter a backward Southern community in quest of justice, and in the awesome examples of courage in the daily lives of men like Dr. T. R. M. Howard of Mound Bayou, and the men of Belzoni, Mississippi.

When we have reached the stage of systematic and organized selfless sacrifice for the future of our children, the 300 years of oppression which our ancestors endured will not have been in vain. We then will have vindicated their suffering by making a maximum contribution to civilization through strengthening the foundations of democracy in our nation and, thereby, strengthening the structure of democracy and equality for all peoples throughout the world.

Emancipation: History's Fantastic Reverie

DR. DWIGHT DUMOND

Dwight Lowell Dumond, a native of Kingston, Ohio, earned his Bachelor of Arts degree at Baldwin-Wallace College, (1920) the Master of Arts degree at Washington University, (1928), and the Doctor of Philosophy degree at the University of Michigan (1929).

Dr. Dumond is a member of the Society of American Historians of the American History Association and served on the Association Committee on Teaching of History in Schools and Colleges in 1943. He was a member of the Mississippi Valley History Association and was a member of the organization's Executive Committee from 1939 to 1940 and its President from 1948 to 1949. He has memberships in the Southern History Association; Michigan Academy of Arts, Sciences, and Letters; the Masonic Lodge; and the Research Club of the University of Michigan. He was a Commonwealth Foundation Lecturer at University College (London) from 1938 to 1939. Dr. Dumond is the author of *A History of the United States* (1942), *America in Our Time* (1947), and *Antislavery, Crusade for Freedom in America* (1961), for which he received the Ainsfield-Wolf Award, *America's Shame and Redemption,* (1965).

A professor of history at the University of Michigan since 1939, Dr. Dumond expresses his belief that mankind will no longer await the "dream-come-true" cycle of life in these United States and offers the "Men in Washington" suggestions for the means of saving this na-

tion's "soul." His speech, "Emancipation: History's Fantastic Reverie,"
was delivered at the annual dinner of the Association for the Study of
Negro Life and History, October 17, 1963, at Virginia State College,
Petersburg, Virginia.

*   *   *

It is my settled conviction that the four documents most important
to the building of this nation are the New Testament, the Declaration
of Independence, the Constitution of 1787, and the Emancipation
Proclamation. If we were to add a fifth, it would have to be the
Fourteenth Amendment. The first contains God's plan for individual
salvation and ultimate perfection of the human race. The second is a
testament of faith; a seemingly perfect definition of manhood; an
acknowledgment of man's intellectual capacity and moral responsibility for self-government. The third is the supreme law of the most
perfect establishment in recorded history for the cultivation of man's
spiritual and intellectual freedom. The fourth is the basic charter
of freedom for a large portion of our people, a confession of previous
error and a simple act of justice by the highest authority of the nation. As to the fifth, I say again, as I have said many times, that

> wrapped up in that famous trilogy are the social teachings of Jesus,
> the philosophy of Locke, and the legal principles of Blackstone. . . .
> keep it in the proper historical perspective and everything is there:
> God and man—the natural rights of man—men and government—
> mutual obligations of allegiance and security—due process—equality
> of all men in the endowment of rights, the security of rights, the
> exercise of rights, before the law and in the halls of justice.

The Founding Fathers established a vast store of credit throughout
the world for virtue and high-mindedness by the first sentence of the
Declaration. It was a compendium of Christian faith. It was a pros-
pectus of democratic philosophy. It stated without equivocation the
equality of all men in the sight of God. These men dedicated the nation to freedom, in every age and every place the incontestable right
to know all things and to act by choice. They dedicated the nation
to equality in all things without reservation, so completely in fact that
slavery was swept away north of Virginia and could have been struck
down everywhere by judicial decree.

Some of the men who framed the Constitution may have believed
the Declaration to have been a glittering generality. Some may have
been influenced by greed. Some may have been moral hypocrites.
Some simply lacked perspective, or were devotees of decentraliza-

tion of power, or actually believed in biological inequality and racial inferiority. Or they may have believed in gradualism, and felt they were making adequate provision of the ultimate abolition of slavery. Whatever the cause of their weakness, they failed.

Most people in the country at large were satisfied with the achievement of independence and establishment of a stable government by the Constitutional Convention. This was true of members of the several ratifying conventions. They placed their trust in God without realizing He needs a little help, and that trait has remained constant to the present time. I never cease to be amazed at the ability of Christians to adjust to the most grievous wrongs of civil government. In this first stage of our reverie we established a government based upon the principle of the Declaration but continued slavery, which ate at the vitals of the Union and democratic institutions. Nearly a century later, we freed the slaves by a great civil war without defining emancipation or correcting the glaring weaknesses of political organization. Now, after another century we face a worldwide revolution of immense proportions, still talk in riddles, and seem to think if we wait long enough our troubles will all go away.

Racialism is a myth. Out of it has come a whole progeny of evils. Its survival in the United States is rationally inconceivable. A discussion of it would seem to be outside the realm of scholarship. It belongs to intellectual pygmies who neither know nor respect basic principles of religion, science, or history. It belongs to fantasy and legend. How many people have subscribed to it at any given time or place is a moot question. Too many, of course.

Slavery enshrined the doctrine and the Constitution did not strike it down. The Declaration said all men are endowed by their Creator with the inalienable right to life, liberty, and the pursuit of happiness. The Constitution *said* no person should be deprived of life, liberty, or property without due process of law; but it also *allowed* slaves to be imported for twenty years. It allowed slave masters to roam the entire country seizing people and carrying them off to an infinitude of slavery, and it established a political system incorporating the repugnant principle that men who owned slaves should have extra political power in the Congress and the electoral college. It allowed the states to retain the police powers under which slavery existed and men of color, both slave and free, have been crucified for three hundred years. And the nation dreamed its dream of freedom and equality for all men.

Slavery was two things. It was complete subjection of one man to another by force, recognized and sustained by state law. It was the complete subordination of people of color to white people in all things. Slavery, in short, was an individual relationship and a system. Slave or free, the man of color was always a potential victim of unrestrained sadism and/or incessant mortification. Slavery gave to the dominant whites license to maltreat at pleasure all who were darker in color. The victims were denied all positive and substantive rights. Most important of these were access to the courts and protection by law, access to knowledge and religious instruction, the right to make decisions, including moral judgments, the right to use their talents to the end of an enriched and more satisfying life, and the right to participate in the social and political life of the nation. The inevitable tendency of slavery was to dehumanize the slave and corrupt the slaveholder.

A democratic society is based upon voluntary industry. It is a society in which the individual is allowed as much freedom and is under as little restraint as is consistent with the rights of others; a society based in equity, where all men alike are recipients of impartial justice and protection of rights; a society in which free inquiry and discussion know no restraints; where investigation, reason, and collective intelligence are the basis of action, where political power is uniformly distributed, and where the national conscience is brought to bear in the determination of public policy. Slavery was eternally at war with all of these functional processes.

Slavery forced the church to abdicate its power. It is the duty and high privilege of churchmen to condemn evil, corruption, and despotism in government, to castigate immoral conduct on the part of individuals, and to speak as tribunes in defense of weak, exploited, helpless people. The church is the one agency whose primary responsibility is reformation. It surrendered its stewardship and sprang to the defense of slavery.

Discussion was silenced in the slave states, greatly curtailed in Congress, avoided by statesmen as long as possible. Great intellectuals, humanitarians, free Negroes, anyone who claimed the right to discuss slavery in peaceable assemblies, in churches, and in newspapers were set upon by howling mobs. The guilt of mobs was charged to their victims; public officials claimed the right to withhold protection from persons and property and sometimes joined in the onslaught.

Slaveholders and their minions subordinated the authority of the federal government to that of the states. They insisted upon the right of a state to nullify federal law to protect themselves against the will of a constitutional majority in the nation, when what they really wanted was freedom from restraint to oppress, exploit, and destroy a minority of their own people who were also, and first of all, citizens of the United States. They finally waged war upon the very government and constitution which had allowed them to maintain a powerful aristocracy and to possess extraordinary power in the government. It was a rebellion without justification and without reason.

Nobody knows when Abraham Lincoln came to a realization that preservation of the Union and abolition of slavery were inseparable. Mystic or not, no other man of his day saw a problem in its totality with more clarity. So many anxieties pressed in upon him that a public pronouncement of intent was impossible. He knew full well that the philosophy of slavery and the philosophy of human rights had been contending for a generation and were now locked in a death struggle for control of the nation. He had held fast to no compromise, knowing that compromise at that point would mark the end of constitutional government.

It is amazing how many people turned away from reality in 1861, just as they are doing today. That is what I mean by history's fantastic reverie. They wanted peace by compromise. Then they wanted a war of limited objectives. They were willing to barter away forever the high prerogative of the people to determine public policy in respect to human rights. They were willing to place a premium upon resort to arms by men who lost a decision at the ballot box. They were willing to recognize the power of a section to restrain the whole of a nation. Not so the men—those much maligned radicals —who had put their hands to the task of restoring the authority and prestige of constitutional government; not Lincoln.

Lincoln got some powerful antislavery men into foreign diplomatic posts immediately to correct the notion that slavery was not an issue in the war. No one could have done better on that score: Joshua Giddings, John Bigelow, Richard Hildreth, William Dean Howells, Carl Schurz, Thomas Corwin, Cassius M. Clay, John Lothrop Motley, Anson Burlingame, Zebina Eastman. He finally got some men in command of his armies who knew what the war was about.

It was in the first year of the war that full acknowledgment was made of the end of slavery. Slavery was destroyed by the first shots fired at the Stars and Stripes. An incredulous people were slow to realize the consequences of this action. Even now there are those who would argue the point. The inescapable fact is, however, that slavery was an exercise of force sustained by state law which once broken could never be restored. When slaveholders ran away and slaves ran away, the slaves were free. Slavery was abolished as the armies advanced and broke the exercise of force. Lincoln's Emancipation Proclamation and the Thirteenth Amendment completed the work begun on the battlefield.

Unfortunately emancipation, like slavery, meant nothing divorced from the interpretations placed on it. No man could now hold another in legalized bondage. The Thirteenth Amendment put that point beyond reversal by courts or a later Congress. It did not free the Negroes from control by the whites, or provide any safeguards for democratic institutions, or remove the power of former slaveholders and racists from the government. Those who saw the enormity of the problem, the fearful responsibility that faced the country, the glorious opportunity to erect a lasting monument to the dead were so few in numbers as to be treated with the same disdain as was visited upon the early antislavery men.

The South at the close of the war was a spiritual and political vacuum. The men who carried the burden of government at Washington through four agonizing years knew that it would be a wicked and cowardly thing to withdraw its control from the South. They knew that Congressional withdrawal would mean government of the old slave states by and for the whites for a long time. They knew that if the nation did not make decisions, the Southern whites would make them, and that tomorrow would play no part in their scheme of things, only present poverty and the delusion of past glory. They knew the protecting mantle of the federal Constitution must be thrown over these newly emancipated people; that denial of the right of secession was too moderate a restraint upon states' rights; and, that the burden of proof must rest upon those who had forfeited the public trust, in all matters pertaining to the restoration of their political privileges.

It is a false notion that internal peace required acceptance back into the councils of the nation of the men who had attempted to destroy it. This was a return to the old immorality of concession. What was the most important issue in this crisis of the war's end: the political privileges of the whites or the natural rights of three and one-half million Negroes who had been rescued from their oppression? Some men knew the correct answer but their prodigious efforts always fell a little short of providing complete emancipation for the Negro and redemption of democracy in the former slave states.

Men accepted the preservation of the Union, but grudgingly and under duress. They had no choice but to accept the abolition of slavery, but they would not accept emancipation in its broader aspects, nor admit slavery to have been an evil, nor recognize the natural rights of Negroes as persons or their constitutional rights as citizens.

Love for the Union and respect for the federal government were hard to come by. The Lincoln policy of generosity to rebels did not evoke generosity to friends of the government or loyalty on their part. It simply did not work. Men who had waged bitter war soon returned to power. They were heroes. They had done no wrong. People thought of themselves, spoke of themselves, as Southerners. There was almost a complete lack of national sentiment. The Confederate flag was prominently displayed through the years, more often than not with more respect than the Stars and Stripes. Sectionalism in all its virulence remained to plague the nation. It was hostile to social revolution and to national unity. Its evil genius was second-class citizenship for the Negro. It thrived on cultural deficiencies and nourished pride in second-rate achievements. It may well be that these people were incapable of loyalty to anything except their own prejudices.

So we come to the end of another century. We shrank from our responsibilities in 1787, and we did it again in 1865. If we do it now we do not deserve to survive as a free people. All of our glorious history, all the precepts of humanity, the fate of civilization itself, demand that we rouse ourselves from our lethargy, tell the people the truth, face realities, correct the defects of our institutions, and purify our hearts. Mankind will wait upon our reveries no longer. This is a worldwide revolution today, not a family quarrel. It is as great a revolution as the Reformation. Few people grasp its meaning, its intensity, its power. Some people are trying to make money from it; some to gain notoriety; some to win political preferment; but I say to you, and I wish I could say it to every man in Washington today, the only men in public or private life whose words and deeds will live in history are those who stand foursquare for justice and truth, who love their fellowmen about all earthly gain, who reach a helping hand to those who suffer and weep for those who are crucified by hate and prejudice, who sacrifice their wealth, their social position, their public careers if necessary to save this nation's soul. We will never find peace except at the foot of the cross, and if that road is blocked again as it was in 1861, then may God have mercy upon us.

What we have to do is quit dreaming and get down to reality. In an age which demands a concept of world citizenship, men continue to talk about state sovereignty and some aspirants to high office want even to atomize that. State sovereignty is a myth. There never has been any such thing as state sovereignty since 1789, probably not since the Association. All of the power of the states flows to them through the Constitution of the United States and the Constitution is the supreme law of the land. Some governors currently project themselves back 100 years to emulate the Davises, the Yanceys, the Calhouns. They wrap themselves in the folds of the Stars and Bars and set themselves up as sacred symbols of Americanism, of righteousness and honor. They live and dream in a world of fantasy. These men are heroes and prophets to many people. They demand segregation forever as slaveholders demand slavery forever. They are pledged to resist federal law. They set themselves above the national conscience and the courts. Their followers fly the flag of rebellion everywhere and above the Stars and Stripes. They ride through the night to burn and torture and kill. They pride themselves on violence and second-rate achievement.

Men reared in the kind of atmosphere which prevails in these communities are not fit to participate in government. They go to Congress and do everything in their power to prevent enactment of laws to protect the victims of these injustices. Their ideas of justice are corrupt. Their attitude toward poor and unfortunate people is one of contempt. No man who would discriminate against another man because of the color of his skin is fit to participate in the formulation of public policy.

Common sense should have dictated some better security for the Negro than the franchise, unless control of the franchise were given to the federal government. Control of the franchise by state governments has created so many ridiculous situations as to be beyond the pale of respectability. In this case it was tragic. Negroes had to be guaranteed the franchise the same as they had of necessity been enrolled in the Union armies, as a recognition by the highest authority of equality. They had to be guaranteed the franchise for their own self-respect and their own protection. Freedom for the slaves automatically gave to a people fresh from the wars of rebellion an increase of representation if they could get restoration of representation in Congress. The old evil of giving men extraordinary power in government as a reward for oppressing and exploiting their fellowmen was now compounded. An effort was made to prevent this by authorizing a reduction in representation for any state denying the franchise to the Negro, but the vagaries of politics made the provision little else than a monument to incompetence. It was all wrong, even if it had been applied, because that would have deprived the Negro of the franchise and the nation of his voice in public affairs. It was the wrong approach then; it is the wrong approach now in spite of anything the Civil Rights Commission may say. Even assuming, and it is a wild assumption, that these states would rather permit the Negro to have a voice in public affairs than to lose representation, the approach and the principle involved are both morally wrong. What can men be thinking about to offer approval of this sort of evil even on the basis of reducing the political power of the evildoers? The nation has a right to the wisdom and talents of all its people in the conduct of public affairs. It dare not be content with less. The Negro has a right to participate in public affairs on a state and local level. He dare not ever, in any circumstances, agree to less. The idea that voting and office holding is a privilege to be given or withheld by a majority is no longer valid.

The combination of readmission of states and retention of state control of the franchise was a betrayal of everything for which men had fought in the war. Southern whites excluded Negroes from the ballot box, continued to appropriate to themselves all representation based upon the Negro population, and went back to Congress to thwart any cooperative legislation through the years. Their power in party conventions, in the House of Representatives and in the electoral college is so great that both parties vie for its support directly or by indirection and they are already doing it shamelessly in anticipation of the next presidential campaign. Bear in mind also that the filibuster in the Senate is the perfect application of Calhoun's doctrine of nullification. Keeping a bill from coming to a vote is a far more vicious and deadly way to stifle the will of the people than declaring it null and void after it becomes a law. Bear in mind also that chairmanships of committees go to men on the basis of seniority, and Southern whites have compiled a fantastic record for bottling up legislation in Committee. All in all, we are about where we were in 1789.

Finally, the state and local governments were allowed to continue exercise of the police powers, and the courts denied that Congress might intervene to prevent positive denial of equal protection, or to supplement deficiencies in protection of natural rights of the individual. It would seem that Congress had always possessed the power to protect persons in their civil rights, if not on the basis of reciprocity of allegiance and protection, at least by virtue of the Bill of Rights. In fact, the Constitution itself as the supreme law of the land, without congressional legislation, would seem so to protect. It would seem that Congress was empowered to legislate for the protection of persons and property, if not before the Civil War then certainly under the Thirteenth Amendment, because slavery was a comprehensive denial of natural rights and the amendment abolished slavery. It would seem that Congress possessed the power to protect the natural rights (privileges and immunities) of the individual under the Fourteenth Amendment because that amendment forbade any state to abridge such rights of citizens and failure to protect—protection being a basic function of government—is assuredly an abridgment, denial, or contraction. All of this turned out not to be so. States were held to be the depositaries of individual rights, the federal government not to have the power to protect individuals in their rights of persons and property, and privileges and immunities not to mean the natural rights of individuals. The federal government could not protect its citizens one against another, nor punish offenses of one against another. Police powers of the states were left intact. In retrospect, then, everything hinged upon force. The only reformation worthwhile was achieved through Reconstruction governments of the states, which fell when the army was withdrawn. That day came in 1876 because politics demanded that it be withdrawn. We have opened a door now with the equality clause, but I warn you it is a limited achievement. We have no weapon here to enforce protection by local police, prevent police brutality, or cleanse the corruption and degradation of the jury system.

We are still in the depths of a great reverie, dreaming precious days away, talking wonderful words that have been discredited a thousand times over: patience, moderation, gradualism, compromise; but what are we doing actually (1) to acknowledge the awful crime of giving excessive, and at times controlling, political power to men as a reward for oppressing a large portion of our people, (2) to free the conscience of the nation from the restraints of a state with the lowest cultural level in the nation, (3) to give to Negroes the enjoyment of the franchise and more importantly to the nation the benefit of their full participation in the public affairs, to get rid of the filibuster, and to prevent committee chairmen in the House of Representatives from governing by decree. What are we doing to provide protection to persons and property, just and equitable treatment to everyone by state and local officials, justice in the courts, particularly by juries, for persons disliked by the majority in a community to whom all local officials are beholden? What are we doing to bring about a spiritual regeneration which will remove color consciousness from our relationships with other people and permit us to associate freely as human beings and citizens?

Suffering will not go away. Poverty will not go away. Neither will aspiration and hope from the hearts of the oppressed. Men will always love freedom and equality. They will fight for it because they dare not compromise it away. It's a false notion that something can be given to people from whom everything was taken away. It can only be restored, and compromise has no place here, only retributive justice. This is a matter of justice and right or nothing. Why will we not then as a people forget the doubts of our minds, take the problem into the sanctuary of our hearts, and find security and peace in love for our fellowmen? We will not, of course, because we are neither Christians nor gentlemen, and the hour of retribution draws near. The only thing the country understands today is fear: fear of communism, fear of atomic bombs, fear of Negroes. We are starved in mind and soul. We have the greatest opportunity ever given to a people to resume moral leadership of the world in the area of human relationships. We have a great obligation, even necessity, to expand upon our democratic ideals and institutions, but we cannot rise to the challenge. It is my considered judgment that we will not until impending disaster frightens us into action. There must be no more compromise, no more expedience, no more politics. The march for freedom must go on, will go on, even at the fearful risk of civil strife. Man cannot turn back in his quest for justice and the better life.

The Moral Dimensions of the Civil-rights Movement

FATHER THEODORE S. HESBURGH

A notable figure in the Catholic Church and the world community, Theodore Hesburgh has been a leading spiritual and social leader of the middle of the twentieth century. As an educator, he is recognized around the world. Over a dozen universities have conferred honorary degrees upon him.

Since his appointment as President of the University of Notre Dame, he has served as Director of the Woodrow Wilson National Fellowship Corporation; as Chairman of the United States Civil Rights Commission; as Director of the Midwest Universities Research Association; as Director of the American Council on Education; as a trustee for the Rockefeller Foundation; as a member of the United States Advisory Commission on International, Educational, and Cultural Affairs; as Director of Freedoms Foundation; and as President and Director of the Institute of International Education.

Included here is an address given before the meeting of the American Academy of Arts and Sciences, Boston, Massachusetts, November 11, 1964.

* * *

Several years ago I attended a lecture by a distinguished South African scholar at Capetown University on the subject "The Moral Justification of *Apartheid*." After the lecture, we were driving down the Cape to his home university of Stellenbosch when he asked me: "What did you think of my lecture?" I told him that he had convinced me that there was no moral justification of apartheid. "I had hoped to do the opposite," he replied.

It might be said that I hope to do the opposite today: to show that the civil-rights movement here and about the world is not just another economic, political, social, or ethnic movement, although it is all of these, too. There is a deep moral dimension to the whole concern for civil rights in our times. In fact, the moral dimension is the most fundamental aspect of it all. Without it, the movement loses much of its vital dynamism and ultimate thrust. Also, without the moral dimension, the civil-rights movement will never be completely understood, or completely successful either.

Even our political leaders have understood this truth. Many of them have said that we should try to achieve full civil rights for all of our citizens not simply because it will be helpful to our cause in the international field, or because it will make American life more peaceful and productive, but because it is right that this should happen.

As he signed the Civil Rights Act of 1964 into law, President Johnson said:

Our generation of Americans has been called on to continue the unending search for justice within our own borders.

We believe that all men are created equal—yet many are denied equal treatment.

We believe that all men have certain inalienable rights—yet many Americans do not enjoy those rights.

We believe that all men are entitled to the blessings of liberty—yet millions are being deprived of those blessings, not because of their own failures, but because of the color of their skin.

The reasons are deeply imbedded in history and tradition and the nature of man. We can understand without rancor or hatred how this all happened. But it cannot continue.

Our Constitution, the foundation of our republic, forbids it. The principles of our freedom forbid it. Morality forbids it. And the law I will sign tonight forbids it. . . .

"The law says" President Johnson continued

That those who are equal before God shall also be equal in the

polling booths, in the classrooms, in the factories, and in hotels
and restaurants and movie theaters, and other places that provide
service to the public.

We will achieve these goals because most Americans are law-
abiding citizens *who want to do what is right.* . . .

Let us hasten the day when our unmeasured strength and our
unbounded spirit will be free to do the great works ordained to
this nation by the just and wise God who is Father of us all.

If you ponder upon these words, you will see that this is at base
a moral statement of the problem. The appeal is directly to conscience,
to justice, to equality before God, to inalienable rights, to responsibility in freedom, to the law of basic human dignity as ordained by
a wise and just God and echoed in our Constitution and the laws that
specify the civil rights that our Constitution proclaims. The appeal
of our President is most forceful because one cannot reject his conclusions without rejecting his moral principles which are at the base
of what it means to be a human person in the good society.

I am reminded of what often happened during the hearings of the
United States Commission on Civil Rights here and there about the
country. We would come to a particularly difficult moment when any
kind of consensus seemed impossible, either because of the complica-
tion of the problem at hand or the hostility of the audience or wit-
nesses. At this point, one of the staff would slip me a note scribbled
on the inevitable long sheet of yellow legal paper, saying, in effect,
"Better give them some theology." All of us can legitimately differ
about ways and means, about possible solutions to seemingly impossible problems. But ultimately, anyone who understands anything
of the Judeo-Christian tradition at the base of Western culture must
hold some common principles about the nature and destiny of man
which alone validate the society in which we live. It is characteristic
of our ambivalent age that all too few people ever consciously consider these fundamental philosophical and theological principles, but
yet, consciously or unconsciously, they are there, and in a time of
great conflict they will be recognized, appealed to, and, however
incoherently, understood.

It has always been to me a curious reality that among the multitudinous books that our age produces one finds so very few that
address themselves to the moral foundations of democracy, or cor-
relatively, to the moral dimensions of human rights. Professor John
Hallowell of Duke University has written such a book. He justifies it
in a few words: "Our democratic institutions require a philosophy of
life to sustain them. . . . Without a clear understanding of why the

institutions exist, we shall have neither the means of defending them intellectually, nor the resolution to defend them by force when the occasion demands it."[1] And again,

> Democracy rests upon a faith in man as a rational, moral, and spiritual creature, and it is as much aspiration as it is fact. The ideals of democracy never have been and never will be achieved with perfection—they are goals constantly to be striven for, but never perfectly realized. In the last analysis, democracy is "a venture of faith in the moral and spiritual possibilities of men when entrusted with freedom."[2]

Sir Richard Livingstone, one-time Vice Chancellor of Oxford University, made the same point, on both the philosophical and theological level, in a book he wrote during the last war. He was addressing himself to another crisis, but I find his words relevant today as we face the major crisis of our own times, the drive towards a more complete realization of civil rights. Sir Richard says:

> We shall not understand ourselves and our predicament unless we realize what has happened during the past fifty years. Every civilization grows up round and with a system of beliefs and values, which are its vital principle, the nerve which feeds and keeps it healthy. If that principle perishes, if that nerve is cut, then the structure of society which depends on it still remains, but the life has gone out of it, its self-renewing power is gone, and it declines first into decay and then into death. Those who have lived through the last fifty years have witnessed the steady and progressive destruction of the soul of Western civilization. . . .
> The soul of Europe is partly Greek and partly Christian. The vital force of our civilization comes from two sources, beyond which no others count seriously, from Palestine and from Greece. We may believe in Christianity. We may not like it, but whether we deplore it or not, the main source of Europe is Christianity . . . the mass of people drew and still draw the best part of their beliefs and standards of life and conduct from Christianity, however confused and diluted the channels through which they pass. To attack Christianity was to attack the spiritual life of Europe, to weaken it was to weaken that life . . . and so we get our modern civilization—a civilization of means without ends, with ample body, but with a meager soul, with a rich inheritance, but without clear values

---

[1] *The Moral Foundations of Democracy* (Univ. of Chicago Press, Chicago, Illinois), p. 67.
[2] *Ibid.,* pp. 128-129.

or a ruling principle. . . . There is a phrase in Plato which exactly describes our condition . . . the danger of living "by habit without an intellectual principle."[3]

I take it that what Hallowell and Livingstone are telling us is that moral dimensions are historically, philosophically, and theologically discernible, but often taken for granted except in time of crisis, when we come running to them to justify our cause, to inspire heroism, to bolster courage, and to convince ourselves that the battle is really worth fighting. The deeper the crisis, the deeper our principles should run, the more clarionlike they should sound, the more clearly should they be enunciated. The last three Presidents have told our nation that the present crisis in civil rights is the greatest and most important domestic problem facing our nation. Clearly, then, it is again a time for basic principles.

While the principles at issue have recently been enunciated often enough, and clearly enough, as, for example, in the statement of President Johnson quoted above, the foundations of the principles are all too often assumed rather than demonstrated. Even our founding Fathers held these truths to be self-evident: That man is endowed by his Creator with certain inalienable rights and that among these are life, liberty, and the pursuit of happiness. This is the tradition, rightly enough, but there is more to it than the mere statement and what it assumes, and wrongly assumes, to be philosophically self-evident. It is not self-evident apparently to those who rule a third of the human race today and hold in practice that man has only those rights conceded to him by the state.

Where does one begin then? Since we are talking about human rights and the problems incident to our common humanity, we might well begin by considering more deeply what a human person is, for it is the human person who alone is the subject on earth of these inalienable rights which somehow originate in his nature. It is the human person, too, who bears the responsibility to respect these human rights. It is likewise the human person who is endowed with that inherent dignity and destiny that make a denial of these rights not merely a bad political, economic, or social situation, but a devastating spectacle of the inhumanity of man to man.

To consider the human person is to enter the realm of metaphysics, the mystery of being as uniquely realized in the inner sanctuary of the individual human being. The metaphysical tradition of the West

---

[3] *Crisis of Civilization in the Deeper Causes of the War* (Allen and Unwin Ltd.), pp. 98-99, 103-104.

defines the person in terms of individuality and independence. The person exists not as migrant bird against the fall sky, the sound of wings, the flash of light against color, but as a reality which subsists spiritually, constituting a universe unto itself, a relatively independent whole within the great overarching whole of the universe and deriving from the Transcendent Whole which is God. A person lives in self-possession, a master of himself, capable of containing himself, thanks to intellect and freedom. This same tradition sees in God the infinite essence of personality, since the very existence of God consists in the infinite and absolute superexistence of knowledge and love.

The individuality of the human person is not like the individuality of other corporeal beings, because personality is not directly related to matter, man's body, but has its roots in spirit, man's immortal soul.

The best description of human personality that I know of comes from Jacques Maritain's *Principes d'une politique humaniste*.

What do we mean precisely when we speak of the human person: When we say that a man is a person, we do not mean merely that he is an individual, in the sense that an atom, a blade of grass, a fly, or an elephant is an individual. Man is an individual who holds himself in hand by intelligence and will. He does not exist only in a physical manner. He has a spiritual superexistence through knowledge and love; he is, in a way, a universe in himself, a microcosm, in which the great universe in its entirety can be encompassed through knowledge; and through love, he can give himself completely to beings who are to him, as it were, other selves, a relation for which no equivalent can be found in the physical world. The human person possesses these characteristics because in the last analysis man, this flesh and these perishable bones which are animated and activated by a divine fire, exists "from the womb to the grave" by virtue of the very existence of his soul, which dominates time and death. Spirit is the root of personality. The notion of personality thus involves that of totality and independence; no matter how poor and crushed he may be, a person, as such, is a whole and subsists in an independent manner. To say that man is a person is to say that in the depths of his being he is more a whole than a part, and more independent than servile. It is to say that he is a minute fragment of matter that is at the same time a universe, a beggar who communicates with absolute being, mortal flesh whose value is eternal, a bit of straw into which heaven enters. It is this metaphysical mystery that religious thought points to when it says that the person is the image of God. The value of the person, his dignity, and his rights belong to the order of things naturally sacred which bear the imprint of the Father of being, and which have in Him the end of their movement.[4]

The moral conscience of the human person tells him many things: what is morally right and morally wrong, a knowledge, more or less developed, of what is generally called the natural law, and the rights that any human person possesses simply because he is a person, an independent whole who is master of himself and his acts, who can know his destiny, what is to his ultimate good, who is not a means, but an end. The natural law means nothing if it does not say that the human person has a right to be respected for what he is, and what he is for. As Maritain has said, there is, by virtue of man's ontologically unchanging human nature, an order or disposition which human reason can discover and according to which the human will must act in order to attune itself to the essential and necessary ends of the human being.

There is, of course, progression in the sensitivity of man's conscience and in his perception of the full meaning of the natural law, the full extension of the rights of man. The fact is that during ancient and mediaeval times, more attention was often paid to the obligations than to the rights of man. The eighteenth century finally saw more emphasis on human rights, although, at times, somewhat exclusively. Now today the wheel has come full round. One of the most stirring documents of our times, Pope John's *Pacem in Terris*, is totally cast in the framework of rights and duties. The transitional paragraph, following the opening outline of human rights, bears quoting here:

The natural rights with which we have been dealing are, however, inseparably connected, in the very person who is their subject, with just as many respective duties; and rights as well as duties find their source, their sustenance, and their inviolability in the natural law which grants or enjoins them. Therefore, the right of every man to life is correlative with the duty to preserve it; his right to a decent standard of living with the duty of living it becomingly; and his right to investigate the truth with the duty of seeking it evermore completely and profoundly.

Once this is admitted, it also follows that in human society, to one man's right there corresponds a duty in all other persons: the duty, namely, of acknowledging and respecting the right in question. For every fundamental human right draws its indestructible

---

[4] *The Social and Political Philosophy of Jacques Maritain* (Charles Scribner's Sons, N.Y., 1955) p. 14.

moral force from the natural law, which in granting it imposes a corresponding obligation. Those, therefore, who claim their own rights, yet altogether forget or neglect to carry out their respective duties, are people who build with one hand and destroy with the other.[5]

There is one more basic consideration which must be studied here: that of human equality in regard to rights, or, as it is often more specifically stated: equality before the law. Historically, this basic truth, a necessary consequence of all that has been said of human dignity, natural law, and human rights, has been honored more in the breech than in the keeping. Philosophically, there have been those who could easily rationalize slavery in all its multitudinous forms: the great slave class of the Greeks and Romans, the lower-caste untouchables of India, the millions enslaved and transported from Africa in the name of white superiority, the economically enslaved of the Industrial Revolution, the millions enslaved today in the name of the the Marxist-Leninist myth to promote the eventual millennium of the Proletariat. As was declared by a Nazi at Nuremberg, there was in their judgment "a greater distance between the lowest forms still called human and our superior races than between the lowest man and the highest monkey." This noxious poison of racism is still with us in many forms today, and often enough science is prostituted in an attempt to make it intellectually respectable.

Human equality has an almost equal enemy in those who confuse equality with egalitarianism. The human person is not an abstraction; he lives as an individual in time and space. Individually human persons are unequal in many ways, both natural and acquired: in talent, ability, virtue, intelligence, beauty, grace, energy, and health. To all of these natural or acquired inequalities, one must add those that result from long generations of injustice, persecution, exploitation, the whole weight of sorrow that results from bad men and bad institutions These inequalities of time and place do not create a new species of man, or produce a man less entitled to his rightful equality before the law and equality of opportunity for all things human. The basic mistake of the idealistic egalitarians is that they refuse to look at the reality of the human situation. They are disturbed by any hierarchy of values. Everything must be leveled. Mediocrity must be the order of the day. There is no place for the superior, no matter in what context it is achieved. Creative genius of any kind must be put into their

---

[5] *Pacem in Terris*, Paulist Press Edition, (Paulist Press, Glen Rock, New Jersey, 1963), Par. 28, 29, 30.

preconceived straitjacket. Culture must be, and really is in their society, horribly drab. There are no mountains or valleys among men, only plains. All this is a perversion of human equality, is again an overemphasis on rights at the expense of obligations. Egalitarians may indeed speak the right words at times, and engage in good causes, but their music is dissonant when one considers that equality in rights is only a moral beginning. Performance differs from person to person. All should have an equal opportunity, but then if history is any guide, within the democracy of equal men there will always be the aristocracy of excellence.

Once more, I believe that of all the philosophers I have read on this subject, Jacques Maritain best puts the whole problem of equality in clearest perspective:

"If you treat a man as a man, which means if you respect and love the secret he bears within him and the good of which he is capable as an individual person, then to that extent you make effective in yourself his equality or unity in nature with yourself.

"In the experience of misery, in the sorrows of great catastrophes, in humiliations and distress, under the blows of the executioner or the bombs of total war, in concentration camps, in the hovels of starving people in big cities, in common necessity, the doors of solitude fly open and man recognizes man. Also man knows man when the sweetness of a great joy or a great love for a moment makes the eye pure. In helping his fellows or being helped by them, in sharing the same elementary actions and the same elementary feelings, in beholding his neighbor, the humblest gesture shows him, in others and in himself, human nature's common resources and common goodness, a goodness that is primitive, rudimentary, wounded, unconscious, and repressed. At one stroke the real equality and community of nature is revealed to him as a most precious good, an unknown marvel, a fundamental stratum of existence."

The order which prevails in society is by nature moral. Grounded as it is in truth, it must function according to the norms of justice, it should be inspired and perfected by mutual love, and finally, it should be brought to an ever more refined and human balance in freedom.[6]

This now brings us to a question which I have been asked before. When appearing once before a hearing of the Senate Judiciary Com-

---

6 Maritain

mittee, Senator Eastland asked me: "What are civil rights?" On that occasion, which was less friendly than this, since my appointment to the Civil Rights Commission was in contention, I answered more briefly: "Civil rights are the rights granted to every American citizen under the Constitution." Even in the short seven years since that day, the specificity of civil rights has grown appreciably, but the basic principles are the same.

It appears to me that we avoid some of the deviations mentioned above, and place ourselves in the most propitious moral stance, if rights are placed in the context of equality of opportunity to exercise both one's rights and one's responsibilities. Fundamentally, what we are seeking for everyone is the equal opportunity to have free access to everything that bears upon the full development of all of our human capabilities. This means many things in modern American society. First and foremost, it means the right to life. In one county in Mississippi, there was a murder, several shootings, whippings, and beatings during the first five months of this year, without a single indictment of the guilty parties. In one city of 10,401 people, Macomb, Mississippi, there have been thirty-five bombings, burnings, and beatings this year without punishment, even of the parties who admitted guilt. A Negro citizen of that state told me that his right to life was as tenuous as the good will of every white citizen, since any one of them could take his life with impunity. To develop oneself humanly, one must first live.

Then there is the right to become involved in the political life of the city, the state, the nation. This today is abridged in many ways, first, by the denial of voter registration, then by the denial of the vote to those registered, and, finally, by fraudulent miscounting of the votes cast. All of this is further vitiated by the lack of representation, indeed the misrepresentation, of many Negroes in the South, and by the inability of many to take any personal part in the political life of their community by holding office.

Next consider the equality of educational opportunity. Juridically, this was settled more than ten years ago by the *Brown* decision of the Supreme Court. In fact, only 1.2 percent of the Negro population in the South has been integrated in the past ten years, and in the North, the great majority of Negro children are condemned to inferior segregated schooling because of the pattern of segregated housing. Here we have the perfect vicious circle: Negroes are poorly educated because Negroes are poorly educated. The products of inferior schools staff the schools that gave them an inferior education to produce another generation of poorly educated children and so *ad infinitum.*

The simple moral mandate here is to break the vicious circle, and on every point of its circumference. This will involve radical educational reorganization in the South and a change of housing patterns in the North, but again, equality is a mercurial element that must be captured by the continued dynamism of a drive for human progress in any society. This must be done without impairing the quality of education for anyone, and it can be done if we prize equality enough to give it a chance to operate in the life of every American. It will be costly, but the moral imperative is deaf to financial considerations. It must be done because it is right. If we can afford to spend fifty billion dollars every year for defense, we can afford to spend whatever is necessary to elevate the quality of life in America. This, after all, is what we are defending. Without equal opportunity for education on all levels, the door to every other opportunity is automatically closed. We cannot appeal to the weight of past negligence to foreclose the opportunities of the present and the future. We have had enough of conversation. What we need now is imaginative plans and action.

Another large area of opportunity that remains to be opened to minorities in America is housing. Anyone with the money can buy the highest priced car on the market. However, the Negro pays twice as much for his house as the white purchaser, and to compound his problem, he is restricted for the most part to buying only those houses that the white citizen no longer wants in neighborhoods that whites have deserted. Whatever one says of rights, there is a vast and silent conspiracy to keep this immoral situation as it is. Bankers, builders, and realtors, often aided and abetted by public federal financing, close the normal housing market to Negroes and other minorities. Again, the moral imperative is clear. Every American should have equal opportunity to buy a decent home in a wholesome neighborhood, wherever his heart desires and his means permit. Our moral blindness in this situation has given us a divided America, an ugly America replete with black ghettos. We can spend 40 billion dollars to get a man on the moon where no life exists, and yet we continue to condemn millions of human beings to substandard, unsanitary, and dilapidated housing. We allow children to grow up in city jungles, to attend disgraceful schools, to be surrounded with every kind of physical and moral ugliness, and then we are surprised if they are low in aspiration and accomplishment. Some say: "Why don't they move?" And I ask you, "Where?" Of the hundreds of millions of dollars of FHA-assisted private housing, less than 1 percent has benefited the Negro, because of the closed market. The moral judgment is clear enough. First grant equality of opportunity and then criticize poor performance, if indeed there is then poor performance. But poor performance in an impossible situation is no reason for withholding the equality of opportunity to improve the situation.

Equality of economic opportunity is likewise on this list. This, of course, is meaningless without the educational opportunity to qualify oneself. Here, too, we face the vicious circle of denial. Negroes have historically been educated only for menial jobs because menial jobs only are available to Negroes. In times of economic crisis, the Negro is the first fired, naturally, since he was the last hired. Because he makes on the average only half as much as the white citizen, many other opportunities that cost money are closed to him. He presents a dismal picture of personal failure to his children; his wife must work, which further corrodes his family life. Thus, each new generation, reared in failure, has no great aspiration to the success that appears impossible. Failure breeds failure and misery begets more misery.

Then there is the matter of the administration of justice, equality before the law. I think it a fair appraisal of history, ancient and modern, to say that the poor have always fared badly with the instrumentalities of justice. Perhaps the many injustices that often accounted for their being poor made them troublesome and sometimes violent, but, once more, the fruits of injustice are no excuse for further delaying justice. If the poor happen to be highly visible, as the Negroes are, then they fare even more badly.

Think of your chances for justice in a county where no member of your race is on the police force, or among the jail personnel, or on the judge's bench, or in the jury box. Add to this situation that of a state where there are only four Negro lawyers and they are intimidated from handling civil-rights cases, and there is only one white member of the bar who will promote this kind of justice until he is summarily disbarred.

We have a magnificent record of federal enforcement in many difficult areas like kidnapping, espionage, and inter-state auto theft, but somehow the area of infringement of basic civil rights, even the murder of those promoting their own and others' rights, has generally eluded all of our electronic expertise. What do we do? Perhaps tighten the blindfold on the figure of Justice so that justice indeed is color blind and all men are equal before the law. We might also promote a new passion for justice in all of our law schools. A former president of the American Bar Association has just recently perpetrated a monumental intellectual fraud in misrepresenting the meaning of the proposed Civil Rights Act in an effort to defeat its passage, financed incidentally by public money from his state.

Lastly, there is the matter of equal access to public accommodations, now clearly a matter of civil rights. Have you ever imagined what it would be like to be insulted ten or twenty times a day? To travel and not know whether you would be able to find a place to wash or eat or rest or sleep, despite the fact that you were surrounded by facilities apparently open to the public? To be looked upon as something unclean when all you wished was a haircut or to try on a suit you would like to buy? To have to drink from a special fountain, to sit in a special seat, the worst one? To be always the last served, if you were allowed to be served at all, to be made to feel inferior even amidst people who were clearly your inferior as persons, to have to do all the menial work, to always be the servant if not the clown, to expect nothing and generally get what you expected? This is the life of second-class citizenship to which we have generally subjected our Negro brethren until most recently. When they began finally to resent it, we were the most surprised people in the world. They actually wanted to eat in the same places where we eat, to swim where we swim, to rest where we rest, to pray where we pray, even to be buried where we are buried. The fact that they surprised us by the vehemence of their desire to enjoy the same human rights and the same human dignity that we claim for ourselves is perhaps the measure of our own moral blindness. Had we not heard for centuries: "Do unto others as you would have others do unto you"?

What is our moral obligation as a nation? To make possible basic human dignity at the very least; to judge human persons for what they are and how they perform when given an equal chance, not by their color, a fact over which they have no control or no choice; to make equality of opportunity a reality in the whole spectrum of human development; this at least would begin to open up the closed society.

The litany of inequality might go on, but I believe that we have at least said enough to establish the depth and range of the moral dimension of the civil-rights movement. One more point should be emphasized. Morality is not just one decision; it is a system. The problem of civil rights in America today is an organic problem of many closely articulated parts. The total problem cannot be solved by tinkering with a solution to one of the segments of the problem. We must have an integral moral solution, across the whole spectrum of the problem, if equal opportunity, human rights, and human dignity are to be realized in our times.

The equal opportunity to vote creates further problems without equal opportunity for education. Equal opportunity for education is an empty phrase without equal opportunity for housing. Equal opportunity for housing is meaningless without economic opportunity, which, in turn, is an empty promise without educational opportunity. Justice before the law is chimerical without participation in the instrumentalities of justice. And, none of this will come to pass in a truly humane fashion until each American is convinced that he cannot detach himself from the problem at hand, for each one of us is involved, and every part of our nation is involved. No man is an island in this total sea of inequality. When one man's dignity is cruelly wounded, every man suffers indignity. When one man is denied equality, none of us is really free. And when all of this happens on a wholesale scale, the whole quality of our life as a nation is debased.

How did we arrive at the ugly impasse we so often see today? President Johnson said in the statement quoted at the beginning of this paper that: "The reasons are deeply imbedded in history and tradition and the nature of man." A brief look at history might help us understand the agonizing rise and fall of tension, the fluctuations in the moral relationships between whites and Negroes in this country. This is, of course, a two-sided history, increasingly so in recent years and months.

We must begin with the state of slavery, more or less passively accepted by both sides for about two centuries, mainly because the Negro could not do very much about it and the whites did not want to do much about it because of economic considerations. However, America's stated morals finally came to the surface under the pressure of Abolitionists. There was a bloody war, Lincoln's Emancipation Proclamation, and the Fourteenth and Fifteenth Amendments to bring the Constitution up to date.

After an initial good start, there appeared the original white backlash—a reaction to the excesses of the carpetbaggers. The thrust of this backlash was, as institutionalized for the next eight or nine decades, to keep the Negro in his place, definitely a place inferior to that of the whites. The *Plessy* decision of the Supreme Court further silenced any moral inquietude regarding the "separate but equal" situation that resulted. Thus, for almost a century after the Emancipation Proclamation, what was proclaimed did not come to be, and one finds all too little moral concern from any public or private source during this whole period. At best, the whites were paternalistic; at worst, they were oppressive and morally insensitive for the most part.

What was the turning point, the new day for civil rights? First, there was World War II which meant greater mobility for Negroes in service or war industries, greater employment opportunity under the stress of labor shortages in the North, East, and West, a breath of new interest from President Roosevelt—but still, for most Negroes, depressingly servile work in industry and the armed forces. President Truman began the work of integration in the services. The *Brown* decision of 1954 reversed the earlier Supreme Court decision of *Plessy,* outlawing separate but equal in education. The walls began to crumble.

President Eisenhower signed the first civil-rights bill in eighty years, and established the Civil Rights Commission. Shortly after its first biennial report, another and stronger civil-rights bill appeared. About this time, less than ten years ago, the real birth of the Negro's civil rights movement took place. In Montgomery, Alabama, Mrs. Rosa Parks, who had many times moved to the rear of the bus when told to do so, one day refused to move. When the driver stopped the bus and threatened to call the police, she said, "Then just call them." The second key event came in North Carolina when some young Negro students staged the first sit-in. No one would have guessed that these two Negro actions would result, within a few short years, in another federal law outlawing for all time what had been the accepted, although immoral, custom of many generations. What was the thrust of the movement that grew from these two seemingly unimportant events?

Philosophically, the roots go deep. In the pre-Christian era, there was the action of Socrates, more than two thousand years ago, that first lit the flame. Socrates drank hemlock rather than concede the right we grant our citizens in the First Amendment. Aristotle quoted Antigone to argue that "an unjust law is not a law." The two greatest intellects in the Christian tradition, Augustine and Thomas Aquinas, agreed that any human law contrary to natural or divine law ought not to be obeyed. In the American tradition, we have Henry Thoreau's essay on *Civil Disobedience*; that inspired Gandhi's doctrine of non-violence. Together they provide the best descriptive name for the Negro civil-rights movement of the past few years: nonviolent civil disobedience. It has many dangerous offsprings, some clearly illegitimate, but this should not distract from the inherent moral dynamism that, from the first, characterized the best part of the Negro civil-rights movement.

To return for a moment to its most recent forebears: Thoreau and Gandhi. In 1846, Sam Staples, the town jailer, interrupted Thoreau's tranquil life at Walden Pond and put him in jail because he refused to pay his poll tax to a government that imprisoned and returned runaway slaves, thus upholding slavery. He was somewhat upset to be released the next day because apparently his Aunt Maria paid the tax for him. Thanks to Aunt Maria's action, we have Thoreau's personal protest in print today. It is the text by which all the world best knows Thoreau. I shall only give the headlines of his thesis, the bare bones of Thoreau's argument:

> Can there not be a government in which majorities do not virtually decided right and wrong, but conscience? . . . Must the citizen ever for a moment, or in the least degree, resign his conscience to the legislator? . . . The only obligation which I have a right to assume is to do at any time what I think right. . . . a wise man will not leave the right to the mercy of chance, nor wish it to prevail through the power of the majority. . . . Unjust laws exist: shall we be content to obey them, or shall we endeavor to amend them, and obey until we have succeeded, or shall we transgress them at once? . . . If the injustice is part of the necessary friction of government, let it go, let it go, perchance it will wear smooth. . . . but if it is of such a nature that it requires you to be the agent of injustice to another, then I say, break the law. Let your life be a counter friction to stop the machine. I think that it is enough that they [the Abolitionists] have God on their side . . . any man more right than his neighbors constitutes a majority of one already. . . . Under a government that imprisons anyone unjustly, the true place for a just man is also a prison.

True to his word, when Emerson asked Thoreau what he was doing in jail, Thoreau replied, "What are you doing outside?" Thoreau concludes: "A minority is powerless while it conforms to the majority . . . but it is irrestible when it clogs by its own weight. If the alternative is to keep all just men in prison, or give up . . . slavery, the state will not hesitate which to choose."

This was heady doctrine, even back in 1846, but its relevance did not escape either Gandhi or Martin Luther King. Gandhi saw civil disobedience as a constitutional form of persuasion, as a way to reach the minds and hearts of people and thus to mold the law. Thoreau, in one brief phrase, gave Gandhi an insight to a new element adding greater moral weight to the doctrine of civil disobedience. "How much more eloquently and effectively he can combat injustice who has experienced a little in his own person."[7]

---

[7] *Walden and Civil Disobedience* (Boston: Houghton Mifflin, 1957), pp. 236, 240, 243, 244, 245.

Gandhi made an eloquent plea to his countrymen for this new element of nonviolent, suffering civil disobedience, implicit in Thoreau:

Nonviolence in its dynamic condition means conscious suffering. Rivers of blood may have to flow before we gain our freedom, *but it must be our blood*. Things of fundamental importance to people are not secured by reason alone, but have to be purchased with their suffering (what else characterized the early Christian martyrs in the face of an all-powerful Roman Empire?) *Suffering is infinitely more powerful than the law of the jungle* for converting the opponent and opening his ears, which are otherwise shut, to the law of reason.

Gandhi concludes: "The appeal of reason is to the head, but the penetration of the heart comes from suffering. It opens up the inner understanding in man."[8]

One last footnote is in order to show how this theme is reflected, most recently, in Pope John's *Pacem in Terris*. Once more, as in Thoreau, the focal emphasis is on conscience.

"As authority rests chiefly on moral force, it follows that civil authority must appeal primarily to the conscience of individual citizens, that is, to each one's duty to collaborate readily for the common good of all." Pope John then makes the point that only God can ultimately command the human conscience, and adds:

". . . those, therefore, who have authority in the state may oblige men in conscience only if their authority is intrinsically related with the authority of God and shares in it. By this principle, the dignity of the citizens is protected.

". . . Since the right to command is required by the moral order and has its source in God, it follows that if civil authorities pass laws or command anything opposed to the moral order and consequently contrary to the will of God, neither the laws made nor the authorizations granted can be binding on the consciences of citizens, since 'God has more right to be obeyed than men'" (Acts 5:29.[9]

I have already said that this is heady doctrine and, as such, can easily lead to abuses. Arnold Toynbee, in his monumental study of human civilizations, wonders at the patience, forebearance, and good will of America's Negro citizens, despite their cruel human lot. Martin Luther King's "Montgomery Improvement Association" gave

[8] *Walden and Civil Disobedience.*
[9] *Pacem in Terris, ed. cit.,* pars. 48-51.

American Negroes a way to begin to redress their wrongs in an open, nonviolent way through civil disobedience. The many other movements that followed were predicated more or less on the same Gandhian premise that voluntary human suffering in the cause of justice would most effectively and eloquently change the pattern of injustice. The passage of the 1964 Civil Rights Act is ample demonstration of the effectiveness of nonviolent civil disobedience, especially in the most difficult area of public accommodations. So much for history.

Now the whole civil-rights movement seems to be entering into a new phase which may well reverse the gains of the recent past, since the moral foundations outlined above are being more and more abandoned in many of the latest manifestations of the movement.

Most unfortunately, nonviolence is often giving way to violence, which loses the moral force and persuasion so essential to Thoreau, Gandhi, and King. Civil disobedience must also consist in direct noncompliance with what is essentially an unjust law, so that there is clearly established an open, honest protest that has some direct relationship with injustice. Opening water faucets to deplete a water supply, clogging highways to the World's Fair, or booing the President who was at the moment championing a new civil-rights law is simply another form of injustice, insensitivity, or inhumanity—alienating friends and confirming enemies. Looting, inane destruction of property, hooliganism and violence, personal injury, and irresponsibility are as far from the moral foundations espoused by the true promoters of civil rights as injustice is far from justice, order from disorder, humanity from inhumanity. As Martin Luther King said, commenting on the race riots of Harlem, Brooklyn, and Rochester: "My position on nonviolence and my continued adherence to nonviolent philosophy are well-known. I do not think violence can solve the problem in New York, nor can it solve the problem in Mississippi" (Syracuse Post-Standard, July 28, 1964). Or as Gandhi said earlier: "Suffering is infinitely more powerful than the law of the jungle."

Suffering there has been, and violence has not only risen in the North and among Negroes. Between June 12 and September 19 of this year, in fourteen counties of Mississippi, there have been thirty-two Negro churches burned or bombed. Imagine the reaction if this had happened to white churches or synagogues in Boston, New York, or Chicago. Clearly violence is no answer.

We might, then, summarize the moral case for nonviolent civil disobedience as legitimate only when all legal redress has failed to change an unjust law. The Lutheran Church in America, at its 1964 biennial convention, stated this clearly: "If and when the means of legal recourse have been exhausted or have been demonstrably inadequate, Christians may then choose to serve the cause of racial justice by disobeying a law that clearly involves the violation of their obligations as Christians."

However, the disobedient person must be nonviolent to preserve his moral stance. He must engage in meaningful protest, not indiscriminate demonstration, and he must be willing to accept the legal penalty for his action. Moreover, the basic aim of nonviolent civil disobedience is always the same as regular litigation, to challenge the law and to bring it to a test under the regular legal procedures, only in this case by disobeying it and suffering the consequences.

Who can predict the future, who can forecast further progress, if the waters are continually muddied by a perversion of civil disobedience? At best, we can assume that the patience, forebearance, and good will of which Toynbee wrote are apparently wearing thin, even at a time that seemed to be the dawn of victory. All of these symptoms, however, ultimately point to a profound malady that I suspect has only one great geographic focal point in modern America—the dismal slums of our great cities that can only produce, as long as they are allowed to exist, a continuous caldron of pent-up human frustration, born of miserable living conditions, blighted neighborhoods, overcrowded rooms, broken marriages and promiscuity, education all in the wrong direction, unsanitary, unhealthy, and dilapidated living conditions, playgrounds only in crowded streets, children perverted by all around them, poverty, crime, rape, dope, and drunkenness. Everything here speaks of human failure and perpetuates a primordial, primitive human misery. Again, how to break out of this basically immoral and inhuman circle of frustration?

If we can spend forty billion dollars to put a man or two on the moon, and fifty billion annually on defense, then I take it that our affluent society can afford a similar amount to bulldoze our slums into oblivion and to recreate the hearts of our cities. I fully realize that more than physical conditions must be recreated, that there is needed a new moral revolution within the deprived Negro community itself, based on a new pride in what human dignity and human equality can mean in America. As the late President Kennedy said, "Let us make a beginning."

I said earlier that every great moral system asks man to go beyond his natural condition. The human condition of the world today is ambiguous, to say the least, in the whole area of civil rights. The situation in our own beloved land, the so-called showcase of democracy, is one of great and growing tension. If the great moral tradition we have inherited says anything to us today, it must say this: we are free to deny the human condition, but it will remain what it is despite our denial. We can try to forget it by indulging in the multitudinous distractions that our age offers. Or, we can accept the human situation for what it is: a great moral challenge to demonstrate in these our times that man is growing, not standing still or falling back; that human dignity means so much to us that we wish to share it with all our fellow countrymen, indeed with all the world; that human equality need not be a bitter and frustrating travesty, but a bright reality to which all of us are committed in the depth of our hearts and souls; and, finally, that all of us recognize each of these tasks as a deeply human moral obligation to which we, too, are willing to pledge today, as our forefathers did in their day, our lives, our fortunes, and our sacred honor.

The Need for a Program of
International Economic Aid

DR. MORDECAI JOHNSON

Dr. Mordecai Johnson, president emeritus of Howard University, has been an influential leader in educational circles for more than thirty-five years. At a testimonial dinner given in Dr. Johnson's honor after his retirement, his successor President Nabrit eulogized him as a "scholar, teacher, minister, administrator, educator, and champion of the rights of all people."

Dr. Johnson was only thirty-six years old when he was appointed to the presidency at Howard University. Because of his planning and hard work, he gained prominent stature in the academic world.

In June, 1959, some 650 distinguished citizens representing fourteen North Atlantic Treaty Organization nations assembled in London for the first Atlantic Congress. Dr. Johnson, a member of the Board of Directors of the 110-man United States Delegation, was selected as one of five plenary speakers. The address he delivered follows, wherein he, the son of a slave, made himself the "ardent and moving defender of the underdeveloped people, particularly those in Africa."

Your Lordship, Mr. President, Distinguished Members of the NATO Congress:

I am glad beyond measure to be here and to speak to you on behalf of the Fourth Committee, which has to do with the relationship between the NATO countries, the Atlantic community, and the underdeveloped peoples.

I suppose one of the reasons why you have been so kindly constrained to invite me is because I am one of those underdeveloped peoples and you would like to hear about the world from the way it looks down under. I am indeed from among the underdeveloped peoples; I am the child of a slave. My father was a slave for twenty-five years before the emancipation; my mother was born in slavery; I have lived practically all my life on the territory of former slave states, so when you hear me talk you are dealing with the real underdeveloped thing.

Yet I have early in my life come into contact with what I conceive to be the noblest and best element in the Western world namely those Christian educational missionaries who founded the first colleges and universities for Negroes. I am today working in a university founded by them on the basis of principles which are precious to the Western world, for when these men founded Howard University they put it on the cornerstone of the inherent dignity and immeasurable possibilities of the human individual as such, and they enrolled slaves and the children of slaves with their own sons and daughters without hesitation and without fear, being confident that on that campus they would be able to bring them all to maturity, to responsibility and democratic and Christian creativity. I am indebted to those men for the development of my powers, for teaching me how to live freely from the deepest inclinations of my being, and for giving me the power to give my life away freely for causes that I love. So you are not only listening to the child of a slave who can give you authentic words from down under, you give heed at this moment to one who knows the deepest and purest traditions of the Western world, who loves those traditions, who reveres the men who handed them to him, and who loves the community of peoples out of whom they have come.

COLD WAR IN SECOND PHASE

Now I am very tired. It has been a struggle for me to be able to stay here, but I have a message for you; I have had it in my heart for a long time. But when a man is tired he may speak poorly, when he finds merely that his words are inadequate to say well what he wants to say. Please keep in mind that I speak with the highest esteem for the members of the Atlantic community, and that whatever I say is intended, as my father used to say when he preached, to stir up your pure minds in order that the cause that is precious to you may come to victory on the highest level.

As I read all the papers that have come into my section, I find that they are all certain that the second phase of the war between the Atlantic community and the Soviet Union has already begun, and that is the economic phase. I have always looked upon the economic purposes of the Soviet Union as their primary purposes, so that in my humble judgment we are just now beginning to confront the central and most powerful purposes of the Soviet Union and her allies. In my humble opinion there is no appraisal of what is going to come to us better than can be found in the twenty-fifth chapter of Matthew, in which it says, "And at midnight there was a cry made, 'The bridegroom is at hand. Go ye out to meet him'." I have a feeling that the bridegroom of our Western civilization is at hand, and that we are now at the parting of the ways; that when we meet this economic offensive we are going to meet the most powerful opposition of ideas, the most vigorously intelligent handling of the economic and spiritual factors of life in a revolutionary way that any group of people in the world has faced, and we are going either to adjust ourselves to meet that onslaught of idea-power and economic organizational power with a vigorous readjustment of our lives, or we are going down and possibly lose any power to control the trend of history for years to come. But if we do meet it boldly, realizing from the beginning that it will involve the use of all of our powers to the maximum extent, we may be able to pursue a course of action which will not only lead to victory but which will lift our democratic life to a higher level of functioning than we have ever known before, and give us a radiant power over the lives and affections of men around this world, such as we have not had in five hundred years.

REAPPRAISAL NECESSARY

Now if this is going to happen to us, I think we need to do two things that are somewhat uncongenial to us. We have got to go back and make a re-estimate of our enemy, and we have got to acquire some humility in the appraisal of ourselves. Up to this time we have been looking at the military side of our enemy, his totalitarian organization, and his aggressive subversion, and we have been filled with disgust and fear, and we have been facing him primarily with military organization, cohesive and powerful economic organization. We have rather paid little or no attention to the central focus of what he is about in this world. Now we have got to look at that central focus, and if we are wise, I think we will not allow our emotions of revulsion to prevent us from appraising him on the level represented by his highest and most intelligent and pure-hearted devotee. It is a great mistake to appraise any movement like the movement represented by the Soviet Union and the Chinese people by continually listing their faults. God has never yet been able to choose a faultless movement for the projection of His powerful purposes. One pure-hearted man at the head of a thousand men, 50 percent of whom are full of faults, is able by the inspiration of his purity of heart, his moral power, to keep them in cohesive union, to bring to their assistance forces that are primarily selfish in character, and to bring about a change in human affairs that could not be calculated beforehand.

We must try to take a look at the Soviet Union through the eyes of their purest, most devoted, and honorable men. When you do that you will see that at the central part of the Communist movement there is a simple and great faith. It is a faith that, with the scientific and technical intelligence which we have at our disposal in the modern world, if we put it in the hands of the right men, the struggle for existence in this world could be overcome in a worldwide way and that poverty, squalor, ignorance, disease, and early death could be conquered and the foundation laid for a great society in which culture would be available to all human beings.

ACHIEVEMENTS ARE ASTONISHING

These men believe this with a passion that is not exceeded by any movement in the world except early Christianity. They are all responding to it every day and every hour with an enthusiasm which is nothing short of remarkable. On the ground of Russia and the Chinese soil they are making achievements of one kind or another which have astonished us, and they are preaching it now around the world with an evangelistic enthusiasm that is immense. This message that they have is very fittingly addressed to the underdeveloped peoples of the world, of whom there are 1,200,000,000, all of whom have a scale of living which is under a hundred dollars per capita per year; all of whom are living in a primarily agricultural civilization, and a very poor type of agriculture at that; all of whom are living in countries in which there is very little industry to supplement agriculture; all of whom are impoverished in the field of scientific and technical intelligence; and to most of whom it makes no difference how much money you would give them, they would have no governmental personnel prepared to make a wise and well-coordinated use of scientific and technical plans and projections.

TECHNICAL AID OFFERED

The Soviet Union is saying to these people, "Here we come to you from among those who, like yourself, have suffered. We have come not to make you strong and powerful so that you could dominate, exploit, and humiliate your fellows, we have come to show you how to treble and quadruple your agricultural production, to supplement your agriculture with the industries which we will show you how to establish, to lend you scientific and technical personnel, to sit down and talk with you about plans for the further development of your country, to lend you money at rates so low that you will see in an unequivocally clear manner that we are not trying to make a profit on you, and we are prepared to devote ourselves to this task for months and years solely because we believe that there is in you the power to conquer the struggle for existence in your country, and we want to have the joy of seeing you do that."

If we do not see that in them, we shall have no power to deal with them because it is there—it is there. In pursuit of that purpose they are prepared to enter into a pure-hearted relationship with the people of Asia and Africa. Now, what do I mean by that? In spite of the fact that they do not have any metaphysics akin to our religion, they have something that is very important—they have radical, universal ethics in their relationship to the black and brown and yellow peoples of the world. They have said in their literature—do not misunderstand this —"We take our position quite contrary to the Second International. We are not out to organize the white working people of the world. We are out to organize the working people of the world, and we say it to all of our workers everywhere, in Africa, in Asia, and in the homelands of the colonial powers, 'Make solidarity with workers. Pay no attention to their national origin. We want to unite the workers of the world for a great society in which the struggle for existence is conquered, and all are led to a new freedom on the basis of that conquest'."

Now they stand on a territory that constitutes one-fourth of the land areas of this world. They have one-third of the population of this world, and they have now established themselves in a place where they know that we no longer have the military power to dis-lodge them. Eight hundred million of these one billion two hundred million people that are underdeveloped are on the border of the Soviet Union and of China, so close that they have to cross no water to reach them. They can also touch their hands any time of day, and they can speak to them without a long-distance telephone.

MILLIONS ARE APPREHENSIVE

But all these eight hundred million people are black and brown and yellow Asiatics who in times past have suffered at the hands of the peoples whom we represent, and who have some fear of us. They look at what the Soviet Union and the Chinese people have done by their faith with admiration, and they are proud to believe that if they could have the right kind of relationship with any group of people in this world, they themselves could do that.

We are up against an immense antagonist. How many of these people does he have to win? Why, if he won India alone he would all but tip the scales of the majority population of the human race and, in a few months after that, might turn the tables on us and put us in the minority of the world. We are up against a great antagonist with a great passion, with an immense achievement as a result of that passion, and with a profound faith that he is getting ready to turn the corner which leads to our graveyard—no, which leads to the graveyard and to the grave which we are digging for ourselves. He believes that.

SELF-APPRAISAL IS NEEDED

Now let us take a look at ourselves. I said the next thing we have got to do is to acquire some humility in the appraisal of ourselves. We are going to enter this contest with a great handicap. We speak of ourselves in a highly complimentary fashion as the free peoples of the world. Indeed we are, and the one who is speaking knows how true that is, for in our domestic institutions we are the freest and most flexibly organized people in the world. We are most sensitive to the will of the people, and we have developed parliamentary institutions which are precious to the whole of the human race and which we rightly want to preserve. But it takes a great man like Toynbee to tell us that in the relationship with the people of Asia and Africa this is not so of us; that for 500 years we have been aggressors against them, we have attacked and conquered nearly all of them, we have exploited their natural resources in a manner which they consider to have been unjust, and we have often segregated and humiliated them on the land of their fathers and in the presence of the graves of their mothers. They remember these things, and in this hour when they are called upon to choose between us and the Soviet Union, there is in their hearts a fear of us which they cannot easily eradicate.

WESTERN NATIONS DIVIDED

In the second place, we are still wounded; we are divided in our minds today by moral habits which have descended from the colonial system which we have not yet been able to overcome. We present an equivocal picture in what we are doing now. The underdeveloped peoples of the world have only to look at Africa to see how divided our minds are. On the one hand, we see the noble British one by one freeing their peoples from the colonial yoke, freeing them deliberately, supporting them in their freedom, and inviting them in their freedom to "come back to your mother country which is now for you no longer an empire but a commonwealth." Every now and then we see the noble French rise with a passionate gesture and say to their peoples, "Are we holding you? Then be free," and then under their breath they say in prayer, "But do come back. We want you to be with us." The other day we saw a declaration from the Belgians saying, "This pathway of freedom is what we intend to pursue. Our plans are in the making and will be ready." Now you look at Africa: it is magnificent to see that some 70 million of the peoples have been freed under these circumstances by members of this organization. But there are one hundred and ten million of Africans who are neither free nor under mandate, still dominated politically, still having their natural resources exploited, not for their good but for the good of those who exploit. We see on the shores of Africa instances of the most deliberate and cruel segregation and discrimination of the inhabitants of the country on the land of their fathers and in the presence of the graves of their mothers. Nobody can look at Africa without knowing that we are divided in our minds and that we have not yet been able to summon either the political power or the moral power to overcome that division. Though the God of our fathers has vetoed the colonial system and closed the open gates of the world against it, we are still reluctant to turn it loose, and we may yet shame ourselves by admitting one more venture to reopen those gates.

May I say to you again, we have as yet been able to put no great world-encircling concept in the place of the colonial system to which we have been devoted for some 500 years and which is now fallen.

What greater idea do we have now of a world-encircling nature that we can offer these underdeveloped peoples of Asia and Africa, of which they can be members just as we, in which they can be respected just as we, they can move freely out of their own spontaneous enthusiasm just as we? I suggest to you that we do not yet have one. There are no great words coming from us today regarding that city that hath foundations that was made for the whole human race of one blood; and because we do not have it, we are in some difficulty in approaching these Asiatics and Africans.

MOTIVES ARE WRONG

I have sat often in these meetings when we talk about what we want to do for them economically, and I have sat for a whole hour and heard us talk tactics, heard us talk self-interest, heard us saying that we must do these things in order to protect ourselves without one word of pure-hearted love for these people, without one single intimation that we are moved by a sense of obligation to do these things for them because it is a great thing to be in a position to create freedom in this world.

When those early white men came to the place where I was to be educated, they came to ask nothing—nothing. They looked at me when my trousers were not pressed, and my face was not clean, and said, "Mr. Johnson, will you read?" They knew I was no mister, but they knew what I could be, and they came there for only one purpose, for the joy that was set before them in making a man out of me and turning me loose in the world. I tell you that one of the great, great differences in our preparations is that we seem to have lost the power to speak to these Asiatics and Africans that way; and so our program of economic helpfulness is an adjunct and a servant of our military activities. We talk about it that way in our congresses and parliaments. We say to our people, "Why are we asking you for $3 billion, why? Because we have got to have it to defend ourselves, to take care of our self-interest." If we ask for a little more money in addition to that, attached thereto, we say, "Of course, we cannot give all of our money for that purpose, we have got to have a benevolent margin which we give away simply because they need it." I will tell you that up until this date, the greater portion of all that we are now devoting to the people of Africa and Asia in the field of economic help, even as an adjunct and accessory to the military, is in the field of benevolence that is not beyond condescension. There is as yet no substantial sum of money and no substantial program developed for them purely out of the motive to make them free from the struggle of existence and to give them a chance to be men.

PRESENT AID INADEQUATE

Let me say again—I told you you must watch me and bear with me —only those who love greatly can talk this way. I say to you that as I look at this great economic program, it seems to me to be on the periphery of our interest, almost an afterthought. It has never sat in the chair directly in front of us and grasped the central focus of our hearts. We have a great military program, which represents the greatest power of provisional planning and coordination that we are capable of. In the Marshall Plan and other great projects, we have had great programs of development protective of and stimulative of each other, which are ample cause for admiration among men. But our program of economic helpfulness is a puny vein and comes into our minds as an afterthought, never having received prolonged thought from us, prolonged affection, and robust attention. Moreover—I am trying to be hard, and my purpose is, as my father used to say, to stir up your pure minds—that program is dependent today too largely upon little droplets of annual appropriations which expire on June 30 and which permit no planning and give no index that we have any purpose to devote ourselves to this objective in an unequivocal manner beyond one year.

CENTRALIZATION IS LACKING

Again, there is no central organization in existence of our making, which plans to use and to coordinate all the economic powers that we have for this purpose and to see to it that they work. I tell you, ladies and gentlemen, we are going into the fight of a determinative lifetime, and we are not prepared. We are not prepared. We are not morally prepared. We are not purely prepared in our hearts in their orientation towards the thing that we want to do for these people. We are not committing ourselves to any long-range purpose when we know that it may take years and years to develop the economies of these people. We have no great central organization for talking with them, for listening to their ideas or exchanging ideas with them, for approach in cooperation with them, for applying a fit measure to them.

It is hard for me to say these things to those that I love, but it is so, and it points to a weakness so great that God Himself, who loves you, must weep when He looks at it for fear that, walking so boldly and in such a self-congratulatory manner into the battle of your life-time, you may fail and ruin the thing that He has loved you for from the foundation of the world.

EQUALITY MUST BE RECOGNIZED

Now if the chairman will bear with me for a minute, I will say swiftly what I think we have got to do. The first thing we have got to do is not economic, it is religious. The first step that we must take is to put the colonial system behind us in our minds and renew our allegiance to the Christian world view, regarding the nature of human nature and the possibilities of a free human society in this world, based on these considerations. The British know what I mean; you great Frenchmen, who pioneered the Illumination, know what I mean; you great Germans, who have meditated upon socialism long before the idea was born among the Russians, you know what I mean. I mean the thing that Abraham Lincoln meant when he said, "Govern-ment of the people, for the people, and by the people, dedicated to the proposition that all men are created equal," all men! And he said, "I have never had a political idea in my life that was not based upon this great proposition, and when I read that proposition I not only see the slaves set free but I see the last tyranny lifted from the back of the last man."

The world is in front of our eyes, with just a few hours away from the children of any people on earth. Our missionaries and our scientists tell us that every child in this world who is normal shares with us the essential dignity and higher possibilities of human life that are im-measurable. Now look this world in the face. We are either going to dedicate ourselves to serve that world, on the conviction that all men are created equal, or else we are going to turn our faces away and morally die and deserve to die because, having seen the God that we have seen and turned our faces away, it is better that we had not been born.

The next thing we have got to do, and we shall need the help of God to do it and the help of each other, we have got to give our consent to the Eternal's veto on the colonial system and turn all the strength of these Atlantic powers to the liquidation of the remaining remnants of the colonial system in Africa. We have got to listen to the cries of these 110 million black Africans who are crying out against political domination, economic exploitation, segregation, and humiliation, as if we were listening to the words of our own children, and we have got to say to them, as we have never said, "I tell you, my son, this is Britain that hears you, this is France that hears you, this is Belgium that hears you, this is Portugal that hears you, this is Germany that hears you, this is your Uncle Samuel that hears you, and I'm coming and I am going to do what you want to be done, so help me God, as if I were performing a great act of expiation before God and making a demonstration before the whole world of the purity of my purposes toward you." We have got that to do, and if we think that it is at all possible for us to influence the people of Asia in the way that we need to influence them without doing this, we mistake human nature and the order of this universe.

MORAL RESPONSIBILITY CITED

In the third place, we must accept the moral responsibility towards the people of Asia that is indissolubly connected with the enormous scientific and technical knowledge, organizational resources, and constructive powers that we have, and we have got to go to them with a pure heart and say, "We have come to you not to offer you aid for the sake of your military helpfulness, not to hand you economic assistance as people put a halter on a bag of oats before a mule's mouth in order that while you are eating the oats, we may lead you along the pathway to take up a load which otherwise, of your own free will, you would not take, but to offer you this program purely in order that you may be free in the same sense that we are free, in order that you may conquer the struggle for existence in your territory in the way that we are conquering it, and in order that you may be members with us of that great society which we have in our hearts and which we intend shall cover this world."

COORDINATED EFFORT NEEDED

We ought in the next place to take this whole business out of the range of benevolence, put it before us not as an accessory to our military program but as the greatest of all programs in itself—listen to me—for which the military program, as big as it is, is only a fence-building and protecting operation, to handle the program in the central focus of our being, to accept it as an obligation not to be done with our cigar money, nor with our chewing-gum money, nor our cigarette money, but to be done, if necessary, with our very blood, because we cannot live in our hearts and see them suffer impoverishment the way they suffer and hold what we have and eat the bread we have in peace. We must cease to think about little benevolent annual drops of money. We are no mere jugglers of money. We are the greatest producers of scientific and technical intelligence in the world, of the most diversified scientific and technical intelligence; we know more about the multiplication of agricultural products than any group of human beings in the world. We know more about building up great dairy herds and pure milk supplies than any group of people in the world. We know more about lending money, borrowing money, the effective use of money. We know more about trade, and all these things that have to do with the building up of a great economic order.

This thing that I am talking about calls upon us to use all of these things in a coordinated fashion to an end which we determine to do or die if we do not do it. If we will do this, we have got to have an organization to do it with. I do not know enough to tell you what organization to use. I can tell you what kind it has got to be. It has got to be akin to this great military organization that spoke to us this morning; it has got to be led by minds that understand economic procedures through and through; it has got to be as diversified as the populations of the earth to which we go; it has got to be a planning organization that can send a team of men into any country and help them in a few days to discover the natural resources there, the soil there, the possibilities of development there, and come back with a program that they have talked over with the people; and men who after they have got that program know what scientists and technicians to choose, what administrative organizers to choose, and send them there and keep them there until the work is done.

PROGRAM WILL BE COSTLY

I see we have used up nearly all my time, and I have got to quit reluctantly. This is going to cost us something. It may cost us as much as one-tenth of all the productive power of the Western World. It may even come to the place where it costs us the necessity to recoil from our high standard of living substantially in order that the money thus sacrificed may be put into this program—pulling back our standard of living in order that we may lift up the standard of life all over this world, and deserve the gratitude of the men who are looking to us for leadership. I tell you that this is a program for which we were born in the world. It is as if God were standing before us today saying to you, "My sons, this is what I brought you into the world for. Don't be afraid. Go on and do it for me. Nothing that you suffer will be too great. I'll give you the power to bear it, and I will make your name loved and respected and honored all over this world." If we do it, we will entirely transform the relations that have existed between us and the peoples of Africa and Asia for nearly five hundred years. We will give them hope such as they have never had in all these years, and they will know that it came from us because we loved them. It will infuse our democratic institutions with a new and radiant life and put them upon a higher level than they have ever been in all their lifetime, and it will place us in a position where we can look at the Communists and say to them, "Khrushchev, you miscalculated. You thought that we were morally incapable of this, and therefore you had to deceive us. Now, let us sit down and talk. What you say you want to do for this world, can't you see that I am doing it? Why can we not do it together? What you say you want to do for the world and you cay you cannot do without totalitarian power, do you not see I am doing it with freedom and flexibility and listening to the wish of the people? Turn away from your methods, my son. Come with your brethren in the Christian world who are your brothers indeed, and let us do these things together."

CLOSING

Now you will forgive me, will you not, for taking the chairman's time, but I had a message for you that was so big that a stone would have burst unless it got it out of its system. Hear me now, for even in these times men like you ought to listen to a stone.

Desegregate and Integrate to What End?
DR. BENJAMIN MAYS

Benjamin Mays, born in Epworth, South Carolina, earned the Bachelor of Arts degree from Bates College, and the Master of Arts and Doctor of Philosophy degrees from the University of Chicago.

His professional experience ranges from college teacher to church pastor to college president. He has contributed to a number of community, civic, and national efforts over a period of years.

He has been Executive Secretary of the Tampa (Florida) Urban League and National Student Secretary of the YMCA. He has served as Director of the Study of Negro Churches in the United States for the Institution of Social and Religious Research and has been President of the United Negro College Fund. He was a United States representative at the Oxford Conference on Church, Community, and State at Oxford University and a representative for the United States YMCA at the Plenary Session of the World Committee in Stockholm. He was a delegate to the First and Second Assemblies of the World Council of Churches in 1948 and 1954, respectively, and was a member of the 1939 Youth Conference at Amsterdam and the World Conference of the YMCA at Mysore, India.

He is currently a member of the National Committee of the Mid-century White House Conference on Youth, the United States Advisory Committee for the United Nations, the National Advisory Council to the Peace Corps, the United States National Commission for UNESCO, and a former member of the Board of the National Council of the Churches of Christ of the United States. After relinquishing the post of Dean of the School of Religion at Howard University, Dr. Mays was appointed President of Morehouse College in 1940 and served in that position until 1966.

He is recipient of the second annual award from Texas State University for outstanding work in human relations and the Christian Culture Award from Assumption University, Windsor, Ontario, Canada. His book *The Christian in Race Relations* (1954) is one of several he has written in the fields of religion and race relations along with his numerous contributions included in encyclopedias, newspapers, and magazines.

"Desegregate and Integrate to What End?" is the question Dr. Mays asked and sought to answer in the thought-provoking speech delivered at Livingstone College on February 11, 1964. Included here also is the great "Eulogy of Dr. Martin Luther King" delivered on the occasion of his funeral at Morehouse College in Atlanta, Georgia, April 9, 1968.

*   *   *

We spend millions upon millions, we demonstrate, we sit-in, picket, boycott, go to jail, and some have died trying to desegregate and trying to integrate the United States. For what? To what end? The press, the radio, and TV have devoted more time to this question in the last ten years than to any other single topic. Congress is wrangling over it. Desegregate and integrate for what?

Here we must distinguish clearly between desegregation and integration. It is strange to me how learned people and scholars have been using integration since 1954 when they really meant desegregation. I think I was first or among the first to cry out against this misuse of the word integration. Desegregation means the absence of segregation.

When the courts opened public schools and universities, golf courses and swimming pools, abolished segregation on dining cars, in interstate travel, and on buses and abolished the white primary, they were not integrating the facilities. They were desegregating them. When sit-ins, boycotts, and picketing opened restaurants, hotels, and motels, this too was desegregation—not integration. This is also true when a church votes to drop the color bar. The church is desegregating, not integrating. Desegregation means the absence of segregation.

To integrate means to unite together to form "a more complete, harmonious or coordinate entity." It means to organically unify, to form a more perfect entity. In other words, integration means "unification and mutual adjustment of diverse groups or elements into a relatively coordinated and harmonious society and culture."

In an integrated society, fellowship, comradeship, and neighborliness have no limits or boundaries based on nationality, race, or color. Associations will be formed mainly in the realm of spiritual, mental, and cultural values. There will be no laws against interracial marriages, and custom will recognize the validity of every man and every woman to marry whomever he or she pleases without any kind of penalty being imposed upon the couple by society. Integration is largely spiritual. It is even possible for a married couple to live in the same house, bearing and rearing children, fussing and feuding without ever becoming thoroughly integrated, without ever being unified in their purposes and outlook on life.

Although there is a vast difference between desegregation and integration, desegregation is an indispensable step in the march toward integration. All barriers that keep integration from developing must be destroyed. Desegregation creates the atmosphere, plants the seed, tills and fertilizes the soil so that integration can sprout and grow in a normal fashion.

Since 1935 when the Appellate Court of the state of Maryland ruled that the University of Maryland had to accept Murray, the NAACP Legal Defense and Educational Fund, the NAACP, the Southern Christian Leadership Conference, the Congress of Racial Equality, and the Student Nonviolent Coordinating Committee have spent millions upon millions of dollars to get America desegregated. Desegregate and integrate to what end? This is the question.

I hope to develop the thesis that desegregation and integration are not ends in themselves but mere means to ends of intrinsic worth and great value.

Certainly, the end of desegregation, in church and school, in train and plane, on land and sea, in hotel and motel, in employment and recreation, is not to be with white Americans. It is not to give one a false notion of his worth, to make him believe that he has arrived, that he has risen higher in the world, that he, automatically, is more important as a person because he can eat in the finest restaurant, sleep in the swankiest hotel, and work side by side with any American and socialize freely. These are not the ends of a desegregated and eventually an integrated society. If these were the ends, they aren't worth the sacrifice. Americans, disguised as Communists, intent on overthrowing the United States government, Nazis spreading the poison of hate, the members of the Ku Klux Klan, the wealthy who make their millions in the underworld of prostitution, alcoholism, and dope can and do enjoy these luxuries unsegregated and without embarrassment.

Desegregation is not and certainly should not be designed to perpetuate or create an inferiority complex in Negroes or a superiority complex in whites to the end that we feel that desegregation can come about only one way—only if we abolish all banks and insurance companies, all churches and educational institutions, all newspapers and magazines, all businesses and professions built and established with Negro brain and sweat, however good or promising they may be. Rather, the aim should be to incorporate everything that is good and everything that is needed into the mainstream of American life.

To state the case more positively, the end of desegregation, and eventually integration, should be to unshackle the minds of Negro youth, loose the chain from the Negro's soul, free his heart from fear and intimidation so that he will be able to develop whatever gifts God has given him and share the fruits of his mind and soul with humanity around the globe in the arts and sciences, in the professions and sports, in business and industry, in medicine and mental health, in music and dance, and in painting and sculpture.

To be unshackled, to improve the mind, to mold the character, to dream dreams, to develop the body, to aspire for greatness or to strive for excellence is the birthright of every child born into the world. And this birthright is given not by Christianity nor by democracy but by God and by virtue of the fact that the child is born. And no society has the right to smother ambition, to destroy incentive, to stifle growth, to curb motivation, and circumscribe the mind.

To do this to anyone, it seems to me, is an unpardonable sin. And yet we can never know how this nation has allowed potentially great minds, both Negro and white, to go uninspired and uncultivated by providing no schools at all during 246 years of slavery, and since emancipation, until fairly recently, very inadequate schools. How many Joseph Charles Prices, W. E. B. DuBoises, Booker T. Washingtons, George Washington Carvers, Mary McLeod Bethunes, Charles Clinton Spauldings have died without ever having had a chance to develop their minds for the good of the nation? But all this is beside the point. Nothing can be done now to undo the tragic events of history. "The moving finger writes and having writ moves on. Nor all your wit nor piety can lure it back to cancel a half line of it; nor all your tears wash out a word of it."

The individual was born to grow in body, mind and soul—just as the seed is planted to sprout and grow without artificial interference. So the end of desegregation is to free the mind and soul of Negro people so that Negro youth can reach for the stars and grasp after the moon. Someone has beautifully said:

Thank God a man can grow. He is not bound with earthward gaze to creep along the ground, though his beginnings be but poor and low. The fire upon his altar may grow dim, the torch he lighted may in darkness fail and nothing to kindle it avails. But high beyond his dull horizon's rim, Arcturus and the Pleiades beckon him —thank God a man can grow.

We seek to desegregate the South not only to free the Negro's mind but the mind of the white South as well. Prejudice and segregation have contributed their share toward keeping our Southland below par both economically and educationally. The time we should have spent developing our economy and utilizing the manpower of every Southerner, we have used much of it trying to keep one group down. Desegregation is not only good for the Negro but for the nation. It is my considered judgment that eyes have not seen, ears have not heard, and prophets have not dreamed what the South has yet to contribute to the nation in mind, heart, and spirit once it is freed of its prejudice and fears.

We strive to desegregate and integrate America to the end that this great nation of ours, born in revolution and blood, "conceived in liberty and dedicated to the proposition that all men are created free and equal," will truly become the lighthouse of freedom where none will be denied because his skin is black and none favored because his eyes are blue; where the nation is militarily strong but at peace; economically secure but just; learned but wise; where the poorest will have a job and bread enough and to spare, and where the richest will understand the meaning of empathy. For if democracy cannot function interracially as well as intraracially in the United States, I fear for its survival in the world. The battle for democracy is being fought out at this very moment in the streets of America and in the Congress of the United States.

We strive to desegregate and integrate America to the end that the Christian gospel which we preach may become a reality in our time. It is sheer hypocrisy to expound brotherhood and foster caste, to preach Christian fellowship and deny it to certain racial groups because they are Africans or Negroes, to declare a universal church and deny membership to certain groups as if the Church of God were nothing but a private or social club, to expound the sacredness of the human person and give segregated differential treatment in hospitals and clinics, and sheer hypocrisy to worship a God with our lips in whom we do not believe and in whom we do not trust. These are the ends which we seek in our effort to desegregate our country and pave the way for an integrated society.

But along with desegregation and integration go a heavy responsibility. The more we clamor for a desegregated society, and clamor we must, the more obligated we become to carry our full weight in the community, state, and nation. All sane men know that coercion of some kind must be applied to uproot entrenched wrongs supported by law, custom, and religion. It is clear as day that most of the social changes that have come about recently came through court action or some kind of demonstrations.

But you, my dear young friends, must remember that there is no substitute for academic excellence. There is no dichotomy in the civil-rights struggle. Although Hamilton Holmes did not sit-in and demonstrate in Atlanta, and did not go to jail, yet it was just as essential for the civil-rights struggle that Holmes sat-in in the laboratories and libraries at the University of Georgia, the first Negro to enter, graduating with membership in the Phi Beta Kappa. That too is a part of the civil-rights struggle. It was necessary to get many of the hotels and restaurants in Atlanta opened to Negroes through demonstrations. But it was also important to get Leroy Johnson elected Senator in Georgia and Rufus E. Clement elected to the Atlanta School Board. This too is a part of the civil-rights struggle. We must continue to struggle for civil rights until America is what she claims to be. But it is also important to have Carl Rowan, Ambassador to Finland, now Director of U.S. Information Service. This too is a part of the civil-rights struggle.

The color bar at the University of Mississippi had to be broken, and federal marshals had to be used to keep Meredith there; but it is equally important for the civil rights cause that Bob Weaver is the Head of the Housing and Home Finance Agency and that a South Carolina Negro is a member of the Supreme Court of the State of New York and that a Negro is Attorney General of the State of Massachusetts. It isn't either-or, it is both-and—civil rights and academic excellence.

Desegregation and eventually integration present a special challenge to Negroes and especially to Negro youth. No allowance will be made for our shortcomings because for 245 years our ancestors were slaves and for another 100 years we were enslaved again through segregation by law and by custom. No allowance will be made for our poverty in that the average income of the Negro family is only about 55 percent of that of the average white family. When competence is needed in science, whether in government, industry, or education, no allowance will be made for the inferior schools Negroes have had to attend for decades upon decades. The only comment you will hear: "Negroes are not qualified. They failed the test." When a man of experience is needed to fill a certain post, no allowance will be made for the fact that the Negro has never been given a chance to get the kind of experience needed for that job. He will be passed by and the only comment—"No Negro could be found with the proper qualifications."

What am I trying to say? I am trying to tell you with every ounce of my 177 pounds that you, with low income, poor academic backgrounds before college, unfortunate home conditions, disabled ancestors for three and a half centuries—you are now required to compete in the open market with those who have been more favorably circumstanced than you for several centuries. Our inadequacies will be printed in the press, flashed over the radio, and screened on TV. Nobody will explain the reason.

What can you do? You can blame it on the past. But it will do no good. You can accuse the environment, but this will not change your conditions. You can curse and rave only to develop ulcers. You can wring your hands and cry only to find that nobody is moved by your tears.

What can you do? There is only one thing you can do as new opportunities open up to you. You can accept as valid the Chinese proverb: "It is better to light a candle than to curse the darkness." The only thing left for a poor man to do to overcome his poverty is to find a good job, work hard, and save. The only thing a sick man can do to gain health is to follow the doctor's advice and be sensible.

The illiterate man who would overcome his ignorance must burn the midnight oil and study long and hard.

Such is your plight and mine. For he who starts behind in the great race of life must forever remain behind or run faster than the man in front. The man who is handicapped by circumstances over which he had no control must work harder than the man who had no such handicaps to overcome. Deprived of the best schools, reared in homes economically below standard, denied the opportunity to read good books in elementary and high schools, robbed of the opportunities to qualify for the best jobs, you are, almost overnight, challenged to meet the competition of the modern world.

Whether we like it or not, we must read more and socialize less, study more and frolic less, do more research and play less, write books and articles and become recognized in our respective fields. It is better by far to be known by the articles we write than by the bridge we play; by the books we publish than by the house we live in. It is better to have our students rave about our great teaching than about our beautiful cars. It is better to have our colleagues envious of our scholarship and research than of our houses and land.

I am sure Marian Anderson is economically secure, but Marian Anderson will be known not by her wealth but by her songs. John Fitzgerald Kennedy was a millionaire. But he got into history not by his millions but because he taught America that if things need to be changed we don't have to wait a hundred years to change them, we can change them now. Nobody cares how Socrates dressed—whether he wore shoes or walked barefooted. But the name of Socrates is immortalized. Nobody cares how Mahatma Gandhi dressed or rode— half naked or third class. History will claim him as one of the great men of all times.

Jesus was a despised Jew and a carpenter, but he is known as the Son of God and the Saviour of the World. Nobody thinks of George Washington's wealth. He is the father of his country. Nobody worries about Lincoln's poverty, he is the great emancipator. Shakespeare is known by *Hamlet* and *Macbeth,* Milton by *Paradise Lost,* Darwin by *The Origin of Species,* W. E. B. DuBois by *The Souls of Black Folk,* James Weldon Johnson by *God's Trombone,* Booker T. Washington by Tuskegee, and Joseph Charles Price by Livingstone. Let me ask you with what will your name be associated in the years ahead?

Alumini, faculty, and friends, we have assembled here today to celebrate the eighty-fifth anniversary of the founding of Livingstone

College and to pay homage to that good and great man, Joseph Charles Price. We have every right to rejoice and be glad. The AMEZ Church has a right to rejoice and be happy. The alumni, faculty, and students can walk these grounds with dignity and pride. The accomplishments of your graduates are outstanding. Your history is noteworthy.

But I must tell you that Livingstone in order to be true to its past, to the sacrifices the church has made, and in order to be true to its founder, Joseph Charles Price, greater things than these, Livingstone must do. Livingstone cannot live on the reputation of its deceased and contemporary alumni, as great as that reputation is. Each graduating class must produce its share of distinguished men and women. The truth of the matter is, that in order to be as great as former Livingstone graduates, you must be greater; and in order to accomplish more than they, you must accomplish more.

I must also tell you that Livingstone's future, as all private colleges similarly circumstanced, is not guaranteed in the stars. The future of the private college is no easy road. Every private college must fight for its life, and in the battle for survival, the competition is ruthless and at times unethical. Though adorned in polite English, fluent speech, college degrees, and a veneer of Christian piety, mankind is still a rather selfish animal.

The Livingstone of tomorrow will not be the Livingstone of yesterday. Livingstone will more and more be competing with every college and university in the United States for the best students. Livingstone more and more will be competing with every college and university in the United States for the best teachers. Livingstone more and more will be competing with every college and university in the United States for money from the same millionaires, the same foundations, and the same corporations. Only the Livingstone alumni and the AMEZ Church will be your exclusive domain. I predict that your future health will depend largely upon the increasing support you will get from these two sources—alumni and church.

As desegregation gives us larger and larger opportunities, let us not forget that these bring with them larger responsibilities. Negroes, under crippling conditions, have done exceedingly well, but not well enough to pass. We have not been accepted into the mainstream of American life. We have not yet made our case in politics, business, and education. The confidence we need in all these areas is not yet there. And yet the Negro's future in America is brighter than ever before. I look to the future with the courage and hope of Tennyson in "Ulysses":

'Tis not too late to seek a newer world.
Push off, and sitting well in order smite
the sounding furrows; for my purpose holds
to sail beyond the sunset and the baths
of all the western stars until I die.
It may be that the gulfs will wash us down;
It may be that we shall touch the Happy Isles,
and see the great Achilles whom we knew.
Tho' much is taken, much abides; and tho'
we are not now that strength which in old days
moved earth and heaven, that which we are, we are,—
"One equal temper of eroic hearts,
made weak by time and fate, but strong in will
"To strive, to seek, to find, and not to yield."

Eulogy of Dr. Martin Luther King, Jr.

DR. BENJAMIN MAYS

To be honored by being requested to give the eulogy at the funeral of Dr. Martin Luther King, Jr., is like asking one to eulogize his deceased son—so close and so precious was he to me. Our friendship goes back to his student days at Morehouse College. It is not an easy task; nevertheless I accept it, with a sad heart and with full knowledge of my inadequacy to do justice to this man. It was *my desire* that if I predeceased Dr. King, he would pay tribute to me on my final day. It was *his wish* that if he predeceased me, I would deliver the homily at his funeral. Fate has decreed that I eulogize him. I wish it might have been otherwise, for, after all, I am three score and ten and Martin Luther is dead at thirty-nine.

Although there are some who rejoice in his death, there are millions across the length and breadth of this world who are smitten with grief that this friend of mankind—all mankind—has been cut down in the flower of his youth. So, multitudes here and in foreign lands, queens, kings, heads of governments, the clergy of the world, and the common man everywhere, are praying that God will be with the family, the American people, and the President of the United States in this tragic hour. We hope that this universal concern will bring comfort to the family—for grief is like a heavy load: when shared it is easier to bear. We come today to help the family carry the load.

We have assembled here from every section of this great nation and from other parts of the world to give thanks to God that He gave to America, at this moment in history, Martin Luther King, Jr. Truly God is no respecter of persons. How strange! God called the grandson of a slave on his father's side, and the grandson of a man born during the Civil War on his mother's side, and said to him: *Martin Luther, speak to America about war and peace; about social justice and racial discrimination; about its obligation to the poor; and about nonviolence as a way of perfecting social change in a world of brutality and war.*

Here was a man who believed with all of his might that the pursuit of violence at any time is ethically and morally wrong; that God and the moral weight of the universe are against it; that violence is self-defeating; and that only love and forgiveness can break the vicious circle of revenge. He believed that nonviolence would prove effective in the abolition of injustice in politics, in economics, in education, and in race relations. He was convinced, also, that people could not be moved to abolish voluntarily the inhumanity of man to man by mere persuasion and pleading, but that they could be moved to do so by dramatizing the evil through massive nonviolent resistance. He believed that nonviolent direct action was necessary to supplement the nonviolent victories in the Federal courts. He believed that the nonviolent approach to solving social problems would ultimately prove to be redemptive.

Out of this conviction, history records the marches in Montgomery, Birmingham, Selma, Chicago, and other cities. He gave people an ethical and moral way to engage in activities designed to perfect social change without bloodshed and violence; and when violence did erupt it was that which is potential in any protest which aims to uproot deeply entrenched wrongs. No reasonable person would deny that the activities and the personality of Martin Luther King, Jr., contributed largely to the success of the student sit-in movements; in abolishing segregation in downtown establishments; and that his activities contributed mightily to the passage of the Civil Rights legislation of 1964 and 1965.

Martin Luther King, Jr., believed in a united America; that the walls of separation brought on by legal and *de facto* segregation, and discrimination based on race and color, could be eradicated. As he said in his Washington Monument address: *"I have a dream!"*

He had faith in his country. He died striving to desegregate and integrate America to the end that this great nation of ours, born in revolution and blood, conceived in liberty, and dedicated to the proposition that all men are created free and equal, will truly become the lighthouse of freedom where none will be denied because his skin is black and none favored because his eyes are blue; where our nation will be militarily strong but perpetually at peace; economically secure but just; learned but wise; where the poorest—the garbage collectors—will have bread enough and to spare; where no one will be poorly housed; each educated up to his capacity; and where the richest will understand the meaning of empathy. *This* was his dream, and the end toward which he strove. As he and his followers so often sang: "We shall overcome someday; black and white together."

Let it be thoroughly understood that our deceased brother did not embrace nonviolence out of fear or cowardice. Moral courage was one of his noblest virtues. As Mahatma Gandhi challenged the British Empire without a sword and won, Martin Luther King, Jr., challenged the interracial wrongs of his country without a gun. And he had the faith to believe that he would win the battle for social justice. I make bold to assert that it took more courage for King to practice nonviolence than it took his assassin to fire the fatal shot. The assassin is a coward: he committed his dastardly deed and fled. When Martin Luther disobeyed an unjust law, he accepted the consequences of his actions. He never ran away and he never begged for mercy. He returned to the Birmingham jail to serve his time.

Perhaps he was more courageous than soldiers who fight and die on the battlefield. There is an element of compulsion in their dying. But when Martin Luther faced death again and again, and finally embraced it, there was no external pressure. He was acting on an inner compulsion that drove him on. More courageous than those who advocate violence as a way out, for they carry weapons of destruction for defense. But Martin Luther faced the dogs, the police, jail, heavy criticism, and finally death; and he never carried a gun, not even a knife to defend himself. He had only his faith in a just God to rely on; and the belief that "thrice is he armed who has his quarrels just." The faith that Browning writes about when he says: "One who never turned his back, but marched breast forward; Never doubted that clouds would break; Never dreamed that right though worsted wrong would triumph; Held we fall to rise, are baffled to fight better; Sleep to wake."

Coupled with moral courage was Martin Luther King, Jr.'s capacity to love people. Though deeply committed to a program of freedom for Negroes, he had love and concern for all kinds of peoples.

He drew no distinction between the high and the low; none between the rich and the poor. He believed especially that he was sent to champion the cause of the man farthest down. He would probably say that *if death had to come, I am sure there was no greater cause to die for than fighting to get a just wage for garbage collectors.* He was supra race, supra nation, supra denomination, supra class, and supra culture. He belonged to the world and to mankind. Now he belongs to posterity.

But there is a dichotomy in all this. This man was loved by some and hated by others. If any man knew the meaning of suffering, King knew. House bombed; living day by day for thirteen years under constant threats of death; maliciously accused of being a Communist; falsely accused of being insincere and seeking the limelight for his own glory; stabbed by a member of his own race; slugged in a hotel lobby; jailed thirty times; occasionally deeply hurt because friends betrayed him—and yet this man had no bitterness in his heart, no rancor in his soul, no revenge in his mind; and he went up and down the length and breadth of this world preaching nonviolence and the redemptive power of love. He believed with all his heart, mind, and soul that the way to peace and brotherhood is through nonviolence, love, and suffering. He was severely criticized for his opposition to the war in Vietnam. It must be said, however, that one could hardly expect a prophet of Dr. King's commitments to advocate nonviolence at home and violence in Vietnam. Nonviolence to King was total commitment not only in solving the problems of race in the United States but in solving the problems of the world.

Surely this man was called of God to do this work. If Amos and Micah were prophets in the eighth century, B.C., Martin Luther King, Jr., was a prophet in the twentieth century. If Isaiah was called of God to prophesy in his day, Martin Luther was called of God to prophesy in his time. If Hosea was sent to preach love and forgiveness centuries ago, Martin Luther was sent to expound the doctrine of nonviolence and forgiveness in the third quarter of the twentieth century. If Jesus was called to preach the Gospel to the poor, Martin Luther was called to give dignity to the common man. If a prophet is one who interprets in clear and intelligible language the will of God, Martin Luther King, Jr., fits that designation. If a prophet is one who does not seek popular causes to espouse, but rather the causes he thinks are right, Martin Luther qualified on that score.

No! He was not ahead of his time. No man is ahead of his time. Every man is within his star, each in his time. Each man must respond to the call of God in his lifetime and not in somebody else's time.

Jesus had to respond to the call of God in the first century, A.D., and not in the twentieth century. He had but one life to live. He couldn't wait. How long do you think Jesus would have had to wait for the constituted authorities to accept him? Twenty-five years? A hundred years? A thousand? He died at thirty-three. He couldn't wait. Paul, Galileo, Copernicus, Martin Luther the Protestant reformer, Gandhi and Nehru couldn't wait for another time. They had to act in their lifetimes. No man is ahead of his time. Abraham, leaving his country in obedience to God's call; Moses, leading a rebellious people to the Promised Land; Jesus, dying on a cross; Galileo, on his knees recanting; Lincoln, dying of an assassin's bullet; Woodrow Wilson, crusading for a League of Nations; Martin Luther King, Jr., dying fighting for justice for garbage collectors—none of these men were ahead of their time. With them the time was always ripe to do that which was right and that which needed to be done.

Too bad, you say, that Martin Luther King, Jr., died so young. I feel that way, too. But, as I have said many times before, it isn't how long one lives, but how well. It's what one accomplishes for mankind that matters. Jesus died at thirty-three; Joan of Arc at nineteen; Byron and Burns at thirty-six; Keats and Marlow at twenty-nine; Shelley at thirty; Dunbar before thirty-five; John Fitzgerald Kennedy at forty-six; William Rainey Harper at forty-nine; and Martin Luther King, Jr., at thirty-nine.

We all pray that the assassin will be apprehended and brought to justice. But, make no mistake, the American people are in part responsible for Martin Luther King, Jr.'s, death. The assassin heard enough condemnation of King and of Negroes to feel that he had public support. He knew that millions hated King.

The Memphis officials must bear some of the guilt for Martin Luther's assassination. The strike should have been settled several weeks ago. The lowest paid men in our society should not have to strike for a more just wage. A century after Emancipation, and after the enactment of the thirteenth, fourteenth, and fifteenth Amendments, it should not have been necessary for Martin Luther King, Jr., to stage marches in Montgomery, Birmingham, and Selma, and go to jail thirty times trying to achieve for his people those rights which people of lighter hue get by virtue of their being born white. We, too, are guilty of murder. It is time for the American people to repent and make democracy equally applicable to all Americans. What can we do? We, and not the assassins, represent America at its best. We have the power—not the assassins—to make things right.

If we love Martin Luther King, Jr., and respect him, as this crowd surely testifies, let us see to it that he did not die in vain; let us see to it that we do not dishonor his name by trying to solve our problems through rioting in the streets. Violence was foreign to his nature. He warned that continued riots could produce a Fascist state. But let us see to it also that the conditions that cause riots are promptly removed, as the President of the United States is trying to get us to do. Let black and white alike search their hearts; and if there be prejudice in our hearts against any racial or ethnic group, let us exterminate it and let us pray, as Martin Luther King, Jr., would pray if he could: *Father, forgive them for they know not what they do.* If we do this, Martin Luther King, Jr., will have died a redemptive death from which all mankind will benefit.

Morehouse College will never be the same because Martin Luther came by here; and the nation and the world will be indebted to him for centuries to come. It is natural, therefore, that we here at Morehouse and President Gloster would want to memorialize him to serve as an inspiration to all students who study in this Center.

I close by saying to you what Martin Luther King, Jr., believed: *If physical death was the price he had to pay to rid America of prejudice and injustice, nothing could be more redemptive.* And, to paraphrase the words of the immortal John Fitzgerald Kennedy, permit me to say that Martin Luther King, Jr.'s, unfinished work on earth must truly be our own.

Race Relations and World Upheaval

DR. LISTON POPE

Liston Pope is an eloquent pleader for the emancipation of the nonwhite peoples of the earth. Graduating from Duke University in 1929, he later received the Doctor of Philosophy degree from Yale University and the Doctor of Sacred Theology degree from Boston University.

He has served as the Gilbert L. Stark Professor of Social Ethics at Yale University since 1938, and was Dean of the Yale University Divinity School from 1949 to 1962. His literary contributions include *Millhands and Preachers*, *Labor's Relation to Church and Community* (editor), and *The Kingdom beyond Caste*.

He has held a number of significant posts in distinguished organizations: He was a trustee of the Phelps-Stokes Fund; Chairman of the Interseminary Committee of the National Council of Churches; member of the Central Committee and Executive Committee of the World Council of Churches; Chairman of the Executive Committee of the American Association of Theological Schools; and currently is a member of the Board of Directors of the Urban League.

The following speech was delivered for the Human Relations Council of Houston, Texas, at the University of Houston, during Human Rights Week on December 12, 1963.

* * *

This week is being widely observed as Human Rights Week, celebrating the fifteenth anniversary of the adoption by the United Nations of the Universal Declaration of Human Rights. That remarkable document set forth "the inherent dignity and . . . equal and inalienable rights of all members of the human family." But for us in the United States the struggle to define and guarantee equal rights for all our citizens goes back for a hundred years.

Five score years ago one of our greatest forefathers gave forth a proclamation that those who had hitherto been slaves in this nation should thenceforth be free. Today we are engaged in a great battle over civil rights, testing whether this nation, conceived in liberty and dedicated to the proposition that all men are created equal, can realize at last the intent of that proclamation. The battleground is not confined to the historic hills of Gettysburg or even to the legislative halls of Washington. It stretches out to include hundreds of public schools across the land, streets of Birmingham and housing projects in Chicago, job opportunities in New York and voting rights in Mississippi.

The struggle over justice and freedom and opportunity for nonwhite peoples stretches out, indeed, to cover most of the world at this moment. In 1939 at the outset of the second world war, approximately 750 million people—one-third of mankind and nearly all of them nonwhite—were living under colonial rule dominated by white nations. Today less than thirty million people, nearly all of them in Africa, continue to be under white dominion. In the last twenty-five years independence has come to the vast populations of Asia, and today Kenya became the twenty-sixth nation in Africa to win its independence since the end of World War II. Today these emancipated peoples are not only shaping their own destiny, courageously or falteringly; they are also affecting the policies of the entire world and stimulating the aspirations of nonwhite peoples everywhere, including those of millions of our nonwhite fellow Americans.

And so it is that discussion of race relations can no longer be focussed on Connecticut or Texas alone, or on the South or the North, or on the United States. So far as race relations are concerned anywhere in the world, the way in which any minority is treated is no longer exclusively the business of the majority immediately involved. Hitler massacred the Jews, and this was one important factor that led to the death of thousands of American boys on battlefields. When the Union of South Africa has race riots, their flame sears the whole world and especially the entire continent of Africa, causing other peoples in Africa to become restless and embittered.

Whenever a racial incident occurs in the United States, the Communist propaganda network tells the whole world about it, and the hundreds of millions of nonwhites in Africa and in Asia have their doubts about us increased. It is notorious that when an American makes a speech in either Africa or Asia, the first question in the discussion that follows almost invariably has to do with the status of the Negro in America. In a world struggle, what we do to our neighbors at home has become as important for the outcome as what we do to our enemies abroad.

In short, race relations anywhere have become the concern, the legitimate concern, of people everywhere. The race problem has become one of the paramount issues of our time. The future of our Western civilization may depend to a considerable degree on our ability to dissolve racial tensions. If the colored peoples of Asia and Africa are alienated from the Western nations, and doubtless that is Russia's long-range strategy, and more recently Communist China's as well, we shall have lost the major part of our struggle in the world. And Communist nations have already all but succeeded in convincing many nonwhite peoples that they are their champions against the alleged imperialism and chauvinism of the Western powers. Against such weapons bombs are helpless, and we had better realize that Russia's proclamation of racial equality can be combatted only by a better demonstration of equality than Russia herself can provide. Russia's own practice is far from perfect in this connection, of course, especially in relation to her Jewish minority.

The contemporary struggle in the world is not a power struggle only. An equally important struggle is underway for racial and social justice and for the minds and loyalties of vast multitudes of nonwhite people who comprise the majority of mankind. Russia is a power state, but she professes to be primarily a revolutionary force, a force to liberate the oppressed and to elevate the underprivileged of the earth.

Actually, the revolution in the contemporary world is much older and wider than the Communist movement. The rise of submerged masses toward equality goes back to the American Revolution and to the French Revolution of the Eighteenth century, before Karl Marx was even born. Russia's version of the world revolution represents a betrayal of basic human freedoms, despite her claim to be democratic and her appropriation of the term "people's democracy."

But our problem in the United States is not only that of resisting Russia's pretensions and designs, as important as that problem is. Our task is that of understanding and realizing our own concepts of democracy and freedom in human relations. If we are concerned about the rights of Negro Americans or Mexican-Americans or Japanese-Americans, our solicitude is not based primarily on our desire to create a better image of America abroad or to fortify our foreign policy. Rather, we are determined to do what is right as we understand the right, to be just in a society dedicated to justice, to be free and to help all our people to be free in a land illumined from its beginning by "freedom's holy light." The Americans at Bunker Hill and Yorktown and the Alamo and Gettysburg and Iwo Jima did not act as if they believed "freedom" and "equality" to be only slogans or political rallying cries. No more can we if we would be their worthy heirs.

Most especially in this centennial year of the Emancipation Proclamation we are heirs of the vision of Abraham Lincoln. That proclamation, to be sure, was very largely a stratagem of war, but its intrinsic content reflected Lincoln's vision of an America united and free. Lincoln's greatness arose from his simplicity, his majesty from his humility. A gaunt, homespun man he was, ridiculed in his own day as a railsplitter and backwoodsman, hated for subsequent decades in the South as a symbol of Northern interference and of bitter defeat. Today we honor him, North and South alike, as having been perhaps the greatest American. A common man he was, and we have done well to place his image on our most common coin, so that every child knows from the beginning that unforgettable face. But there was about him an aura of greatness, and its light burns brighter with the passing years.

We paid little attention to Lincoln's memory in the South when I was growing up in North Carolina. Too many could still remember the terrible years of war and Reconstruction. And though we all revere him now for his personal greatness, for many decades Lincoln's work of emancipation has remained unfinished in the United States and throughout the world. He emancipated the slaves, but the Negro is not yet free. He fought for freedom, but many still are in bondage. Lee surrendered to Grant at Appomattox, but the Union is not yet restored on all questions of racial policy.

Slavery was abolished, but new tyrannies arose, partly from necessity, partly from rapacity, partly from fear. The Negro remained a servant and a social inferior, as tenant farmer or domestic servant or common laborer. Technically enfranchised, he could seldom vote; indicted, he was often presumed guilty; suspected, he was frequently banished or lynched. Judged before the War Between the States by his qualities as a first-rate slave, he was judged thereafter by his ability to adjust to second- or third-rate conditions of life, to inferior wages, houses, schools, hospitals, railroad cars, restaurants, hotels, motion-picture theatres, and all things else.

While the South was devising new methods to control the Negro, or "to keep him in his place" (as the expression came to be), the remainder of the nation was developing comparable methods for management of other racial minorities. Immigrants (and especially Jews) in the East, Orientals in the West, Mexicans in the Southwest—all were welcomed as cheap labor and repudiated as equal human beings. The South built its segregated ghettos for Negroes at the edge of town; a similar result was achieved in Northern cities by the insertion of restrictive covenants in deeds to property. Southern universities barred Negroes; universities elsewhere often barred them too, from the student body and from the faculty, and established quotas for Jews. Barriers to full rights of citizenship for Negroes were matched by similar obstacles for Mexicans and Orientals. Everywhere in America the barriers went up: the old stock must be protected from the immigrant, the Christian from the Jew, the white people from the Negro. Regional differences in the treatment of racial minorities became less and less significant, and were largely matters of degree.

In the case of the Negro, particularly, obstacles were artificially constructed. As Vann Woodward has demonstrated in his book, *The Strange Career of Jim Crow,* barriers were constructed by state legislation in the respective Southern states. They did not result simply from bitterness in the years just after reconstruction. The federal troops left the South in 1877; for the next twenty years, approximately, relations between the Negro and the white in the South were rather informal, undefined, casual, chaotic. Then in two decades, beginning about 1890, nearly every Southern state passed legislation reimposing the poll tax in an effort to disfranchise the Negro and the poor white against the Populist movement, and other restrictive legislation was enacted, requiring separate railway transportation, separate railway and bus stations, separate public facilities, and all the rest. If you say that legislation cannot change the human heart, it should be remembered it can change conduct, as it did in the first instance when the barriers were erected.

In the last few years the tides have been running rapidly in the other direction. We have probably made more progress in race relations in America in the past two decades than in the previous century, though we have only begun. Many changes have taken place. Negro baseball players have been admitted to the big leagues, and Jackie Robinson and his successors of his race have become heroes for the sandlot gangs. This is very important: we can remember that prejudice against immigrants was diminished by the fact that football and baseball players with unpronounceable names became heroes to the kids. Professional football is largely desegregated, as seen in the Dallas Cowboys and most other teams. A Negro, Dr. Ralph Bunche, has achieved one of the highest posts in international affairs and has been awarded the Nobel Peace Prize. A number of college fraternities have defied their national organizations by admitting Negroes and Jews to membership, even when it cost them their national affiliation. There are several thousand Negroes in white Southern universities, most of them having been admitted without incident. The President of the United States ordered the elimination of segregation in the armed services, and integration has been widely achieved. Lynching has virtually disappeared.

Significant changes have occurred in economic opportunities for minority groups. Traditionally, Negroes were confined largely to roles as domestic servants or tenant farmers. When they entered industry at all, it was as unskilled employees, and opportunities for training and advancement were very poor. During the Second World War an unprecedented number of Negroes entered factories, and a number of states have established fair employment practice commissions to make sure that members of minority groups are treated fairly as to wages, promotions, and the like.

Not all the inequities have been removed by any means; even now the average family income for the Negro family is less than two-thirds that of the average income for the white family, but vast progress has been made. And the maximum development of our economy, nationally and in particular localities, requires that our economic policies shall be color-blind from now on.

Traditionally Negroes were excluded largely from white-collar jobs that would bring them into direct contact with the general public—such jobs as clerks in department stores, secretaries or receptionists in offices, and the like. In many parts of the country Negroes and Japanese-Americans and members of other minority groups have now been admitted to such jobs. The riots and the boycotts that had been freely predicted have failed to materialize, and most members of the public appear hardly to notice the skin color of the person waiting on them.

The labor unions have played a leading role in the creation of equal opportunities for Negroes, and especially the CIO, which has been officially opposed to segregation in its unions from the very beginning. There are those that say that the CIO had led the fight, second to the Supreme Court, to break down racial barriers in America. There are still unions which exclude Negroes or give them second-rate membership, but they are out of line with their national leadership.

As for the churches, it has been said that "eleven o'clock on Sunday morning is the most segregated hour in the week." One could qualify that conclusion; eleven o'clock on Saturday night is even more segregated in most residential areas, for the country-club set, and other purely social clubs are in general more completely uniracial than are the churches. If the statement is properly hedged about and seen in perspective, however, it must be granted that the church is probably the most racially segregated major institution in America, at least as it is represented in its local manifestations. Great national and world church gatherings are the exception to the usual practice, and they inspirit us for the future. But it is at the level of the local church and community, where people must live and work and worship face to face, day after day, that the crucial test will come. At this level, the churches, North and South, have lagged behind the Supreme Court as the conscience of the people on questions of race, and they have fallen far behind trade unions, factories, schools, department stores, athletic gatherings, and most other major areas of human association as far as achievement of integration in their own life is concerned.

But in the light of the Bible, in the doctrines of the Jewish community and of the Christian Church, in centuries of experience since Pentecost (when the church was born)—before all these tribunals the practice of racial segregation or discrimination before God or in the church stands condemned. And deep in their own hearts most thoughtful Christians, North or South, in South Africa or in Singapore, know that this is true.

Whatever the culpability of the churches, more recently there have been many marks of penitence on their part. The National and World Councils of Churches, and many of their constituent bodies, have denounced segregation and have pledged themselves to work for a nonsegregated church in a nonsegregated society. Slowly but surely they are moving toward that end. Though nonsegregated congregations in American Protestantism still comprise only about 15 percent of the total number of congregations, this percentage is eight times as great as that of ten years ago. In some denominations the figure is much higher than this national average. And comparable or even greater changes have taken place during the last decade in most church-related institutions such as schools, colleges, and hospitals. The movement toward integration has been at an uneven rate in the various denominations and regions of the country, but it has affected them all, including a number of churches and educational institutions in the South.

Slowly, how slowly, the mending of the breach proceeds, but it does proceed. It should be remembered that most of the Christian churches in the world still refuse to practice discrimination or segregation. If the church as a whole had capitulated, it would have utterly lost its integrity and completely denied its Lord. Whatever the regional defections may be, it is the very nature of the Church to be an inclusive and integrated community of the faithful. And it is its task to give leadership to efforts toward justice and equality in the wider society. If the ministers of Houston could find the courage and open-mindedness to invite Presidential candidate John F. Kennedy to Houston to discuss with them the political implications of his faith as a Roman Catholic, these same ministers have the right to expect that discussion and action on racial questions in their churches and community will be frank and open.

For two decades now we have been moving, in many important spheres of our common life, toward the realization in race relations of our democratic ideals. In the last year the pace has been greatly accelerated; in retrospect the years of 1963 and 1964 may seem to have been the years of great decisions. Prisons have been filled and blood has already been spilled in the streets of our cities in racial demonstrations; the conflict next year may be worse than that of this year unless our nation moves with more than "all deliberate speed." Two hundred thousand persons could march on Washington this year without serious incident, but that remarkable nonviolent demonstration is no guarantee of a peaceful future. A Civil Rights Bill containing minimum guarantees languishes in Congress, obstructed at every turn by cynical legislators; passage of such legislation will represent only a beginning, but the fate of this bill will be an augury of things to come, for good or ill. Desegregation of schools and universities proceeds in crucial instances in token fashion only. Men of good will favor better jobs and homes for members of minority groups, but not next to themselves.

When all is said and done, the acid test of our democracy will doubtless come in the conduct of her citizens rather than that of her existing political leaders alone. In a speech delivered before the Chamber of Commerce in Columbia, South Carolina, last week, former Governor Leroy Collins of Florida urged his fellow Southerners to full partnership in the struggle for racial justice. He said:

We have allowed the extremists to speak for the South—the very ones whom we in the South have had to struggle against in our towns and in our state capitals for much of the progress we have made . . . How long are the majority of Southerners going to allow themselves to be caricatured before the nation? How many Sunday School children have to be dynamited to death? How many Negro leaders have to be shot in the back? How many Governors have to be shot in the chest? How many Presidents have to be assassinated?

Governor Collins continued:

Too many politicians down our way have been hoodwinking the people on the civil-rights issue. They have been trying to pretend, for their own personal and political advantage, that the changes which are coming over the hill really are not there. They talk defensively of "states' rights" when they and we well know that there can be no such thing as a state's right to default on a national duty.

As individuals and members of groups we can make our convictions known to our legislators. But we can also act directly, by trying to keep open channels of communication between racial groups and by breaking down segregation in the groups—industries, political parties, churches, social clubs, fraternities—to which we belong. Voluntary groups are among the last outposts of white exclusiveness. The question is not whether a group of people have a right to choose their close friends; of course they do. In a democracy, the question also is, "Does every person have a right to be chosen without regard to color or race or national origin?" As Lowell once put it, "Democracy does not mean that I am as good as you are, but that you are as good as I am."

The Judeo-Christian faith agrees with the ideals of democracy and the findings of science in proclaiming the unity and equality of all men everywhere. Science has proved that racial differences, if they exist in nature at all, are very elusive, and the term "race" has become practically meaningless scientifically. Two old definitions of prejudice are supported by the findings of science: "Prejudice is being down on what you are not up on," and "Prejudice is a vagrant opinion without visible means of support." The ideals of democracy likewise affirm that all men are created equal and have certain inalienable rights. But there continues to be a great gap between our official American creed and our actual racial practice.

The Judeo-Christian faith goes even further than science or the philosophy of democracy. Despite the bad practice of the churches, they teach that men are not only equal, but also brothers; they must not only tolerate each other, but must actually love each other, because God loves them all equally. God did not make the Negro to be a hewer of wood and a drawer of water; He made him a living soul, as precious as any other.

The findings of science, the political ideals of democracy and religious faith all coincide in the quest for racial equality; if that quest is forsaken or its fruition much longer delayed, the greatest faiths and truths of our civilization must be rejected as error and hypocrisy. We must choose between racial segregation on the one side and science, democracy, and Christianity on the other. A civilization, like a personality, can remain schizophrenic for only a limited time without rushing to its own self-destruction.

Happily, we are moving toward unity in race relations, and toward reconciliation with each other. We must hasten, for the time is short. But justification is coming for the faith of a tall man—a gaunt man so tall that his sheltering shadow will fall across centuries—a homespun man of the people who believed that the people, though often fooled, at last would find their way.

As Governor Collins affirmed in his speech in South Carolina:

The principle that all men are created equal is an idea that can never be stopped—not by custom, not by prejudice, not by hate, not by murder, not by armies, not by an mortal force. It may be thwarted, it may be delayed, its triumph may be at great cost and sacrifice, but it will keep coming on and on, for it has the invincibility of simple truth, justice and right. . . . Above all else it is the moral duty of our generation to plow under racial injustice everywhere in the United States, and to plant new opportunities for the generations which will come along after us and reside in this green part of our old planet.

Reversing the Spiral toward Futility
DR. SAMUEL PROCTOR

Samuel Proctor received the A.B. degree from Virginia Union University, holds the B.D. degree from Crozer Theological Seminary, and the Th.D. degree from Boston University.

Early in his professional career, he taught at Virginia Union University, where he later became Dean of the School of Religion. He also appeared as chapel preacher at Bucknell University, Pennsylvania State University, Hampton Institute, and Cornell University, among others. He served as the President of North Carolina Agricultural and Technical College from 1955 to 1960. He was appointed associate director of the Peace Corps in 1965 before serving as special assistant to the national director of the Office of Economic Opportunity in 1966. Recently, he has been appointed Vice-President for Special Programs at the University of Wisconsin.

This address expresses Proctor's concern for making all of us aware of the steps that we must take to bridge that gap in the Negro's culture which separation and discrimination have produced.

* * *

The burden of this address is that for eighty years, since the beginning of the concept of racial separateness as a national institution, there has been a cause-and-effect, one-two punch operating so effectively in Negro life that now one can hardly tell what is cause and what is effect, which is punch number one and which is number two. The product of discrimination is used to prove that discrimination is fitting and proper. This process has been moving like a whirling spiral carrying the Negro on towards futility. One may understand the maze of urban school problems, the violence of last summer, and the apathy and inertia of hordes of teen-agers in terms of this spiral having spun to a dead halt at the point of futility.

This is one more metaphor used to capture a grim reality that we will have to live with for a few more summers. We have used all sorts of appellatives for this phenomenon; we have called those trapped at the end of this spiral the "culturally deprived," the "culturally diversified," the "socially retarded," the "subculture," and you name it!

The fact is that we have finally come to focus on the consequences of discrimination in opportunity—opportunity in education and in employment. We have a half million youth out of school and out of work, "dropouts," half of whom are Negro. And no one knows how many "dripouts" there are, those who are still on the rolls, loitering in the halls, smoking in the rest rooms, and strolling in and out of classes without homework.

These young people are at the end of this spiral toward futility. More than half of them were reared in homes with only the mother in charge. Half of their parents reached less than the seventh grade in school. Their schools were overcrowded, understaffed, and their teachers were the products of the same circumstances, only ten years earlier and therefore without the benefit of the ten years of greatest progress in these schools—the ten years since the 1954 Supreme Court decision against segregated schools.

This picture is further embroidered by the fact that these young people customarily saw only white faces in the advertisements picturing successful living, only white men in important business positions, no Negro clerks in the big stores. They had no reason to be convinced that hard work would be rewarded with a good job. Only a handful of Negroes in New York and Washington had really good jobs. One could make money playing ball, dancing, and singing. But, lacking these talents, there was little else to hope for. Therefore, the backwaters of fear, hostility and defeatism have stagnated in the minds and hearts of these youngsters. We have a major engineering job to do if this situation is to be changed. We cannot substitute statistics for effort, semantics for concern or talkfests, and banquet speeches for hard work. We need to discover what causes this spiral to spin on toward futility, and try to stop it, put it in reverse, and cause it to move toward fulfillment and success.

Let us look at the spiral. It begins with those first experiences of rejection and that early awareness that society has a special niche for the Negro. Even though there are all of the replicas of the larger "white" world present in some form in the Negro ghetto, the unspoken understanding is that the world is for others, not "our kind." In order to survive this arrangement, feeling whole and aspiring, one has to pull all kinds of tricks on his mind. The worst kind of schizophrenia is frequently the result.

The spiral churns on from rejection to fear. Fear of big words, fear of printed tests, fear of large, clean rooms, fear of police, fear of failure, fear of embarrassment, fear of interviews. I recall a basketball player at our college who had been recruited out of one of our big city's slums. He had played out his eligibility and still needed a few hours and grade points to graduate. When he saw the world closing in on him, he packed to leave the campus and return to the slums. He had been turned down so many times in life that he considered no alternative but defeat. He was afraid to try some of those long shots. My wife and I learned about him, put him up in our guest room as an experiment, and let him work for his board and tuition. Today, rather than lurking in the shadows and leaning on the bars of that town, he is a teacher helping other youngsters to climb out of their apathy. It required someone to bend down over him, displace his defeatism with confidence, open a door and help him through.

This fear crystallizes into hostility. What concerns me most today is that unthinking and recalcitrant whites will want to do political and psychological battle with Negro youth, translate their irritation over aggressive Negro efforts into a grand silence of belligerence and resistance. They have no way of assessing the hostility that rejection and fear have already generated, and the consequences can become—event yet—a bloody, rather than a nonviolent, pursuit of the Negroes' objectives.

It is just as likely that instead of fighting, Negroes by the millions will spend madness and indignation among themselves and lapse into resignation, defeat, and futility. Here is where the spiral delivers them now! Everybody loses. The unskilled, angry people are a burden. Unproductive citizens and semiliterate crowds in the streets are the easy prey of every vice, the victims of every form of exploitation, and will not always follow the most responsible leadership—and everybody loses!

This issue is especially relevant for you. You train the nation's teachers, those who have the earliest and the longest contact with the young. These teachers colleges are now becoming just colleges. You have the elasticity to grow, and I predict that you will be the ones to take the expanding enrollments and teach most Americans for the next twenty years. Your disciples can begin now, with the inspiration that you will give them, and they can bring to bear on this problem their new insights, their strength of heart and breadth of vision. And they can start that spiral moving in the other direction in September.

In Nigeria I saw thirty-five Peace Corps Volunteers at the University of Neukka begin their tour of duty under the most trying circumstances. They were called spies. A postcard inadvertently dropped and highly publicized had infuriated their African students. Martin

Luther King was arrested in Birmingham, and four Negro children were killed in a Sunday School by white terrorists. How much more could one ask for to kill the first Peace Corps effort in Nigeria?

But the volunteers studied their situation and learned it well. They could not afford to parrot worn clichés about Africans, Negroes, democracy, communism, or colonialism. This "savvy" gained them the respect of their students. They lived and played and worked with them, defying all of the old concepts of how white colonials should deal with Africans. And they won! Some of them returned to that staff after their tours ended. In Nigeria the Peace Corps has nearly six hundred and when the postcard was dropped, we had less than sixty.

We can flood this country with teachers capable of seeing the world through the eyes of the deprived minority youth and make this the most wonderful achievement in American education. With your leadership, they will start that spiral moving the other way this September. Rejection must be corrected by acceptance. This does not mean giving a Negro high praise for low performance. But it does mean a little extra attention to convince him that he and his problems are no surprise and all in a day's work. The necessity for this varies, and soon it will fade as a new crop comes to flower, but now it is necessary.

Acceptance is one step from confidence and self-assurance. How can white coaches take Negro athletes and prepare them to play before strangers and keep them poised and confident? Do coaches know more than we? Granted they have a built-in system of immediate rewards, the applause of the crowds and newspaper clippings. But we need to find comparable motivating devices in English and math. It has been done, and with a deep desire I believe it can still be done.

A young Negro teacher in Newark is now drawing attention to her work because she is taking hardened junior high school girls from one of the toughest neighborhoods and making them love opera, symphonies, and serious drama. She puts in long hours and has poured much effort into her work. But she testifies that the rewards are worth it. Parents came to one of her performances of *The Mikado* and wept to see their daughters pursuing this type of endeavor. These were tears of joy at something worthwhile and not tears of grief in a court room or a morgue.

One does not work alone in this. Our major universities are stirred up, and Wisconsin has a new institute of human relations, as one example, addressing itself to this issue. The major foundations are

now discovering Negro youth. One is preparing a massive program
to strengthen Negro college placement programs. This will be a pace-
setting device. When their brothers, cousins, and uncles get better
jobs, they will want to learn more, faster.

The churches have grown skeptical of trusting individual com-
municants to play private roles in this area, and they have committed
their resources to change the character and face of America. Last
summer the students who volunteered to go to Mississippi were
shocked to learn that the churches had quit hiding their heads in
the sand and had come forth with an orientation program at one of
our fine colleges. This commitment was reassuring to those making
their first gestures toward brotherhood. The government is clear on
this. Our President could not speak more succinctly than he has on
equal opportunity. So, be my guest! It is right. It is acceptable. It is
necessary. It is patriotic. It is professionally challenging and personally
rewarding.

Recently I sat in a briefing session for personnel managers of one
of our largest corporations. The leader, speaking on company policy,
said this:

Up to now we have sought only the top 5 percent of a class, the
cream. We have had also minimum standards beneath which we
will not go for anybody. In recognition of the special problems of
Negroes in preparing for our types of jobs, we will not only go after
the top 5 percent but we will hire Negroes who clear our minimum
standards by a safe margin and who show potential for growth.

This is all that Whitney Young and Julius Thomas of the Urban
League have advocated. Our country has established special programs
for agriculture, adult education, the blind, the deaf, the orphaned,
and the immobile child who needs a visiting teacher. Even though
it is certainly more difficult to formalize, we are saying now that the
same attention and concern should be brought to bear on the Negro
child as he feels his way out of the blight and limitations of segregated
education in the ghetto into the broad stream of education where all
Americans flow.

One day we will look back with great pride on the manner in which
education in the United States took on the clinical aspects of integration, that day-by-day tedium of making the delicate actions routine
and the risky decisions standard procedure. Our gratification is even
deeper as we ponder the alternatives of hatred, neglect, chaos, and
disorder. When you have succeeded in assuring acceptance and estab-

lishing confidence, the next step is obvious, melting hostility and belligerence.

A few weeks ago I stood in the lobby of an all-Negro YMCA in a big Midwestern town reading the report of the death of the missionary physician in the Congo. I must have exclaimed my shock and dismay loudly, for a youngster with a mop came up behind me and said, "What's wrong with that? What is he out there for? You mean you're crying because they killed a white man?" This is the hostility that results from rejection and fear. He seemed to be showing off a little. I could not believe that he was earnest. But the prospect of this is frightening.

Let us not stand by, enjoying the status of our profession, fighting for salaries and tenure, and miss this opportunity to focus on a serious American issue, a splendid opportunity to show the world how a dynamic democracy can recover from an illness and renovate itself without bloodshed and violence and hasten to prove to the Negro Americans that what made them so angry no longer exists. Let us join hands in building a multiracial republic of law and justice and equality. This attitude will inspire affirmative openness rather than hostility.

This affirmative openness that becomes the propulsion towards fulfillment and success is not easy to come by, because a Negro youngster —and even more so for my generation—never really knows when his environment has changed from hostility or indifference to acceptance. After all, he can be heralded as a fast-moving halfback, kissed by the homecoming queen in public on Saturday, and then discover Sunday afternoon that the luxury apartments going up in a new subdivision are closed to his "twice-degreed" family doctor. He seeks a summer job at the local hotel and all of the bellmen are now white. He goes on his first plane flight and the seat next to him is the only one that remains vacant. His team is planning a banquet for the coach and the country club has turned them down because their policy has not changed yet. This is 1965! U.S.A.!

Whereas many worthwhile changes have beckoned to him and encouraged him to believe that his environment is amicable and trustworthy, still the vestiges of racism are cloistered in innumerable crevices of his experience. They reach out and grab him when he is least expecting it.

More than that, the encouraging news about things changing is not validated in his total mode of living if his existence is typical of the masses of Negroes. Housing is still rigidly proscribed, the poverty of his neighborhood remains indelible, his parents are locked in job categories that will not change for them. The capital required to buy a home would never be accumulated on their minimal earnings. So he is caged in a ghetto, unexpected and unwanted outside of it, and his participation in the life of the community is always peripheral.

So it will take some extra effort to penetrate the callousness that custom wears on the mind of the young Negro. A Saturday picnic is a tease. Membership in one hobby club is a joke. There must be some consistency in a corridor of his experience that proves to him that a solid change has begun. It could happen in his school experience.

Last year I visited a sophisticated Eastern preparatory school for boys—the $2500 variety. In a student body of nearly four hundred there were five Negroes. Four of them had a Negro roommate, and the fifth lived alone until he dropped out. That was the 1963–1964 school year and I had been invited to help the students to understand something about America's race problem. What could I say that would offset the image of the Negro that was so glaring on that campus? The Negro boys had been admitted and then quarantined like they had the measles. It is like inviting the rabbi to dinner and serving pork chops or your Hindu friends and serving hamburger!

I repeat, affirmative openness comes as an involuntary neurological response to life after there has been sufficient experience to prove that the world is at least neutral—if not friendly. This must be clearly understood. One who has known nothing but rejection and the cool indifference of a prosperous, fun-loving society does not suddenly leap to hedonic glee because a resolution was passed. The habit of withdrawn suspicion and caution in every interracial contact takes time to change.

Therefore, in order to hold our Negro pupils responsible for attaining performance at par, we must continue to work at the problem of neutralizing the environment of their student world. Returning to that prep school for a moment, when I asked one of the brighter Negro boys how he felt about this ostracism, he climbed the summit of sagacity and came to his faculty's defense. He said, "After all, these teachers grew up in Eastern suburbs where no Negroes lived, attended Eastern colleges where they saw Negroes only occasionally, and they think we are happy living together. They don't mean to insult." So, he continued, "while it makes us appear to be something between a vegetable and a human to be set apart like this, we'll prove to them that we are human."

Now just why should he be expected to compete in the school on par, overcome his deficiencies that hang on from segregated early school experience in a poor community, learn to love books that he could not get to look at in an all-white library back home, and in addition to this have the adult sense at age fourteen to rationalize the insensitive bias of experienced school administrators?

As we prepare teachers for the nation, we can go a long way toward this goal, the assurance of a pattern of experience in our own institutions, the creation of an atmosphere on our campuses that will send out waves of teachers, every June, all over America, wanting to see the nation guarantee to every citizen that no grand conspiracy is operating against him. Hardly can any other group take on such an assignment and have such potential for accomplishment. And I believe that this is the challenge you want!

I have talked of the typical Negro youth. There are many who have been helped through this maze, some quite by accident, and they are happy that they had sufficient guidance and encouragement that they could be selective about their environment. They could choose those stimuli that they would let cross the threshold of consciousness and reject those others. They became deaf to the insults and ignored the indignities. As a blind man learns the safe way home, they have tipped through society like walking on eggs. They have practiced "feeling whole" and equal and they have designed life accordingly.

When my brother and I were finishing high school the depression was whipping our town with long, persistent lashes. College seemed no live option. We had played horns in the high school band, so we applied to the Navy as musicians. We were rejected. Negroes did not blow horns in the Navy in 1937. They cooked, scrubbed, and waited on officers. They did not blow horns. But we took this in stride. We had enjoyed a happy home with loving parents who had been blessed with education. We joked it out. We selected other stimuli and barred this discouragement from our perceptive mass!

My brother loved music more than I. He pressed on through college and finished in music. He was drafted in 1941 and eventually was sent to the Army Music School at Fort Meyer. For twenty-two years he has been a Chief Warrant Officer Band Master and is now the Band Master at Stewart Air Force Base in Newburgh, New York. And we have helped a sister through a Masters, another brother through dental school, and the baby brother through medicine.

Not every Negro needs to do that to succeed. Not everyone will succeed. But this was possible over the past twenty years under the most adverse circumstances. It was possible given the added ingredient that a family was cohesively bound together and parents had the resource of a Presbyterian mission college education to make available to their children. This is not typical of Negro society. Half of Harlem's youth live with one parent and not 8 percent of Negro mothers have been to college. We just cannot expect every Negro to be a Ralph Bunche, run a thousand yards a season for the Cleveland Browns, or bat .300 for the Braves to make it in life.

Without paternalism and cheap, showy condescension, the educators of our land must make a fast break beyond the structures of mores that punish a child for being born of Negro parents and find ways of reducing the subtle, hostile practices of racism to a minimum.

This raises a final issue. How can this be done without the highest motivation on the part of teachers and the cultivation of a concern for others that is the byproduct, the fallout of high religion. Human nature is prone to protect an advantage. We don't like to talk about "original sin" but we must deal with it. In the comic strip "Peanuts" Linus says to Charlie Brown: "Do you know what the whole trouble with you is?" Charlie Brown replies: "No, and I don't want to know!" Then they stare at each other. The stare is broken when Linus says, "The whole trouble with you is that you don't want to know what the whole trouble with you is!"

Educators are not exempt from the atavistic drag of human failure and egocentricity. We are not supermen. We just cannot pick up from here and go out as world-changers unless something changes us first.

We have declared that as a nation we must not use our public institutions for religious training. But if people are there, religious training will happen. You can no more hide your beliefs than you can sneak daybreak past a healthy rooster. Your arched eyebrows, your voice inflection, your hands, your subclauses, and where you put that "neverthless" in a paragraph will be dead giveaways. A teacher cannot look down on life in Olympian detachment. He is involved and his students know it. A teacher-education program that fails to challenge the hierarchy of values that we deliver to our young through the classrooms is deficient and neglectful.

A teacher must have a responsible working hypothesis that answers the questions: Why are we here? Where are we going? What is our destiny? What is the best way? Is the universe on our side? Is life a game of chance? Is there purpose in it all?

You cannot peddle a Catholic answer. You cannot sell a Baptist salvation formula. You cannot require an Episcopalian creed and Methodist hymn singing. But the questions must be raised and the students must see in the teacher a living incarnation of at least one set of viable answers that can be lived out to its logical extremity!

And one of these answers must be on how to treat other creatures of God who happen to be different. Shall I hate them? Shall I endure them? Shall I tolerate them? Shall I separate them? Shall I destroy them? Shall I respond to their need in respect and love, try to see the world through their eyes and then begin to find real value in my life by reversing the spiral toward futility in theirs, so help me God!

PART THREE
Government Officials

Once considered strictly a local matter, the American Negro's thrust for dignity has now engaged the attention of leadership at all governmental levels where ways and means are being sought for creating a just society. The *Brown* decision of 1954 was no magic formula for the establishment of social justice. All challenges to the Southern *status quo* have been met with an avalanche of new statutes, designed to perpetuate the traditional system of segregation. The fact that certain local and national government leaders have dared to sidestep "the law of the land" can in no way detract from the consistent and continuing efforts of those government officials who have given their time, support, influence, and sagacity to the passage of those bills which have introduced in state legislatures and in Congress for the purpose of ensuring basic rights for all.

Whether it be President Johnson addressing the nation from the White House, Ralph Bunche focusing on America's role in the international arena before the United Nations, or Adam Clayton Powell roaring his contempt for those who have made a mockery of democracy in their dehumanization of America's 20 million blacks—all have one thing in common in their rhetoric: they are fighting against tradition that would deprive any citizen of his rightful chance because of the accident of color.

DEMOCRACY
—Langston Hughes

Democracy will not come
Today, this year
　Nor ever
Through compromise and fear.

I have as much right
As the other fellow has
   To stand
On my two feet
And own the land.

I tire so of hearing people say,
Let things take their course.
Tomorrow is another day.
I do not need my freedom when I'm dead.
I cannot live on tomorrow's bread.

Freedom
Is a strong seed
Planted
In a great need.
I live here, too.
I want freedom
Just as you.

Equality in 1984
BERL I. BERNHARD

Berl Bernhard, former Staff Director of the United States Commission on Civil Rights, received the B.A. degree from Dartmouth and the LL.B. degree from Yale. He was admitted to the bar in the District of Columbia in 1954 where he served as a law clerk to the U.S. District Judge for the following two-year period. After two years in private practice, he was appointed to the United States Civil Rights Commission in 1958. He was recipient of the Arthur S. Flemming Award in 1960, and was selected as one of the ten outstanding young men in the United States by the United States Junior Chamber of Commerce in 1962.

The speech below was an address given at the Commencement ceremonies at Central State College, Wilberforce, Ohio, June 2, 1963.

* * *

Knowledge and discontent are one. To know is to hope; to hope is to aspire. Men who aspire to equality and who sense its imminence, but who are time after time denied it, except when it pleases others, are bound to grow discontented. So we find the fever of discontent burning hot today; hotter than it ever has before. More Negroes go to bed angry at night and fewer sleep it off. The remarkable band of Negroes who have surmounted the pits of prejudice, hurled defiance at unlawful racial barriers, struggled to attain that education so readily given to others, and painfully learned the art of leadership against all odds, have fired with hope the great mass of American Negroes. And as hope spreads, discontent abounds. A century after emancipation, we are torn by racial insurgency. And yet the well-intentioned white majority looks at Negroes, at their turbulent rejection of implied inferiority, and are perplexed. "Don't they recognize the magnitude of achievement in the past decade?" they ask. "Why can's the Negro be patient just a little longer?" In this innocence, they also ask, "Why can't I be left alone to work with whom I choose, live with whom I choose, and have things the way I've always had them?"

This is the temper of the society into which you emerge this day, nearly a full decade after the unfulfilled promise of the Supreme Court's school-segregation decision. Since that decision, the course of human events has changed with a rapidity surpassed only by technology. What was true ten years ago is not true today. Today's truth will be replaced outright by tomorrow's reality. What will the future bring you? Every graduating student has a vested interest in that question. Many of you have more than the usual motivation to inquire. What will America be like for you—not one or two, but three decades after the *Brown* decision?

The year then is 1984, a date of special significance to the readers of George Orwell's book about the absolute state. In 1984, you will be at your professional peak. You will be at or near the top of your lifetime earning power. You will be educating your own children and, I would hope, taking an interest in improving your community and your nation. To look into the future has always been hazardous, but to fail to is equally dangerous. We must assume the risk and attempt to predict the course of history with whatever means are available. Barring the ravages of an international war, American society should be rather well ordered by 1984. The full-blown crises in race relations should be settled one way or the other by then, as should the crises of urban redevelopment and other domestic problems of similar urgency. This must be so for they are in a condition of crisis, and crisis cannot be prolonged indefinitely.

CAN HUMAN RELATIONS ALSO BE PLANNED?

By 1984 many problems will be resolved and many ends achieved. But how can we predict whether the means we are using will lead to the ends we seek? In the realm of physical things, we have some opportunities for measurement. You can look at Washington, D.C., for example, and see to a degree what Philadelphia was like a few years ago. You can look at Philadelphia today and see how an old city can renew itself in its urban housing, its business center, and its judicious combination of rail and road transportation. You can also look at Los Angeles and see, in its profusion of highways in search of a downtown, what Philadelphia could have been like today—and what rudderless Washington may well be like in 1984 without incisive changes in policy and control.

But in human relations we rarely see the past and the future together. If you look only at the remarkable acceleration in the drive for civil rights during the past decade, you can easily conclude that all citizens of this republic will live peaceably together in full legal and social equality in the America of 1984. But if you look instead at the defiance of law and misuse of authority in race relations today, you may just as easily see another future. Peace and good will were not part of the vision conjured up by Orwell in his frightening book. He said: "If you want a picture of the future, imagine a boot stamping on a human face—forever." The boot has been stamping on the face in Mississippi and Alabama during the past year. Crouched beside the boot has been a new and brutal symbol of misused authority —the police dog. But it seems clear enough that the watchful eye of the press, the growing firmness in the application of our national law and the emerging national conscience will dispel this Orwellian behavior in the not-too-distant future.

We still live under a system of guarantees provided by our Founding Fathers. They are stated in the Constitution of the United States, which was tested against a Balkan concept of states' rights in a civil war a century ago and found supreme. No American has to *earn* his constitutional rights or in any way prove himself worthy of them. They are his *at birth* and *by birth* regardless of his color, his religion, his extraction, or the affluence or poverty of his parents. This is the law, and though petty tyrants and embittered racists may twist and squirm in its grasp, it will prevail. It is reaching right now, on the heels of protest demonstrators, into the rural backwaters of the Deep South. It should surprise no one that a penniless, uneducated white in some Deep Southern backwoods should get drunk on cheap moonshine and go burn a Negro church. It should surprise no one that an embittered Negro youth without education or incentive or experience with decent behavior should mug someone on a Northern street. Talking human rights to either of these individuals would be like speaking a foreign tongue.

BEYOND EQUAL RIGHTS

Newsman Eric Sevareid has observed:

Those agitating for their rights are bound to win, somehow, not only because their present aims are limited and unarguable, but because they have succeeded in involving us all, whoever we are, wherever we live within the nation's frontiers.

But he added:

Desperation, like war, ennobles some among its victims and debases others. No true people's revolution was ever neat, clean, or devoid of sad anomalies.

There are indeed sad anomalies today and there may be more tomorrow. We may justly believe that the boot will no longer be in the face in 1984 and that equal rights will have been won for all. But will equal rights be enough? The answer, I believe, is no.

RACE CAUGHT UP IN STATUS-SEEKING SUBURBANIZATION

If certain current trends continue, such cities as Baltimore, Cleveland, Chicago, Detroit, Philadelphia, and St. Louis may be entirely Negro communities by 1984. Washington may attain that dubious distinction long before that. This has nothing to do with the birth rate. It has to do with the white movement to all-white suburbs to find better housing and better schools than exist in the decaying downtown cores. It has to do, too, with the tightening noose of the suburbs around the congested central city. And despite the President's housing order, Negroes are still excluded from the suburbs. In Washington, the Negro population has reached 54.6 percent. But the Negro population of the Washington metropolitan area as a whole is only 24 percent, about the same as it was in the time of Abraham Lincoln. The congestion of Washington's central city increases as the percentage of Negroes increases. In the suburbs, this percentage has decreased over the past decade. Highway placement, park dedications, and like devices have driven the few suburban Negroes back into the city.

In many respects, this picture is not confined to Washington but represents a pattern common to many urban areas. The one principal exception lies in the fact that Washington, unlike all other cities, does not govern itself. It suffers from decades of neglect by the national Congress that is empowered to govern it.

If this general urban trend continues, all of the agony and effort to break down the destructive "separate but equal" doctrine will have been wasted. It is a contemporary paradox that the Negro in the South fights to get into the neighborhood school and the Negro in the North fights to get out of it. The reason is the same in both cases—to get a better education. It is traditional for school assignment to embrace neighborhood populations and, in the North, concentration of minority groups in the central city has meant attendance at rundown schools in blighted neighborhoods, obsolete textbooks, an inadequate curriculum, and usually less qualified teachers. Separate has never equaled equal in North *or* South. While educational standards are generally higher in the North and dramatically improved in some communities that have remedial programs for the underprivileged, in general, conditions in the South today are no better than they were at the time of the *Brown* decision.

INEVITABLE DOWNWARD SPIRAL OF FORCED SEGREGATION FACTORS

Residential segregation means poorer schools. Poorer schools mean inadequate education. Inadequate education means inferior jobs. Where then is equality? But pause a moment—I have drawn a portrait of but one possibility, and this is a developing *apartheid* that may result in Negro self-government. May not Negro governments be expected to extend rights to Negro citizens equal to those that white-dominated governments have extended to white citizens? In the end, Elijah Muhammad may have realized his dream in a manner he did not expect. What his Black Muslim movement and its pattern overlook, however, are the basic reasons for wanting desegregation—to enjoy equal rights and opportunities, yes, but also to end the conflict between members of the white and Negro communities who, knowing little of each other, find themselves in growing hostility and tension.

HISTORY AND PERVERSION OF THE AMERICAN SPIRIT

These tensions of today recall vividly the predictions of Alexis de Toqueville. This young French nobleman during the 1830's made some uncannily accurate observations about America. First, he saw as a supreme paradox the founding of a free society upon a system of slave labor. He saw the presence of millions of enslaved Negroes as "the most formidable of all the ills that threaten the future of the nation." He predicted that emancipation would not of itself solve the problem and that it would intensify rather than alleviate racial prejudice. He predicted that the conflict would terminate in a civil war. He was right on all four counts. But he also predicted that the conflict might devolve into the extirpation of one race by the other— a spectacle that we can only visualize today as an armed conflict between a nation-size Ku Klux Klan and a powerful Black Muslim army.

What can the history of the past teach us about the present so that we can use it to mold a better future? Concerning the Negro, it tells us that he first came here, not a slave at all, but as an indentured servant, bound over to a master for a period, after which he had his freedom. Such freedmen abounded in early America as master mechancis in the communities. Free Negroes even worked for the owners of Southern plantations. But by the first quarter of the eighteenth century, as slave labor began to be more profitable for agriculture and native industry, the social privileges of the free Negroes were gradually diminished. It was also decreed during this period that a manumitted slave could not rise to equality with white persons. Finally, the conflict over slavery led to civil war in America and to emancipation of the slaves by President Abraham Lincoln.

But it was only the beginning. The Proclamation became effective a full century ago. What of the long dark night between then and now? Why was there inaction for so long? Undoubtedly, the premature death of Lincoln blighted the movement toward freedom. Certainly the succession to the Presidency of Andrew Johnson, a Southern segregationist whose policies returned the former Confederates to power, played a significant part. And later, when a significant civil-rights gain was made in the public-accommodations legislation of 1875, its effect was largely cancelled out by the controversial Hayes-Tilden election and the politically motivated withdrawal of federal troops from the South. The remaining Reconstruction governments promptly collapsed. All that had survived of the first efforts to establish racial equality in the United States were three constitutional amendments and a panoply of unenforced federal legislation. The nation wanted no more confrontations between the peoples of its regions; the nation was weary of war and argument, and it was willing to forget the past and even blink at the present in order to have some peace.

After Lincoln, you can examine American Presidents all the way up to Franklin Delano Roosevelt before you find any significant interest in civil rights. His era, perhaps, signaled the great reawakening of America's social conscience. This reawakening seems largely due to his public statements, to his appointment of Negroes to office, and to his creation of a civil-rights section in the criminal division of the Department of Justice. Even more active in terms of executive accomplishment was the administration of President Harry S. Truman. It was he who created a Presidential Committee on Civil Rights and who said to the committee: "I want our Bill of Rights implemented in fact. . . . We are making progress, but we are not making progress fast enough."

From this point on, things began to move forward for the American Negro—and, needless to say, for the American ideal of equal rights for all citizens. The reasons were manifold: the emergence of the United States as the leader of the free world, the industrialization of the South, the migration to urban areas, a general improvement in the economy, and the increasingly complex and sensitive network of communications that focused a watchful eye on every part of the nation.

BEGINNING OF RETURN TO THE AMERICAN WAY

The decade of 1950–1960 saw three salient actions, all of them quite different from one another but all destined to play significant parts in our national struggle for equal rights. In 1954, there was the landmark decision of the Supreme Court in the school-segregation cases. Three years later, there was the Civil Rights Act of 1957, the first positive Congressional expression of an expanding federal role in civil rights since 1875. It strengthened federal power to enter suits in cases of voting denials; it elevated the civil-rights section of the Department of Justice to the status of a division, and it created the United States Commission on Civil Rights. Though the Commission is a fact-finding agency alone and has no power of enforcement, it will, I believe, be seen by history as a major and dynamic force for the realization of civil rights in America. It has done things that no group or other agency could do. It established national goals, conceived legislation, criticized inaction, uncovered and exposed denials in many fields and places, prodded the Congress, nagged the

Executive department, and aided the courts. Above all, it has lacerated, sensitized, and perhaps even re-created the national conscience.

The third great action came on February 1, 1960, when four students from the Agricultural and Technical College of Greensboro, North Carolina, entered a variety store. They made several purchases, sat down at the lunch counter, ordered coffee, were refused service because they were Negroes, and remained in their seats until the store closed. Thus the nonviolent direct-action movement began. During this decade the actions of the judiciary, the Commission, and the Negro students attacked the problem sharply and from three different vantage points. Many, many other significant actions, public and private, happened before and after these events, of course. I mention these three because they seem especially significant to me. I would also like to point out that all three of these actions came about because Negroes either directly or indirectly worked to bring them about. This is meritorious not only because self-help is always the best means of self-advancement, but because the American Negro did not ignore a moral duty to fight for his rights. This moral duty was recognized recently by Pope John XXIII. In his encyclical of April 10, 1963, His Holiness declared:

> Racial discrimination can in no way be justified . . . for, if a man becomes conscious of his rights, he must become equally aware of his duties. Thus he who possesses certain rights has likewise the duty to claim those rights as marks of his dignity, while all others have the obligation to acknowledge those rights and respect them.

Even more recently, Protestant Episcopal Presiding Bishop Arthur Lichtenberger, in writing of the racial crisis, emphasized this moral duty:

> It is not enough . . . to exhort men to be good. Men, women, and children are today risking their livelihood and their lives protesting for their rights. We must support and strengthen their protest in every way possible. . . .

THE HARD ROAD OF THE CONCERNED

For those of you who are Negro, will life be immeasurably better than it was for your parents? I will hazard the prediction that you will have it harder than the Negro of the past generation. The weaker member of this group could always justify his lack of achievement on the ground that he was discriminated against; it made a handy excuse. The stronger member became an active worker in the cause. He had something to aspire to. He could shout and sing and march and carry signs with his comrades. He could burn with zeal, be part of a national fraternity based upon a program of absolute virtue—the medieval chivalry of the twentieth century; the triumph of good over evil. There are many whites who have envied the Negro this cause; it is good to submerge your identity in something important and right and to be able to work for it in the company of your friends. Some of you may enjoy this same privilege, though the reasons for it should be snuffed out within a few years. But you will face a much harder job. For, while you have a right to vote, to send your children to decent schools, to equal protection under the law, even to an end to discrimination in housing, you have no right, legally speaking, to walk into a given place of business and demand employment. Many groups are working to end discrimination in employment, and the day will come when employers will bend over backwards to accommodate qualified Negro applicants. But, in that job, you will be required constantly to prove yourself. There is an old parental saying from the Jewish heritage: "My son, in order to be silver, you must be gold." You will have to concentrate more intensely than your white counterpart, show more interest, work longer and harder, and more carefully discipline your conduct in and out of your place of business. It will be hard, but, in my opinion, you will make the longest stride forward of any generation of Negroes in American history by doing it.

For those of you who are white, I submit that this matter concerns you deeply; indeed, you have equal cause for concern. You bear the burden of the white man's guilt in his conduct toward the Negro. You will have more immediate mobility than your colored friends; you will be able to work for equal rights in areas and ways that are still denied to them. You can add an important dimension to their struggle for social equality and, by doing so, you will strengthen yourself, your community, and your nation.

All of you are being thrust into an ailing society sorely in need of your ingenuity to develop new and even more effective remedies. The NAACP's monumental legal battles, CORE's sit-ins and Freedom Rides, the Southern Christian Leadership Conference's protest demonstrations—all of these and more will go on. But even as these actions jolt the American mind with the realities of discrimination and segregation, you must fashion new tools to accomplish two complementing needs—first, to combat highly sophisticated forms of discrimination and second, to heal simultaneously the wounds suffered in the battle for equality. We all have a personal and critically important stake in this struggle to close the gap between the proclamation of freedom and its practice in America. As we struggle with our enemies without, we must build additional strength within. To let our heritage be eroded means the fall of what the Great Emancipator so aptly called "the last best hope of earth."

The issue is nothing less than this. *The law demands it.* We have the guarantees written into the Constitution that the Supreme Court, in its May 27 decision in *Watson v. Memphis,* has made clear are "warrants for the here and now," and "not merely hopes to some future enjoyment of some formalistic constitutional promise." *Morality pleads for it.* The Judeo-Christian ethic forbids discrimination and demands adherents to right such wrongs. *Our economy argues for it.* The Negro as a consumer has more potential for American business than Canada or the Netherlands; bringing his average salary to parity with the white man could add $20 billion to the gross national product. *National survival cries for it.* We have been bady wounded in our international struggle with communism by the comparison of our practices with our avowed principles.

We have no more time to waste. What each of us does from this moment on may mean the difference between an America of freemen or a nation in which every man wears the badge of bondage. This, to us, may be the ultimate significance of 1984. Will it be hand clasping hand or the boot pressing into the human face? *Don't assume the outcome. Work to determine it.* The dedication of others is not enough. Your good intentions alone will not do. The future cannot be delegated.

The Forward March of Democracy

DR. RALPH J. BUNCHE

Ralph Bunche, best known for his services in the United Nations, completed his undergraduate work at U.C.L.A. He received the M.A. and the Ph.D. degrees from Harvard University. He rose from instructor in Political Science to Professor at Howard University, and then became Head of the Department of Political Science in 1939 and served in that capacity until 1950. He was Professor of Government at Harvard University from 1950 to 1952.

An expert on anthropology and colonial policy, he became active in government work shortly after the outbreak of World War II. He served successively as Senior Social Science Analyst in charge of research on Africa and other colonial areas for the Office of Strategic Services and is currently serving as Undersecretary of the United Nations.

He has been a member of the Board of Higher Education of New York City, a trustee of Oberlin College, and a member of the Board of Overseers at Harvard University. He is past President of the Political Science Association.

Ralph Bunche has received numerous awards, among them the Springarn Medal by the National Association for the Advancement of Colored People, the Nobel Peace Prize, the Theodore Roosevelt Association Medal of Honor, and the Third Order of St. Francis Peace Award.

His complete honesty and sharp insight into the racial ferment of our day have made the speech below a valuable contribution to this volume. The speech was delivered at the forty-fifth Annual Convention of the NAACP, Dallas, Texas, July 4, 1954.

* * *

I have flown out here just for this occasion not because I have anything new or of particular importance to say, but simply because I want to be a part of and want to do whatever I can to aid the great crusade which the NAACP leads. I am here not only because I am a Negro and proud of it. I have come because I am an American and proud of it; because I have a fervent belief in democracy as the only way of life worthy of free men; because I believe that winning full equality and full integration for the Negro citizen is indispensable not only to him but to the nation; because I believe that proving the ability of democracy to have unqualified application to all people irrespective of race or religion is imperative to the cause of freedom throughout the world, to our nation's international prestige and to our leadership of the free peoples; because I believe that proving the virility of our democracy is one of the strongest blows we can strike at aggressive communism (the Communists, incidentally, after a delay—the unanimous Court decision left even their propagandists speechless for a while—tried weakly to dismiss the Court's decision as just a propaganda move); and finally, because I have children and am determined to do all that I can to ensure that they will be complete Americans on the same basis as every other American and without the handicaps of race which you and I have had to suffer. Those are enough reasons to have induced me even to walk out here from New York, if it were necessary.

What little I have to say can be plainly said and briefly. After all, the most eloquent and meaningful statement that has been made in this year or in many another year, or that is likely to be made for sometime to come, was made in May in this nation's Supreme Court. I have never imagined that legal phraseology could be so beautiful, that a court's decision could read like poetry. But that is because the decision of the Court in the school segregation cases marked encouraging progress in democracy, advance in the removal of the racial stigma from the innocent children of a very large segment of the nation's population, and confidence in our ideals, our Constitution, and the good sense and decency of the American people.

When the forward march of democracy is being expressed, the language, the words, and the grammar are of little significance—it would be beautiful and inspiring in any language—even in sign language. It would still have been music to the ears of everyone who believes in democracy and the equality and dignity of man if the Court, instead of its meticulously phrased legal language had just said—unanimously: "There ain't gonna be no more segregated schools." We would have hailed the decision just the same and then we might have taken up a generous collection to send whoever wrote the opinion to an integrated school to learn grammar.

But the Court's decision is merely on paper. The question everyone asks is "Will it be implemented?" I say, of course it will be implemented. Indeed, in some places voluntary steps are already being taken to that end. The Communists, naturally, scoff at it, say that it is only a gesture in the Cold War and that it will never be implemented. Now could any good Americans support and join the Communists in that stand? Here is a new kind of guilt by association, a new test of good Americanism and loyalty.

I am confident that the objectives of the Court's decision will be realized because the American people are traditionally law-abiding and have a deep reverence for their way of life and their institutions of government. If the practice should ever be sanctioned that individuals and local and state government are entitled to select the decisions of the courts which they will respect and the laws they are inclined to observe, that will signal the collapse of our system of government and the beginning of an era of anarchy and chaos. Who is willing to pay this fatal price merely to prevent white and black children from sitting side by side in a public school? Who would give aid and comfort to the Communists by defying the judgment of the highest court in the land, for clearly only the Communists could profit from the undermining of our institutions?

There has probably never been a major decision of the Supreme Court that pleased everyone. Certainly, for many years the Negro, constituting one-tenth of the population, vigorously disliked and greatly suffered from the doctrine of "separate but equal" enunciated by the Court in *Plessy v. Ferguson.* We knew it was false. We knew it was unjust. We suffered much deprival and humiliation under it. We knew by bitter experience that "separate" automatically meant unequal, that the very philosophy of the doctrine signified inferior status for an entire group of American citizens. Negroes, being good Americans, cherishing the American way of life, did not try to defy the Court, did not threaten violence, did not claim the right to take the law into their own hands. Rather, in the typical American and democratic way the Negro set about, through his organizations and with the sympathetic assistance of an increasing number of fair and democratic white Americans, to convince the American public, the government, and the courts that this doctrine was wrong and fundamentally incompatible with the principles and ideals of our Founding Fathers and our Constitution. And all the while the Negro played the role of the good citizen—he paid his taxes, served his society in every capacity, gave his life for his country willingly and courageously on battlefields the world over even though he died under the shadow of "separate but equal" and usually while serving in segregated military units. That he will never have to do again, since the policy of integration is eliminating segregation in the armed forces.

In response to this effort, in the light of the remarkable progress made by the Negro in less than a century since release from the still greater injustice of bondage, and with knowledge of the adverse reaction of peoples throughout most of the world to the underprivileged status of the Negro in America, all nine of the members of the nation's highest tribunal, three of whom are sons of the Southland— one, indeed, from this great state—reversed *Plessy v. Ferguson* and nullified the doctrine of "separate but equal."

That is the way democracy works; it is the only way it can work. That is why democracy is the only system under which minority groups have a chance to gain and enjoy their rights and to throw off the shackles of minority status. The Negro American, better than most, I suspect, values the American way of life and respects American institutions.

I cannot help but wonder whether finally in this problem of relations between the races—and I do not specify the South, for this
is a national and not a sectional problem—we are not approaching the
stage in which reason can begin to supplant emotion—and by emotion I mean blind prejudice. What really is at issue? Surely we do
not agree with the proposition that our country must remain in the
camp of democracy and must march always at the head of the democratic forces of the world. There are but two world forces really, the
free and democratic peoples and the Communist. The Negro asks
only that American democracy march on its black as well as its
white feet. Most white Americans, I believe, agree with this thesis.
For clearly our maximum national strength and unity are indispensable to meet the threat which international communism opposes to our
freedom.

Now I know that it is often said that it is hard for people to change
their racial attitudes, that it is too much to expert that the white
people of the South, accustomed as they are to seeing the Negro
segregated and regarding him as they do as something different and
apart and implicitly if not explicitly inferior, could readily (some
bitter-enders say ever) accept him in an equal and unsegregated role.
No student of society and human psychology would deny the difficulties. They are undoubtedly complex. Ingrown social attitudes and
prejudices are stubborn. But there are reasons for believing that the
difficulties can easily be exaggerated and often are. One of the most
convincing is the ease with which so many white citizens of the South
accept Negroes without prejudice or qualification outside of the
South and increasingly in it. I have myself seen too many instances
of that to ever believe that the generality of the white citizens spend
very much of their time worrying about whether the Negro will be
put on a level of equality with them. People can be stirred up about
the issue, to be sure, politicians exploit it, and it may come as a
shock to some when for the first time they find themselves in the company of Negroes on this basis. But with many, I think, this is more
reflex than prejudice—it is the more or less automatic reaction of the
community mores which are absorbed by individuals and which are
perpetuated largely through indifference and the unwillingness of very
many to risk criticism in the community by breaking with the mores,
no matter how outmoded they may have become.

What I mean to say is that the prejudice of the white American
against the Negro is more veneer than deep grain and can be peeled
off with little damage of pain. There are fears, superstitions, shib-
boleths about this problem of race which, as experience has shown,

quickly explode and vanish whenever an institution or a community summons the courage to take a moderately bold step away from segregation and discrimination.

I do not contend that prejudice is a myth. I do say that it is not as vigorous, deep-rooted, and omnipresent as it once was, and that with many it is today worn as a loose garment.

A while back I spoke of the application of reason to the problem of the reflex. Let us pursue that a bit further. A great many of us who are Negroes have come to this Convention from far-off places by train, plane, and bus. On those interstate carriers we sit next to our white fellow citizens, eat next to them, and sleep next to them. You cannot get much closer to a person than in the seats of a plane, train, or bus. A great many of our white fellow passengers are from the South. I travel about all the time but I have not noticed any who seemed to be very unhappy or suffering very much because of the presence of a Negro passenger. My own experience is that most often they wish to engage in friendly conversation and not infrequently say that they regret the unfair treatment accorded the Negro.

Still, when the passengers, having traveled on the interstate carrier for long distances without any semblance of separation or segregation and in at least polite harmony and amity, alight at the airports or stations, they must suddenly adopt another pattern of behavior—they must separate and segregate, they must seek separate eating places, separate waiting rooms, separate rest rooms, often separate taxis, and even separate drinking fountains. When the NAACP held its annual convention in Atlanta a few years ago, the segregation regulations in the Municipal Auditorium were relaxed, even on the separate drinking fountains in the lobbies. I drank quite fully out of a fountain marked "white" and suffered no ill effects at all.

Let me underscore one thought. The Negro believes that it is a great thing to be an American, to live in a free society, to walk in dignity as a man, to vote to pay taxes, to be a fully responsible citizen. It is a great thing. The South believes so too, for there are no more devoutly patriotic citizens in this land and none more stout-hearted on the battlefields when our nation must be protected than the sons of the South. And the black sons of the South have always been there too, fighting and dying shoulder to shoulder with their white brothers. Who therefore better than the white Southerner can understand the Negro's burning desire to become an American in full, to win acceptance, to be permitted to make his maximum contribution to the nation that is his own, to join hands with all of his fellow citizens in building on these American shores and plains the greatest and strongest and most democratic society that mankind has ever known?

What I have said, has been said not at all in a spirit of chiding or needling. I know that in the South there are far too many people of good will in both races to warrant that, people who are earnestly devoted to interracial harmony and progress and working tirelessly toward that end.

After all, this problem of race is now less than it used to be a problem of economics and politics and more a problem of our minds, our thinking and concepts. It is the mental images, the stereotypes that we have to combat. One of the great obstacles to more rapid progress toward integration of the Negro in the mainstream of American life is the fact that there is, as one of my good friends wrote to me the other day, an "almost universal concept of an American as a white Anglo-Saxon Protestant." He went on to say and I think he is right that "even we Negroes tend to think of an American in such terms," that is, in terms of an ethnic-religious concept of national type. I agree with his conclusion that there is need now to reconcile the concept of who is an American with the tenets of our political philosophy and the facts of our political history.

For we in America not only have democracy—not perfect democracy to be sure, but still the most advanced in the world—but we have built it on unique foundations—a union of peoples more diversified in origin than any society has ever known. From the beginning of our history, we have been diversified culturally and racially. Ours has been a great experiment in human potentiality, perhaps the most challenging and certainly the most dramatic in the history of human society. We have set out here to demonstrate that peoples of all racial strains, of all colors, creeds, and cultures, of widely varying backgrounds, can as equals learn to live and work and play together and be molded into a firm unity by the attraction and force of noble ideals mutually shared—the dignity and worth of the individual, the equality of men under God, and the conception of the state as the democratic expression and the servant of free men and women.

We have made remarkable progress along that course and have developed our great national strength and unity on that solid foundation. We are still building, still perfecting our democracy, and in some aspects of our life, at a considerably accelerated pace. In the field of race relations, for example, I believe that there has been more progress in the last decade than in all the years before.

This pace can be quickened when we really correct our mental images in such way as to permit our thought reflexes to perceive a typical American as brown, black, and yellow as well as Nordic, Catholic as well as Protestant, Jew as well as Christian.

Speaking of images, there seem to be some white Americans, though I hope not very many, who are inclined to suspect that Negroes are almost inevitably disloyal. This, I think, is mainly a reflection of bad conscience. They know the Negro has suffered much injustice and therefore assume that his resentment is directed against his country. They do not know the Negro and typically are unfamiliar with the Negro's magnificent record of toil, sweat, and sacrifice for his country. They do not know that there have never been more than a handful of Negro Communists and there has never been a Negro traitor against his country, though there have been more than enough against their race. They need to know that the Negro has fought valiantly for American liberty from Crispus Attucks to the foxholes of Korea. And he will always do so against any enemy of the country he has helped mightily to build. Some, of course, may question the Negro's loyalty with the deliberate intent of discrediting Negro organizations and Negro leadership. Others take the position, whether honestly or not is beside the point, that any time a Negro demands equality he must be a Communist. That would make for an awful lot of Communists in this country.

Now that the progress that is being made and the encouraging spirit of the new times have been so dramatically signaled by the Supreme Court, the Negro and all others who strive for intergroup democracy must guard against complacency. The struggle is not won, by any means. There is a long, hard row still to hoe before the rich harvest of full integration can be reaped.

And, mind you, the continuous struggle will be not entirely with intransigent whites. We must face it, there will be some Negroes amongest us who will claim to prefer segregation to integration. For some strong vested interests have developed behind the walls of segregation. Inevitably, there will be some who are too weak, too timid, too lacking in self-confidence, too incompetent, or just too plain lazy to wish to risk competition in the open field beyond the ghetto. Others, quite immorally, will deliberately choose to defend that segregation upon which their present Jim Crow-created jobs and status depend at the expense of the birthright and dignity of their entire group of more than 15 million Negroes. They prefer being comfortable and relatively safe to being men. In this climax stage of the Negro's struggle for first-class citizenship all such modern version Uncle Toms will be carefully noted, I am sure, and their supine and dishonorable role will be properly dealt with in the annals of Negro history. In this democracy, they are entitled to their views, but not to our respect.

Some, especially in the field of education, have already begun the effort to safeguard their positions by reassuring their white superiors, in effect, that the Supreme Court decision did in fact go too far, since the Negro is very happy with separate schools and prefers not be integrated. They trot out the well-worn clichés which are the stock in trade of those among the white group who have insisted all along that there is really nothing wrong with the pattern of race relations since separation is what both races desire. They will try to undermine the Court's opinion by blandly asserting that Negro students prefer separate schools, that separate schools for Negroes afford better opportunities for developing Negro leadership than well integrated ones, that the Negro prefers to be in a homogeneous group, i.e., with himself, to being with other Americans, and will find Jim Crow education more convenient and less costly. In other words, they deny the basic thesis of the Court, namely that separate cannot be equal. And worse still, they do so by parroting the words of the racial bigots about the Negro perferring to be "with his own kind."

I am a Negro and can speak only for myself, and I say to this that I do prefer to be with my "own kind," but my "own kind" are Americans, all Americans, and I do not give a hang what their color or religion may be so long as they believe in our way of life and our democratic destiny. I suspect that most Negroes feel the same way.

I am rarely an angry man but when I hear or read of such sellouts by obsequious, favor-seeking, so-called Negro leaders, my blood boils no little.

I think there can be little honest doubt as to what the Negro wants and what his thinking is on such matters.

He wants for his children the best education possible on the same basis as other American children and under conditions which will not scar them with the psychological wounds of inferiority through enforced segregation. And he knows from long and bitter experience that this can be only in integrated schools.

He wants the best job for which he is qualified wherever he can get it, whether he will be working with black, white, or yellow Americans or any combination of them. He wants to be freed of the handicap of race in earning an honest living.

He wants to vote and hold public office, to be free to live in homes anywhere, to be transported in public conveyances, to receive medical services, to enter all public places as an American and not as something apart, as something different, as something to fear, despise, or avoid, as an unwanted straggler from a black ghetto.

Surely every fair-minded person will realize that no American should be subjected to this sort of treatment or forced to think and act always in terms of ghetto psychology.

We must move resolutely forward and I am sure that we will move forward. I think it is no idle dream to expect that by the date of the centennial anniversary of the Emancipation proclamation in 1963 the back of the entire system of segregation and discrimination will be permanently broken.

But I say most solemnly to the members of my race and their friends in the other races, we must have faith in our democratic system and its institutions, we must have faith in the reason, the good hearts, and the fairness of the American people. In our struggle upward let us always be wise, statesmanlike, and unstrained. May we never stoop to rancor or bitterness. May we as good citizens of our country always act with a deep sense of responsibility not only to our group but to our society and nation as a whole. The Supreme Court decision has afforded us a unique opportunity for constructive work. Let us undertake vigorous but wise efforts to help the American communities make the transition from segregation to integration as calmly and painlessly as possible. This is no time for boasting, for gloating, for indulgence in either cant or vindictiveness. This is the time to serve our country's interest even more than our own. We can do so by helping it to fulfill its magnificent democratic promise and thereby to make it stronger, greater, more firmly united than it has ever been. And this at the very hour of its sternest challenge and therefore its greatest need. Never in our nation's history could we less afford disunity.

Above all, let everyone of us be dedicated to the proposition that always in our individual attitudes, our action and conduct we will give incontrovertible proof that the Negro citizen is a good and valuable citizen, devoted to his country and ever at its service.

What we all, white and black alike, must ceaselessly seek after is the means of living together simply as people. The philosophy of our Founding Fathers, our Constitution, the tenets of our religions all tell us this is the way of the good life, this can be done. It is being done and will be done.

All Americans, we will all be brothers.

Cities and Racial Minorities: Atlanta's Approach

MAYOR WILLIAM B. HARTSFIELD

While serving as mayor of Atlanta, William Hartsfield had a vision of better things for the human race. He was one of the South's outstanding moderate leaders in solving day-to-day urban problems. The good performance record of the city of Atlanta in race relations is a monument to his hard work and dedicated leadership.

Born in Georgia and educated in the schools of that state, he invested his talents for progressive development of Atlanta, his birthplace. He served in the Atlanta City Council and in the State Legislative before becoming mayor of Atlanta.

Mayor Hartsfield's philosophy and approach to race relations are exemplified in the remarks which he gave during the 1964 Marshall-Wythe Symposium at the College of William and Mary in Virginia.

* * *

I have long since learned that it is quite impossible to document or even to outline the problems of any one city and then attempt to apply them equally to all other cities. It is beyond our understanding and appreciation to evaluate any but the most obvious aspects of municipal politics in a comparative sense. And I do not propose to do it here.

I shall attempt to tell you how we in Atlanta tried to handle the problem of racial minorities and their accommodation in the past fifteen years or so, a period of great change and social readjustment in the South generally as well as in our city. Superlatives unknown to us today would be necessary to describe completely the breaking away from old bonds and what this means to all people in this country.

When I first became mayor of Atlanta, in 1937, I was elected under what was known as the white primary—a device through which white citizens of the South had traditionally decided upon their officials. The ratification was effected through the general election, but the conclusion was often foregone if not decided outright by the lack of opposition. This pattern was the same in all levels of government, in the South, and had been so since before the turn of the century.

But the winds of social change were blowing, even in 1937. A Negro citizen of Texas brought suit in his state, charging that the white primary was a device chiefly for the disfranchisement of Negroes and thus constituted a denial of constitutional rights and guarantees accorded by the Fourteenth Amendment. The Supreme Court, as you know, decided in his favor, and from that time on, the days of the white primary in the South were numbered. Some hard-core resistance was evident in the few states, as they tried various responses to the Court's decisions. None were of any lasting value, and soon the limited political participation of the Democratic Party was transformed into a more representative group.

Sooner or later as I talk about Atlanta and its experiences in these days of trial and political upheaval, I will mention a fact proudly recorded by all those who value what has happened in our city. Atlanta has six Negro colleges and universities. The presence of these institutions of higher education, together with the confluence of businessmen in the Negro community, make up a very fine group of educated men and women. They were and are instrumental in furnishing through their ability an ideal sort of leadership that is so necessary for good race relations.

The city of Atlanta, soon after I had reached the mayor's office, began a program of improved liaison between the two races. Negro citizens were encouraged to come to City Hall and air their grievances and present their requests for improvements if they wished to do so. What is probably even more important, city officials began attending meetings of Negro citizens and evidencing some interest in Negro civic affairs. This was not always looked upon with approbation by some in the white community, but I felt that the first step was a recognition of a basic equality of citizenship status.

In the early 1940's, in another very important development, the state of Georgia abandoned the poll tax as a requirement for voting. As a result, large numbers of Atlanta Negroes registered. Then in 1946, the federal courts, after a local suit was brought, ordered the Negro citizens of Georgia admitted to vote in the primary election. Since the largest number of intelligent and literate Negroes were in Atlanta, as mentioned earlier, the state's largest city, it was only natural that this large registration would have its greatest effect in Atlanta.

But the rural areas of the state did not like the development one little bit. Atlanta's course of racial tolerance has aroused great antagonism and opposition in the state legislative halls and of course with the great majority of state officials. This was particularly the case in our state of Georgia because the county-unit system of voting greatly favored the rural sections and made Atlanta almost a helpless pawn in gubernatorial and statewide politics generally.

Then in 1954 came an even more momentous Supreme Court decision, as segregation of public schools was ended under the equal-protection clause of the Fourteenth Amendment. The result was to induce still greater opposition to Atlanta's by now firm position on racial matters. The state legislature immediately enacted a series of lamentable but nevertheless real state laws compelling Atlanta and other cities to stay within the rigid pattern of segregation. These laws, together with the highly inflammatory speeches of candidates in rural areas and entrenched county-unit system representatives, made the course of smooth race relations a difficult one for several years. Atlanta, however, to the credit of her people, held to the established policy of racial tolerance and human dignity, a position which gave to others in the South a beacon they could follow in those acrimonious days.

In swift succession after that came a series of Supreme Court decisions which knocked down the punitive state laws, and then the county-unit system itself was decreed unconstitutional in 1962. With the large urban population of Georgia now unfettered, the people could help to silence the vocal rural politicians. No longer were Atlanta and other cities held up to be the state whipping boys for the opposition of rural elements to racial and social change.

As we all know, it is a fact that throughout this period I have alluded to, when change was taking place at all levels from the national and international to the local, the Negro citizen became increasingly vocal and demanding in his natural quest for full citizenship and the attainment of the rights of the American dream. While it has been relatively slow in some other parts of the South, and even in other parts of Georgia, this trend has accelerated in Atlanta through the increased Negro registration and voting.

With better public-health standards and an increasing immigration, the number of Negro citizens within the city of Atlanta has been constantly increasing. Since Negroes are the low income group, it is but natural that the central parts of the city would show the greatest percentage of rise. This is true in many other cities as well. The white citizen, with higher income producing greater mobility, moves to the suburbs. The Negro, meanwhile, expands, often slowly and painfully, into the next block or two. Over a period of months and years, this process takes place until whole sections of the central city area are overwhelmingly Negro.

An off shoot of the changing demographic complexion of the city is the potential discord between Negroes and whites as the changes occur. A number of Negro organizations, as one might well expect, have tended to give in to the very human temptation of boasting about their political power in the cities. Some of this boasting is perhaps the natural expression of citizenship and pride in what they can accomplish as a group, but the kind of racial inbalance which underlies it, compounded over a long period of time, can have serious consequences. There is an element of animosity which might be aggravated by bad feeling between city and suburb. Already there exists, in Atlanta and elsewhere, quiet but effective effort to discourage Negroes from moving into the suburbs. Most often this is done through a failure or refusal to zone property where the income range would indicate Negro occupancy.

And there are other more subtle devices used toward the same end. We know about the unwritten agreements among real estate agents, open opposition by people in the neighborhoods, and sometimes violent threats which serve to make the tight ring enclosing Negroes in the downtown areas.

The result, in purely political terms, is that in many of our cities the Negro is becoming increasingly dominant both in numbers and in the amount of pressure he can generate, while white citizens flee to distant suburbs. Particularly does this problem exist in Washington, D.C. The basic reason there is the inflexibility of the District boundary line.

Subjectively, then, this trend poses the greatest racial problem of American cities. Is it good for the white citizen to continue in increasing numbers to move to distant suburbs, while the lower income group, which in most cases is the American Negro, continues to take over the secondhand house in the city? Eventually, the Negro will also take over its management and control.

This will not be good for either race. For the white man, it constitutes abandonment of a great economic potential in the center, with the millions of dollars of investment in institutions and services. There is no substitute for a strong central local government, able to do the big things in the community and to take the big problems. For the Negro, his elevation to control would mean segregation by abandonment, and would subject him to the pressures and imperfections of the worse element of his own group. For the community, it would mean racial animosity.

What can be done is the worry of many city officials, who look beyond the next election and who are genuinely interested in the future of their localities. They are attempting to devise a dual system of education which will stress the interdependence of the various groups in the society. They are emphasizing to the white suburbs the impossibility of conducting a unified approach to local problems by giving over the central part of the community completely. To the Negroes, they are devising training in the administration of local government, and it takes little convincing that declining real estate values leave less than adequate revenue for city government.

Of course, the ideal solution is for all citizens to live together in peace and harmony. This is above all else the goal toward which we must strive. In the years to come, it is the hope of us all that this may be the case.

In Atlanta, specifically, we have been trying to bring about a balance both in political control and in the composition of the citizenship which is the eventual voice of the people. For years we had done little to make constructive progress in the direction of redressing that balance, and there is still much to be done. One effort has been to annex large areas of the outlying suburban population, so as to bring white citizens back into voting participation in the Atlanta city government.

In the meantime, over the long run, there must be encouragement for better educational opportunity among Negro citizens. As the Negro wins his rights, often through the courts and the law, he too must realize that his greatest effort must be to win acceptance in what has been largely a white society. As his opportunity is enhanced, the Negro citizen will become more mobile. Some are already feeling the benefits of white-collar employment in industry and in government. Better income will take the Negro to the suburbs, and likewise I believe increased income and opportunity will tend to move Negroes into the nation at large more than they are at the present time.

So often, the American Negro has been used as a prime example of the way that racial factors are instrumental in human behavior patterns. The real truth of the matter is that environmental factors, probably more so among members of that race than others, have combined to give observers the impression of other influences. It has been the long years of extremely low income levels, the lack of education, or of education for menial tasks, and finally the fear of unequal treatment, which have tended to concentrate the Negro in the section where he was first freed and to impede his general progress as a group.

World events, though, today have put the Negro in the limelight of the news. His dramatic appeals for equal rights, so reflective of our Declaration of Independence of two hundred years ago, have occupied the front pages of newspapers and the prime time of radio and television. Some of the news has been in the Negro's best interest; some has not. Publicity is a heady wine, and sometimes the long-term goals can become clouded in the desire for attention.

Laws setting up equal rights for all citizens are inevitable in our democratic society. And I believe we should have the laws. But that is not the end. What happens after the laws are enacted? Social interaction of the kind which produces meaningful cooperation across the entire breadth of the society will be the product of both races learning to have respect for each other. Before the American Negro as a group, and we have notable exceptions to that generalization as well as others we make, can enjoy the full sweet fruits of first-class citizenship in every part of this country, he must work hand in hand with his white compatriots to become acceptable each to the other. The day must come when the Negro votes independently and not as a Negro. A high level of liaison and close communication must be maintained between the races at all times until then.

Civic clubs, newspapers, radio, and television in Atlanta have performed great public service in exposing the better elements of both groups to each other. For years, the white people of the South have thought they knew the Negro best. As a matter of fact, of course, they knew only the servants, and the servant often told his white employer only what the employer wanted to hear. Many times, in my own experience, I have introduced some outstanding Negro citizen to a white group, only to have some of them tell me later that they didn't know there were such fine educated Negroes in our city. That is a commentary upon the great lack of communication which has existed up to now in many areas of the South.

As I have indicated in public speeches and in campaigns, the American Negro is in a difficult period in his quest for rights and acceptance. The specter of extremism is raising its head. Here and there, the inescapable, perhaps, temptations of political expedience arise. I am sometimes concerned about the tendency which is being established by the encouragement of schoolchildren to boycott their classes. And when hysterical demonstrators fling themselves under bulldozers, how can respect for law and order be upheld? I feel that some of these demonstrations we have witnessed in the past few months have been like digging holes in wet sand. In my humble opinion there is more real progress to be made in dignified pressure exercised through public hearings, and through the registration of people who can then vote for good officials, rather than the flashy headline of publicity gimmicks. After the famous freedom rides through Alabama, I remarked to one of our local Negro leaders that an election campaign resulting in the election of a moderate governor in Alabama was worth a thousand freedom rides.

Too many Negro leaders, in short, seem to me to be clamoring for places of power, for national attention. On the other hand, too many white politicians are now willing to do whatever it takes to capture a mass vote. And the resultant atmosphere is not a healthy one for the real progress which will show up in better race relations twenty-five or fifty years from now.

Good race relations, ladies and gentlemen, must be built upon the solid foundations of morality, decency, and mutual good will. It must be the product of a sincere desire to do unto others as we would have them do unto us.

In summary, our cities are the bedrock of our democracy. How and whether we solve the problems there will be a long step toward the solution of them nationally. We must not let our cities disintegrate and divide into two hostile groups, the central city and the suburbs. We must go to work on this problem immediately, before the evil is more solidly entrenched.

In the meantime, and for the indefinite future perhaps, we must work at the business of finding ways and means of living together in peace and harmony. Each race must endeavor to bring its own lower element to a higher standard. Better education, better economic opportunity, and high moral standards ought to gradually bring both races closer together.

We must find ways to live together in this great democracy in peace and harmony or else risk its future destruction and decay.

A Tragic Moment in American Life

VICE PRESIDENT HUBERT HUMPHREY

Hubert Horatio Humphrey, Jr., ex-Vice-President of the United States, was awarded the A.B. degree at the University of Minnesota in 1939, the A.M. degree at the University of Louisiana in 1940. Prior to his active political life he served on the teaching staffs of the University of Louisiana and the University of Minnesota. From June to November, 1944, he was the state campaign manager for the Roosevelt-Truman Committee. After serving as Mayor of the City of Minneapolis, 1945–48, he was elected United States Senator from Minnesota in 1948, in 1954, and in 1960. He was elected Senate Majority Whip in 1961.

As early as 1948 at the time of the Democratic National Convention, he established himself as a liberal in the Civil Rights field. Later he became Chairman of the President's Council on Equal Opportunity and President of the Commission on Equal Employment Opportunity. In addition to holding membership in the American Political Science Association and the American Academy of Arts and Sciences, he holds keys of Phi Beta Kappa and Delta Sigma Rho.

"A Tragic Moment in American Life" was delivered at the National Alliance of Businessmen in South Huntington, Long Island, New York, on April 5, 1968. This stirring presentation was in response to the assassination of Dr. Martin Luther King, Jr. the night before.

* * *

This is a very tragic moment in American life.

I have been with the President and the Cabinet this morning. We have been meeting with the outstanding leaders of the civil rights movement in America, leaders of the Negro community in our nation. We've had a soul-searching morning—we've had a very soul-searching meeting.

These are very difficult moments to know what to say. But I suppose what is best to say is what flows from your heart, as well as from your mind.

In an hour of tragedy, one's true character and soul come to light. Whatever that tragedy might be, and surely we are now as individuals required to literally open our soul, look at it—our spirit, look at it—and see if it is what we want it to be.

Last night, Dr. Martin Luther King, Jr., died a martyr's death. His death snatched from American life something rare and precious, the living reminder that one man can make a difference—that one man, by the force of his character, the depth of his convictions, and the eloquence of his voice—can alter the course of history.

What a testimonial to individualism, what a testimonial to dignity and to human purpose—for Martin Luther King had the courage to challenge the intolerance, the injustice, inadequacies and inequities of the society in which he lived—a nation that he loved—a nation of which he was a citizen—and a nation for which he prayed and worked.

We grieve today for Martin Luther King and his family—and what a tragic loss it is to the family. In so doing, we grieve as well for ourselves and for our nation.

There is something of shame in all of this. This nation of law and order has its Presidents shot down, and has its spiritual leaders assassinated, and has those who walk and speak and work for human rights beaten, and some killed.

My fellow Americans, we cannot let this happen! Every one of us must resolve that it shall never, never, never happen again. To do less is to be unworthy of our heritage.

Dr. King touched the hearts of all people when he cried out in that memorable message in Washington a few years past, and you remember it—

I have a dream that my four little children will one day live in a nation where they will not be judged by the color of their skin, but by the content of their character.

The greatness of a nation is not in its size or its wealth, but rather, in how you wish to use these things. The true test of a nation is not in its power, but the character of its men and women.

Martin Luther King was voicing more than his personal dream. How I can still hear those words ring out from the Lincoln Memorial—

I have a dream.

That dream that he talked about is my dream—and I know it's your dream. Indeed, it is America's dream.

What will Martin Luther King's death mean to the American people? If it becomes a signal for black Americans to strike out in vengeance—in rage—in retaliation, as some have said—then we will have made a mockery of all for which he lived and died. This man was an apostle of non violence in the cause of social justice, even as he was taken by an act of violence.

What will Martin Luther King's death mean if it leads white Americans in a spirit of weariness and futility to turn from the tortuous road which leads to progress and equality. If this happens, we will have strengthened that very doctrine which he defied, the sense that the world has gone mad, and mortal man cannot set it right.

The murder of Dr. Martin Luther King does not mean—at least it does not mean to me—that as a nation we have somehow lost our way.

We can do what we want to do, my fellow Americans. We are not the innocent victims of raging forces if we seek to control our destiny, if we exercise self-discipline, if we live by the ideals that we preach.

An assassin's bullet can no more indict an entire society in 1968 than it could in 1865 or in 1963—and people wept then, as we weep now. Good people, hundreds of millions of them.

We are still as we were yesterday—a nation that is strong and vital and proud of man's deeds, and blessed by God's gifts. But the test of a people, like that of a man, is not how well it accepts its good fortune, but how it responds to adversity.

It is in the worst of time, ladies and gentlemen, that we must do our best. It is precisely at such moments, when our complacency is shattered by the thunderbolt of tragedy, that a nation has a chance to move forward and achieve greatness.

If the death of Martin Luther King can place in sharper focus the evils with which he daily struggled, then it can lead us to action and to a re-application of faith in ourselves and in our nation.

Let us then find comfort in Dr. King's own words,

"If you are cut down in a movement which is designed to save the soul of a nation, then no other death could be more redemptive."

You can almost say—

"O death, where is thy sting. O grave, where is thy victory?"

So my fellow citizens, let us find honesty today in the awareness that what Martin Luther King sought for his own people, is in the best interests of all of the people—and to me there can be just one people, one citizenship.

I wish I could have stood here first and led you in the Pledge of Allegiance. Our children repeat it quite often; adults tend not to as often as we should.

But there is a great lesson of citizenship and a morality in what we have taught our young and should remember in our maturity—"one nation, under God, indivisible, with liberty and justice for all."

That's what we're talking about. All people, all God's children, all American citizens.

Let us find purpose and unity in the words Dr. King spoke as he accepted the Nobel Peace Prize:

"I have the audacity to believe that people everywhere can have three meals a day for their bodies, education and culture for their minds, and dignity and equality and freedom for their spirits."

The words of a great American. The spirit of this nation—"life, liberty and the pursuit of happiness."

Jefferson said the only legitimate objective and purpose of government is the health, well-being, and the happiness of the people. This is America. This is what it's all about. This is what we mean to the world and to ourselves—if we would but only listen and only believe.

Now there are many things that we as Americans can do together. For example, we can pass without further delay the Civil Rights Bill now pending in Congress. We cannot have an integrated bunker at Khe Sanh and segregated neighborhoods at home. Now let's just get it straight, gentlemen—we can't do it!

We cannot ask men to die for their country and not let them live in it. We cannot have a man bear the uniform of the United States and fight gloriously and bravely and then deny him an equal chance when he returns. It can't be done and, if it is, then all that we talk about is a mockery.

We are at a very, very important point in history. We are deciding now in our time whether this will really be a government of the people, and by the people, as well as for the people.

We're going to have to decide whether or not American citizenship means full citizenship for everyone or just some. And there is no decision we can make except that full equality of opportunity, full equality of treatment, of education, is in the entitlement of every citizen that bears the most honored title in the world—citizen of the United States!

So we can pass this legislation, and I hope we will. I think we will and I want you to tell the Congress that we should.

We can mobilize the resources, both public and private, that will banish the specter of poverty from our land. Not overnight, I know that. There are no instant solutions to the problems of centuries and generations. But beginnings are imperative.

What every man needs above everything else is hope—and it is the hopelessness and the despair that grips people in far too many areas of America today.

The National Alliance of Businessmen is a vital factor in this effort and I want to thank you. I think one of the greatest things that has happened in America in recent years is this new sense of social conscience in the American business community.

But we've got to put it to work with renewed energy. The time is running out, and who has more to lose than those who have everything to lose. So may I suggest that, in the spirit of decent government, good morals, and good economics, we redouble our efforts to provide full opportunity.

In this instance we speak of jobs. We speak of training and we speak of meaningful jobs, productive jobs. With jobs come self-reliance and self-respect.

Your action in providing jobs for the hardcore unemployed and jobs for these disadvantaged young people this summer can be the first resounding answer to the senseless tragedy of Memphis.

Ladies and gentlemen, words will not suffice—deeds—action—it is imperative that we produce results.

We can root out the last vestiges of discrimination, and segregation and inequality. We can do it in our schools, in employment and in housing, and in public services.

We can—and we must—commit ourselves unreservedly to the broad program of action that was recommended in the National Advisory Commission on Civil Disorders, so that America will not become two societies—one black, one white, separate and unequal.

This must never become our America. This would violate the very words I spoke a few moments ago: "one nation, under God, indivisible with liberty and justice for all." We dare not indulge ourselves in national hypocrisy.

As individuals, we can search our own souls for the remnants of prejudice and injustice. We can fearlessly stand up now for human dignity and freedom for everybody, white and black, whatever a man's creed or national origin, just as Dr. King stood. For those who speak evil of another man, may I urge you to speak well of another man. Remonstrate with those who would defile the meaning of our democracy. Hold high the hand of your neighbor who speaks up for America and what it means.

Lincoln was right—it is the last best hope of earth. But you know what else he said: "We shall either nobly save it or meanly lose it." And every generation has to decide that issue.

We have to decide it this day, just as we had to decide it on that day that John Kennedy was stricken, just as America had to decide it on that day that Abraham Lincoln was shot down.

Every so often it seems as if divine providence tests us, and I think that the test is upon us now as never before. But I also believe that our tragedy can be our victory.

Remember the words of a great Englishman who once said—

"If a man has nothing to do for his country, he shall have no love for it."

There are far too many in America today who have been denied their chance to do something for this country. Some of the reason of denial I do not know. But it is a fact that amongst far too many of our youth, and particularly among Negro youth, unemployment runs as high as 35 percent. The unemployed young people stand idly on a street corner, bitter, and listening all too often to the purveyors of division and hate.

We must speak up for the love of this country with more than words. Yes, we must speak up with jobs, with homes, with good neighborhoods, with education, with help and, above all, with dignity.

People must have a sense of pride that their hopes can be realized.

I happen to believe that we can summon the courage for reconciliation in this nation. I believe that we can reject and we must reject the cowardice of violence—the cowardice of violence.

If we do—if we do recognize the testament in the life and death of Martin Luther King, if we do rededicate ourselves to the mission of healing the torment of our poor and hungry, our deprived and illiterate, then truly, then truly this tragedy will be remembered, not as the moment when America lost her faith, but as the moment when America found her conscience.

My fellow Americans, in our own way each and everyone of us must search deeply into our very being. We need to ask ourselves this day,—

"Am I really worthy of the heritage of this land? What did I contribute to it? What is it that I shall leave and others did not?"

I ask you to save lives. I ask you to convert human waste into human worth. I ask you to be worthy of having been created in the image of your maker. If we are, America will be a better land because we walked here, we worked here, and we lived here.

Thank you very much.

The Fight to Free Ourselves
A Crisis in Civil-rights Leadership
SENATOR JACOB JAVITS

A native of New York City, Jacob Javits had chosen law as his profession and had practiced in New York as a trial lawyer before he
entered the United States Senate, he served as a member of the 80th
to the 83rd and 85th Congress. From 1955–1957, he was attorney general of New York. During World War II, he served in the European
and Pacific Theatres of operation and was discharged as a lieutenant
colonel.

Javits is the author of *A Proposal to Amend the Anti-Trust Laws,
Discrimination U.S.A., Order of Battle,* and *A Republican's Call to
Reason.* As a member of the liberal wing of the Republican Party, he
has consistently championed the cause of civil rights.

The first speech, "The Fight to Free Ourselves," was delivered at
ceremonies marking the 200th anniversary of the dedication of the
Touro Synagogue, the oldest Synagogue in the nation, in Newport,
Rhode Island, September 15, 1963. "A Crisis in Civil-rights Leader-
ship" was delivered at the Law Day ceremonies sponsored by the
Philadelphia Bar Association in Independence Square, Philadelphia,
Pennsylvania, May 1, 1963.

* * *

When this small synagogue was dedicted in Newport 200 years ago,
liberty was the theme of our age. This temple was born and nurtured
in a setting that was as inspirational as it was historic.

This site in the colony of Rhode Island—which Roger Williams
founded as a citadel of religious liberty, opening its arms to the oppressed from across the seas—is as symbolic of the heritage of our
nation as any piece of earth could be.

The letter to this congregation from George Washington, with the
immortal words that the United States "gives to bigotry no sanction,
to persecution no assistance"—words that were written before even the
Bill of Rights in the Constitution was adopted—is as symbolic of the
soul of our nation as any document could be.

Thus, on this bicentennial celebration, we can look at this splendid temple with passion and with pride; and with the knowledge that in places such as this, the human spirit was first ennobled in the United States; and the American Dream was first articulated.

We also cannot help but be reminded of a tableau three weeks ago at another shrine, in Washington, D.C., when liberty was again the theme. There, the spiritual leader of the current civil-rights "revolution" cried to us that the American dream was too long forgotten by too many and too long denied to those so ardently reaching for its realization.

And so, the fight for liberty continues; the crusade for human dignity goes on; the struggle to bring meaning to the American promise is still far from won.

This is a struggle which we must face in the communities no less than in the Congress, in our synagogues and churches no less than in our business establishments and recreational facilities. And as Jews we have a special responsibility to set forth by example and in highly positive deeds the great religious and prophetic tradition to which we are the heirs.

The extent to which this crusade is the major unfinished business of our society was never more dramatized than by published polls this past week which declared that 50 percent of our nation believes that integration is moving "too fast."

Just think of it—if these polls really reflect deep convictions, it means that half of our nation may not yet have freed itself of this sorrowful irrationality.

The synagogues and churches of our land will not be persuaded by such polls; and I hope politicians will not either. For I believe that while the 50 percent of those questioned may have said "too fast," the consciences, when properly appealed to, of those same Americans will give a different answer.

This is the most powerful force in this current struggle—*that the deeply held conscience of the white American is on the side of the Negro, whatever may appear to be his emotions.*

This is why every level of our society must be enlisted to bring about a moral awakening among the American people—or to put it more bluntly, to stir the uneasy consciences of every white American so he may free himself of bias.

This fight to free ourselves is the great, unwritten struggle being waged today in the depths of each individual soul. It is a battle for survival of the American dream, and of the human spirit.

Our minds hear the message: When freedom is denied to one man, it is denied to all; for freedom is noble and indivisible. If we want to enjoy it, it must be extended to everyone; if we want to maintain it, we must fight for it.

These simple truths are enshrined in this synagogue, as they are enshrined in the hearts of every Jew. The accumulated experience of centuries of persecution have equipped the Jewish community—perhaps more than most—with the ability to understand that the security of one minority is no greater than the security of any other minority, just as the denial of liberty to one American threatens the liberty of every American.

It is this identity of interest between the Negro minority and other minorities in the United States which gives this 1963 civil-rights "revolution" strength and effectiveness. It is this identity of interest which should make possible joint and interdependent action to eliminate these injustices from American society.

We cannot allow ourselves to be barred from this struggle, as some misguided Negroes suggest, for an American struggle for the soul of our nation is neither for whites only nor for Negroes only.

The rabbis and priests and ministers who joined the Freedom Marchers in Birmingham; in Gwynne Oaks, Maryland; in Albany, Georgia; in Jackson, Mississippi; and in the other towns and cities—they gave substance to this truth. The 200,000 men and women of all faiths and color who participated in the August 28 march on Washington—a demonstration which enriched our democracy as few events ever have—they recognized this, too.

But not everyone has to march or to picket or to demonstrate in order to make an effective contribution to this fight. But neither can anyone remain aloof—every American must speak his conscience and act its dictates on this racial crisis. Silence has been the greatest weapon for the demagogues. It has caused mankind's darkest hours— as no Jew of modern times can ever forget.

The problem is not confined to the South, as we all know. In the North and among all groups, there are problems of "silence," too—of an unwillingness to implement convictions, a reluctance to be the first to tread on unwalked paths.

A Negro leader once confessed to me, "In the South, we know our enemy; in the North, we don't always know—and that is sometimes more difficult."

This struggle is more than just the number of votes that are needed in the Congress to pass civil-rights legislation; and that it is more than the dramatic confrontations between state and federal power which we have seen in Mississippi and Alabama.

It is, above all, an enormous battle of conscience—which will not be resolved until each individual is willing to take inventory, to realize that the resolution cannot be put off for another day or for another generation; and that now is the time to commit our hearts as well as our minds.

I feel the stirrings of this battle of conscience.

I see it in the letter a woman wrote to *The New York Times,* telling of her search for a way to implement her convictions. She wrote that she went

rather impulsively, to the evening service at a local Negro church. . . . I was welcomed . . . and I recommended such activities to friendly white Americans. Do not be afraid to go it alone at first. Others will follow. And if enough of us show our spirit in some such way, no longer can our Negro leaders feel that there has been no moral awakening or conversion among the American people.

I feel this stirring too, in the mail coming into my office. Few people realize that even a Senator from New York—for six years until this year—had received more mail opposed to civil rights than mail favoring it. But this summer, that trend has sharply reversed. The "good people" are beginning to write, to speak out on what bothers their consciences and what they know is right.

I feel these stirrings too, on the floor of the Senate. There have been days in my fifteen years in Congress when to plead for civil rights was a lonely battle, irritating to the establishment; and the coldness of the reception would hang icily in the air. Today, there is warmth and great understanding that this battle has to be waged now for it relates to the very destiny of our nation.

It is the stirring of conscience, too, an equal opportunity which is forcing businessmen to review their hiring and promotion practices; which is forcing labor unions to review their admission and apprenticeship policy; which is forcing others to examine their reasons for patronizing particular stores, hotels, or restaurants, or for deciding in what community they will live; and what schools they want their children to attend. It is this stirring of conscience which is awakening Americans to their personal opportunities to afford equal opportunity to our fellow Negro Americans in myriad ways not affected by laws.

The battle will be won when this conscience can be translated into action. If we can succeed in doing this now, our nation will be nourished and enriched; our society will be fuller and stronger. And we will free ourselves at last.

No one can speak against the backdrop of Independence Hall without feeling the fervent historical spirit of our democracy and our Constitution. Those who wrote the words—"We hold these truths to be self-evident, that all men are created equal . . ."—were engaged, during an embattled hour of world history, in a struggle to defend the rights of man.

Today, that struggle is still the very theme of our existence. Unhappily and significantly, we have a long way to go to realize this objective which gave birth to our nation. As a people, we do not like to admit that. We prefer to talk about the progress, nearly 200 years after the Declaration of Independence and 100 years after the Emancipation Proclamation, when in nearly every aspect of our national life in such a large part of our nation we are still living in defiance of the basic truth that "all men are created equal, that they are endowed by their Creator with certain inalienable rights. . . ."

Is progress really meaningful, the Negro asks, if it cannot be assuredly measured in one man's lifetime? Is it substantial progress when there is so much intransigent opposition by whole states and their governments to equal opportunity, even as to the right to vote?

I believe our reluctance, as a nation, to recognize what truly needs to be done in civil rights represents a dreadful danger to our society. For the Negro community in America today is stirring as it has never stirred before. It is bitter and impatient and it is searching for outlets for its frustration which, unless satisfied, can only lead to extremism and disaster. Let us beware of what we sow lest we reap bitterness.

Those who think this is an exaggeration are, I believe, closing their eyes to events around them.

Two weeks ago, the United States Civil Rights Commission issued a hair-raising summation on conditions of denial of basic rights to Negroes in the State of Mississippi. With devastating suddenness, some of our highest officials and leading newspapers—North and South—pounced on the Commission for having the audacity to suggest that the President should "explore" the legal authority he possesses to withhold federal funds from Mississippi until that state complies with the Constitution and the laws of the United States. They called this suggestion cruel, unusual, dangerous, drastic, and radical. And in the process, they managed to ignore the awful truth of what the Commission's Mississippi Advisory Committee—all Mississippians—had to say:

We find that the existing conditions under which our Negro citizens must live are in the main intolerable, with a continuing deprivation of rights, and an ever-present threat of police brutality and economic reprisal against any citizen who attempts to break the established pattern of segregation.

Even the first reaction of the President of the United States was negative to the Commission's reports. A day after the report was published, he said, in reply to a question, "I don't have the power to cut off the aid in a general way . . . and I would think it would probably be unwise. . . ." Subsequently, at a later news conference and in a letter to the Commission, the President recovered, indicating that the suggestion was not such an unreasonable idea, that it is at least deserving of consideration. One had the feeling that whatever his initial judgment on the recommendation, he at least recognized that it raised some very pointed questions regarding the morality of our federal government subsidizing, in some of its programs, racist lawlessness in Mississippi—and there is no question that it does.

When leading voices in our nation find it so easy to attack the Commission for a suggestion to "explore," and find it so hard to point up its findings of terror, is it so surprising to see the Negro grow more suspicious and disillusioned over his efforts to achieve the legitimate objectives of American citizenship?

The Negro essayist, James Baldwin, says, "The brutality with which Negroes are treated in this country cannot be overstated, however unwilling white men may be to hear it." This theme is raising an awful echo in many hearts.

The challenge I pose today is that we must not refuse to hear the sounds of restlessness. On this Law Day, when we are called upon to rededicate ourselves to the ideals of equality and justice, we must face this issue—with more than words, but with acts and leadership. There is in our nation today a crisis of leadership on civil rights, as indicated by the difficulty in bringing about broad public acceptance for the recognition of the rights of man and in establishing the means by which these rights may be asserted in the law.

This crisis of leadership is an especially great challenge to the legal profession. The opportunities for the skilled and organized legal profession to meet the challenge of our national civil-rights problems and to assume the leadership in their solution has never been greater.

Lawyers should be the most ardent advocates of laws to implement these rights, and they should be the most ready to represent those who suffer under the injustice of discrimination and segregation. Leadership in obtaining civil-rights legislation should appeal particularly to the lawyer, for he knows that the social penalty for suppressing legiti-

mate aspirations for equality is violence and disorder of the very kind
we see now in Mississippi.

The lawyer knows, too, that law sets a standard to which all men
can repair and gives tongue to grievances which might otherwise seek
extralegal remedy.

There has been a real failure in the Congress to assume the proper
responsibility for civil-rights measures and a failure by the President
to ask for the needed legislation. The reluctance to proceed with the
vigor and completeness which the situation requires is a tragic mistake. For I am convinced that without legislative enactments, the bases
for serious trouble are present.

There is, first, the hardening of the segregationist opposition in such
places as Mississippi when it becomes clear that desegregation is inevitable and yet, when adequate law does not exist to curb intransi-
gence. There is the growing feeling among Negroes that the processes
of law are too difficult to bring relief and too slow to materially help
in their situation. There is also the danger of a slackening of the pace
of the drive for equal opportunity in areas outside the South, where
lack of zeal is bound to creep as long as Congress remains unmoved
by the mounting crisis in civil rights.

I know of few efforts which would be as productive in this field as
the intensified action of the organized bar. It could give prestige to
the civil-rights struggle which it does not now enjoy. It would assure
a trained and effective judgment on the legality and practicality of
civil-rights measures which are projected. It would lend backing to
the most effective legal representation for those who are the objects
of discrimination and segregation violative of our Constitution.

It is not unusual in states where segregation maintains its hold for
lawyers to be intimidated, ostracized, and to have economic sanctions
visited on them for taking civil-rights cases. So, too, special anti-
barratry statutes complicate and bedevil such representation. At the
very least, the support of the bar would give needed backing and
encouragement to such lawyers who stand in such dangerous loneliness
in communities where their causes are unfriendly.

Until now, lawyers and the bar on the national level have not taken
an adequately vocal stand on the side of upholding minority rights.
We have neither been sufficiently outspoken nor have we acted, as
well we might, to awaken the social conscience of our fellow citizens.
The bar has rarely spoken out in times of crisis when its persuasive
influence might well have been helpful to the national interest. It has
rarely sought to obtain a consensus of opinion in the legal community

and has all too infrequently been unwilling to stand behind it. It has rarely asked the President or the Congress to take note of its position.

In the recent Oxford, Mississippi, incident, it was not until after violence had taken place that the organized bar spoke out. The people of Mississippi and the entire nation could have benefited greatly by the persuasive effort of the legal profession's speaking out in favor of upholding federal law. Yet the necessity of abiding by the Court's rule of law was never urged with clarity and strength; the profession remained silent. It did not openly confront the forces which opposed the rule of law.

This is a day for plain speaking. In the face of growing Negro frustration over a crisis of leadership in civil rights, we must all face our responsibilities. It is in this spirit that I have issued to the bar today this call to action on civil rights. Here is truly a dedication for Law Day worthy of the character and spirit of the day.

Right to Vote

PRESIDENT LYNDON B. JOHNSON

Lyndon Baines Johnson, the thirty-sixth President of the United States, has been a man of action throughout his political career. As majority leader of the United States Senate, he helped to direct the 1957 and 1960 Civil Rights Acts through the Senate. As the President, he personally spearheaded the enactment of the comprehensive Civil Rights Act of 1964, and even more recently, the new law of 1965 guaranteeing every American the right to vote.

His country wisdom, plain talk, and understanding heart are reflected in the speeches which have been selected for this volume. His "Right to Vote" message was delivered at the first session of the eighty-ninth Congress on March 15, 1965. It was on June 4, 1965, that he delivered the Commencement address, "A Candle of Understanding" at Howard University, Washington, D.C.

* * *

I speak tonight for the dignity of man and the destiny of democracy.

I urge every member of both parties—Americans of all religions and of all colors—from every section of this country—to join me in that cause.

At times history and fate meet at a single time in a single place to shape a turning point in man's unending search for freedom. So it was at Lexington and Concord. So it was a century ago at Appomattox. So it was last week in Selma, Alabama.

There, long-suffering men and women peacefully protested the denial of their rights as Americans. Many were brutally assaulted. One good man—a man of God—was killed.

There was no cause for pride in what has happened in Selma.

There is no cause for self-satisfaction in the long denial of equal rights of millions of Americans.

But there is cause for hope and for faith in our democracy in what is happening here tonight.

For the cries of pain, and the hymns and protests of oppressed people, have summoned into convocation all the majesty of this great government, the government of the greatest nation on earth.

Our mission is at once the oldest and most basic of this country: to right wrong, to do justice, to serve man.

In our time we have come to live with the moments of great crisis. Our lives have been marked with debate about great issues—issues of war and peace, issues of prosperity and depression. But rarely, in any time, does an issue lay bare the secret heart of America itself. Rarely are we met with the challenge, not to our growth or abundance, or our welfare or our security—but rather to the values and the purposes and the meaning of our beloved nation.

The issue of equal rights for American Negroes is such an issue. And should we defeat every enemy, and should we double our wealth and conquer the stars and still be unequal to this issue, then we will have failed as a people and as a nation.

For with a country as with a person, "What is a man profited, if he shall gain the whole world, and lose his own soul?"

There is no Negro problem. There is no Southern problem. There is no Northern problem. There is only an American problem.

And we are met here tonight as Americans—not as Democrats or Republicans—we are met here as Americans to solve that problem.

This was the first nation in the history of the world to be founded with a purpose. The great phrases of that purpose still sound in every American heart, North and South: "All men are created equal"— "Government by consent of the governed"—"Give me liberty or give me death." And those are not just clever words and those are not just empty theories. In their name Americans have fought and died for two centuries and tonight around the world they stand there as guardians of our liberty risking their lives.

Those words are a promise to every citizen that he shall share in the dignity of man. This dignity cannot be found in a man's possessions. It cannot be found in his power or in his position. It really rests on his right to be treated as a man equal in opportunity to all others. It says that he shall share in freedom, he shall choose his leaders, educate his children, provide for his family according to his ability and his merits as a human being.

To apply any other test—to deny a man his hopes because of his color or race or his religion or the place of his birth—is not only to do injustice, it is to deny America and to dishonor the dead who gave their lives for American freedom.

Our fathers believed that if this noble view of the rights of man was to flourish, it must be rooted in democracy. The most basic right of all was the right to choose your own leaders. The history of this country in large measure, is the history of the expansion of that right to all of our people.

Many of the issues of civil rights are very complex and most difficult. But about this there can and should be no argument. Every American citizen must have an equal right to vote. There is no reason which can excuse the denial of that right. There is no duty which weighs more heavily on us than the duty we have to ensure that right.

Yet the harsh fact is that in many places in this country men and women are kept from voting simply because they are Negroes.

Every device of which human ingenuity is capable has been used to deny this right. The Negro citizen may go to register only to be told that the day is wrong, or the hour is late, or the official in charge is absent.

And if he persists, and if he manages to present himself to the registrar, he may be disqualified because he did not spell out his middle name or because he abbreviated a word on the application.

And if he manages to fill out an application he is given a test. The registrar is the sole judge of whether he passes this test. He may be asked to recite the entire Constitution, or explain the most complex provisions of state law and even a college degree cannot be used to prove that he can read and write.

For the fact is that the only way to pass these barriers is to show a white skin.

Experience has clearly shown that the existing process of law cannot overcome systematic and ingenious discrimination. No law that we now have on the books—and I have helped to put three of them there —can ensure the right to vote when local officials are determined to deny it.

In such a case our duty must be clear to all of us. The Constitution says that no person shall be kept from voting because of his race or his color. We have all sworn an oath before God to support and to defend that Constitution.

We must now act in obedience to that oath.

Wednesday I will send to Congress a law designed to eliminate illegal barriers to the right to vote.

The broad principles of that bill will be in the hands of the Democratic and Republican leaders tomorrow. After they have reviewed it, it will come here formally as a bill.

I am grateful for this opportunity to come here tonight at the invitation of the leadership to reason with my friends, to give them my views, and to visit with my former colleagues.

I have had prepared a more comprehensive analysis of the legislation which I had intended to transmit to the Clerk tomorrow, but which I will submit to the Clerk tonight. But I want to really discuss with you now, briefly, the main proposals of this legislation.

This bill will strike down restrictions to voting in all elections—federal, state, and local—which have been used to deny Negroes the right to vote.

This bill will establish a simple, uniform standard which cannot be used, however ingenious the effort to flout our Constitution.

It will provide for citizens to be registered by officials of the U.S. government if the state officials refuse to register them.

It will eliminate tedious, unnecessary lawsuits which delay the right to vote.

Finally, this legislation will ensure that properly registered individuals are not prohibited from voting.

I will welcome the suggestions from all the members of Congress—I have no doubt that I will get some—on ways and means to strengthen this law and to make it effective. But experience has plainly shown that this is the only path to carry out the command of the Constitution.

To those who seek to avoid action by their national government in their home communities—who want to and who seek to maintain purely local control over elections—the answer is simple.

Open your polling places to all your people.

Allow men and women to register and vote whatever the color of their skin.

Extend the rights of citizenship to every citizen of this land.

There is no constitutional issue here. The command of the Constitution is plain.

There is no moral issue. It is wrong—deadly wrong—to deny any of your fellow Americans the right to vote in this country.

There is no issue of states' rights or national rights. There is only the struggle for human rights.

I have not the slightest doubt what will be your answer.

But the last time a President sent a civil-rights bill to the Congress it contained a provision to protect voting rights in federal elections. That civil-rights bill was passed after eight long months of debate. And when that bill came to my desk from the Congress for my signature, the heart of the voting provision had been eliminated.

This time, on this issue, there must be no delay, or no hesitation, or no compromise with our purpose.

We cannot, we must not refuse to protect the right of every American to vote in every election that he may desire to participate in.

And we ought not and we cannot and we must not wait another eight months before we get a bill. And I do not make this request lightly, for from the window where I sit with the problems of our country I recognize that from outside this chamber is the outraged conscience of a nation—the grave concern of many nations—and the harsh judgment of history on our acts.

But even if we pass this bill, the battle will not be over. What happened in Selma is part of a far larger movement which reaches into every section and state of America. It is the effort of American Negroes to secure for themselves the full blessings of American life.

Their cause must be our cause too, because it is not just Negroes but really it is all of us, who must overcome the crippling legacy of bigotry and injustice. And we shall overcome.

As a man whose roots go deeply into Southern soil I know how agonizing racial feelings are. I know how difficult it is to reshape the attitudes and the structure of our society.

But a century has passed—more than 100 years—since the Negro was freed. And he is not fully free tonight. It was more than 100 years ago that Abraham Lincoln, a great President of another party, signed the Emancipation Proclamation. But emancipation is a proclamation and not a fact.

A century has passed—more than 100 years—since equality was promised. And yet the Negro is not equal.

A century has passed since the day of promise. And the promise is unkept.

The time of justice has now come. And I tell you that I believe sincerely that no force can hold it back. It is right—in the eyes of man and God—that it should come. And when it does, I think that day will brighten the lives of every American.

For Negroes are not the only victims. How many white children have gone uneducated and how many white families have lived in stark poverty—how many white lives have been scarred by fear because we have wasted our energy and our substance to maintain the barriers of hatred and terror.

And so I say to all of you here and to all in the nation tonight that those who appeal to you to hold on to the past do so at the cost of denying you your future.

This great, rich, restless country can offer opportunity and education and hope to all—all black and white, all North and South, sharecropper and city dweller. These are the enemies—poverty, ignorance, disease—they are our enemies, not our fellow man, not our neighbor. And these enemies too—poverty, disease, and ignorance—we shall overcome.

Now let none of us, in any section, look with prideful righteousness on the troubles in another section or the problems of our neighbors. There is really no part of America where the promise of equality has been fully kept. In Buffalo as well as in Birmingham, in Philadelphia as well as Selma, Americans are struggling for the fruits of freedom.

This is one nation. What happens in Selma or in Cincinnati is a matter of legitimate concern to every American. But let us look within our own hearts and our own communities, and let each of us put our shoulder to the wheel to root out injustice wherever it exists.

As we meet here in this peaceful, historic chamber tonight, men from the South, some of whom were at Iwo Jima, men from the North, who have carried Old Glory to far corners of the world and brought it back without a stain on it, men from the East and from the West, are all fighting together without regard to religion or color or region in Vietnam. Men from every region fought for us across the world twenty years ago.

And now, in these common dangers and these common sacrifices, the South made its contribution of honor and gallantry no less than any other region of the great republic, and in some instances—a great many of them—more.

And I have not the slightest doubt that good men from everywhere in this country—from the Great Lakes to the Gulf of Mexico, from the Golden Gate to the harbors along the Atlantic—will rally now together in this cause to vindicate the freedom of all Americans. For all of us owe this duty, and I believe that all of us will respond to it.

Your President makes that request of every American.

The real hero of this struggle is the American Negro. His actions and protests—his courage to risk safety, and even to risk his life—have awakened the conscience of this nation. His demonstrations have been designed to call attention to injustice, designed to provoke change, designed to stir reform. He has called upon us to make good the promise of America. And who among us can say that we would have made the same progress were it not for his persistent bravery and his faith in American democracy?

For at the real heart of battle for equality is a deep-seated belief in the democratic process. Equality depends not on the force of arms or tear gas, but depends upon the force of moral right—not on recourse to violence but on respect for law and order.

There have been many pressures upon your President—and there will be others as the days come and go—but I pledge you tonight that we intend to fight this battle where it should be fought, in the courts and in the Congress and in the hearts of men.

We must preserve the right of free speech and the right of free assembly. But the right of free speech does not carry with it, as has been said, the right to holler "fire" in a crowded theatre. We must preserve the right to free assembly, but free assembly does not carry with it the right to block public thoroughfares to traffic.

We do have a right to protest and a right to march under conditions that do not infringe the constitutional rights of our neighbors. And I intend to protect all those rights as long as I am permitted to serve in this office.

We will guard against violence, knowing it strikes from our hands the very weapons with which we seek progress—obedience to law, and belief in American values.

In Selma, as elsewhere, we seek and pray for peace. We seek order. We seek unity.

But we will not accept the peace of stifled rights, or the order imposed by fear, or the unity that stifles protest. For peace cannot be purchased at the cost of liberty.

In Selma tonight—and we had a good day there—as in every city, we are working for a just and peaceful settlement. And we must all remember—after this speech I am making tonight, after the police and the FBI and the marshals have all gone, and after you have promptly passed this bill—the people of Selma and the other cities of the nation must still live and work together. And when the attention of the nation has gone elsewhere they must try to heal the wounds and to build a new community. This cannot be easily done on a battleground of violence, as the history of the South itself shows. It is in recognition of this that men of both races have shown such an outstandingly impressive responsibility in recent days—last Tuesday, and again today.

The bill that I am presenting to you will be known as a civil-rights bill. But in a larger sense, most of the program I am recommending is a civil-rights program. Its object is to open the city of hope to all people of all races.

Because all Americans just must have the right to vote. And we are going to give them that right.

All Americans must have the privileges of citizenship regardless of race. And they are going to have those privileges of citizenship regardless of race.

But I would like to caution you and remind you that to exercise these privileges takes much more than legal right. It requires a trained mind and a healthy body. It requires a decent home, and the chance to find a job, and the opportunity to escape from the clutches of poverty.

Of course people cannot contribute to the nation if they are never taught to read or write, if their bodies are stunted from hunger, if their sickness goes untended, if their life is spent in hopeless poverty just drawing a welfare check.

So we want to open the gates to opportunity. But we are also going to give all our people—black and white—the help that they need to walk through those gates.

My first job after college was as a teacher in Cotulla, Texas, in a small Mexican-American school. Few of them could speak English and I could not speak much Spanish. My students were poor and they often came to class without breakfast—hungry. And they knew, even in their youth, the pain of prejudice. They never seemed to know why people disliked them, but they knew it was so because I saw it in their eyes.

I often walked home late in the afternoon after the classes were finished wishing there was more that I could do. But all I knew was to teach them the little that I knew—hoping that it might help them against the hardships that lay ahead.

Somehow you never forget what poverty and hatred can do when you see its scars on the hopeful face of a young child.

I never thought then in 1928 that I would be standing here in 1965. It never even occurred to me in my fondest dreams that I might have the chance to help the sons and daughters of those students—and to help people like them all over this country.

But now I do have that chance and I will let you in on a secret—I mean to use it.

And I hope that you will use it with me.

This is the richest and most powerful country which ever occupied this globe. The might of past empires is little compared to ours.

But I do not want to be the President who built empires, or sought grandeur, or extended dominion.

I want to be the President who educated young children to the wonders of their world.

I want to be the President who helped to feed the hungry and to prepare them to be taxpayers instead of tax-eaters.

I want to be the President who helped the poor to find their own way and who protected the right of every citizen to vote in every election.

I want to be the President who helped to end hatred among his fellow men and who prompted love among the people of all races and all regions and all parties.

I want to be the President who helped to end war among the brothers of this earth.

And so at the request of your beloved Speaker and the Senator from Montana, the majority leader, Mr. Mansfield, and the Senator from Illinois, the minority leader, Mr. Dirksen, and Mr. McCulloch and others, members of both parties, I come here tonight not as President Roosevelt came down one time in person to veto a bonus bill; not as President Truman came down one time to urge the passage of a railroad bill. But I come here to ask you to share this task with me and to share it with the people we both work for.

I want this to be the Congress—Republicans and Democrats alike— which did all these things for all these people.

Beyond this great chamber—out yonder in the fifty states are the people we serve. Who can tell what deep and unspoken hopes are in their hearts tonight as they sit there and listen? We all can guess, from our own lives, how difficult they often find their own pursuit of happiness; how many problems each little family has. They look most of all to themselves for their future.

But I think that they also look to each of us.

Above the pyramid on the great seal of the United States it says in Latin, "God has favored our undertaking."

God will not favor everything that we do. It is rather our duty to divine His will. I cannot but believe that He truly understands and that He really favors the undertaking that we begin here tonight.

A CANDLE OF UNDERSTANDING
LYNDON BAINES JOHNSON

Dr. Nabrit, my fellow Americans: I am delighted at the chance to speak at this important and this historic institution. Howard has long been an outstanding center for the education of Negro Americans. Its students are of every race and color and they come from many countries of the world. It is truly a working example of democratic excellence.

Our earth is the home of revolution. In every corner of every continent men charged with hope contend with ancient ways in the pursuit of justice. They reach for the newest of weapons to realize the oldest of dreams, that each may walk in freedom and pride, stretching his talents, enjoying the fruits of the earth.

Our enemies may occasionally seize the day of change, but it is the banner of our revolution they take. And our own future is linked to this process of swift and turbulent change in many lands in the world. But nothing in any country touches us more profoundly, and nothing is more freighted with meaning for our own destiny than the revolution of the Negro American.

In far too many ways American Negroes have been another nation: deprived of freedom, crippled by hatred, the doors of opportunity closed to hope.

In our time change has come to this nation too. The American Negro, acting with impressive restraint, has peacefully protested and marched, entered the courtrooms and the seats of government, demanding a justice that has long been denied. The voice of the Negro was the call to action. But it is a tribute to America that, once aroused, the courts and the Congress, the President and most of the people, have been the allies of progress.

Thus we have seen the high court of the country declare that discrimination based on race was repugnant to the Constitution, and therefore void. We have seen in 1957, 1960, and again in 1964, the first civil-rights legislation in this nation in almost an entire century.

As majority leader of the United States Senate, I helped to guide two of these bills through the Senate. And, as your President, I was proud to sign the third. And now very soon we will have the fourth— a new law guaranteeing every American the right to vote.

No act of my entire administration will give me greater satisfaction than the day when my signature makes this bill too the law of this land.

The voting-rights bill will be the latest, and among the most important, in a long series of victories. But this victory—as Winston Churchill said of another triumph for freedom— "is not the end. It is not even the beginning of the end. But it is, perhaps, the end of the beginning."

That beginning is freedom; and the barriers to that freedom are tumbling down. Freedom is the right to share, share fully and equally, in American society—to vote, to hold a job, to enter a public place, to go to school. It is the right to be treated in every part of our national life as a person equal in dignity and promise to all others.

But freedom is not enough. You do not wipe away the scars of centuries by saying: Now you are free to go where you want, or do as you desire, and choose the leaders you please.

You do not take a person who, for years, has been hobbled by chains and liberate him, bring him up to the starting line of a race and then say, "you are free to compete with all the others," and still justly believe that you have been completely fair.

Thus it is not enough just to open the gates of opportunity. All our citizens must have the ability to walk through those gates.

This is the next and the more profound stage of the battle for civil rights. We seek not just freedom but opportunity. We seek not just legal equity but human ability—not just equality as a right and a theory, but equality as a fact and equality as a result.

For the task is to give 20 million Negroes the same chance as every other American to learn and grow, to work and share in society, to develop their abilities—physical, mental, and spiritual—and to pursue their individual happiness.

To this end equal opportunity is essential, but not enough, not enough. Men and women of all races are born with the same range of abilities. But ability is not just the product of birth. Ability is stretched or stunted by the family you live with, and the neighborhood you live in, by the school you go to and the poverty or the richness of your surroundings. It is the product of a hundred unseen forces playing upon the little infant, the child, and finally the man.

This graduating class at Howard University is witness to the indomitable determination of the Negro American to win his way in American life.

The number of Negroes in schools of higher learning has almost doubled in fifteen years. The number of nonwhite professional workers has more than doubled in ten years. The median income of Negro college women tonight exceeds that of white college women. And there are also the enormous accomplishments of distinguished individual Negroes—many of them graduates of this institution, and one of them the first lady ambassador in the history of the United States.

These are proud and impressive achievements. But they tell only the story of a growing middle-class minority, steadily narrowing the gap between them and their white counterparts.

But for the great majority of Negro Americans—the poor, the unemployed, the uprooted, and the dispossessed—there is a much grimmer story. They still, as we meet here tonight, are another nation. Despite the court orders and the laws, despite the legislative victories and the speeches, for them the walls are rising and the gulf is widening.

Here are some of the facts of this American failure.

Thirty-five years ago the rate of unemployment for Negroes and whites was about the same. Tonight the Negro rate is twice as high.

In 1948 the 8 percent unemployment rate for Negro teen-age boys was actually less than that of whites. By last year that rate had grown to 23 percent, as against 13 percent for whites unemployed.

Between 1949 and 1959, the income of Negro men relative to white men declined in every section of this country. From 1952 to 1963 the median income of Negro families compared to white actually dropped from 57 percent to 53 percent.

In the years 1955 through 1957, 22 percent of experienced Negro workers were out of work at some time during the year. In 1961 through 1963 that proportion had soared to 29 percent.

Since 1947 the number of white families living in poverty has decreased 27 percent while the number of poorer nonwhite families decreased only 3 percent.

The infant mortality of nonwhites in 1940 was 70 percent greater than whites. Twenty-two years later it was 90 percent greater.

Moreover, the isolation of Negro from white communities is increasing, rather than decreasing, as Negroes crowd into the central cities and become a city within a city.

Of course Negro Americans as well as white Americans have shared in our rising national abundance. But the harsh fact of the matter is that in the battle for true equality too many are losing ground every day.

We are not completely sure why this is. We know the causes are complex and subtle. But we do know the two broad basic reasons. And we do know that we have to act.

First, Negroes are trapped—as many whites are trapped—in inherited, gateless poverty. They lack training and skills. They are shut in slums, without decent medical care. Private and public poverty combine to cripple their capacities.

We are trying to attack these evils through our poverty program, through our education program, through our medical care and our other health programs and a dozen more of the Great Society programs that are aimed at the root causes of this poverty.

We will increase, and we will accelerate, and we will broaden this attack in years to come until this most enduring of foes finally yields to our unyielding will. But there is a second cause—much more difficult to explain, more deeply grounded, more desperate in its force. It is the devastating heritage of long years of slavery; and a century of oppression, hatred, and injustice.

For Negro poverty is not white poverty. Many of its causes and many of its cures are the same. But there are differences—deep, corrosive, obstinate differences—radiating painful roots into the community, and into the family, and the nature of the individual.

These differences are not racial differences. They are solely and simply the consequence of ancient brutality, past injustice, and present prejudice. They are anguishing to observe. For the Negro they are a constant reminder of oppression. For the white they are a constant reminder of guilt. But they must be faced and they must be dealt with and they must be overcome, if we are ever to reach the time when the only difference between Negroes and whites is the color of their skin.

Nor can we find a complete answer in the experience of other American minorities. They made a valiant and a largely successful effort to emerge from poverty and prejudice.

The Negro, like these others, will have to rely mostly on his own efforts. But he just can not do it alone. For they did not have the heritage of centuries to overcome, and they did not have a cultural tradition which had been twisted and battered by endless years of hatred and hopelessness, nor were they excluded—these others—because of race or color—a feeling whose dark intensity is matched by no other prejudice in our society.

Nor can these differences be understood as isolated infirmities. They are a seamless web. They cause each other. They result from each other. They reinforce each other.

Much of the Negro community is buried under a blanket of history and circumstance. It is not a lasting solution to lift just one corner of that blanket. We must stand on all sides and we must raise the entire cover if we are to liberate our fellow citizens.

One of the differences is the increased concentration of Negroes in our cities. More than 73 percent of all Negroes live in urban areas compared with less than 70 percent of the whites. Most of these Negroes live in slums. Most of these Negroes live together—a separated people.

Men are shaped by their world. When it is a world of decay, ringed by an invisible wall, when escape is arduous and uncertain, and the saving pressures of a more hopeful society are unknown, it can cripple the youth and it can desolate the man.

There is also the burden that a dark skin can add to the search for a productive place in society. Unemployment strikes most swiftly and broadly at the Negro, and this burden erodes hope. Blighted hope breeds despair. Despair brings indifference to the learning which offers a way out. And despair, coupled with indifference, is often the source of destructive rebellion against the fabric of society.

There is also the lacerating hurt of early collision with white hatred or prejudice, distaste, or condescension. Other groups have felt similar intolerance. But success and achievement could wipe it away. They do not change the color of a man's skin. I have seen this uncomprehending pain in the eyes of the little Mexican-American schoolchild that I taught many years ago. But it can be overcome. But, for many, the wounds are always open.

Perhaps most important—its influence radiating to every part of life —is the breakdown of the Negro family structure. For this, most of all, white America must accept responsibility. It flows from centuries of oppression and persecution of the Negro man. It flows from the long years of degradation and discrimination, which have attacked his dignity and assaulted his ability to provide for his family.

This, too, is not pleasant to look upon. But it must be faced by those whose serious intent is to improve the life of all Americans.

Only a minority—less than half—of all Negro children reach the age of eighteen having lived all their lives with both of their parents. At this moment, tonight, little less than two-thirds are at home with both of their parents. Probably a majority of all Negro children received federally aided public assistance sometime during their childhood.

The family is the cornerstone of our society. More than any other force it shapes the attitude, the hopes, the ambitions, and the values of the child. And when the family collapses it is the children that are usually damaged. When it happens on a massive scale the community itself is crippled.

So, unless we work to strengthen the family, to create conditions under which most parents will stay together—all the rest: schools, and playgrounds, and public assistance, and private concern, will never be enough to cut completely the circle of despair and deprivation.

There is no single easy answer to all of these problems. Jobs are part of the answer. They bring the income which permits a man to provide for his family.

Decent homes in decent surroundings and a chance to learn—an equal chance to learn—are part of the answer.

Welfare and social programs better designed to hold families together are part of the answer.

Care for the sick is part of the answer. An understanding heart by all Americans is another big part of the answer.

And to all these fronts—and a dozen more—I will dedicate the expanding efforts of the Johnson administration.

But there are other answers still to be found. Nor do we fully understand even all of the problems. Therefore, I want to announce tonight that this fall I intend to call a White House conference of scholars, and experts, and outstanding Negro leaders—men of both races—and officials of government at every level.

This White House conference's theme and title will be 'To Fulfill These Rights." Its object will be to help the American Negro fulfill the rights which, after the long time of injustice, he is finally about to secure; to move beyond opportunity to achievement; to shatter forever not only the barriers of law and public practice, but the walls which bound the condition of man by the color of his skin; to dissolve, as best we can, the antique enmities of the heart which diminish the holder, divide the great democracy, and do wrong—great wrong—to the children of God.

And I pledge you tonight this will be a chief goal of my administration, and of my program next year, and in years to come. And I hope, and I pray, and I believe, it will be a part of the program of all America.

For what is justice? It is to fulfill the fair expectations of man.

Thus, American justice is a very special thing. For, from the first, this has been a land of towering expectations. It was to be a nation where each man could be ruled by the common consent of all—enshrined in law, given life by institutions, guided by men themselves subject to its rule. And all—all of every station and origin—would be touched equally in obligation and in liberty.

Beyond the law lay the land. It was a rich land, glowing with more abundant promise than man had ever seen. Here, unlike any place yet known, all were to share the harvest.

And beyond this was the dignity of man. Each could become whatever his qualities of mind and spirit would permit—to strive, to seek, and, if he could, to find his happiness.

This is American justice. We have pursued it faithfully to the edge of our imperfections, and we have failed to find it for the American Negro.

So, it is the glorious opportunity of this generation to end the one huge wrong of the American nation and, in so doing, to find America for ourselves, with the same immense thrill of discovery which gripped those who first began to realize that here, at last, was a home for freedom.

All it will take is for all of us to understand what this country is and what this country must become.

The Scripture promises: "I shall light a candle of understanding in thine heart, which shall not be put out."

Together, and with millions more, we can light that candle of understanding in the heart of all America.

And, once lit, it will never again go out.

Special Message to the Congress on Civil Rights, February 28, 1963

PRESIDENT JOHN F. KENNEDY

John Fitzgerald Kennedy, brilliant author and statesman, has been ranked by some with Lincoln because of his forthright stand in the civil-rights crusade. Born in Brookline, Massachusetts, he was graduated from Harvard University, and immediately became active in the political arena. He served as United States Senator from Massachusetts from 1953 to 1961.

Profiles in Courage was written while he was recovering from an operation necessitated by injuries incurred as a skipper of a World War II torpedo boat. It won for him the Pulitzer Prize for Biography in 1957. In addition, he wrote *Why England Slept, Strategy of Peace,* and *To Turn the Tide.*

As thirty-fifth President of the United States, John F. Kennedy demonstrated an unusual versatility in language. He had an ardent concern for the welfare of man in society, and he strongly believed in the necessity for all citizens to participate in democratic governmental processes. Though he appealed to the intellect, his intimacy of manner gave conviction to his purpose. His proficiency was enlivened by a style that was clear, candid, precise, and direct.

Kennedy's speaking was a significant factor in his rapid rise to political heights. In the speeches presented in this volume, he succeeded in keeping Americans sensitive to their moral obligations, to the nation, and to the Negro as an American citizen. Even prior to his assassination on November 22, 1963, he was revered by Negro Americans for the forthright direction and concern he had given to the civil rights movement.

The "Special Message to Congress on Civil Rights" was delivered on February 28, 1963; and his "Radio and Television Report to the American People on Civil Rights," June 11, 1963, following a day of disorder which occurred at Tuscaloosa, Alabama, after the United States District Court had ordered that two Negroes be admitted to the University of Alabama.

* * *

SPECIAL MESSAGE TO CONGRESS ON CIVIL RIGHTS,
FEBRUARY 28, 1963

To the Congress of the United States:

"Our Constitution is color blind," wrote Mr. Justice Harlan before the turn of the century, "and neither knows nor tolerates classes among citizens." But the practices of the country do not always conform to the principles of the Constitution. And this message is intended to examine how far we have come in achieving first-class citizenship for all citizens regardless of color, how far we have yet to go, and what further tasks remain to be carried out—by the executive and legislative branches of the federal government, as well as by state and local governments and private citizens and organizations.

One hundred years ago the Emancipation Proclamation was signed by a President who believed in the equal worth and opportunity of every human being. That proclamation was only a first step—a step which its author unhappily did not live to follow up, a step which some of its critics dismissed as an action which "frees the slave but ignores the Negro." Through these long 100 years, while slavery has vanished, progress for the Negro has been too often blocked and delayed. Equality before the law has not always meant equal treatment and opportunity. And the harmful, wasteful, and wrongful results of racial discrimination and segregation still appear in virtually every aspect of national life, in virtually every part of the nation.

The Negro baby born in America today—regardless of the section or state in which he is born—has about one-half as much chance of completing high school as a white baby born in the same place on the same day—one-third as much chance of completing college—one-third as much chance of becoming a professional man—twice as much chance of becoming unemployed—about one-seventh as much chance of earning $10,000 per year—a life expectancy which is seven years less—and the prospects of earning only half as much.

No American who believes in the basic truth that "all men are created equal, that they are endowed by their Creator with certain unalienable rights," can fully excuse, explain, or defend the picture these statistics portray. Race discrimination hampers our economic growth by preventing the maximum development and utilization of our manpower. It hampers our world leadership by contradicting at home the message we preach abroad. It mars the atmosphere of a united and classless society in which this nation rose to greatness. It increases the costs of public welfare, crime, delinquency, and disorder. Above all, it is wrong.

Therefore, let it be clear, in our own hearts and minds, that it is not merely because of the Cold War, and not merely because of the economic waste of discrimination, that we are committed to achieving true equality or opportunity. The basic reason is because it is right.

The cruel disease of discrimination knows no sectional or state boundaries. The continuing attack on this problem must be equally broad. It must be both private and public—it must be conducted at national, state, and local levels—and it must include both legislative and executive action.

In the last two years, more progress has been made in securing the civil rights of all Americans that in any comparable period in our history. Progress has been made—through executive action, litigation, persuasion, and private initiative—in achieving and protecting equality of opportunity in education, voting, transportation, employment, housing, government, and the enjoyment of public accommodations.

But pride in our progress must not give way to relaxation of our effort. Nor does progress in the executive branch enable the legislative branch to escape its own obligations. On the contrary, it is in the light of this nationwide progress, and in the belief that Congress will wish once again to meet its responsibilities in this matter, that I stress in the following agenda of existing and prospective action important legislative as well as administrative measures.

I. The Right to Vote

The right to vote in a free American election is the most powerful and precious right in the world—and it must not be denied on the grounds of race or color. It is a potent key to achieving other rights of citizenship. For American history—both recent and past—clearly reveals that the power of the ballot has enabled those who achieve it to win other achievements as well, to gain a full voice in the affairs of their state and nation, and to see their interests represented in the governmental bodies which affect their future. In a free society, those with the power to govern are necessarily responsive to those with the right to vote.

In enacting the 1957 and 1960 Civil Rights Acts, Congress provided the Department of Justice with basic tools for protecting the right to vote—and this administration has not hesitated to use those tools. Legal action is brought only after voluntary efforts fail—and, in scores of instances, local officials, at the request of the Department of Justice, have voluntarily made voting records available or abandoned discriminatory registration, discriminatory voting practices, or segregated balloting. Where voluntary local compliance has not been forthcoming, the Department of Justice has approximately quadrupled the previous level of its legal effort—investigating coercion, inspecting records, initiating lawsuits, enjoining intimidation, and taking whatever follow-up action is necessary to forbid further interference or discrimination. As a result, thousands of Negro citizens are registering and voting for the first time—and many of them in counties where no Negro had ever voted before. The Department of Justice will continue to take whatever action is required to secure the right to vote for all Americans.

Experience has shown, however, that these highly useful acts of the eighty-fifth and eighty-sixth Congresses suffer from two major defects. One is the usual long and difficult delay which occurs between the filing of a lawsuit and its ultimate conclusion. In one recent case, for example, nineteen months elapsed between the filing of the suit and the judgment of the court. In another, an action brought in July, 1961, has not yet come to trial. The legal maxim "Justice delayed is justice denied" is dramatically applicable in these cases.

Too often those who attempt to assert their constitutional rights are intimidated. Prospective registrants are fired. Registration workers are arrested. In some instances, churches in which registration meetings are held have been burned. In one case where Negro tenant farmers chose to exercise their right to vote, it was necessary for the Justice Department to seek injunctions to halt their eviction and for the Department of Agriculture to help feed them from surplus stocks. Under these circumstances, continued delay in the granting of the franchise—particularly in counties where there is mass racial disfranchisement—permits the intent of the Congress to be openly flouted.

Federal executive action in such cases—no matter how speedy and how drastic—can never fully correct such abuses of power. It is necessary instead to free the forces of our democratic system within these areas by promptly ensuring the franchise to all citizens, making it possible for their elected officials to be truly responsible to all their constituents.

The second and somewhat overlapping gap in these statutes is their failure to deal specifically with the most common forms of abuse of discretion on the part of local election officials who do not treat all applicants uniformly.

Objections were raised last year to the proposed literacy-test bill, which attempted to speed up the enforcement of the right to vote by removing one important area of discretion from registration officials who used that discretion to exclude Negroes. Preventing that bill from coming to a vote did not make any less real the prevalence in many counties of the use of literacy and other voter qualification tests to discriminate against prospective Negro voters, contrary to the requirements of the Fourteenth and Fifteenth Amendments, and adding to the delays and difficulties encountered in securing the franchise for those denied it.

An indication of the magnitude of the overall problem, as well as the need for speedy action, is a recent five-state survey disclosing over two hundred counties in which fewer than 15 percent of the Negroes of voting age are registered to vote. This cannot continue. I am, therefore, recommending legislation to deal with this problem of judicial delay and administrative abuse in four ways:

First, to provide for interim relief while voting suits are proceeding through the courts in areas of demonstrated need, temporary federal voting referees should be appointed to determine the qualifications of applicants for registration and voting during the pendency of a lawsuit in any county in which fewer than 15 percent of the eligible number of persons of any race claimed to be discriminated against are registered to vote. Existing federal law provides for the appointment of voting referees to receive and act upon applications for voting registration upon a court finding that a pattern or practice of discrimination exists. But to prevent a successful case from becoming an empty victory, insofar as the particular election is concerned, the proposed legislation would provide that, within these prescribed limits, temporary voting referees would be appointed to serve from the inception to the conclusion of the federal voting suit, applying, however, only state law and state regulations. As officers of the court, their decisions would be subject to court scrutiny and review.

Second, voting suits brought under the federal civil-rights statutes should be accorded expedited treatment in the federal courts, just as in many state courts election suits are given preference on the dockets on the sensible premise that, unless the right to vote can be exercised at a specific election, it is, to the extent of that election, lost forever.

Third, the law should specifically prohibit the application of different tests, standards, practices, or procedures for different applicants seeking to register and vote in federal elections. Under present law, the courts can ultimately deal with the various forms of racial discrimination practiced by local registrars. But the task of litigation, and the time consumed in preparation and proof, should be lightened in every possible fashion. No one can rightfully contend that any voting registrar should be permitted to deny the vote to any qualified citizen, anywhere in this country, through discriminatory administration of qualifying tests, or upon the basis of minor errors in filling out a complicated form which seeks only information. Yet the Civil Rights Commission, and the cases brought by the Department of Justice, have compiled one discouraging example after another of obstacles placed in the path of Negroes seeking to register to vote at the same time that other applicants experience no difficulty, whatsoever. Qualified Negroes including those with college degrees have been denied registration for their inability to give a "reasonable" interpretation to the Constitution. They have been required to complete their applications with unreasonable precision—or to secure registered voters to vouch for their identity—or to defer to white persons who want to register ahead of them—or they are otherwise subjected to exasperating delays. Yet uniformity of treatment is required by the dictates of both the Constitution and fair play—and this proposed statute, therefore, seeks to spell out that principle to ease the difficulties and delays of litigation. Limiting the proposal to voting qualifications in elections for federal offices alone will clearly eliminate any Constitutional conflict.

Fourth, completion of the sixth grade should, with respect to federal elections, constitute a presumption that the applicant is literate. Literacy tests pose especially difficult problems in determining voter qualification. The essentially subjective judgment involved in each individual case, and the difficulty of challenging that judgment, have made literacy tests one of the cruelest and most abused of all voter qualification tests. The incidence of such abuse can be eliminated, or at least drastically curtailed, by the proposed legislation providing that proof of completion of the sixth grade constitutes a presumption that the applicant is literate.

Finally, the Eighty-seventh Congress—after twenty years of effort —passed and referred to the states for ratification a constitutional amendment to prohibit the levying of poll taxes as a condition to voting. Already thirteen states have ratified the proposed amendment and in three more one body of the legislature has acted. I urge every state legislature to take prompt action on this matter and to outlaw the poll tax—which has too long been an outmoded and arbitrary bar to voting participation by minority groups and others—as the Twenty-fourth Amendment to the Constitution. This measure received bipartisan sponsorship and endorsement in the Congress—and I shall continue to work with governors and legislative leaders of both parties in securing adoption of the anti-poll tax amendment.

II. Education

Nearly nine years have elapsed since the Supreme Court ruled that state laws requiring or permitting segregated schools violate the Constitution. That decision represented both good law and good judgment—it was both legally and morally right. Since that time it has become increasingly clear that neither violence nor legalistic evasions will be tolerated as a means of thwarting court-ordered desegregation, that closed schools are not an answer, and that responsible communities are able to handle the desegregation process in a calm and sensible manner. This is as it should be—for, as I stated to the nation at the time of the Mississippi violence last September:

... Our nation is founded on the principle that observance of the law is the eternal safeguard of liberty, and defiance of the law is the surest road to tyranny. The law which we obey includes the final rulings of the courts, as well as the enactments of our legislative bodies. Even among law-abiding men, few laws are universally loved—but they are uniformly respected and not resisted.

Americans are free to disagree with the law but not to disobey it. For in a government of laws and not of men, no man, however prominent or powerful, and no mob, however unruly or boisterous, in entitled to defy a court of law. If this country should ever reach the point where any man or group of men, by force or threat of force, could long defy the commands of our court and our Constitution, then no law would stand free from doubt, no judge would be sure of his writ, and no citizen would be safe from his neighbors.

The shameful violence which accompanied but did not prevent the end of segregation at the University of Mississippi was an exception. State-supported universities in Georgia and South Carolina met this test in recent years with calm and maturity, as did the state-supported universities of Virginia, North Carolina, Florida, Texas, Louisiana, Tennessee, Arkansas, and Kentucky in earlier years. In addition, progress toward the desegregation of education at all levels has made other notable and peaceful strides, including the following forward moves in the last two years alone:

Desegregation plans have been put into effect peacefully in the public schools of Atlanta, Dallas, New Orleans, Memphis, and elsewhere, with over sixty school districts desegregated last year—frequently with the help of federal persuasion and consultation, and in every case without incident or disorder;

Teacher training institutes financed under the National Defense Education Act are no longer held in colleges which refuse to accept students without regard to race, and this has resulted in a number of institutions opening their doors to Negro applicants voluntarily;

The same is now true of Institutes conducted by the National Science Foundation;

Beginning in September of this year, under the aid to Impacted Area School Program, the Department of Health, Education, and Welfare will initiate a program of providing on-base facilities so that children living on military installations will no longer be required to attend segregated schools at federal expense. These children should not be victimized by segregation merely because their fathers chose to serve in the armed forces and were assigned to an area where schools are operated on a segregated basis;

In addition, the Department of Justice and the Department of Health, Education, and Welfare have succeeded in obtaining voluntary desegregation in many other districts receiving "impacted area" school assistance; and, representing the federal interest, have filed lawsuits to end segregation in a number of other districts;

The Department of Justice has also intervened to seek the opening of public schools in the case of Prince Edward County, Virginia, the only county in the nation where there are no public schools, and where a bitter effort to thwart court decrees requiring desegregation has caused nearly 1,500 out of 1,800 school-age Negro children to go without any education for more than three years.

In these and other areas within its jurisdiction, the executive branch will continue its efforts to fulfill the constitutional objective of an equal, nonsegregated educational opportunity for all children.

Despite these efforts, however, progress toward primary and secondary school segregation has been too slow, often painfully so. Those children who are being denied their constitutional rights are suffering a loss which can never be regained, and which will leave scars which can never be fully healed. I have in the past expressed my belief that the full authority of the federal government should be placed behind the achievement of school desegregation, in accordance with the command of the Constitution. One obvious area of federal action is to help facilitate the transition to desegregation in those areas which are conforming or wish to conform their practices to the law.

Many of these communities lack the resources necessary to eliminate segregation in their public schools while at the same time assuring that educational standards will be maintained and improved. The problem has been compounded by the fact that the climate of mistrust in many communities has left many school officials with no qualified source to turn to for information and advice.

There is a need for technical assistance by the Office of Education to assist local communities in preparing and carrying out desegregation plans, including the supplying of information on means which have been employed to desegregate other schools successfully. There is also need for financial assistance to enable those communities which desire and need such assistance to employ specialized personnel to cope with problems occasioned by desegregation and to train school personnel to facilitate the transition to desegregation. While some facilities for providing this kind of assistance are presently available in the Office of Education, they are not adequate to the task.

I recommend, therefore, a program of federal technical and financial assistance to aid school districts in the process of desegregation in compliance with the Constitution.

Finally, it is obvious that the unconstitutional and outmoded concept of "separate but equal" does not belong in the federal statute books. This is particularly true with respect to higher education, where peaceful desegregation has been underway in practically every state for some time. I repeat, therefore, this administration's recommendation of last year that this phrase be eliminated from the Morrill Land Grant College Act.

III. Extension and Expansion of the Commission on Civil Rights

The Commission on Civil Rights, established by the Civil Rights Act of 1957, has been in operation for more than five years and is scheduled to expire on November 30, 1963. During this time it has fulfilled its statutory mandate by investigating deprivations of the right to vote and denials of equal protection of the laws in education, employment, housing, and the administration of justice. The Commission's reports and recommendations have provided the basis for remedial action both by Congress and the executive branch.

There are, of course, many areas of denials of rights yet to be fully investigated. But the commission is now in a position to provide even more service to the nation. As more communities evidence a willingness to face frankly their problems of racial discrimination, there is an increasing need for expert guidance and assistance in devising workable programs for civil-rights progress. Agencies of state and local government, industry, labor, and community organizations, when faced with problems of segregation and racial tensions, all can benefit from information about how these problems have been solved in the past. The opportunity to seek an experienced and sympathetic forum on a voluntary basis can often open channels of communication between contending parties and help bring about the conditions neccessary for orderly progress. And the use of public hearings—to contribute to public knowledge of the requirements of the Constitution and national policy—can create in these communities the atmosphere of understanding which is indispensable to peaceful and permanent solutions to racial problems.

The federal Civil Rights Commission has the experience and capability to make a significant contribution toward achieving these objectives. It has advised the executive branch not only about desirable policy changes but about the administrative techniques needed to make these changes effective. If, however, the Commission is to perform these additional services effectively, changes in its authorizing statute are necessary and it should be placed on a more stable and more permanent basis. A proposal that the Commission be made a permanent body would be a pessimistic prediction that our problems will never be solved. On the other hand, to let the experience and knowledge gathered by the Commission go to waste, by allowing it to expire, or by extending its life only for another two years with no change in responsibility, would ignore the very real contribution this agency can make toward meeting our racial problems. I recommend, therefore, that the Congress authorize the Civil Rights Commission to serve as a national civil-rights clearing house providing information, advice, and technical assistance to any requesting agency, private or public; that in order to fulfill these new responsibilities, the Commission be authorized to concentrate its activities upon those problems within the scope of its statute which most need attention; and that the life of the Commission be extended for a term of at least four more years.

IV. *Employment*

Racial discrimination in employment is especially injurious both to its victims and to the national economy. It results in a great waste of human resources and creates serious community problems. It is, moreover, inconsistent with the democratic principle that no man should be denied employment commensurate with his abilities because of his race or creed or ancestry.

The President's Committee on Equal Employment Opportunity, reconstructed by executive order in early 1961, has, under the leadership of the Vice-President, taken significant steps to eliminate racial discrimination by those who do business with the government. Hundreds of companies—covering seventeen million jobs—have agreed to stringent nondiscriminatory provisions now standard in all government contracts. One hundred four industrial concerns—including most of the nation's major employers—have in addition signed agreements calling for an affimative attack on discrimination in employment; and 117 labor unions, representing about 85 percent of the membership of the AFL-CIO, have signed similar agreements with the Committee. Comprehensive compliance machinery has been instituted to enforce these agreements. The Committee has received over 1,300 complaints in two years—more than in the entire seven and a half years of the Committee's prior existence—and has achieved corrective action on 72 percent of the cases handled—a heartening and unprecedented record. Significant results have been achieved in placing Negroes with contractors who previously employed whites only —and in the elevation of Negroes to a far higher proportion of professional, technical, and supervisory jobs. Let me repeat my assurances that these provisions in government contracts and the voluntary nondiscrimination agreements will be carefully monitored and strictly enforced.

In addition, the federal government, as an employer, has continued to pursue a policy of nondiscrimination in its employment and promotion programs. Negro high school and college graduates are now being intensively sought out and recruited. A policy of not distinguishing on grounds of race is not limited to the appointment of distinguished Negroes—although they have in fact been appointed to a record number of high policy-making judicial and administrative posts. There has also been a significant increase in the number of Negroes employed in the middle and upper grades of the career federal service. In jobs paying $4,500 to $10,000 annually, for example, there was an increase of 20 percent in the number of Negroes during the year ending June 30, 1962—over three times the rate of increase for all employees in those grades during the year. Career civil servants will continue to be employed and promoted on the basis of merit, and not color, in every agency of the federal government, including all regional and local offices.

This government has also adopted a new executive policy with respect to the organization of its employees. As part of this policy, only those federal employee labor organizations that do not discriminate on grounds of race or color will be recognized.

Outside of government employment, the National Labor Relations Board is now considering cases involving charges of racial discrimination against a number of union locals. I have directed the Department of Justice to participate in these cases and to urge the National Labor Relations Board to take appropriate action against racial discrimination in unions. It is my hope that administrative action and litigation will make unnecessary the enactment of legislation with respect to union discrimination.

V. Public Accommodations

No act is more contrary to the spirit of our democracy and Constitution—or more rightfully resented by a Negro citizen who seeks only equal treatment—than the barring of that citizen from restaurants, hotels, theatres, recreational areas, and other public accommodations and facilities.

Wherever possible, this administration has dealt sternly with such acts. In 1961, the Justice Department and the Interstate Commerce Commission successfully took action to bring an end to discrimination in rail and bus facilities. In 1962, the fifteen airports still maintaining segregated facilities were persuaded to change their practices, thirteen voluntarily and two others after the Department of Justice brought legal action. As a result of these steps, systematic segregation in interstate transportation has virtually ceased to exist. No doubt isolated instances of discrimination in transportation terminals, restaurants, restrooms, and other facilities will continue to crop up, but any such discrimination will be dealt with promptly.

In addition, restaurants and public facilities in buildings leased by the federal government have been opened up to all federal employees in areas where previously they had been segregated. The General Services Administration no longer contracts for the lease of space in office buildings unless such facilities are available to all federal employees without regard to race. This move has taken place without fanfare and practically without incident; and full equality of facilities will continue to be made available to all federal employees in every state.

National parks, forests, and other recreation areas—and the District of Columbia Stadium—are open to all without regard to race. Meetings sponsored by the federal government or addressed by federal appointees are held in hotels and halls which do not practice discrimination or segregation. The Department of Justice has asked the Supreme Court to reverse the convictions of Negroes arrested for seeking to use public accommodations; and took action both through the courts and the use of federal marshals to protect those who were testing the desegregation of transportation facilities.

In these and other ways, the federal government will continue to encourage and support action by state and local communities, and by private entrepreneurs, to assure all members of the public equal access to all public accommodations. A country with a "color blind" Constitution, and with no castes or classes among its citizens, cannot afford to do less.

VI. Other Uses of Federal Funds

The basic standards of nondiscrimination—which I earlier stated has now been applied by the executive branch to every area of its activity—affects other program not listed above:

Although President Truman ordered the armed services of this country desegregated in 1948, it was necessary in 1962 to bar segregation formally and specifically in the Army and Air Force Reserves and in the training of all civil-defense workers.

A new executive order on housing, as unanimously recommended by the Civil Rights Commission in 1959, prohibits discrimination in the sale, lease, or use of housing owned or constructed in the future by the federal government or guaranteed under the FHA, VA, and Farmers Home Administration program. With regard to existing property owned or financed through the federal government, the departments and agencies are directed to take every appropriate action to promote the termination of discriminatory practices that may exist. A President's Committee on Equal Housing Opportunity was created by the order to implement its provision.

A Committee on Equal Opportunity in the Armed Forces has been established to investigate and make recommendations regarding the treatment of minority groups, with special emphasis on off-base problems.

The U.S. Coast Guard Academy now has Negro students for the first time in its eighty-seven years of existence.

The Department of Justice has increased its prosecution of police-brutality cases, many of them in Northern states—and is assisting state and local police departments in meeting this problem.

State employee merit systems operating programs financed with federal funds are now prohibited from discriminating on the basis of race or color.

The Justice Department is challenging the constitutionality of the "separate but equal" provisions which permit hospitals constructed with federal funds to discriminate racially in the location of patients and the acceptance of doctors.

In short, the executive branch of the federal government, under this administration and in all of its activities, now stands squarely behind the principle of equal opportunity, without segregation or discrimination, in the employment of federal funds, facilities, and personnel. All officials at every level are charged with the responsibility of implementing this principle—and a formal interdepartmental action group, under White House chairmanship, oversees this effort and follows through on each directive. For the first time, the full force of federal executive authority is being exerted in the battle against race discrimination.

CONCLUSION

The various steps which have been undertaken or which are proposed in this message do not constitute a final answer to the problems of race discrimination in this country. They do constitute a list of priorities—steps which can be taken by the executive branch and measures which can be enacted by the eighty-eighth Congress. Other measures directed toward these same goals will be favorably commented on and supported, as they have in the past—and they will be signed, if enacted into law.

In addition, it is my hope that this message will lend encouragement to those state and local governments—and to private organizations, corporations, and individuals—who share my concern over the gap between our precepts and our practices. This is an effort in which every individual who asks what he can do for his country should be able and willing to take part. It is important, for example, for private citizens and local governments to support the State Department's effort to end the discriminatory treatment suffered by too many foreign diplomats, students, and visitors to this country. But it is not enough to treat those from other land with equality and dignity—the same treatment must be afforded to every American citizen.

The program outlined in this message should not provide the occasion for sectional bitterness. No state or section of this nation can pretend a self-righteous role, for every area has its own civil-rights problems.

Nor should the basic elements of this program be imperiled by partisanship. The proposals put forth are consistent with the platforms of both parties and with the positions of their leaders. Inevitably there will be disagreement about means and strategy. But I would hope that on issues of constitutional rights and freedom, as in matters affecting our national security, there is a fundamental unity among us that will survive partisan debate over particular issues.

The centennial of the issuance of the Emancipation Proclamation is an occasion for celebration, for a sober assessment of our failures, and for rededication to the goals of freedom. Surely there could be no more meaningful observance of the centennial than the enactment of effective civil-rights legislation and the continuation of effective executive action.

RADIO AND TELEVISION REPORT TO THE AMERICAN PEOPLE ON CIVIL RIGHTS
JOHN F. KENNEDY

Good evening, my fellow citizens:

This afternoon, following a series of threats and defiant statements, the presence of Alabama National Guardsmen was required on the University of Alabama to carry out the final and unequivocal order of the United States District Court of the Northern District of Alabama. That order called for the admission of two clearly qualified young Alabama residents who happened to have been born Negro.

That they were admitted peacefully on the campus is due in good measure to the conduct of the students of the University of Alabama, who met their responsibilities in a constructive way.

I hope that every American, regardless of where he lives, will stop and examine his conscience about this and other related incidents. This nation was founded by men of many nations and backgrounds. It was founded on the principle that all men are created equal, and that the rights of every man are diminished when the rights of one man are threatened.

Today we are committed to a worldwide struggle to promote and protect the rights of all who wish to be free. And when Americans are sent to Vietnam or West Berlin, we do not ask for whites only. It ought to be possible, therefore, for American students of any color to attend any public institution they select without having to be backed up by troops.

It ought to be possible for American consumers of any color to receive equal service in places of public accommodation, such as hotels and restaurants and theaters and retail stores, without being forced to resort to demonstrations in the street, and it ought to be possible for American citizens of any color to register and to vote in a free election without interference or fear or reprisal.

It ought to be possible, in short, for every American to enjoy the privileges of being American without regard to his race or his color. In short, every American ought to have the right to be treated as he would wish to be treated, as one would wish his children to be treated. But this is not the case.

The Negro baby born in America today, regardless of the section of the nation in which he is born, has about one-half as much chance of completing a high school as a white baby born in the same place on the same day, one-third as much chance of completing college, one-third as much chance of becoming a professional man, twice as much chance of becoming unemployed, about one-seventh as much chance of earning $10,000 a year, a life expectancy which is seven years shorter, and the prospects of earning only half as much.

This is not a sectional issue. Difficulties over segregation and discrimination exist in every city, in every state of the Union, producing in many cities a rising tide of discontent that threatens the public safety. Nor is this a partisan issue. In a time of domestic crisis men of good will and generosity should be able to unite regardless of party or politics. This is not even a legal or legislative issue alone. It is better to settle these matters in the courts than on the streets, and new laws are needed at every level, but law alone cannot make men see right.

We are confronted primarily with a moral issue. It is as old as the Scriptures and is as clear as the American Constitution.

The heart of the question is whether all Americans are to be afforded equal rights and equal opportunities, whether we are going to treat our fellow Americans as we want to be treated. If an American, because his skin is dark, cannot eat lunch in a restaurant open to the public, if he cannot send his children to the best public school available, if he cannot vote for the public officials who represent him, if, in short, he cannot enjoy the full and free life which all of us want, then who among us would be content to have the color of his skin changed and stand in his place? Who among us would then be content with the counsels of patience and delay?

One hundred years of delay have passed since President Lincoln freed the slaves, yet their heirs, their grandsons, are not fully free. They are not yet free from the bonds of injustice. They are not yet freed from social and economic oppression. And this nation, for all its hopes and all its boasts, will not be fully free until all its citizens are free.

We preach freedom around the world, and we mean it, and we cherish our freedom here at home, but are we to say to the world, and much more importantly, to each other that this is a land of the free except for the Negroes; that we have no second-class citizens except Negroes; that we have no class or caste system, no ghettos, no master race except with respect to Negroes?

Now the time has come for this Nation to fulfill its promise. The events in Birmingham and elsewhere have so increased the cries for equality that no city or state or legislative body can prudently choose to ignore them.

The fires of frustration and discord are burning in every city, North and South, where legal remedies are not at hand. Redress is sought in the streets, in demonstrations, parades, and protests which create tensions and threaten violence and threaten lives.

We face, therefore, a moral crisis as a country and as a people. It cannot be met by repressive police action. It cannot be left to increased demonstrations in the streets. It cannot be quieted by token moves or talk. It is a time to act in the Congress, in your state and local legislative body, and, above all, in all of our daily lives.

It is not enough to pin the blame on others, to say this is a problem of one section of the country or another, or deplore the fact that we face. A great change is at hand, and our task, our obligation, is to make that revolution, that change, peaceful and constructive for all.

Those who do nothing are inviting shame as well as violence. Those who act boldly are recognizing right as well as reality.

Next week I shall ask the Congress of the United States to act, to make a commitment it has not fully made in this century to the proposition that race has no place in American life or law. The federal judiciary has upheld that proposition in a series of forthright cases. The executive branch has adopted that proposition in the conduct of its affairs, including the employment of federal personnel, the use of federal facilities, and the sale of federally financed housing.

But there are other necessary measures which only the Congress can provide, and they must be provided at this session. The old code of equity law under which we live commands for every wrong a remedy, but in too many communities, in too many parts of the country, wrongs are inflicted on Negro citizens and there are no remedies at law. Unless the Congress acts, their only remedy is in the street.

I am, therefore, asking the Congress to enact legislation giving all Americans the right to be served in facilities which are open to the public—hotels, restaurants, theaters, retail stores, and similar establishments.

This seems to me to be an elementary right. Its denial is an arbitrary indignity that no American in 1963 should have to endure, but many do.

I have recently met with scores of business leaders urging them to take voluntary action to end this discrimination and I have been encouraged by their response, and in the last two weeks over seventy-five cities have seen progress made in desegregating these kinds of facilities. But many are unwilling to act alone, and for this reason, nationwide legislation is needed if we are to move this problem from the streets to the courts.

I am also asking Congress to authorize the federal government to participate more fully in lawsuits designed to end segregation in public education. We have succeeded in persuading many districts to desegregate voluntarily. Dozens have admitted Negroes without violence. Today a Negro is attending a state-supported institution in every one of our fifty states, but the pace is very slow.

Too many Negro children entering segregated grade schools at the time of the Supreme Court's decision nine years ago will enter segregated high schools this fall, having suffered a loss which can never be restored. The lack of an adequate education denies the Negro a chance to get a decent job.

The orderly implementation of the Supreme Court decision, therefore, cannot be left solely to those who may not have the economic resources to carry the legal action or who may be subject to harassment.

Other features will be also requested, including greater protection for the right to vote. But legislation, I repeat, cannot solve this problem alone. It must be solved in the homes of every American in every community across our country.

In this respect, I want to pay tribute to those citizens North and South who have been working in their communities to make life better for all. They are acting not out of a sense of legal duty but out of a sense of human decency.

Like our soldiers and sailors in all parts of the world they are meeting freedom's challenge on the firing line, and I salute them for their honor and their courage.

My fellow Americans, this is a problem which faces us all—in every city of the North as well as the South. Today there are Negroes unemployed, two or three times as many compared to whites, inadequate in education, moving into the large cities, unable to find work, young people particularly out of work without hope, denied equal rights, denied the opportunity to eat at a restaurant or lunch counter or go to a movie theatre, denied the right to a decent education, denied almost today the right to attend a state university even though qualified. It seems to me that these are matters which concern us all, not merely Presidents or Congressmen or Governors, but every citizen of the United States.

This is one country. It has become one country because all of us and all the people who came here had an equal chance to develop their talents.

We cannot say to 10 percent of the population that you can't have that right; that your children can't have the chance to develop whatever talents they have; that the only way that they are going to get their rights is to go into the streets and demonstrate. I think we owe them and we owe ourselves a better country than that.

Therefore, I am asking for your help in making it easier for us to move ahead and to provide the kind of equality of treatment which we would want ourselves; to give a chance for every child to be educated to the limit of his talents.

As I have said before, not every child has an equal talent or an equal ability or an equal motivation, but they should have the equal right to develop their talent and their ability and their motivation, to make something of themselves.

We have a right to expect that the Negro community will be responsible, will uphold the law, but they have a right to expect that the law will be fair, that the Constitution will be color blind, as Justice Harlan said at the turn of the century.

This is what we are talking about and this is a matter which concerns this country and what it stands for, and in meeting it I ask the support of all our citizens.

Thank you very much.

The Promise of Democracy
SENATOR ROBERT F. KENNEDY

Robert Frances Kennedy, son of Joseph Patrick and Rose (Fitzgerald) Kennedy, earned his Bachelor of Arts degree at Harvard and the Bachelor of Laws at Virginia Law School. Admitted to the Massachusetts bar in 1951 and the United States Supreme Court in 1955, having served as attorney in the criminal division of the Department of Justice in Washington, 1951–1952, he later received appointments as assistant counsel to the United States Senate permanent subcommittee on investigation (1953), chief counsel to the minority (1954), chief counsel to the United States Senate select committee on improper activities in labor management (1957–1960). He held the post of attorney general of the United States, 1961–1964. He was elected as United States senator from New York in 1965.

Among the books which he has authored are *The Enemy Within, Just Friends and Brave Enemies,* and *Pursuit of Justice.*

A serious contender for the Democratic nomination in the presidential campaign of 1968, he was assassinated in Los Angeles on June 5, 1968.

"The Promise of Democracy" is representative of his position as a liberal on the Civil Rights question in America. It was delivered at the annual meeting of the Missouri Bar Association in Kansas City, Missouri, September 27, 1963.

* * *

I am grateful for the opportunity to talk with this distinguished group.

Yours is one of the strongest and most vital bar organizations in the country. That you have won the American Bar Association's top Award of Merit twice within the last four years is an honor that speaks for itself—and I am impressed too by several other examples of your leadership in matters of civic concern.

Your scheduling of a discussion on the representation of the indigent accused is only one such example.

Everything I have read and heard about your activities suggests courage, high principle, and true engagement with the social realities of our time. You are to be congratulated.

But it is regrettable that the same spirit is not shared by all lawyers and public officials throughout the country. If it were, our nationwide problems in civil rights would be much less severe than they are.

To a far greater extent than most Americans realize, the crisis in civil rights reflects a crisis in the legal profession—in the whole judicial system on which our concept of justice depends.

I'd like to discuss three legal propositions with you. Each of them is part of a time-honored and noble tradition—and each of them, today, is being used to threaten the very foundations of law and order in this country.

The first is the proposition that it is proper and just to avail one-self of every legal defense to test either the validity or the applicability of a rule of law.

The second is that a court decision binds only those persons who are a party to it.

The third is that a court-made rule of law should always be open to re-examination, and is susceptible to being overruled on a subsequent occasion.

All three ideas are basic to our system of justice; none of them needs any explanation or defense to an audience of skilled advocates such as yourselves.

But today we have only to pick up a newspaper to see how these honorable principles—used in isolation, invoked in improper contexts, espoused as absolutes, and carried to extremes—have placed the sanctity of the law in jeopardy.

Separately and in combination, they are being proclaimed by lawyers and public officials as the justification for tactics to obstruct the enforcement of law and court orders—as the rationale, that is, for withholding justice and equality from the grasp of millions of our fellow Americans.

We are all familiar with the catch-phrases of that rationale, and with the air of righteous indignation in their utterance.

The argument goes something like this:

Brown versus the Board of Education is not the law of the land; it governs only one particular set of facts and is binding only upon the litigants of that case.

Only when each separate school district, each state, and each new set of administrative procedures has been tested and judged on its own merits can it be said that a binding decision has been reached.

And furthermore—so the argument goes—a decision like *Brown*, repugnant to certain segments of the population and clearly difficult to enforce, may conceivably be overruled as bad law.

To resist it, therefore, is merely to exercise one's constitutional right to seek reversal of a judicial ruling.

When stated that way and surrounded by rhetoric, the argument can be made to have a gloss of respectability. It can even take on the disguise of patriotic, high-minded dissent. Indeed, it is a position publicly espoused today by the governors of two states, by a past president of the American Bar Association, and by a federal district judge who recently overruled the *Brown* decision on grounds that its findings were erroneous.

We cannot blame a layman—even a reasonably fair-minded layman —for being confused and misled by this kind of reasoning.

But to lawyers, it smacks of duplicity. When it comes from the mouths of other lawyers, we must recognize it as professionally irresponsible. And when it comes from the mouths of public officials, we must recognize it as nothing more or less than demagoguery.

Let's go over those three legal principles one at a time. Let's examine each of them and look for the danger that lies within it.

What do we really mean, as lawyers, when we say that it is proper and constitutional to avail oneself of every legal defense?

Surely the Canons of Ethics make clear the impropriety of using dilatory tactics to frustrate the cause of justice.

We have only to imagine that principle being constantly applied across the board, in day-to-day litigation, to see that for all its validity it must be met by a counter principle—a concept that might be called the principle of good faith.

Every lawyer knows—though his clients may not—that nothing but national chaos would result if all lawyers were to object to every interrogatory, resist every subpoena *duces tecum* and every disposition, seek every possible continuance and postponement, frame unresponsive pleadings, and resist court orders to a point just short of contempt.

We know that tolerances are built into the system. We know what the margins for evasion and dilatory practices are—and we also know that the system would be hard put to stand up under a concerted effort to exploit them all.

There must obviously be a strong element of good faith, of reciprocity and cooperation, if our court system is to work at all. Take away that good faith, elevate the right to avail oneself of a technicality into an absolute—and you bring the very machinery of law to a standstill.

What about the second proposition—that a court decision binds only those who are a party to it? Clearly, this too is a principle that conceals as much as it says.

Every lawyer knows—though his clients may not—the distinction between the holding of a case and its rationale. We know that although the holding contains a specific disposition of a particular fact situation between the litigants, its reasoning enunciates a rule of law that applies not merely to one case but to all similar cases.

Often there is room for much discretion and honest disagreement as to when cases are alike or unalike. But clearly, in the matter of desegregation, there can be little or no room for argument in good faith as to when one situation is different—in the legal sense—from another in which the law has been laid down.

The county is different, the names of officials are different, but the situation—in all legally significant respects—is identical.

There is something less than truth in a lawyer who insists, nine years after the *Brown* decision and a hundred years after the Emancipation Proclamation, that a law of the land, a guarantee of human dignity and equality, is merely a law of a case.

We come now to the third principle—that a courtmade rule of law is always open to re-examination and must be viewed as susceptible to being overruled.

No one can prove in strict logic that any given case will never be overruled. But with regard to the *Brown* decision, I think we can all agree that the probability of its permanence is so overwhelming as to counsel the abandonment of anyone's hope for the contrary.

The decision was, after all, a unanimous one. Since 1954 there have been six vacancies in the Supreme Court, which means that by now a total of fifteen justices have endorsed it.

True enough, it was in itself an overruling of *Plessy v. Ferguson*, fifty-six years before. But that reversal had been widely expected through several generations of legal thought. The whole pattern of American and world history pointed to the abolishment of the "separate but equal" concept; and the reform established by the *Brown* decision was all but inevitable.

Moreover, and more importantly, it is clearly a decision that the vast majority of the American public holds to be morally correct.

To suggest, at this point in history, that there is any real likelihood of the *Brown* decision's being reversed is irresponsible to the point of absurdity.

No lawyer would advise a private client to contest the validity of a decision as solidly established and as often reiterated as this one; he would not want to victimize his client by raising frivolous questions.

Yet a client is being victimized every time this frivolous question is raised today—and the client is the American public itself.

Right now, all over the nation, the struggle for Negro equality is expressing itself in marches, demonstrations, and sit-ins. It seems very clear to me that these people are protesting against something more than the privations and humiliations they have endured for so long.

They are protesting the failure of our legal system to be responsive to the legitimate grievances of our citizens. They are protesting because the very procedures supposed to make the law work justly have been perverted into obstructions that keep it from working at all.

Something must be done—and it's a job that can only be done by members of the legal profession.

First, we have got to make our legal system work. We have got to *make* it responsive to legitimate grievances, and to do this we must work to prevent the unscrupulous exploitation of all the obstructive devices available within the system.

Only when our judicial system offers fair and efficient adjudication does it deserve the public confidence; and it seems to me that American lawyers everywhere have a clear obligation to make that confidence justified.

Second, we have a job of education to do. The public must be better informed about the nature of our legal system—and this includes a better understanding of each of the principles and counter-principles I have discussed with you today.

Only if we are able to instill that understanding will people with grievances begin to realize that there is a practical and realistic alternative to street demonstrations and sit-ins.

But we have to make sure both that there *is* an alternative, and that the nature of that alternative is clearly understood.

If we can accomplish this, I believe we will begin to see a new phase in the movement for civil-rights—an increased awareness that sit-ins and demonstrations do not in themselves cure social evils.

They serve to awaken the public conscience, and they can form a means of protest when no other means are available, but they will not dictate solutions; they can only alert us to the problems.

And in the long quest for solutions, we lawyers have a great deal to offer.

We are part of an intricate system that has developed over the centuries as man's best hope for resolving disputes and appraising policies—for working out solutions to problems.

If this system of law—of equal justice for all—can be kept viable, and if people of all backgrounds and of all races and creeds can begin to fully understand and fully take advantage of it, then—and only then—will we stand to realize the promise of democracy, both for ourselves and for the world.

Marching Blacks, 1965: Black Position Paper for America's 20,000,000 Negroes
CONGRESSMAN ADAM CLAYTON POWELL

Courageous and controversial, Adam Clayton Powell captured the imagination of his adherents in Harlem for the more than twenty years that he represented them in the Congress of the United States. He was educated at Colgate University and Columbia University. He has served as minister of the Abyssinian Baptist Church, with one of the largest congregations in the United States since 1937. He is author of *Is This a White Man's War?, Stage Door Canteen, Marching Blacks, Adam Clayton Powell,* and *Keep the Faith Baby.*

Time and time again Powell has spoken out against the white power structure in America for not yielding to justice and fair play in its treatment of the Negro. At times belligerent and at other times urbane, he has used all the tools of political agitation in his effort to gain social and economic equality for minority groups.

"Marching Blacks, 1965: A Black Position Paper for America's 20 million Negroes" was delivered at the annual banquet of the Ebenezer Missionary Baptist Church in Chicago, Illinois, on May 28, 1965.

* * *

Periodically in the conduct of American foreign policy, an important and comprehensive document is published outlining the official position of our government on a particular problem of foreign affairs.

This document is known as a "White Paper."

It is, in effect, a position paper, a statement of high purpose setting forth the historical reasons why the United States intends to alter its existing policy and pursue a new course in that area of foreign affairs.

An example was the famous White Paper on China in 1950.

Tonight, I would like to submit for your thoughtful consideration the topic: "Marching Blacks, 1965: A *Black* Position Paper for America's 20 million Negroes."

Twenty years ago, back in 1945—before the U.S. Supreme Court decision outlawing racial segregation in public schools, before the Montgomery bus boycott, before Birmingham or the March on Washington, I wrote a book called *Marching Blacks.*

Marching Blacks was the result of fifteen years of victories—victories in the picket lines on the sidewalks of New York City, victories at the bargaining table, victories in opening up new jobs for black people.

For a while, these victories continued and were repeated around the country. Then, a debilitating lull set in. Black people suffering from molting Uncle Tom leadership weakened in the fervor of their crusade as the white-conceived doctrine of "gradualism" took over the civil-rights movement.

Then, without warning, the explosive force of the Black Revolt thundered into reality. The black masses displaced our so-called "Negro leaders." And a new battlecry was framed by two words: "Freedom now!"

Victories were many in the Black Revolt, but still, no radical changes occurred in America's social structure.

Why? Because a revolt is only an interlude of social protest, a temporary resistance of authority.

To sustain these victories, to radically alter the face of white America and complete its cycle, the Negro Revolt must change into a Black Revolution. As the Negro Revolt was our Sunday of protests, so the Black Revolution must become our week of production.

This can only be done by Black people seeking power—audacious power.

Audacious power belongs to that race which believes in itself, in its heroes, in its successes, its deeds, and yes, even its misdeeds.

Audacious power begins with the stand-up-and-be-counted racial pride in being black and thinking black—"I am black, but comely, oh ye daughters of Jerusalem."

Audacious power is the determination of black people to be mayors, United States Senators, presidents of companies, members of stock exchanges; the power to decide elections and the capability to alter the course of history.

But one word blocks the realization of these goals: how?

Once black people have decided to pursue audacious power in the building of the Great Society, what steps do we take?

Tonight, I offer these steps and this is my Black Position Paper.

(1) Black organizations must be black led. The extent to which black organizations are led by whites, to that precise extent are they diluted of their black potential for ultimate control and direction.

(2) The black masses must finance their own organizations, or at least such organizations must derive the main source of their funds from black people. No other ethnic or religious group in America except Negroes permits others to control their organizations. This fact of organizational life is the crucible for black progress. Jews control Jewish organizations (there are no Italians or Irish on the board of directors of B'nai Brith). Poles control Polish-American organizations. But the moment a black man seeks to dominate his own organizations, he's labeled a "racist." And frightened black Uncle Toms quickly shun him and cuddle up to Mr. Charlie to prove their sniveling loyalty to the doctrine that "white must be right."

(3) The black masses must demand and refuse to accept nothing less than that proportionate percentage of the political spoils such as jobs, elective offices, and appointments which are equal to their proportion of the population and their voting strength. They must reject the shameful racial tokenism that characterizes the political life of America today. Where Negroes provide 20 percent of the vote, they should have 20 percent of the jobs.

This is not true of other ethnic groups who usually obtain political favors far in excess of their proportion. A good example for comparison are Chicago's Negroes and Polish-Americans. According to the 1960 census, there were 223,255 Polish-Americans and 812,637 Negroes in Chicago. There are now three Polish-American Congressmen from Chicago and only one Negro Congressman. Thus, with approximately one-fourth as many persons as Negroes, Polish-Americans nonetheless have three times as many Congressmen. That kind of inequity is not due to racial discrimination. It is due to racial apathy and stupidity.

(4) Black people must support and push black candidates for political office first, operating on the principle of "all other things being equal." This is a lesson you Chicago Negroes might well learn. In last April's primary in the heavily black Sixth Congressional District, you Chicago black people actually elected a dead white man over a live black woman. Only a few days ago, a young white candidate who only had going for him the fact that he was young and white, defeated an intelligent, dedicated black woman backed by all major civil-rights groups for alderman in a predominantly black ward.

(5) Black leadership in the North and the South must differentiate between and work within the two-pronged thrust of the Black Revolution: economic self-sufficiency and political power. The Civil Rights Act of 1964 has absolutely no meaning for black people in New York, Chicago, or any of the Northern cities. *De jure* school segregation, denial of the right to vote, or barriers to public accommodations are

no longer sources of concern to Northern Negroes. Civil rights in the North means more jobs, better education, manpower retraining, and development of new skills. As Chairman of the House Committee on Education and Labor, I control all labor legislation such as minimum wage, all education legislation, including aid to elementary schools and higher education, the manpower training and redevelopment program, vocational rehabilitation and of greater importance today, the "War on Poverty." This is legislative power. This is political power. I use myself as an example because this is the *audacious power* I urge every black woman and man in this audience to seek—the kind of political clout needed to achieve greater economic power and bring the black Revolution into fruition.

(6) Black masses must produce and contribute to the economy of the country in the proportionate strength of their population. We must become a race of producers, not consumers. We must rid ourselves of the welfare paralysis which humiliates our human spirit.

(7) Black communities of this country—whether it is New York's Harlem, Chicago's South and West sides, or Philadelphia's North side —must neither tolerate nor accept outside leadership—black or white. Each community must provide its own local leadership, strengthening the resources within its own local community.

(8) The black masses should only follow those leaders who can sit at the bargaining table with the white power structure as equals and negotiate for a share of the loaf of bread, not beg for some of its crumbs. We must stop sending little boys whose organizations are controlled and financed by white businessmen to do a man's job. Because only those who are financially independent can be men. This is why I earlier called for black people to finance their own organizations and institutions. In so doing, the black masses guarantee the independence of their leadership.

(9) This black leadership—the ministers, the politicians, businessmen, doctors, and lawyers—must come *back* to the Negroes who made them in the first place or be *purged* by the black masses. Black communities all over America today suffer from *absentee black leadership*. The leaders have fled to the suburbs and not unlike their white counterparts in black communities, use these communities to make their two dollars, then reject those who have made them in the first place as neighbors and social equals. This kind of double-dealing must stop.

(10) Negroes must reject the white community's carefully selected *ceremonial Negro leaders* and insist that the white community deal

instead with the black leadership chosen by black communities. For every *ceremonial Negro leader* we permit to led us, we are weakened and derogated just that much.

(11) Negroes must distinguish between desegregation and integration. Desegregation removes all barriers and facilitates access to an open society. Integration accomplishes the same thing, but has a tendency to denude the Negro of pride in himself. Negroes must seek desegregation, thereby retaining pride and participation in their own institutions just as other groups—the Jews, Irish, Italians, and the Poles have done. Negroes are the only group in America which has utilized the word, "integration," in pursuing equality.

(12) Demonstrations and all continuing protest activity must always be *nonviolent.* Violence even when it erupts recklessly in anger among our teen-agers must be curbed and discouraged.

(13) No black person over twenty-one must be permitted to participate in a demonstration, walk a picket line, or be part of any civil rights or community activity unless he or she is a registered voter.

(14) Black people must continue to defy the laws of man when such laws conflict with the law of God. The law of God ordains that "there is neither Jew nor Greek, there is neither bond nor free, there is neither male nor female: for ye are all one in Christ Jesus." Equal in the eyes of God, but unequal in the eyes of man, black people must press forward at all times, climbing toward that higher ground of the harmonious society which shapes the laws of man to the laws of God.

(15) Black people must discover a new and creative total involvement with ourselves. We must turn our energies inwardly toward our homes, our churches, our families, our children, our colleges, our neighborhoods, our businesses, and our communities. Our fraternal and social groups must become an integral part of this creative involvement by energizing their resources toward constructive fund raising and community activities. *This is no time for cotillions and teas.*

These are the steps I would urge all of America's 20 million black people to take as we begin the dawn of a new day by walking together. And as we walk together hand in hand, firmly keeping the faith of our black forebears, let us glory in what we have become and are today. Glory in the golden legacy of our shackled and tortured past.

Glory in the remembered greatness of black civilizations which built civilizations when white men huddled in caves.

Glory in the proud heritage of black heroes like Crispus Attucks, Sojourner Truth, Dorie Miller, and millions of black men whose blood, spilled all over the world in America's eight wars, has watered the lush foliage of American democracy and given it the beauty of ever-lasting life.

Glory in that mighty fortress of our strength—the Christian faith—"Oh Christ the solid rock I stand, all over ground is seeking sand!"

Brothers and sisters, I bring history up to date tonight. In closing, let me reach back again to those twenty years—1945—to my book *Marching Blacks*. Written in 1945, *Marching Blacks* survives in the potency of its message for black people twenty years later. All of you sitting out there this evening, in the glittering majesty of your black skins, are the *Marching Blacks* of 1965.

As a call to new greatness, as a call to the timelessness of our culture in the catalogues of human existence, as a call to cleave together in the building of the Great Society, I leave the following words from *Marching Blacks* written in 1945 with you on this evening of 1965:

This is what I am a product of—the sustained indignation of a branded grandmother, the disciplined resentment of my father and mother, and the power of mass action of the church. I am a new Negro—a marching black.

America has come upon easy days. We have grown soft. We need to return to the radicalism that made us what we were. Here the *New Negro* stands. That is why he is misunderstood. The *New Negro* is as radical—no more, no less—than Jefferson, Clay, Webster, and Tom Paine. . .

He will not stop until out of the rubble of present-day religion there rises an edifice that includes all races, all creeds, and all classes.

He will not stop until a people's democracy is born out of the rotten decaying political life of America.

The black man is out to save America, to salvage its best, and to take his position in the vanguard of those building an international order of brotherhood.

What will the white man's world do? Continue on its suicidal way to end ingloriously in a form of mass hara kiri? Try to stand outnumbered against the "fresh might" of a billion and a half non-Western people? If it does, the white man is finished— that is, the old white man. . . . The white voice that will trumpet in the South and call the people from their shame and decay will not echo from the vaulted corridors of the capital in Montgomery, Alabama. Somewhere along a black road turning the wearily exhausted red clay with a broken plow, shoeless and in blue jeans, some white will catch a glimpse of the Glory Road that the blacks have gone up.

He will sound the call, answering which men will find a new world waiting for them.

The trumpet call that will summon the new white man from the standards of "white man's civilization" may not be heard in gilded halls, but it will be heard across the fields and through the valleys in sharecroppers' shacks, in mines and mills, on heaving seas wherever the common man precariously seeks out his meager existence.

The black man continues on his way.

He plods wearily no longer—*he is striding freedom road with the knowledge that if he hasn't got the world in a jug at least he has the stopper in his hand!*

He is ready to throw himself into the struggle to make the dream of America become flesh and blood, bread and butter, freedom and equality. He walks conscious of the fact that he is no longer alone— no longer a minority.

He does not want the day of victory to be obtained through violence and bloodshed.

But of one thing he is positive. In the words of Sherwood Eddy, writing in his *Pilgrimage of Ideas*—"in the wrong way or the right way, through violence or nonviolence, it will surely come!"

Glory Hallelujah!

Let the Future Roll On
CARL ROWAN

Carl Rowan, one of America's foremost journalists, received the A.B. degree at Oberlin College and the M.A. degree at the University of Minnesota. As a newspaperman he gained valuable experience with the *Minneapolis Tribune* for fourteen years. In 1961 he became Deputy Assistant Secretary of State for Public Affairs. He was appointed United States Ambassador to Finland in 1963. Roman was Director of the United States Information Agency, 1964–65; since that time he has been a columnist for the Chicago *Daily News* and Publishers Newspaper Syndicate. *South of Freedom,* his first book, gained wide acceptance and this led him to write *Go South, Sorrow, Wait Till Next Year,* and *No Need for Hunger.*

Rowan has received numerous honors and awards for his writings. He was the recipient of the Sidney Hillman Award for Best Newspaper Reporting in 1952; he was selected as one of the ten outstanding young men in America by the United States Junior Chamber of Commerce in 1954; he received the Sigma Delta Chi Award in 1954 for the best general reporting on the segregation cases pending before the United States Supreme Court; he received the American Teamwork Award of the National Urban League in 1955; the Foreign Correspondent Medallion for articles on India in 1955; and the Foreign Correspondent Medallion for articles on Southeast Asia and coverage of the Bandung Conference in 1956.

The address included here was delivered at the NAACP Annual Convention "Youth Night" in Washington, D.C., on June 24, 1964.

* * *

Mr. Frazier, young leaders of the NAACP, ladies and gentlemen:

Mine is an extremely difficult task tonight. At a time when our hearts are full of apprehension about the fate of the three civil-rights workers in Mississippi, when we fear the momentary reporting of another shameful act of bestiality, at a time when you are yearning for deeds, I stand before you to talk.

For if this is a moment for action it is also a time for clear thinking and thoughtful planning.

I stand before you, then, to talk about what must be your most heartfelt concern and this nation's gravest domestic problem.

But it is so difficult to think sense or to talk sense or to listen to sense in a moment of ugly provocation. I remember Seneca's words: "A hungry man listens not to reason, nor cares for justice, nor is bent by any prayers."

When the Negro hungers for human dignity and is served up the ugly bones of social barbarism, perhaps it is too much to expect him to listen calmly to reason, or to weigh justice carefully, or to be bent by the prayers of those who know that the fate of our entire nation, our entire civilization, is wrapped up in this struggle to which you young people have devoted so much of your time and energy.

Still, I am happy to have the opportunity to speak to you tonight. I welcome this opportunity to say what I feel and what I believe you and I must do if we are to serve the cause of human freedom— not merely the cause of Negro freedom, or of liberty in the United States, but the freedom of a threatened mankind that thrashes about in a dark plethora of conflicts.

Let me, at the outset, pay personal tribute to the NAACP. This is one of the two organizations that were doing the tough and lonely jobs in the days before you were born—in those days when few Americans thought it sociable or profitable to make the civil-rights struggle their business. Those of us who hold high positions in government and industry today (and our "tribe" increases quite rapidly) dare not forget, and we do not forget, that without the long struggle in the courts and in the arena of public opinion by the NAACP, we would be far short of where we are today.

And I should like to pay special tribute to you young people. I respect you because you are wise enough to *stand for something*, and I admire you because against all kind of odds, and in the face of all manner of intimidations, you have moved resolutely to make your principles and your ideas a vital part of the fabric of America. By your courage to protest peacefully, even when so often faced with harassments and ugly violence, you have breathed new life and dignity into that First Amendment to our Constitution which guarantees the right of the people peaceably to assemble and to petition for redress of their grievances; by your willingness to face police dogs, fire hoses, and tear gas, you have shown the majority of America how base and evil a segment of our society is; and because in doing these things you have jarred America's conscience and awakened her sense of decency, you have given this nation a new appreciation of those ideals and principles to which we have given lip service for two centuries.

In this regard, when the front pages are full of stories about St. Augustine, Florida, and Philadelphia, Mississippi, it would seem easy to despair. But I beg you to remember that God leads men into deep waters not to drown them, but to cleanse them. Surely the towns and cities of America have been immersed in the deep waters of social conflict of racial readjustment these last few years, but there is genuine evidence that the heart and the spirit of America are being cleansed.

I note, for example, that when the NAACP last met in Washington —in 1947—hotel policies were such that the delegates stayed in private homes. This is progress, though surely not enough to satisfy you and me in this hour of our history.

For those of you who may nonetheless be tempted to despair, let me go back to World War II to those bleak moments in the fall and winter of 1940 when Nazi bombings of Britain had reached a horrible crescendo. London seemed almost leveled, Coventry was smashed, Birmingham was blasted. It was in this moment of tribulation that Britain's grand and gallant leader, Winston Churchill, said to his people:

Do not let us speak of sterner days. These are not dark days; these are great days—the greatest days our country has ever lived; and we must all thank God that we have been allowed each of us according to our stations, to play a part in making these days memorable in the history of our race.

I say with humble respect to all who have suffered, who have gone to jail, who have died in America's great struggle to widen the horizons of human freedom, that these are not dark days. They will be reckoned as the greatest days through which our country ever lived; they will be memorable days in the history of our race if you and I and the American people embrace the future in such a way as to ensure that no civil-rights martyr suffered or died in vain.

The future is up to us—to you and me. We face a future of unprecedented hope; or it can be a future of the greatest possible tragedy —not for the Negro, but for all America. I speak, of course, of the fact that in what surely must be regarded as one of its finest hours, the United States Congress has passed overwhelmingly a bill outlawing racial practices that have caused three centuries of humiliation and hardship for Americans of African descent. In a few days that bill will be the law of the land. At that moment, Americans will have spread before them a new standard of decency for our society—and a challenge to rise up to that standard.

The passage of that bill is a great achievement. I am sure that your children and my grandchildren will see its importance far clearer than we. But you and I ought to recognize that this historic breaching of cloture, this display of bipartisan leadership, this showing of White House resolution, is a sign that the United States intends to meet head on the kind of challenge on which other civilizations have foundered. You and I have a responsibility to our children, yes, but we also have a responsibility to help our country meet that challenge.

And let me say that even in the far corners of the world the significance of this action by Congress is clearly seen.

A newspaper in Taiwan said that "It will gradually exert an influence over the whole world just like the Declaration of Human Rights," And the Trinidad *Guardian* said that "The United States bill has advanced the cause of civil rights for everyone."

I note that in this country men already debate as to what this new law will mean. I can tell you what it will mean: only what you and I and the rest of the American people make it mean. And I am going to speak to you frankly about what I think the American Negro's course ought to be in his efforts to turn this law into real liberties and opportunities that will give American boys of every race, color, and creed an even chance in that hard race that we call the pursuit of happiness.

To make my first point, I must go back to 1961, when a young Negro came to my office in the State Department and challenged me with a question that went like this:

> How best do we Negroes move to wipe out injustice? In all this whole crazy world it is we who have been most reasonable. We have stayed with the law, followed the path of reason, and we have seen the law defied and reason rejected out of hand.
>
> Yet in faraway lands we have seen great uprisings of passion—passion that embraced violence—bear early fruits of freedom. Even in our own land, we have seen the passions of boys and girls sitting-in, kneeling-in, wading-in, riding-in, produce great changes.
>
> So is it not true that we must also reject reason and move to these techniques of passion?

To answer, I quoted these lines from Khalil Gibran's great book, *The Prophet:*

> Among the hills, when you sit in the cool shade of the white poplars, sharing the peace and serenity of distant fields and meadows—Then let your heart say in silence, "God rests in reason."
> And when the storm comes, and the mighty wind shakes the forest, and thunder and lightning proclaim the majesty of the sky,—then let your heart say in awe, "God moves in passion." And since you are a breath in God's sphere, and a leaf in God's forest, you too should rest in reason and move in passion.

What the prophet is saying to you and me and what I said to that youth is that we must never be foolish as to abandon reason—nor too timid to pour forth in passion our hatred for injustice.

Now let me repeat: it is not easy to be both reasonable and forceful about matters which involve our deepest emotions. But we must succeed in this; if we fail, first-class citizenship shall forever be a goal beyond our grasp.

Let me state the wisdom of Khalil Gibran in terms that have more direct bearing on your lives and mine:

You youth are too young to remember the tension and excitement that marked the entrance of a hard-swinging youngster named Jackie Robinson into big-league baseball. You don't remember how, when Jackie stepped to the plate, millions of brown arms (and other millions of white ones) vicariously helped him swing his bat or field a grounder —people who knew that what Jackie put in the box score would be a measure of the success of what then was thought to be a great experiment. And millions more Americans knew that as much as anything, Jackie had to win a public-relations battle. We know now that he did all these things in rare and superb style.

What is the result? The All-Star Team just selected by the players of the National League has an all-Negro outfield—and a Negro first baseman for good measure. Of the sixteen stars chosen in both the American and National Leagues, six are Negroes—a development that speaks rather eloquently of the success with which Robinson knocked down one of the country's oldest and silliest barriers.

I tell this story to illustrate the fact that progress in race relations must be made in many ways, on many fronts. There *is* need for peaceful demonstrations, for picketing, for lawsuits, for the many legitimate devices that aroused Negroes and concerned white Americans have devised to call their grievances to the attention of the American people.

But calamity awaits us if we forget that when all the protesting is done, there must also be those superbly qualified Negroes who can serve as pioneers in another way—those who by their superior abilities and personalities can open the door to wider opportunities. And once the pioneers have blazed the trail there must be followers capable of showing that the pioneers were no freaks. In baseball, the Larry Dobys, Roy Campanellas, Don Newcombes, and Willie Mayses were ready and able to do just that. And as we have just seen, Willie Mays was elected by 240 out of a possible 241 votes to this year's National League All-Star Team.

It is not easy to see, and it may seem inappropriate in this time of stress, but a situation comparable to baseball in the late 1940's exists in government and industry today. The trails have been or are being blazed. Bright new opportunities await the talented ambitious Negro in an assortment of professions and skills. For example, in the last year I have had at least twenty-five inquiries from newspapers, magazines, and television stations asking me to recommend young Negroes with skill and training in journalism. Now I am living evidence that you don't get rich in journalism; but you do eat regularly, and with an appetite whetted by the satisfaction that you are part of the vital process of enlightening human society, most of whose troubles as you will know rise from its lack of enlightenment.

For the good of the country you young people must prepare hurriedly to fill these communications posts and to blaze some new trails in many other areas for generations yet to come. I recognize that in some youth circles today a jail record is a badge of courage; I am constrained to remind you that a Phi Beta Kappa key is also a badge of honor—and no less a vital one in our struggle.

As the Civil Rights Bill takes effect, many new barriers inevitably must fall. How many fall, and how quickly, will still depend on how many of you youths are pounding at the door of opportunity—but pounding now not simply with the sledge hammer of racial anger and frustration, but hammering also with so fragile a thing as a diploma which sometimes will knock down more doors than will sledge hammers.

I note that in his keynote address, your great leader, Roy Wilkins, exhorted Negroes to "be smart rather than loud." That took courage on the part of Roy Wilkins, courage in a day when the Negroes' frustration and anger are such that any Negro who talks this way runs the risk of being called a "moderate," or worse, an Uncle Tom. But Mr. Wilkins was saying what the Negro must know and do if he is to win equality in a society where the mere numerical facts of life say that he cannot reach his goal through force and anger alone.

I say that not to cow you because of our minority status. Many a man with the smaller army and the smaller resources has wound up victorious because he turned out to be smarter than the other fellow, because he had the courage to go by his intellect rather than his emotions.

Let me again go back briefly to the troubles of Great Britain in World War II. As you know, Britain survived the ghastly bombings of 1940. But later, seven days after the Normandy invasion, another desperate threat came out of the skies over Britain. The first V-1 rocket exploded in the center of London, inaugurating a new, impersonal, more ruthless era of terror. It had been rumored since 1939 that the Nazis were working on secret weapons to attack Britain, and now rumor had become fact; pilotless aircraft; flying bombs with brains; speeding robots bearing death!

But Britain met this challenge through planning, perception, organization, and discipline. Using radar, fast P-51s, P-47s, and Spitfires intercepted and destroyed many of these rockets, sometimes in a truly ingenious way. One Spitfire pilot ran out of ammunition and made the great discovery that he did not need a gun to down one of these flying bombs. Weaponless and frustrated, he flew closer to one of the rockets until his wing tip was under the wing tip of the V-1, then he tipped his wing sharply and flipped the V-1. This upset the robot's gyros and it crashed short of its target.

Human ingenuity and daring added a vital new weapon to the fighter plane, the barrage balloon, and later the proximity fuze—the weapons with which Britain successfully withstood the assault of the forerunners of the deadly missiles that now grace the arsenals of the world.

How can we too add brain power to muscle power?

You know and I know that there will be some ignoble responses to the Civil Rights Act of 1964. The Negro will be smart if he lets the indignity, the ignobility, the ugliness be on the other side. You are aware and surely deplore the fact that no Negro sits in the Senate and thus none could vote for the Civil Rights Bill. But even in this there is a point worth remembering: the seventy-three votes in favor of that bill must be considered the symbol of white America's conscience at work—true enough, a conscience prodded and jarred by you and other Negro youth, by a new Negro militancy. But the fact remains that *it is* the conscience of white America which has helped to spell out this new standard of our society. And I say that before we rush rashly and irresponsibly into any adventures to prove what the new law does or does not mean, we ought to see how far this conscience of America will go in producing compliance with the new standard. We ought to let white Americans themselves show who intends to honor America and her new expression of ideals and who intends to dishonor this country by assuming the role of outlaw.

Do not mistake me. I do not counsel timidity or blind patience. I have made it clear over the years that while I attempt to be reasonable, I make no effort to be patient in the face of blatant injustice and indignity.

You and I would be doing the country and the cause of human freedom a disservice if we failed to utilize the new rights and opportunities guaranteed under this law—or if we failed to ask of the nation compliance on every count. But that is different from announcing to the press that at 2:30 tomorrow afternoon we intend to go test Joe's Greasy Hamburger Joint. What does it really prove when the world already knows that Joe is a bigot whose conscience and brain could be crammed into one of his salt shakers.

The wiser approach, it seems to me, is to move in a dignified way, a smart way, to use this bill to widen the horizons of freedom in those areas that are amenable, though perhaps reluctant, to change.

Don't use an elephant gun to hunt toads. Joe inevitably will get his comeuppance under the law—and under circumstances where no one can doubt that it is he who is the troublemaker.

May I close by suggesting a short code of conduct that I think young people might follow in the days immediately ahead:

(1) I shall so conduct myself and my protest efforts that no one can ever justly say that I exhibited less dignity, less responsibility, less self-respect than the Civil Rights Law of 1964 embodies and seeks to protect.

(2) Not only shall I oppose those who inject violence and hooliganism into the civil-rights struggle to the great discredit of those who have sacrificed in a dignified way, but I shall not attempt to use this law to stir up trouble for the mere fact of proving that trouble is still easy to find.

(3) At the same time, I shall regard seriously the guarantees of human rights included in this law, so I shall not accept racial indignities and discriminations in meek silence. In the normal course of acting like a full-fledged American citizen, I shall challenge, and ask my government to deal with, all who violate this new law.

(4) I shall not be unmindful of the limitations of law, or of the role of the private citizen, in promoting social change. So I shall so strive toward excellence that I shall be regarded as an asset to the law and its implementation, just as I expect the law to be an asset to me.

I hope that you do not think me presumptuous in suggesting that code, my young friends, but it sums up what I most earnestly wanted to say to you.

Other than that, I can only say, as Churchill did in those bleak days of 1940:

> I do not view the future with any misgivings. I could not stop it if I wished; no one can stop it. Like the Mississippi, it just keeps rolling along. Let it roll. Let it roll on full flood, inexorable, irresistible, benignant, to broader lands and better days.

Yes, let the future roll on. We cannot stop it. But we can put our mark on it.

Emancipation After One Hundred Years
GEORGE L. P. WEAVER

A graduate of Harvard University Law School, George Weaver is currently Assistant Secretary of Labor for International Affairs. He served as the Assistant to the Secretary-Treasurer of the Congress of Industrial Organizations from 1942 to 1955, and from 1955 to 1958 he was the director of the Civil-rights Committee for that organization. He was the assistant to the President of the International Union of Electronics, Radio, and Machine Workers from 1958 to 1960. Prior to this present position, he was Special Assistant to the Secretary of Labor. He has served as a United States delegate and representative at numerous international labor organization meetings.

The address which follows was delivered in commemoration of the one-hundredth anniversary of Emancipation and in celebration of Negro History Week at Central State College, Wilberforce, Ohio, on February 13, 1963.

* * *

It is a great pleasure as well as a signal honor to address you during this particular observance. We are at a decisive period in our history, and our civilization as we know it. In view of this program, it is obvious that you are quite cognizant of this fact, also. We celebrate Citizenship and Negro History Week in a period of great progress. We have far to go, it is true, but as President Kennedy points out, let us measure by how far we have come as well as by how far we must go. And as we all know, we have come a long way since the days of Frederick Douglass.

Since World War II we have been engaged in an ideological conflict such as the earth has not witnessed since the Reformation period. We are seeing the ideals that we subscribe to gaining acceptance. From a sprawling frontier nation in which rigid isolationism and independence was a way of life, to the leader of the earth's free countries has been realized in less than two centuries. This transition has brought with it a realization of the interdependence of peoples and nations.

Our national objectives are developing a more positive form and shape as we shake off the enchantments of years past. We now know that our own security and progress is contingent on the security and progress of all nations. More and more we now recognize that real independence and self-determination for peoples and nations are mandatory if we, ourselves, are to realize a society based upon freedom and justice.

IN THE LENGTHENING SHADOWS OF TWO GREAT MEN

Our civilization—that strange amalgam of all that man has created to date—is on the threshold of the greatest period of enlightenment and plenty since the world began. Yet, there are those who say that science has created a diabolical force that is leading us in the paths of destruction. But I am optimistic for mankind; I believe that science is creating a unifying force that makes self-evident the absolute necessity of men and nations to walk in the paths of brotherhood. And so I feel it most appropriate that we meet today commemorating the spirit of two men who, by their deeds and what they stood for a century ago, hold out to us the promise of greater tomorrows. Frederick Douglass represents the triumph of courage and the spirit—he will represent for the ages the indomitable spirit of man to be free. Abraham Lincoln represents the triumph of wisdom and compassion. We meet today with their examples before us, not alone to sustain us but to kindle in us anew the magnificent flame for which they provided the original spark to light our way to a better, richer, fuller America.

As most of you may know, my main preoccupation these days is the arena of international affairs. And in thinking about what I might say to you today that would be meaningful, I began to think of Abraham Lincoln and Frederick Douglass. I recalled the fact that they knew one another quite well. Each had great respect for the other—the President of the United States and the former slave. Then I began to think of the vast differences in our nation's role in foreign affairs now and a century ago, when Lincoln and Douglass stalked the stage of American history. At that point in time, a century ago, the United States were not very united, and Lincoln was proving an invaluable point in his determination to save the Union, for in saving the Union physically, he also was saving it morally and spiritually.

President Lincoln was sorely pressed on all sides at that time, for America's foreign affairs in 1863 were not too much better than her domestic affairs—although at least the United States was not involved in a shooting war abroad. But the sympathies of England, France, and Spain were definitely pro-Confederate, and in varying degrees all three countries lent physical and moral support to the rebellious South. Somewhat balancing the scales, however, was the fact that the Scandinavian countries, Prussia, and Russia, especially, which had just freed its serfs, lent their moral support to President Lincoln and the North. Communications, transportation, and diplomacy were primitive, and the science of weaponry was in its infancy. This was the picture a century ago when Abraham Lincoln signed the Emancipation Proclamation, and the reverberations of that act have echoed abroad down the years. That piece of paper, signed by an embattled President, amid a bitter, fratricidal war, spelled the beginning of the end for one form of human oppression and provided the world with moral guidelines for the eventual dissolution of other types of human oppression.

Although I have nothing to substantiate my theory, whenever I think of the Emancipation Proclamation, I cannot help but feel that as Lincoln affixed his name to it the indomitable spirit of Frederick Douglass helped guide his hand, for he knew full well that Douglass epitomized the heights to which man could climb once given the opportunity to fulfill his aspirations. And though I well know the Emancipation Proclamation had many political implications, it was as equally immersed in spiritual and moral values.

Thus are we all beneficiaries of the heritage of Lincoln and Douglass. Darkened souls and battered spirits the world over have been brightened and uplifted by the mere recounting of their deeds and what they meant to a troubled people in a divided land. I believe it is up to each generation to renew the traditions and teachings of these two giants, so that oppressed peoples everywhere may ever know what heights humanity can scale in its never ending quest for freedom with justice and dignity. Daniel Webster once said that "God grants liberty only to those who love it, and are always ready to guard and defend it." I know that we here today feel the truth of these words quite deeply. And this idea is the underlying theme behind our own country's relations with other governments and peoples.

EMANCIPATION AND PRESENT REVOLUTION

When I said at the beginning that we are in a momentous period, I meant precisely that. A worldwide revolution is transpiring before our very eyes. Nations and peoples long subjugated by backwardness and exploitation, are rising, like Neptune, from seas of ignorance and distress, to throw off the burden of time and oppression, and take their rightful place in today's society of sovereign states. As a matter of fact, approximately forty-seven nations have gained their freedom since the birth of the United Nations in 1945. And the pride for Americans is not so much that these countries are emerging from darkness to light, for this would be inevitable in the natural course of time, but that the United States of America is encouraging and assisting these peoples with what is surely the most selfless program of help between nations in the history of the world.

Of course we are all aware that this impulse does not stem from a spirit of pure altruism alone. Originally it began as a means of combating the encroachment of a cynical form of Communist colonialism. But it cuts much deeper than that today. The success of the Peace Corps, from its conception only two years ago, tells us much. And it tells people abroad much more; for I think it goes a long way toward making more clear what Stephen Vincent Benét called the "American muse, whose strong and diverse heart so many men have tried to understand."

We have learned much over the years. We know that a strong, self-reliant country, versed in the ways of freedom, aided in the process of economic, social, and spiritual development, will not be an easy prey for Communist ideology. We know that communism flourishes in the conditions of poverty, of hunger, and of unequal opportunity. It has an appeal that all too often succeeds in distorting the legitimate expectations of people just starting to realize the reach of human potential. It is particularly dangerous to those nations—many of them very new on the calendar of statehood—that have not formulated the democratic values essential to the proper functioning of a free society. This is the basic thinking behind the type of assistance we offer those nations desiring help. And I believe it accounts in part for the Peace Corps' dramatic success. Unlike the Soviets, we are not selling ideology but self-development. The only revolution we are exporting is aimed at ignorance, poverty, and disease.

WHAT AMERICAN FOREIGN AFFAIRS MUST MEAN

Now although I point to the Peace Corps and much of our foreign aid program as a success, it is not my thesis that this is any cause for self-congratulation. I think we are just beginning to realize that the game of foreign affairs is really not a game at all where you have a winner or a loser, or a predictable beginning or ending. It is a continuing struggle—a struggle in which there will be no final culmination, just as there will be no culmination in our own struggle for betterment. Like the striving after salvation, it is a continuing thing, constantly testing our mettle as a free people, constantly seeking renewal by each succeeding generation.

Many qualities are needed for the continuation of this struggle, but I would say that the primary need is for staying power. We cannot, *we should not expect* any quick or final resolution of our problems, for we shall, in our time, always face crises, hazards, and reverses. We must condition ourselves to expect this, for such is the period in which we live.

But there are certain satisfactions we may derive from these struggles, not the least of these being the clarifying of our own ideals. In assisting other nations toward social and economic fulfillment, we make more definite our own similar values here at home. As our national objectives are broadened, so are our domestic objectives. As we strive toward real independence and a free and orderly development of three-quarters of the earth's nations, so shall we move toward the same goals for all people in this country. For just as we have learned that to keep a man down one must, himself, stay down there with him, we also know that to raise a man to a better life, one must inevitably uplift himself at the same time. We may derive satisfaction from the fact that as far as western Europe and Japan are concerned, we have long since ceased to send them material aid. They are now partners in aid. Flat on their backs fifteen years ago, they now contribute 40 percent of free-world aid—as much in proportion to their gross product as we do. And we encourage them to increase this amount yearly.

Day after day we find increasing proof in the correctness of our premise that the developing countries need tools and skills, not ideology and guns. We are entering an era in which the diplomacy of economics speaks louder than gunbots, treaties, or protocol. We are seeing additional signs of success in countries like Taiwan, Greece, and Israel that will soon be able to stand on their own feet and join the west European countries and Japan. To a degree not realized by the American people, we are already concentrating our material assistance on a selective basis. Last year, for example, 80 percent of the development loans administered by the Agency for Internationnal Development went to six countries, while two-thirds of our aid to strengthen countries fighting for survival went to nine countries.

Fundamental lessons are being learned, in brief periods of time, not only by other countries, but by our own, too. Five years ago we were not preoccupied with Africa or Latin America. Today in these areas, despite a multitude of problems, we see not only progress and hope, but an increasing realization that the way of the West holds more promise than that of a closed and dogmatic society. Country after country has flirted with rigid centralism only to be disillusioned. And I believe that the greatest disillusionment, which has opened wide the eyes of the unaligned world, came when the Chinese troops made their drive across the Himalayas into India.

Very recently we saw the Congolese in Africa request the United Nations to help in maintaining law and order and the territorial integrity of that strife-torn country. The United Nations acted and thereby averted civil war in the Congo and, incidentally, a possible confrontation between the United States and the Soviet Union. Now the United Nations, with the participation of our country, is taking the initiative toward helping the Congolese to rebuild their economy. An Agency for International Development, headed by Assistant Secretary of State Harlan Cleveland, is now in the Congo helping them to work out a program of peaceful development.

Five years ago there were at best a handful of countries "formally neutral but informally on our side." Today this category is large and increasing. This does not mean that they will blindly follow us on every United Nations vote, but it does indicate that on basic issues we and they are finding a broad consensus of agreement.

The wind is slowly rising in the West and the tide flows with us. We used to feel that we were facing a monolithic apparatus, remorselessly united in both strategy and tactics. Five years ago it was the West, still suffering from the shock of Suez, that was bitterly divided. Today we find the East preoccupied with criticism and countercriticism. We are able to detect signs of a deep cleavage in the Communist world. The attitude toward Stalin, failure in meeting agriculture targets, the position on coexistence, and the thrust into India, the approach to the Cuban crisis—all these are acrimonious issues within the Communist bloc. This is not to say that the threat facing us is less, or that the divisions among the free countries cannot cause difficulties. But it can be said that the free world has entered 1963 economically stronger and politically more respected than it has been since the cold war began.

Let us reflect for a moment on this fantastic period of change through which we are moving.

ON TAKING THE OFFENSIVE WITH CHANGE

Secretary of Labor Wirtz has said,

the presiding fact in our time . . . is the fact of change, and . . . the common denominator of all our difficulties is dealing with change honestly and wisely and constructively. The important thing is how to take the offensive with change and to make it . . . the instrument of man's deliverance, instead of permitting it to become the instrument of his destruction.

This is a noble task, one offering unlimited challenge for each generation of youth.

In this era of accelerated change, of technology triumphant, of exploding population where maps change as fast as women's fashions and where continents are now closer together in time than county seats were yesterday, you are at the doorway to unlimited opportunity. The dominant fact of your generation is that each individual who is well trained has no limit to realizing his ambitions. Color is not the limiting factor to your generation that it was to your parents. Their struggles and sacrifices have diminished this factor. Today, the most important limitations to realizing your ambitions are the ones you circumscribe for yourself. As Franklin Roosevelt said shortly before he died, "The only limit to our realization of tomorrow will be our doubts of today."

The field of international relations, for example, is open to everyone interested in serving our country in a vital, meaningful way, and possessing the necessary qualifications to perform this service. This brings up a subject about which I feel quite strongly—namely, effective preparation for work in the international area. So often these days we see young men and women, fresh out of college and anxious to become involved in the field of foreign affairs, and—I am afraid—not well enough prepared for it.

There are three areas of study which I feel are positively mandatory for a person to be concerned with if he plans a career in the foreign service. They are, first, English or grammar, because there is a great need for communication, a need for self-expression, for writing accurate reports; second, history, because it is important to have a thorough knowledge of our own country's past before one can successfully work with other countries; and finally what I choose to call "the arts of government"—how nations function, how the democratic as well as other processes work. I advise all young people to know these subjects well. There are unlimited careers in all forms of public service, but in these days they go to those best qualified. Bright, fresh talent is always needed in the conduct of our foreign affairs. Remember, the winds and tides that are slowly shifting in our favor are, for the most part man made. America's youth will have to provide the manpower today to favorably control those winds and tides tomorrow.

What a far road we have traveled since Lincoln signed the Emancipation Proclamation. Here we are, a century later in the year 1963. And from today's promontory of time and events it is very clear to me that the Emancipation of a century ago will always serve to guide present and future generations of enslaved peoples to individual freedom and economic fulfillment. Such is the heritage of Abraham Lincoln and such is the example of Frederick Douglass. No words could be more appropriate in closing than these lines from a prayer to the United Nations given in 1942 by President Franklin D. Roosevelt:

Grant us brotherhood, not only for this day but for all our years— a brotherhood not of words but of acts and deeds. We are all of us children of earth—grant us that simple knowledge. If our brothers are oppressed, then we are oppressed. If they hunger, we hunger. If their freedom is taken away, our freedom is not secure.

Our earth is but a small star in the great universe. Yet of it we can make, if we choose, a planet unvexed by war, untroubled by hunger or fear, undivided by senseless distinctions of race, color, or theory.

Civil Rights for Americans
SENATOR STEPHEN M. YOUNG

Stephen Young, United States Senator from Ohio, was graduated from Western Reserve University in 1911 and admitted to the Ohio bar in the same year. He entered political life as special counsel to the attorney general, and served as a member of the Ohio General Assembly from 1913 to 1917. In 1917, he became prosecuting attorney of Cuyahoga County, Ohio. In addition, he was an at-large member from Ohio of the Seventy-third, Seventy-fourth, Seventy-seventh, and Eighty-first Congresses. He has been a member of the United States Senate since 1958. Young is past president of the Cuyahoga County Bar Association and past president of the War Veterans Bar Association of Cleveland.

It was in October, 1962, that the Senator made his virulent oratorical attack, "The Tragedy of Mississippi," against those who precipitated the riot which took place at the University of Mississippi against admitting Negro James H. Meredith. On June 19, 1964, just prior to the enactment of the Civil Rights Act of July 4, 1964, in a short but spirited address, he challenged Americans to take a step forward on the path to mutual tolerance and understanding in the following speech, "Civil Rights for Americans."

* * *

Mr. President, early in 1959, shortly after I took the oath of office in the Senate, in a newsletter which I sent to my constituents in Ohio, as an additional service as their Senator, I wrote:

> This Congress should expand civil rights and protect civil liberties. We should support the Supreme Court of the United States and its decisions as the law of the land. Daily we hear and read arguments for and against segregation and suggestions to compromise troublesome questions of civil rights. There just cannot be any compromise on civil rights. Either you are for the Supreme Court decision or you are resisting law and order. Racial problems are, in reality, moral problems and not political issues. Let us remember at all times, we are the nation which chiseled on our Statue of Liberty:
> "Give me your tired, your poor,
> Your huddled masses yearning to breathe free;
> Send these, the homeless, tempest-tossed to me;
> I lift my lamp beside the golden door."

Today, after near three months of debate, the hour of decision is at hand. I would not feel right if I did not at this time manifest my complete admiration for the majority and minority leaders, the Senator from Montana (Mr. Mansfield) and the Senator from Illinois (Mr. Dirksen), and also for the assistant majority leader, the Senator from Minnesota (Mr. Humphrey), and the assistant minority leader, the senator from California (Mr. Kuchel).

I wish at this time also to manifest my admiration for the diligence and the great work on this legislation which was done by so many of our colleagues in the Senate, including the senior Senator from Pennsylvania (Mr. Clark), and the junior Senator from Michigan (Mr. Hart).

In this hour of crowning glory, when after a worrisome debate of nearly three months, we shall pass this amended bill—which is, in fact, a greatly improved bill over that which was sent to us from the other body—let us not forget that great President John F. Kennedy, who fought for all Americans and brought this matter to a focus within a few months after he became President of the United States.

He was a great spokesman and a great leader who advocated, as Chief Executive of our Nation, that we must accord to all citizens of the United States complete civil liberties and civil rights, and that there were to be no second-class citizens in this nation.

From the sunshine of happiness and joy of Los Angeles in the summer of 1960, to that dark, bitter, desolate day of last November, as a humble Senator of the United States, I walked along with John F. Kennedy all the way from Los Angeles to Arlington. He was right at every turn of the road.

Within a short time we shall close this historic debate. We shall cast our vote. We shall demonstrate to the people of the world that ours must be and will be a nation in which no one is forgotten, where the young have faith, the aged have hope, and where all stand equal before the law, and protected in all their civil liberties.

For too long, 20 million Americans have been denied their basic rights, the basic rights that our forefathers envisioned when they conceived the Constitution of the United States and wrote the Declaration of Independence.

It is left to us to guarantee those rights for all citizens. They have been affirmed in the courts as belonging to all Americans, not to almost all of them.

The breath-taking pace of modern life no longer permits slow, leisurely adjustments to reality. We are not establishing any new rights. We are only seeking to preserve old rights, rights as old as mankind itself.

I have received many letters from uninformed and misguided constituents, as have many of my colleagues. Those people fear that the civil-rights proposal will in some way infringe upon their liberty and their way of life, even in my state of Ohio. There is nothing whatever, of course, in the final amended bill, that has been so thoughtfully debated for a period of nearly three months, that would give to the Negroes of this nation any rights or privileges which they have not enjoyed in my state of Ohio for many years past under the law of my State. I am proud that this is so. What this legislation will do will be to extend those rights to all Americans, regardless of the states in which they live or in which they travel.

I do not want to take much more time on this subject. All of us will agree that passing this fine, amended bill, agreement to it by the

House of Representatives and then sending the bill to the White House so that it may be signed by our President and become the law of the land on a very fitting day indeed—July 4, 1964—will not immediately abolish injustice.

That must come, Mr. President, through the growing understanding and good will of the people of the fifty states of our Union. However, the legislation which we have worked on, and which we shall pass in this chamber within a period of two hours or less, will at last extend the assurances of our Constitution, our Declaration of Independence, and our heritage of freedom to all Americans, regardless of their race or color. It will be a step forward on that long path toward mutual tolerance and understanding.

Along with so many of my colleagues, it will be a happy occasion when I can cast my vote "yea" in favor of the bill.

PART FOUR

Legal Officials

Since the May 17, 1954, decision of the United States Supreme Court, cracks have begun to appear consistently in the wall of segregation. Though principles must be implemented before they can be effective, they must first be established. Thus, the judiciary, through the *Brown* decision, was the first federal agency to give full impetus and meaning to the grand effort to promote equality for all Americans.

Furthermore, the Justice Department, with unprecedented vigor, has been researching the whole area of civil rights and has been an important arm of the federal government in defining the problem and in attempting to translate our national policy into meaningful reality.

The National Association for the Advancement of Colored People maintains a battery of lawyers as a bulwark to its commitment of assisting the Negro to achieve full participation in society. Thurgood Marshall's brilliant efforts in defending the Negro's rights before the nation's highest tribunal are now legendary.

A long series of court decisions gave statutory precedent and virility to the Civil Rights Act of 1964. In addition, scores of courageous lawyers have offered their services to promote lasting reforms that would assist the federal government in its responsibility for securing equality for Negro citizens.

I, TOO
Langston Hughes

I, too, sing America.

I am the darker brother.
They send me to eat in the kitchen
When company comes,

But I laugh,
And eat well,
And grow strong.

Tomorrow,
I'll be at the table
When company comes.
Nobody'll dare
Say to me,
"Eat in the kitchen,"
Then.

Besides,
They'll see how beautiful I am
And be ashamed—

I, too, am America.

The American Negro's New World and New Purpose

JUDGE RAYMOND PACE ALEXANDER

Raymond Pace Alexander, born in Philadelphia, Pennsylvania, was graduated from the University of Pennsylvania and the Harvard Law School. He has been active in civil and criminal trial practice since 1923. Because of his reputation in the legal profession, he has served as counsel for the National Medical Association, the National Baptist Convention, and the Philadelphia chapters of the National Association for the Advancement of Colored People. He was Counsellor for the Haitian Embassy in Washington from 1946 to 1949. As a member of the Philadelphia City Council from 1951 to 1958, he was Chairman of the Committee on Public Property and Public Works. In 1959, he was appointed to his current post as Judge of the Court of Common Pleas in Philadelphia. The American Jewish Congress honored him in 1950 because of his outstanding contribution in the field of civil liberties. He is a member of the board of directors of the Philadelphia Crime Prevention Association, chancellor of the Philadelphia Cotillion Society, and past director of the Philadelphia Council of Churches.

He has been a forthright spokesman, with pen and voice, for the civil-rights cause. Such periodicals as *Crisis, The Journal of Negro*

Education, The Journal of Negro History, and *The Negro History Bulletin,* have projected his scholarly concern in behalf of the Negro American.

"The American Negro's New World and New Purpose" was delivered March 19, 1965, at the Charter Day Ceremonies at Central State College, Wilberforce, Ohio.

* * *

> We cry among the skyscrapers as our
> ancestors cried among the palms in
> Africa. . . . Because we are alone,
> It is night,
> and we are afraid.
>
> — Langston Hughes

Events and happenings change rapidly. One in the position of the writer of these lines, who has chosen his topic and begun work on the text weeks ago, better be aware that some catastrophic event may happen that may cause him not only to readjust his text but his thinking about some one of importance about whom he planned to include in his remarks. The recent assassination of Malcolm X was just such an event. Event number two was quite a different affair. Some one of this dynamic and alert, I hope to believe, student body, learning of my forthcoming visit, favored me with Volume 1, Number 1, of your new student publication "Gripe-Vine," the gripe sheet of the Central State College student body. It is great! Thanks a lot! I liked it and I suggest this as interesting reading for both faculty and student body. Better to get steam off this way and let everybody know what your complaints are about courses, subjects, and cheating to even the dress and selection of the various and sundry "Campus Queens" rather than student demonstrations, picketing, and strikes. I hope you soon have more participation, and communication *vis-à-vis,* with faculty, trustees, and community groups. But I note that you want "more stimulus to the apathetic attitude that is generally found on this campus." I hope you find my address to be a desired stimulus. As to your next question: "Why are there so few controversial speakers at C.S.C.?" seems very difficult to understand when one reads the lines that follow:

The scheduling of more controversial speakers . . . would improve the campus climate tremendously . . . perhaps a *decrease* in speakers who are preoccupied with the so-called "Negro problem" would give all Centralians a chance to breathe more freely.

A plea for "more controversial speakers" . . . and a suggestion for *less* discussion of the "so-called Negro problem" seems completely unrealistic, if not an utter contradiction.

Amid the shallow sham that dominates much of the political debate that is reported daily from the halls of various state legislatures, even yours and mine, the events of the day surrounding America's Negro citizens cry aloud to the restless mind of America's college students for audacious answers. So, this caused the second derailment from my planned smooth track approach.

I am afraid and I hope that some of the things I shall speak about will cause some controversy among your student body in the form of lively discussions, debates, articles, letters, and even gripes in both the "Gold Torch" and the "Gripe-Vine." The more, the better.

And let me advise you that I shall speak about the most important continuing event of our time, the struggle of the American Negro for basic human rights in a society organized and dedicated to the proposition that all men are created equal and endowed with the inalienable rights of free men in a free society. This is *not,* as you most inappropriately term it, the "so-called negro problem"—how could you so demean this great movement? This is an American problem, the Third American Revolution and the greatest domestic problem that has faced this great country since the Civil War.

Let me add for the record a few significant historical quotes as a preface.

Equality consists in the same treatment of similar persons, and no government can stand which is not founded upon justice. Aristotle (384–322 B.C.), *Politics,* Book VII.

The public good is in nothing more essentially interested than in the protection of every individual's private rights. Sir William Blackstone (1728–1780), *Commentaries on the Laws of England,* 1765.

We hold these truths to be self-evident—that all men are created equal; that they are endowed by their Creator with certain inalienable rights; that among these are life, liberty, and the pursuit of happiness. Declaration of Independence, 1776.

Let us consider some of the features underlying this movement. In the great perspective of history they are not unique. They apply equally as well to the revolutions we find have taken place wherever the impact of world affairs have caused great political changes. The impact is universal especially where, almost overnight, several new countries are formed and new governments have been established out of what formerly were Western colonial empires of white domination of almost the entire earth.

Two glaring examples of enormous colonial empires of European-based countries are shown by small Belgium controlling the huge Congo, the heart of rich Africa, a territory eighty times the size of Belgium, and Portugal's colonial empire in Africa and Asia thirty times its own European homeland. Their withdrawal caused the re-emergence of Asian and African peoples and the creation not only of scores of new Asian and African nations and governments but the creation of new relationships, new images, new roles, and new hopes for the nonwhite races of the world. The yellow man, the brown man, and the black man were cast in a new image.

To the Negro American this was not only a new image, but a new world. The question has often been asked: "Was he ready for this sudden change of image?" "Had he been conditioned for his new stature in America?" The answer must clearly be in the negative—but this was no fault of his own doing. The more than two and a half centuries of slavery had completely destroyed the rich cultural values of his African heritage. He was left on his own to survive against persistent and savage attempts to completely strip him of his humanity and his individuality. America's deliberate failure to make any effort to improve the status of the Negro from the very moment of his landing on these shores and to make any effort at the integration of the Negro until a few short years ago made the masses of the Negroes unequal to the sudden change in their world image.

A strong contributing factor was America's failure to permit him to learn of his own history in the textbooks used in the American school system, in none of which appears an honest reference or an encouraging page of the Negro's contribution to the progress and growth of America.

The lack of identity has haunted the American Negro for generations. He has asked himself again and again, "Who am I? What am I?" By and large America's answer has been the one that Dr. Martin Luther King spoke of just a few days ago at a large mass meeting in a Selma, Alabama, church. "White America has told us we are nothing—we are nobody and we are entitled to nothing." He, of course, was referring mainly to the South and explaining why Negroes in most of the South are denied the basic human rights and liberties guaranteed them by our Constitution and Bill of Rights referred to above. Unfortunately, the forefathers of the average Negro today suffered so long in slavery and the terrible oppression of its aftermath, its debasement, and cruelties that he accepted the white man's description of him in varying ways. I personally can attest to the fact that in the relatively short span of my adult years, I have had to battle the apathy and inertia of fellow Negroes who were so brainwashed by these teachings that it was impossible to move them.

Dr. W. E. Burghart DuBois, the great Negro intellectual writer, essayist, and critic, never was disturbed or in doubt about the power inherent in the Negro. He did, however, fear the effect of the white world's judgment of the Negro on the Negro. He described it this way in one of his foremost works, *Souls of Black Folk,*

Behind the thought lurks the afterthought—suppose if all the world is right and we are less than men? Suppose this mad impulse (for freedom and equality) is all wrong, some mock mirage from the untrue—a shriek in the night for the freedom of men who themselves are not yet sure of their right to demand it?

No race of people in the world has suffered so greatly from the loss of its history as the American Negro. Still it is true beyond question that the Negro is an American to a greater degree than that attained by any other American group. He has had, by fate, to draw exclusively upon the American culture, customs, and ideological bloodstream to sustain life for himself and his loved ones while enslaved and striving to keep alive his hopes for future salvation. The Negro now must remake his past in order to make his future. We think of America as one country where a person can come to its shores without a past, and yet he can make it. Not so—the Negro. History must restore what slavery took away. The social damage of slavery and the Negro's easy identification with it because of his skin color must be compensated by pride of race and a knowledge of our achievements of the past. His renewed interest in his history since his transplantation began 350 years ago from Africa may well emerge and become the essential unifier, among other factors, of the many divergent legions of civil-rights movements and their intelligent leaders.

The Negro is profoundly indebted to one man more than any other for the depth and scope of research and writing on the history of the Negro and his contribution to the progress of our country. I refer, of course, to the late Dr. Carter G. Woodson. Dr. Woodson was born of slave parents in Virginia in 1875. He left Virginia at the age of twelve to work in the mines of West Virginia. He returned to school and finished high school at the age of twenty-two. He went to college at Berea in Kentucky where he was referred to as "a brilliant student . . . " and won his Bachelor of Arts Degree. After graduate study and a Master's Degree from the University of Chicago, he began teaching at Howard University. He then returned to study and research at Harvard University where, in 1912, he received the coveted degree of Doctor of Philosophy. He returned to Howard University where he became Dean of the College of Liberal Arts. It was not long until he felt the need to devote his full time—indeed his life—to his chosen study, the history of the American Negro. He became convinced that American historians had either ignored or deliberately misrepresented the enormous contributions of the Negro toward the progress and development of America. He founded in association with others the now famous and world recognized Association for the Study of Negro Life and History in September, 1915, with headquarters in Washington, D.C. This great institution publishes the scholarly *Journal of Negro History* (a quarterly) under the editorship of the brilliant historian Dr. William M. Brewer, as well as the monthly magazine, *The Negro History Bulletin*, edited by the esteemed educator and historian Dr. Charles Walker Thomas.

Dr. Woodson authored singly, or in collaboration with other distinguished scholars, more than thirty well-recognized and accepted scientific works on the Negro. The most widely known are *The Negro in Our History, The History of the Negro Church, Negro Orators and Their Orations, Free Negro Heads of Families in 1930, A Century of Negro Migration,* and *The Beginnings of Miscegenation of Whites and Blacks.* Dr. Woodson died in Washington on April 3, 1950, at the age of seventy-five. This year we celebrate the fiftieth year of the founding of the ASNLH, now located at 1538 Ninth Street, N.W., Washington, D.C., 20001.

Granted now that we in America face a new world, indeed on the whole, a receptive world, and that we are developing a sense of history, long delayed, what shall be the purpose of the Negro from now and into the future?

Should we not call for a "summit meeting" of all the acknowledged leaders in the civil-rights movement to a round-table conference in an endeavor to formalize a joint program of action for those basic human rights still denied the Negro in the social, political, economic, and educational areas of life? These leaders in the order of their standing both in America and abroad and in my own estimation of their contribution to the cause of the Negro are

1. Dr. Martin Luther King, Southern Christian Leadership Conference (SCLC)
2. Roy Wilkins, National Association for the Advancement of Colored People (NAACP)
3. Whitney Young, the National Urban League
4. James Farmer, Congress of Racial Equality (CORE)
5. John Lewis, Student Nonviolent Coordinating Committee (SNCC)

There are no longer any fundamental doctrinal issues that separate these groups or their leaders. Isn't there in fact too much fragmentation with the danger of even greater stratification and division between the groups that have been accepted as spokesmen for the American Negro citizenry? Is not the drain on the treasury of each of these groups admittedly dangerously weakened because of the excessive cost of operating on such a great national scale—too great—and future receipts of a substantial nature too uncertain to continue individual operation? I refuse to believe that any one of these leaders would deny the urgent need to meet to discuss these issues. I am likewise convinced that each leader of each group would, upon an urgent national call from the ranks of the Negro people of America, reply with a resounding "Yes." Who shall sound the call to these leaders, these men in whose hands lie the plans for the virtual destiny of millions of their fellow men, these men who by their program will put America to the continuing litmus paper test of its humanism and its equal treatment of the Negro? I personally call upon the Negro church, the great religious leaders of the masses of the Negro people, too long under eclipse and too long surrendering their traditional roles as spokesmen for their 10 million enrolled church members. I also call upon the restless Negro and white students in colleges, North and South, young men and women of energy and imagination, the "visionaries" who give such impetus and life to these movements, to urge these leaders to cease their bureaucratic differences and sit down at the conference table, work out a common bargaining ground, a consensus, and elect a leader, then merge their forces and formalize in a joint statement a series of resolutions of demands in every area of human rights, and bring these demands to the attention of the President of the United States, the Attorney General, and the leaders of both Houses of Congress. Such a "demand for human rights" based upon a strong legal and moral foundation will be unassailable and will be heralded and praised throughout America and the world. And finally I ask those of you who will make this call to our leaders to urge the distinguished Dr. Martin Luther King, who was recently honored with the bestowal of the 1964 Nobel Peace Prize, to become chairman and spokesman for the group.

I am certain the white churches and synagogues of America, the great Protestant, Catholic, and Jewish leaders will do as they did in their march to Selma, Alabama, give this proclamation their united support.

This group action in essence is what Dr. King has referred to when speaking "of the needless waste of assets" in the various drives for equality of the Negro. In recent weeks following the assassination of Malcolm X, when it appeared that a bitter and costly feuding between his followers and his former Muslim group would erupt in bloodshed, Dr. King offered to mediate the differences between the two groups. These two instances are but straws in the wind of what could happen in the area of agreement between the civil-rights groups if a clarion call for such a summit meeting were made and from the sources above suggested. Great miracles have often been wrought out of the commitment to a cause by a few people.

What of the fate of Malcolm X and the future of the Black Muslim Movement?

Without a doubt Malcolm X was a peculiar, complicated, and egocentric man. He was struck down by a fusillade of bullets from a group of his former followers, now turned assassins. He was killed perversely enough in a hall from which, "for security reasons," all whites were barred. What about this elusive, sensitive character who, from all reports, was changing? In fact, some insist he *had* changed after his trip to Mecca from a once "preacher of hate" of the white man to one, at the moment of his death, who had started preaching brotherhood and wanted to be recognized as a leader, willing to sit down with accepted leaders and negotiate!!

If this was true, then indeed his death in the manner that it happened was a pity. But his life was anything but a blessing for the people whom he professed to love. He and his former Muslim followers set in force a pattern of extremism in hate of everything white that knew no bounds of restraint.

The Black Muslim movement under the leadership of the aging Elijah Muhammad from which Malcolm X withdrew is the pioneer of the Negro far right extremist group, and as far as public attention is concerned, the only one in active operation. Extremists of the far Left such as the Communists, or the far Right such as the John Birchers, the White Citizens Council, the Ku Klux Klansmen, and the Black Muslims find easy access to the minds of empty souls. These people, usually forlorn, confused, and frustrated, are easy prey to the simplistic slogans and absolutist solutions of even the most difficult problems. The Birchites' current slogan is that civil-rights workers, Negro and white, and their program of integration are part of a giant communistic conspiracy to divide and rule America. The White Citizens Council and the KKK claim that America must enforce strict segregation of the races, banish all interracial organizations, all interfaith movements, all foreign or nationality cooperating groups, and thus preserve white Protestantism. And the Black Muslims decry integration and condemn everything white and say "give us a black state in America and we will control our own destiny." At least the Negro did not originate and has no monopoly on such pernicious and anarchic radicalisms of the right, which, if not fought by Americans of every race and color and by the great American clergy—protestants, catholics, and Jews—may spell the doom of the American way of life and indeed the America we honor and love.

A final word on the danger to the American Negro and his present crusade for equal rights and participation in the American society by such movements as that of the late Malcolm X and the Black Muslims. The Negro no longer lives as he did twenty-five years ago, in an isolated community. What he does in Harlem, Philadelphia, Cleveland, Detroit, Chicago, and particularly in the South is broadcast throughout America and the world. Various interpretations are given to whatever may be reported about him or pictured about him, depending upon the attitude of the news media or the place of coverage. The report of the death of Malcolm X, for example, was reported in the foreign press as the result of a giant conspiracy of "white anti-Negro groups" to kill Negro civil-rights leaders. This completely false picture was spread throughout Europe, Asia, Africa, and the Communist world, resulting in violent demonstrations in many of the African countries under the theory that Malcolm X was "an American Lumumba" who fought for the emancipation of the Negro.

I point to the above as a warning note to my fellow Negroes and above all to the great and growing body of young Negroes in the schools and colleges of America, upon whom the destiny of the entire Negro race depends, that a renewed sense of purpose and a clarification of the objectives of the American Negro is a prime necessity. First and foremost, it is imperative that we support every effort on the part of our local, state, and national governments for widespread and total education of the Negro masses, especially those in densely populated ghettos and pockets of poverty areas in the Deep South and their counterparts in the metropolitan cities of the North. There is a heavy responsibility on the part of the professional, upper class, the better circumstanced, and well-to-do-Negro to sacrifice much of his time to help his brother at the lower level and particularly to give liberally of his money to those causes, and there are many, working to this end. He must be willing to speak up and be heard in public meetings before the various Boards of Education, not only for integrated education but for high-quality education by the best and most qualified teachers. He must assert that the Negro taxpayer will support an increase in the tax rate, however high it may be, when funds are needed to build better schools and provide higher salaries for better quality education. The poor of all races are the beneficiaries and our poor, percentage-wise, unfortunately is the greater. And he should be the first to support and insist upon a program of preschool education at the age of two and one half years, and a longer school day and a shorter vacation period.

There is an urgent need for guidance values of Negro children in their early years of life. I have referred above to what history has done to them and their families for more than two centuries. America is paying the cost of this—and we are the victims of that benighted history. As I write these lines (Friday, March 12 at the noon hour), church bells are ringing and the voice of a distinguished New England clergyman, choked with grief, is telling the nation and world in somber tones of the cold-blooded assassination of one of God's ordained and dedicated advocates—the Reverend James J. Reeb—a white minister of Boston, the latest martyr in the cause of racial freedom in America. This selfless God-like human being, formerly of my own city of Philadelphia, who was personally known both to me and my wife, was savagely beaten, as you know, while in the company of two fellow white ministers, also beaten, after joining in a peaceful demonstration in support of the constitutional rights of Negroes to be registered as voters. This was not just white blood spilled, added to the blood of blacks during the last century in their lawful petition to redress grievances as guaranteed by our American law. This was the blood of America, the blood of our country and our laws that was spilled in Selma, and somehow, in some way, America must make good for this loss, this trauma to the dreams and aspirations of a law-abiding people. The pictures of the mounted Alabama "storm troopers" (not policemen) beating down and gassing helpless men, women, and children that Sunday in Selma were shown throughout the world and will never be forgotten. What priceless propaganda for Communist China in their crusade to gain support of the three-fifths colored races of the world against the white minority!

Somehow this reverend Pastor Reeb, as true a martyr as ever revealed in the long history of American tragedy, I predict will be the one who will have sounded the Biblical Macedonian call which will ultimately bring the full force of the American clergy, Protestant, Catholic, and Jewish, North and South, to immediate grips with President Johnson and the nation's leaders to end this continuing tirade of lawlessness in the South. The murder of this brave man exposes to the glaring sunlight the false faces of a morally impoverished South, the superstructure of which is based upon a totally unsupportable theory of intellectual and spiritual acceptance but with a substructure of corrupt and amoral county and state officials—politicians, sheriffs, police, voting registrars, and school superintendents—maintaining a feudal domain, entrenching themselves, to the denial of all privileges to the Negro majority, as overlords of a never changing society, a South which mistakes irrational and cruel impulse for moral judgment.

Next of importance are the need of guidance values and a new awareness for the Negro youth early in life, beginning at preschool age and continuing through the primary and high school years, with concentration on the need for total perfection and discipline. A hierarchy of values and culture is an absolute necessity.

Nothing has been a greater contributing factor to the Negro's lack of "readiness" for full participation in American opportunity today than the grave losses sustained by the Negro because of the traditional treatment of the Negro masses in our schools both North and South. Historically he was segregated by law in the South and provided with a minimum of education given by poorly trained and poorly equipped teachers in totally inadequate buildings. Worse, the term of the school year was substantially less than that of white children. In the North he found himself in ghetto schools, for the most part de facto segregated confronted with a teaching staff with little interest or motivation.

It becomes necessary, therefore, for the Negro to approach the necessity for mass education with a sense of tragedy; that if we fail in this—all else fails. We must inquire in the secondary or high school courses to find those unusual minds of excellence or those with unusual skills in the various sciences—physical, chemical, and biological —in the manual and creative arts, the performing arts of music, drama, acting, and expression—all to the end that the American Negro, heirs of a rich and vaunted African heritage of many centuries with a history of gigantic accomplishments in these and many other fields which leading world authorities now fully support, may rise again to a place long denied the Negro, as one of the truly great races of the world.

We must give up our lives to this test of excellence and supremacy in this struggle for a place among the great races of the world, which in its accomplishment will carry our native America to an even higher place among the nations of the world.

We shall choose this as our mighty project for the next quarter century and we, with God's help, shall pledge our lives to its accomplishment even to the test of death.

May I give heart to my firm belief that if we undertake to establish an hierarchy of values that we shall in the near future accomplish these goals. Let me state with emphasis and assurance that we are *now very much on our way!*

There are at present *hundreds* of highly placed Negro men, and women too, in some of America's leading industries, colleges, and universities all over America. There are, it is estimated after careful study, as many as five hundred on the faculties of highly regarded colleges of our country. Many have received advanced degrees with distinction at some of America's leading colleges. The Negro is no longer accepted "for token purposes" only. He is accepted on the basis of merit and is sought after, looked for, and, if of exceptional merit, offered flattering contracts of employment with generous fringe benefits. Perhaps the most exceptional in this category and perhaps the earliest is the illustrious biochemist, Dr. Percy L. Julian of Chicago. Dr. Julian and the writer were students together at Harvard in the middle twenties. I know of his scholarship and industry. After teaching at Howard University, he developed his own pharmaceutical laboratory in Chicago, with a very successful branch in Mexico. Just three years ago his famed laboratories of biochemical and pharmaceutical products were so successful that Philadelphia's famous Smith, Kline & French Laboratories bought out Dr. Julian's laboratory and its formulas for the very tidy sum of four and one-half million dollars. He was elected to the Board of Directors of that great pharmaceutical combine. This company has three other research chemists of our race and is represented by a Negro lawyer, Charles A. Moore, of our Philadelphia bar.

An awareness of the opportunities that lie ahead for us; an awareness of our objectives and potential with a disciplined approach in our pursuit to the point of perfection, giving the same concentration toward intellectual achievement in the liberal arts and sciences courses and in mathematics, biology, chemistry, and physics (to name only a few) as we do so successfully in athletic perfection, is a necessity. Here I must congratulate you on your perfect season in basketball, with a 23 won and no loss record, and your championship victory last Saturday. Do not, however, permit your interest in and success in athletics become the totality of your ambition! I personally believe that the glory to Central State, while great, would have greater impact on America and the prestige and future of the Negro in the educational and business world had they, for example, become the victors in the famous "College Bowl" competition that we witness on television every Sunday.

For the stimulation of hope in the hearts of my young friends in this audience, and their proud (and sometimes disappointed) parents and for the American record as well, let me enumerate the recent "breakthroughs" in the various colleges and universities of America to which Negro men and women have been called to *teach*. This is a call for excellence in their respective fields, in which no color line exists. Excellence in their particular fields and, equally important, excellence in the science of *teaching* which is so badly needed in our colleges today—good teachers, dedicated teachers, but which is so greatly lacking. May I add a word of history to accord credit to the great pioneers in this field, both Negro and white, who led the fight for integration of the faculties in American colleges and universities.

The Julius Rosenwald Fund was the first to undertake the integration of Negro teachers in white colleges. This occurred in the late 1930's and in the 1940's. Through the efforts of Edwin Embree, Executive Secretary of the fund, Dr. Allison Davis was appointed to and has been an esteemed Professor at the University of Chicago for more than twenty years. Dr. Ira De A. Reid, a brilliant sociologist and humanist (Ph.D., Columbia) and his wife, Dr. Anne Cook Reid (Ph.D., Yale) were perhaps the "John the Baptists" of this movement. Dr. Ira Reid has been on the famed Haverford College faculty since 1948 and is now Chairman of the Department of Sociology. But prior to that he was a combined Rosenwald University Scholar and Professor at Atlanta Union and a Visiting Professor along with his wife at several Northern and Western universities. (Negro "Visiting Professors" in that era humorously called themselves "John the Baptist Missionaries" going into the highways and byways "to prepare thee for the Lord.") During this period Dr. Julian Lewis became a research associate in medicine at the University of Chicago, as did Dr. Hinton at Harvard. Dr. Hylan Lewis, a leading sociologist, turned down an offer of an Associate Professorship at a leading university because ". . . they seek me only as a symbol . . . and my integrity as a scholar is on trial." It was at this time (the late 1940's and early 1950's) that the vogue of "Visiting Professorships" was in full force, undertaken by the American Friends Service Committee with the very salutory purpose of having these Visiting Professors called later for permanent service in American colleges. The third period, which began in the middle 1950's, was undertaken by the Association of American Colleges and Universities, which designated selected Negro scholars as Visiting Lecturers in the liberal arts and humanities in scores of colleges and universities all over the United States. These were the three movements which provided the breakthrough in the integration of Negro scholars in American colleges and universities. Hurriedly, the following names of just a few of several hundred brilliant Negro scholars who make news in this field. The list is growing so rapidly, I am delighted to say, such appointments no longer make headlines and it is difficult to keep records of them.

Professor Wade Ellis, Mathematics, Oberlin College, now approach-his twentieth year.

Professor B. A. Jones, Chairman, Department of Sociology, Ohio Wesleyan.

Professors Charles Lawrence and Hugh Smythe of Brooklyn College.

Professor Arthur Lewis, now a resident scholar at the Institute of International Studies at Princeton and a former Professor at the University of Manchester (England).

Professor M. R. Smith, Anthropology, Stanford University.

Professor Abram L. Harris, famed Negro scholar who died last year, was Professor of Economics and Philosophy at the University of Chicago.

Dr. John Hope Franklin, former Chairman, Department of History at Brooklyn College, was called last year to the Chairmanship of the History Department at the University of Chicago.

Dr. John Turner, Western Reserve University.

Dr. Charles Willie, who was a classmate of Dr. Martin Luther King at Morehouse College, is now Associate Professor at Syracuse University.

Dr. Charles Davis, who began his teaching career at New York University and Princeton, is now Professor of English at Penn State University.

Dr. Adelaide Cromwell Hill is Director of the Department of African Studies at Boston University and well-known and universally esteemed theologian; Dr. Howard Thurman, religious philosopher and mystic, is Dean of Chapel and Professor of Theology at Boston University.

Dr. Mark Hanna Wilkins is an Associate on the faculty at Johns Hopkins University.

I am delighted to report that we have broken through the Deep South. Dr. Arthur C. Banks, Jr. (Ph.D., Johns Hopkins), former Professor at our Atlanta University, is now Exchange Professor of Political Science at Emory University in Atlanta, and I am informed that a Negro, name not known to me at this writing, has been appointed as Instructor at the University of Texas.

The City College of New York called the famed scholar in sociology and the humanities, Dr. Kenneth Clark, many years ago. His contribution to our civil-rights cases in the United States Supreme Court has been widely acclaimed.

Dr. John A. Davis is head of the Department and Professor of Political Science at the City College of New York.

Dr. Robert B. Johnson, son of the late President of Fisk, is on leave from his Associate Professorship at New York University to be with his wife whom he recently married here at Central State College.

In my own city of Philadelphia, we honor Professor William Fontaine, in Philosophy at the University of Pennsylvania, and Dr. Howard E. Mitchell, brilliant young psychologist and Associate Professor at the University of Pennsylvania, who will soon become the Director of Human Relations Projects at the University.

Dr. Andrew Brimmer, presently on leave from the University of Pennsylvania as Professor of Economics at the famed Wharton School, is now with the United States government. He is an Assistant Secretary of Commerce for Economic Affairs.

Philadelphia, justly proud of its liberal tradition and its early efforts in the field of integrated teaching opportunities, leads the country in this respect in integrated medical-school faculties.

At the University of Pennsylvania Medical School there are the following:

Dr. Edward S. Cooper, Assistant Professor of Medicine;
Dr. James H. Robinson, Associate in Surgery;
Dr. John W. Thomas, Associate in Surgery;
Dr. James W. West, Assistant in Medicine.

Recently called to the University of Pennsylvania Medical School beginning April, 1965, is the first Negro woman physician, the talented Dr. Helen O. Dickens, Board Certified in Obstetrics and Gynecology, who for many years was on the faculty of Women's Medical College.

On the faculty of the Graduate School of Medicine at the University of Pennsylvania Medical School are

Dr. Edward Holloway, the pioneer among Negro teachers of medicine in Philadelphia, and Dr. Melvin J. Chisum.

At the Temple University Medical School are Dr. Thomas Georges and Dr. William Lightfoot.

On the faculty of Women's Medical College Hospital are:

Dr. James Batts,
Dr. Maurice Clifford,
Dr. Theodore Hawkins,
Dr. Durward Hughes.

There are doubtless many, many other brilliant pioneers among those of our race called to teach in our great universities to whom homage is due. This is particularly true, I am told, in the Middle West and in the colleges on the Pacific Coast. They deserve our commendation. To them I fervently urge that they combine the art and skill of teaching with the high scholarship in the subjects taught by them so that they—all those who are pioneering in this new opportunity —will be called America's greatest inspiration to the generations of young people to whom they are exposed.

The subjects I have discussed with you tonight are, to borrow a phrase from a great American jurist, "little fragments of my fleece." They are thoughts that are only a small, but important, phase of the total human tragedy—call it the life, if you will, faced by Negroes in America today.

As Negro Americans we cannot sit idly by and await "a mandate of heaven" as a substitute for the hard agony of collective creativeness. America is in an era of unfolding moral process and we are faced with many conflicts and much tragedy. The issues, as I have tried to show are never clearly delineated or settled—but the choice is ours, and happily, we have not come to the end of history.

The Neglected Tool
HOWARD N. MEYER

Howard N. Meyer is a practicing attorney who was a Special Assistant to the United States Attorney General in the Roosevelt and Truman Administrations. Before graduating from Columbia College and Law School, he was an editor of the *Columbia Law Review*.

An avid student of the Civil War and Reconstruction periods, Meyer feels that the truth about that era has rarely been told. He believes that the American Negro's contribution to American thought and history has been neglected. He has pressed the implication of this point of view in articles in *The Crisis, Negro Digest, Commonweal, Negro History Bulletin,* and *The Midwest Quarterly.*

The following address, "The Neglected Tool," was delivered by Mr. Meyer at the 1963 Annual Negro History Week Celebration, sponsored by the Brotherhood of Sleeping Car Porters in New York City.

* * *

For one who has come to learn—a little late in life—that there is much more to American History than is taught in our schools, and that what is taught in our schools is full of falsehoods, it is hard to put a time or subject limit on remarks commemorating Negro History Week. I have a burning conviction that our civil-rights organizations— which have each performed well, under handicaps, in their fields of concentration—must come to grips with the history-teaching problem, if they are ever to make a massive breakthrough. Brotherhood Week, as the politicians like to say in their speeches, should be celebrated all year 'round—but there will be no true brotherhood in our land until Negro History Week is observed all year—not until it becomes unnecessary for there to be a Negro History Week.

The segregationists and some of the so-called "moderates"—the go-slow folk—have a favorite theme whenever someone calls for action: action in the field of voting in the South, housing in the North, job discrimination across the land. They say, first you have to have education. And while they say it they laugh up their sleeves. Because, by and large, they have the most important part of the educational process tied up in a knot!

The significance of mis-teaching history as a method of ensuring preservation of white supremacy was seen ninety years ago by Wade Hampton, even before he had overthrown the lawful government of South Carolina, in a speech in which he said it was the "duty" of the ex-Confederates "to vindicate the great principles for which the Confederacy fought . . . to explain to the world the everliving truths she sought to maintain . . . and to place on the eternal record an appeal . . . to the tribunal of history." His people responded. For the next forty years Confederate veterans' committees censored and saw to it that Southern history books were properly slanted; Southern white scholars fanned out over the country and took over the history writing and teaching in our great universities, almost as if by plan.

By and large they succeeded in creating a picture of American History, frozen into present-day textbooks, which teach that—

Slavery was a beneficial, civilizing institution that was overthrown only when it had outlived its usefulness in training the savage; emancipation was an unnecessary and even unwanted gift presented to helpless Negroes:

Reconstruction in the South after the Civil War was a period of shameful plunder by Negroes and carpetbaggers and proved that ignorant freedmen had been given the vote too soon.

Then comes the real tough one: what happened to the Negro in the South from 1877 onward was such an atrocity that the power of man to lie was not equal to the task of disguising it. Therefore, it is not mentioned at all; or else passed over with a vile wisecrack—those who condemned or recall the multiple political assassinations of the leaders of the Negro people in the South are said to be merely "waving the bloody shirt."

It is no wonder that so many Americans, at least those who have not known or worked with Negroes in school, shop, or factory, still think of them as history's helpless pawns, an inferior people; he reads "Negro" in his newspaper and thinks to himself: "nigger." Of course this is a product of education, has to be fought by education, and reached through the particular part of education that produced it: the mis-teaching of American history. The distorted teaching of history has had its effects on the young Negro too—in giving him feelings of inferiority and hence of submissiveness,—by depriving him of pride in his heritage and a sense of continuity with his past. The work of Carter G. Woodson and W. E. B. DuBois has helped to combat this, but their efforts and the efforts of their heirs, such as Charles Wesley and Rayford W. Logan and Saunders Redding and John Hope Frankilin, must be multiplied on a far broader, and on an integrated basis. We need white freedom teachers and freedom writers to help make possible the speeding up of the integration that the freedom riders have helped along. Every one of us who is a parent, member of a PTA, or who can make himself heard in some other way can join this part of the fight.

We all remember how the U.S. Military Government in Germany, and later the German government itself, to a certain extent, faced the problem of trying to help remake that country into a democracy. One of the big problems was the deep and intense anti-Semitic feeling among the Germans. How did they tackle it? By seeing to it that the facts of recent German history were faced; by opening the eyes of the young and of those who had lived quietly through it to what had been going on in the concentration camps and the crematoria. Half of the American race relations problem of mis-taught history has to be solved similarly. We must face and teach our children, and their parents, what really happened between Negro and white in our country, over the years; how the Negro was lynched, plundered, flogged, and intimidated for half a century after Emancipation, until they retreated and got to "know their place" in the South, and stayed in it until Martin Luther King led thousands who decided that they'd rather walk than ride a bus for a while; until those brave young lads in North Carolina decided that they'd rather sit-in hungry than eat standing up.

The other half of the history teaching problem is to get across the story of how the Negro, throughout our history, has led the fight for his own freedom. It is particularly timely in this Emancipation year to remember that fact above others. America must face her shame in the fact that when the promise of emancipation of 1863 was made a mockery from 1877 to 1954, it was not merely the withholding of a freedom that had been offered on a silver platter to a helpless people. It was the theft of a freedom that had been hard and nobly won by men in arms who in fighting for their own freedom had also helped to save their country—from a treasonable attempt of slaveholders to overthrow the government to protect their property.

When Lincoln came to the point of issuing his proclamation of emancipation, it was the culminaton of a historical process. That process included the work of the abolitionist movement over the years. History books conceal the fact that abolitionism was as "integrated" a movement as the freedom riders of today. William Lloyd Garrison side by side with Frederick Douglass; Wendell Phillips and James McCrummell; Rev. Samuel May and Rev. Samuel R. Ward; Henry Ward Beecher and Henry Highland Garnet.

In the writing and timing of the Proclamation, Lincoln was mightily influenced by individual Negroes such as Douglass, and by the outspoken community actions of free Negroes across the land. I can cite one example of interest here.

Until August, 1862, Lincoln who, while always personally opposed to slavery, was never sure what to do about race relations afterwards, still thought of so-called "colonization" schemes. On August 14, 1862, he discussed his ideas for voluntary departure of Negroes from the U.S. with a Negro delegation. Shortly afterwards, Garrison's *Liberator* reported a resolution passed by a mass meeting of the colored citizens of Queens County who declared—

We have the right to have applied to ourselves those rights named in the Declaration of Independence . . . our answer is this: There is no country like our own. Why not declare slavery abolished and favor our peaceful colonization in the rebel states?

This was but one of the many expressions by Negro Americans that helped Lincoln along the last difficult part of the road that led to the issuance of the great proclamation of freedom.

That proclamation, in turn, finished opening the door that Thomas Wentworth Higginson's pioneer black regiment had pried loose in the Sea Islands of South Carolina.

You will not find in the textbooks used currently in most schools any reference to the testimony, from high sources, of the importance of the Negro soldier to his country in the Civil War. Secretary of War Stanton said, "This whole contest would have gone against us if at the last moment we had not got 200,000 Negroes to come and join our armies and turn the tide of victory on our side." Thousands of pages and hundreds of thousands of words have been written about the Civil War Centennial, without any reference to Lincoln's statement about the loyal black regiments: "Take two hundred thousand men from our side and put them in the battlefield or cornfield against us, and we would be compelled to abandon the war in three weeks."

Half of our historians, segregation-minded, conceal the role of those black regiments in the Civil War; the other half, ashamed of the century of betrayal of the black men who fought for freedom for all Americans, prefer to forget them. Now, as we mount a nationwide effort to bring back to life what has been the dead-letter amendments to the Constitution, we must bring back to the history books the words of Booker T. Washington—certainly no extremist—who said:

The services which the Negro troops performed in the Civil War in fighting for the freedom of their race not only convinced the officers who commanded them and the white soldiers who fought by their side that the Negro race deserved to be free, but it served to convince the great mass of people at the North that the Negroes were fit for freedom. It did, perhaps, more than any other one thing, gain for them, as a result of the war, the passage of those amendments to the Constitution which secured to the Negro race the same rights in the United States which are granted to white men.

For those who think I exaggerate the nature and extent of distortions of history, I can only suggest that they look at the history or social studies textbooks given to their children. A recent and horrible example of the effect of these distortions is found in the opening column of a nationally syndicated columnist, from whom New Yorkers were spared by the newspaper strike. This Mr. Max Freedman had the impudence or the ignorance to write in a column which appeared in the *Washington Post, Philadelphia Inquirer, Chicago News,* and I don't know how many other papers that the "Negro was the absentee client" at the time of the Emancipation.

Let the lesson of Negro History Week, 1963, be that this type of lie and distortion must be exposed and rebutted, unceasingly and tirelessly; that the fight for civil rights will be hindered and incomplete until we pick up the neglected tool—and integrate America's heritage.

PART FIVE

Clergymen

The Negro is now united as never before, and religious leaders in no small way have been responsible for this spiritual and social cohesion. Since the Negro is often excluded from civic, political, and social organizations in his community, he tends to compensate for this isolation by making the church his focus of protest against an environment that exploits and overpowers him.

Though it was the Rosa Parks incident that set off the Negro Revolt, it was certainly through the dramatic figure of Dr. Martin Luther King, Jr., that the Negro community grasped an opportunity to cloak its social and political aspirations under great moral and religious leadership. King's tactic of direct-action protest quickly spread throughout America, and most often it was a "man of the cloth" who was leading the aggressive attack. Indeed it was the fiery enthusiasm of Protestant, Catholic and Jewish clergy that made the 1963 March on Washington a vigorous testimony to the position of the church on civil rights.

One of the most important effects of the Black Revolution was the change it introduced into Christian practice. The church began to meet the issues of segregation and discrimination head on. It abolished the notion that these were simply social and political problems, and accepted its moral responsibility in waging war against racial intolerance. In clarion tones, organized religion bugled its determination to promote the universal fatherhood of God and the brotherhood of man. Though the church has come directly to grips with the problem of racial intolerance, ironically enough it is still among the most segregated institutions in American life. Yet the eminent and distinguished voices included in this section hopefully remind us that the religious community is not leaderless.

FREEDOM TRAIN
—Langston Hughes

I read in the papers about the
    Freedom Train.
I heard on the radio about the
    Freedom Train.
I seen folks talkin' about the
    Freedom Train.
Lord, I been a-waitin' for the
    Freedom Train!

Down South in Dixie only train I see's
Got a Jim Crow car set aside for me.
I hope there ain't no Jim Crow on the Freedom Train,
No back door entrance to the Freedom Train,
No signs FOR COLORED on the Freedom Train,
No WHITE FOLKS ONLY on the Freedom Train.

    I'm gonna check up on this
    Freedom Train.

Who's the engineer on the Freedom Train?
Can a coal-black man drive the Freedom Train?
Or am I still a porter on the Freedom Train?
Is there ballot boxes on the Freedom Train?
When it stops in Mississippi will it be made plain
Everybody's got a right to board the Freedom Train?

    Somebody tell me about this
    Freedom Train!

The Birmingham station's marked COLORED and WHITE.
The white folks go left, the colored go right—
They even got a segregated lane.
Is that the way to get aboard the Freedom Train?

    I got to know about this
    Freedom Train!

If my children ask me, *Daddy, please explain*
Why there's Jim Crow stations for the Freedom Train?
What shall I tell my children? . . . *You* tell me—
'Cause freedom ain't freedom when a man ain't free.

    But maybe they explains it on the
    Freedom Train.

When my grandmother in Atlanta, 83 and black,
Gets in line to see the Freedom,

Will some white man yell, *Get back!*
A Negro's got no business on the Freedom Track!

> Mister, I thought it were the
> Freedom Train!

Her grandson's name was Jimmy. He died at Anzio.
He died for real. It warn't no show.
The freedom that they carryin' on this Freedom Train,
Is it for real—or just a show again?

> Jimmy wants to know about the
> Freedom Train.

Will *his* Freedom Train come zoomin' down the track
Gleamin' in the sunlight for white and black?
Not stoppin' at no stations marked COLORED nor WHITE,
Just stoppin' in the fields in the broad daylight,
Stoppin' in the country in the wide-open air
Where there never was no Jim Crow signs nowhere,
No Welcomin' Committees, nor politicians of note,
No Mayors and such for which colored can't vote,
And nary a sign of a color line—
For the Freedom Train will be yours and mine!

Then maybe from their graves in Anzio
The G.I.'s who fought will say, *We wanted it so!*
Black men and white will say, *Ain't it fine?*
At home they got a train that's yours and mine!

> Then I'll shout, *Glory for the*
> *Freedom Train!*
> I'll holler, *Blow your whistle,*
> *Freedom Train!*
> *Thank God-A-Mighty! Here's the*
> *Freedom Train!*
> *Get on board our Freedom Train!*

Human Dignity—Have We Not All One Father?
DR. EUGENE CARSON BLAKE

Dr. Eugene Carson Blake is not only the Stated Clerk of the General Assembly of the United Presbyterian Church in the U.S.A., but is also one of the leading preachers in America.

A graduate of Princeton University and Princeton Theological Seminary, Blake has been an activist on the religious front for over thirty years. Holder of nearly twenty honorary degrees, Dr. Blake served as President of the National Council of Churches from 1954 to 1957. He was a delegate to the Second and Third Assembly of the World Council of Churches in 1954 and 1961, and he was also a delegate to the Sixteenth, Seventeenth, and Eighteenth General Councils of the World Presbyterian Alliance.

He was recipient of a special award from the Catholic Interracial Council of Chicago, Illinois, in 1964 "for leadership in the cause of interracial justice and good will." The same year the Anti-Defamation League of B'nai Brith (New York) presented him the American Democratic Legacy Award for giving "inspired leadership in the fight for human rights."

Currently, Dr. Blake is a trustee of Occidental College, Princeton Theological Seminary, San Francisco Theological Seminary, The American University, Hawaii Loa College, and the John F. Kennedy Library. He is a member of the Central and Executive Committees of the World Council of Churches and General Board of the National Council of Churches. Concerned with major issues confronting the world today, he is Chairman of the Division of Interchurch Aid, Refugee, and World Service of the World Council of Churches. His position as Chairman of the Commission on Religion and Race of the National Council of Churches and his membership on the National Advisory Council for the "War on Poverty" have placed him in a position of offering his experience in areas of his interest and discernment.

His speech, "Human Dignity—Have We Not All One Father?" was given at the National Interreligious Convocation on Civil Rights in Washington, D.C., on April 28, 1964.

* * *

We are met here in Washington, representatives of the major religious institutions of this nation, at a critical time in the life of the nation and in the life of our churches and synagogues. We are in a contest, a long contest against those in our nation who resist the new pattern of race relations which must be established if the United States of America is to survive as a citadel of freedom.

Those who are preventing the establishment of justice and equality between the races are of two categories: (1) A relatively small number of our fellow citizens who are clearly determined to continue the unjust, un-christian, and irreligious laws and traditions which keep

Negro Americans, and to a lesser extent all racial minorities of color, out of the mainstream of American life, dependent upon the patronizing good will of the white majority. These, though scattered throughout the nation, are represented by the intransigent Southern Senators who are using every legislative device to prevent the Senate from enacting the civil-rights legislation now before it. These opponents of the new freedom and equality of men of all races are united by ancient prejudice, long-established customs, and by fear and by hate. These opponents of racial justice are strong because they are adamant and united; the long battle required to establish a new racial pattern does not seem to threaten their determination. (2) The second category who are also preventing the establishment of racial justice, freedom, and equality, are of much greater numbers—they are those of our fellow citizens who are confused and fearful, some selfishly indifferent, content to sit on the sidelines, who see no clear moral or spiritual issue before the nation, who allow considerations of order, peace, or private profit to neutralize their too general moral commitment to justice or freedom. These are the Americans whom we must win to our side of the contest; we must by our speaking and by our acting draw them into a determined commitment to our just cause, a commitment that is strong enough to stand the strain of disappointment and frustration in the long battle which will continue long after we have won the legislative skirmish now taking place on Capitol Hill. For we will win this contest. New federal legislation must and will be enacted, and the time is now. But important as is this legislation, I remind you that we in the churches and synagogues have a task that will continue long after the legislation is enacted. We must unite the community and the communities of our whole nation to use the law as the national instrument to establish freedom and justice in all the land.

But we will not win the unconcerned or the uncommitted to our side; we, ourselves, will be divided and defeated unless with courage and moral insight the ministers, priests, and rabbis of the nation, supported by the members of their congregations, make it perfectly clear that we face a moral and spiritual issue. Justice, equality, and freedom for all men are right. Segregation, discrimination, and prejudice are wrong. It is as simple as that. On the whole, 1963 and 1964 have been marked by progress. More Americans than ever before are conscious of the need to act. There have been voluntary, uncoerced, widely scattered changes for the better in the racial pattern in all of the areas of our concern. But it is not enough. And as the battle continues, I note that even some of us who should be the leaders of the movement are weakening in our convictions. We become confused and shaken by the arguments of the opposition. We become fearful when we are asked to pay a price. As in war when casualties mount, the will to press on is shaken and men inside begin to wonder whether victory is worth the dreaded sacrifice.

Last August 28, the March on Washington marked the high peak of moral and spiritual determination of the American people, white and Negro, to make the nation face up to revolutionary change in race relations. Since then the strains of battle have threatened the unity of our movement. We have allowed ourselves to be divided about such questions as the legality of demonstrations. We have been beaten in battles for ending *de facto* segregation of education in our Northern cities. We have argued amongst ourselves as to which techniques are effective. The slowness of accomplishment has made some draw back and others reckless. Our unity is threatened, and our will is weakened because we forget the firm basis of morality upon which the cause is based. We who profess faith in the God who spoke through the prophets of Israel and we who believe that that same God was revealed in Jesus Christ are united in the belief that by creation all mankind is one family. The prophet Malachi speaks for us all as he asks, "Have we not all one father? Has not one God created us? Why then are we faithless to one another. . . .?"

The crisis of the nation is no more severe than the crisis in our churches and synagogues. How can any of us ministers, priests, or rabbis stand safely eloquent behind our pulpits, reflecting the moral confusions of American culture in our tactful balanced prose when God is thundering at *His* people, calling them to repent and to be saved? Never in the life of the nation have the churches and synagogues through their best leadership been so fully united intellectually on any moral issue confronting the American people. But such intellectual unity will reveal the weakness and irrelevance of our pulpits, unless from them we speak and in the world we act to persuade our people to commit themselves to the new patterns of justice and freedom that must be established.

Let me then remind you now of the unargued, and I believe, unarguable morality upon which civil-rights legislation and civil-rights action is based. In our several traditions, the Judeo-Christian convictions about God and man are one in asserting: (1) That God made man in His image, which is to say that man is not merely an animal of a complicated sort but is in essence a spiritual being. His worth is not in his vigor, weight, or cleverness but in his origin. Because man, every man, is created by God, he must be treated, despite his sin, as a potential son of God, by covenant between God and man. (2) Right relations among men is based upon a personal concern for each one which we believe is not only our concern but that of God *Himself*. (3) The most important ethical considerations, and perhaps the only ones, are directly related to the effect of our actions upon the life and well-being of other men—all other men.

Look with me then at the aims of two sections of the civil-rights legislation assigned to me, education and public accommodations, in the light of our spiritual and moral agreement. Of all the disabilities put upon minority peoples by our present patterns of segregation and discrimination, these two, in education and in the standing insults to human dignity, are clearly the most immoral in the terms by which I have just described morality.

What has long been known by educators, and ten years ago been established by the courts, is that education of pupils involuntarily segregated by race has such bad effects on the educational process itself that equal educational opportunity is in fact not available to the segregated minority. And I remind you that the educational effect is not much different when the segregated minority school is retained against the Constitution in a Southern state or is maintained in fact by neighborhood racial ghettos in Northern cities. The effect of this inequality of educational opportunity hurts boys and girls, produces teen-age frustration, leading to crime and degeneracy. All of the learned discussion of the value of neighborhood schools is revealed to be quite irrelevant in the light of what segregated schooling is doing to some children of God. That the resolution of these problems will be difficult, North and South, all of us should know. That the problems must be solved, and quickly in the name of God, let school boards and education commissioners remember. It will be costly. We must spend the money. But no religious man dare say that we do not have money or brains enough to do this job. I plead with you all, wherever you live, begin now, if you have not already begun, to solve this school problem in your community. When school boards will not listen, as in Chester, Pennsylvania, or Cleveland, Ohio, demonstrations must be manned and pressed until the school boards listen or are replaced by an aroused electorate. One of our ministers gave his life a few weeks ago for that cause in Cleveland. Others must take his place.

The legislation before the Senate is aimed towards desegregated education in all the nation. We are for that legislation. But an even greater task than passing the legislation is, in each community of the nation, to renew and revive the educational opportunity of good desegregated public and private education for all the children of this land. It was *One* whom *His* disciples called Rabbi, who said to them: "Temptations to sin are sure to come; but woe to him by whom they come! It would be better for him if a millstone were hung around his neck and he were cast into the sea, than that he should cause one of these little ones to sin." And Jesus spoke here of offenses against little children. God forgive us our offenses against them through all these years.

Finally, as serious as offenses against opportunity for children are offenses against the dignity of men. The legislation before the Congress with regard to public accommodations seems in one sense to be the least important title of the law. What good does it do a Negro to be accepted in a fine restaurant if he has a job so poorly paid he can't afford to eat out at all? And white men ask, don't Negroes really like to associate together? It is true that the right to vote, the opportunity for a good education, the chance at any job for which a man is qualified as well as promotion in the job by merit, and finally the opportunity to buy or rent a decent home in which to shelter and raise a family—all these seem of more fundamental and long-range importance than the right to eat a hot dog in a central-city lunch counter. And yet, as far as morality is concerned, the right of human dignity is fully as important in race relations and perhaps even more important than all of these. Those of us who are white need to know what it does to man's soul and spirit when he sees his wife insulted and his children's eyes beclouded when these senseless indignities are suffered and he dare not protest for fear.

The argument against legislating a strong and universally enforceable public-accommodations section to the bill is that such a law impairs the rights of business people to enjoy their property and to use it as they see fit. How can any Christian or Jew sit still when such an immoral argument is voiced? Where in the Holy Bible, in Old Testament or New, can one find a single passage to support the rights of property as against the rights of men? The only moral justification in our society for the rights of property is the protection it affords men against encroachment upon their freedom by other men or by government. Have we learned nothing since the day Amos thundered against those, who for profit, degraded men? Have we become so enamored of things that we forget that we are men created by a just and loving God?

Let any man who wishes to use his property to serve the public and make his living by it, let any such man know now that he must serve all the public without discrimination. He may insist that his customers be clean. So be it. Any man can wash. He may require his customers to dress properly. So be it. In our affluent society even the poor can find a proper jacket or a proper dress to wear. He may require sobriety, quiet, orderliness, and courtesy from those who wish his services. So be it. White people have no monopoly in any of these. But one thing he may not do and be a moral man—he cannot require a dark man to turn white or to enter by another door. This is an insult to another man, his brother by God's creation. No man may so use his property.

And unless we quickly understand what such standing insults in our society do to make peaceful men turn violent, and patient men lose their self-control—we understand neither the first level of morals nor the depth of the crisis that race discrimination has brought to our once proud nation.

Our task, as churchmen, is not to be expert in legislation, or to tell the Congress how to legislate. But it is our task and it is our competence to cut through the fog of immorality that threatens every American home and every church and synagogue, and to say so that everyone can hear and heed—

Thus saith the Lord.
Let justice roll down like waters and righteousness like an ever-flowing stream.
Woe to them who are at ease in Zion and to those who feel secure on the mountain of Samaria.
Behold the days are coming says the Lord God when I will send a famine on the land; not a famine of bread, nor a thirst for water, but of hearing the words of the Lord.
He that hath ears to hear, let him hear.

Dedicated to a Proposition
BISHOP GERALD KENNEDY

For nearly thirty-five years Bishop Gerald Hamilton Kennedy has been on intimate terms with gospel ministry. In a long and active career, he has earned a position of eminence in the world of religion, scholarship, and letters. He was born in Benzonia, Michigan, educated at the College of the Pacific; the Pacific School of Religion, where he took his A.M. and B.D. degrees in 1931 and 1932; and at Hartford Theological Seminary, where he received his S.T.M. and Ph.D. degrees in 1933 and 1934. In addition, he has received honorary degrees from such distinguished institutions as the College of Puget Sound, Nebraska Wesleyan University, Beloit College, Ohio Wesleyan University, Redlands University, Bucknell University, Bradley University, and California Western University.

Dr. Kennedy has been a dominant figure as a lecturer on college and university campuses for a score of years. Among the institutions where he has held lectureships are the Pacific School of Religion, Southern Methodist, Emory, Depauw, Auburn, Colgate, Yale, and Union Theological Seminary. He is a member of the Executive Board of the National Council of Churches, a member of the California State Board of Education, and also serves on the boards of trustees of several institutions of higher learning.

A prolific writer, Bishop Kennedy has written, among others, *His Word Through Preaching, The Best of John Henry Jowett* (ed.), *The Christian and His America,* and *The Methodist Way of Life.*

"Dedicated to a Proposition" is a sermon delivered on the subject of civil rights. It was presented before the Chicago Sunday Evening Club on November 15, 1964.

* * *

"He created every race of men of one stock. . ." (Acts 13:26, N.E.B.).

Our Ambassador to the United Nations, Mr. Adlai Stevenson, wrote a magazine article on "The Hard Kind of Patriotism."[1] Mr. Stevenson pointed out that this nation differs from others in its principle of unity. We are not bound together by a common heritage since we came from many different countries. We are not people of a single culture and we have not been united through conquest. We are, he says, a land "dedicated to a prosposition," and our unity centers around principles. He was referring, of course, to the phrase used by Abraham Lincoln in the "Gettysburg Address." In that crucial, tragic moment of our history the President said that we were testing whether or not the proposition that had given us birth could withstand the strains of civil war.

Today our society has been forced to pay new attention to our faith. On the one-hundredth anniversary of the issuing of the Emancipation Proclamation, Negro Americans by their demonstrations are forcing our society to consider seriously the original proposition which gave us birth. It is a painful time for white as well as for black citizens. We are confronted by our dilatoriness and our willingness to preach one thing while we practice another. We are face to face with the judgment of the denial of our heritage. This is a time of

---

[1] *Harpers,* August, 1963.

suffering and shock. It is a time when we must re-examine who we are, where we came from, and what we believe.

The first thing I want to say is that *we always live by faith.* Or to put it in another way, we live on the basis of propositions which we cannot prove but which we commit ourselves to live by.

It is amazing how much we assume. The so-called scientific laws oftentimes grow out of date. Not long ago it was discovered that inert gases will combine with chemical elements. Through all the previous years it was thought that this was not possible, so that now the scientific textbooks have to be changed and a scientific law has to be amended. When we deal with the material things of life we must live by faith even as we do in the spiritual realm. We are always moving out beyond the evidence and indeed we could not live on what we can prove.

It would seem that economics could be resolved to a few solid rules so that we would know how to be prosperous and how to prevent depression. There comes to my desk a little paper put out by a New York bank which proposes to give the economic trends for the future. I stopped reading it long ago because it does not really say anything. Its articles announce that if such and such a thing does not happen then perhaps this result may be expected. There is so much hedging in economic forecasting that it becomes obvious that nobody really knows. The only sure thing is J. P. Morgan's prediction concerning the stock market, "It will fluctuate." An outstanding CPA told me one time that his work was as much art as science and that ultimately we must depend upon the character of the accountant himself.

Sociology is far from scientific. We cannot say for sure why juveniles become delinquent and we do not know why one boy goes wrong and another boy goes right. Just when we think we have the principles announced there appears so many exceptions that we have to admit our inability to forecast human behavior. People are the most unpredictable creatures in the world and the heart has secrets which no science can explain.

If a man considers a day in his own life, he knows how uncertain things are. He begins with plans which oftentimes are frustrated and the end of the day seldom reveals what he had expected. We plan for the future the best way we can but the wise man knows that the future is beyond his control. My father always used the phrase "the good Lord willing." The older I grow, the more I understand the wisdom of that spirit. Remember the wise word of *the*

Epistle of James, "What is your life? For you are a mist that appears for a little time and then vanishes. Instead you ought to say, 'If the Lord wills, we shall live and we shall do this or that'" (James 4:14–15). God has made our life so that we are driven to commit ourselves to propositions we must live by, but which are always in the realm beyond proof.

I marvel at the ability of men to forecast happenings in the universe. A physical scientist may be able to tell us to a split second the time of the next eclipse of the sun. He may be able to forecast the exact position of Saturn in the year 2000. But that same scientist cannot be sure what his teen-age boy is going to do tomorrow. We live by faith.

Now the second thing that needs to be said is that *life is a dedication.* The strength of the nation lies primarily in a willingness to commit itself to its faith. What we believe was announced by the Founding Fathers in their Declaration of Independence. They had a high regard for the public opinion of the world and when they severed their relationship with Great Britain, they wanted to make sure that the rest of the world knew why they were doing it and what they had in mind. So we have in that great document, not only a Declaration of Independence but really a Declaration of Faith. They wrote: "We hold these truths to be self-evident, that all men are created equal, that they are endowed by their Creator with certain inalienable Rights." America was to be something different for it was to be a land where every man could expect equal justice and equal opportunity regardless of race or class. Some of us have forgotten how through the years New York Harbor has been the gateway to equal opportunity for every man. So when in the darkness of the Civil War slaughter, people stood in the presence of their dead, President Lincoln reminded them again of the ideas for which these men had died. Faith becomes powerful only when it becomes something more than intellectual assent. It calls for complete commitment from those who have announced what they believe.

The future of any society depends on the greatness of its faith and the strength which men dedicate to its fulfillment. In all of our talk these days about defense and foreign aid, we need to keep this truth very clear in our minds. It is an unseen spirit of devotion which produces the power to live by. A nation will find its chief temptation is to compromise in the name of expediency. For as our awareness of our chief purposes grows dim, we become more like the enemy and our allies and friends become confused and uncertain. We cannot conquer without a continuing renewal of our dedication to the purposes of the nation. This means that our chief enemy is always within our borders and, indeed, it is usually within our own hearts. The hesitancy which Americans have felt in taking seriously the commitments of the Declaration of Independence has spelled weakness and not strength. It is time to recover knowledge of the propositions and find a great new voice to proclaim this faith abroad.

The Christian church comes into our world with an idea about man and his ultimate nature. It proclaims the worth of every human creature and the universal brotherhood of all of us. There is no biblical support for prejudice or for the artificial distinctions of color and class. When the church ceases to be dedicated to that philosophy or when it ceases to practice it within its own fellowship, it destroys one of the main foundation stones and it surrenders its claim to universality.

We are committed to a society in which every child has his opportunity. We must be forevermore opposed to saddling any youngster with manmade handicaps. When we put these millstones around the necks of children because they happen to be born in a certain place and of a certain race, we are guilty of denying our Lord. Our compromise in this field has led to nothing but failure. If the church is to have any authoritative word in our time, it must come from commitment to our belief in all men.

In my own poor life and yours this principle of the necessity of dedication finally brings us to judgment. All that we are worth are the propositions we have given ourselves to serve. Our test finally is the extent to which we have been faithful to our principles. The measure of any man's life is ultimately the measure of his dedication to the propositions he accepted.

Logan Pearsall Smith once wrote in his diary: "What a bore it is to wake up every morning the same person!" But it would be very confusing and frustrating to wake up every morning a different person. Actually, the thing that saves us from boredom is to wake up every morning with a sense of privilege and adventure which comes from our commitment to great issues. And if we have a dream of wider brotherhood and more justice, each day becomes a more exciting adventure.

A third thing we need to observe is that *our commitments have become vague.* It is too easy to believe that yesterday was better than today and that our modern problems are unique. It does seem true to me, however, that there is a kind of uncertainty in our contemporary situation which makes it very difficult for us to determine the propositions which are important.

A few years ago the Council of Bishops of the Methodist Church met in Washington, D.C. We called on President Dwight Eisenhower at the White House. The secretary of our Council read to the President the greetings which had been delivered to President Washington by the first Methodist bishop of America, Francis Asbury, more than 150 years before. In his reply to this greeting, the President remarked how simple life seemed to be in those days compared with life today. There were so few government employees and so few international involvements, unlike the present situation. Then he went on to say that the more involved and complicated life becomes, the more important it is that men should have a clear vision of the underlying principles. It is this clear vision that is lacking with us. The complications of our present life blur the sharp lines of our principles.

We see it in the movies. Now and again, there is a picture which is downright suggestive and people with some sense of moral decency are shocked. But in some ways a more serious defect is the motion picture which stays within the laws of decency but offers only a meaningless hodgepodge of activity as our way of life. The thing that troubles me more than anything else in modern pictures is this lack of moral awareness and a loss of the ability to distinguish between what is good and what is evil. It is a tendency which we see in city, state, and national government and is observed in all our society.

This is a disease which attacks the church. The modern church in some ways looks very imposing. We rejoice in the billions of dollars worth of property represented by the churches in America. We can be proud of the number of people who claim membership in American churches, for it is at the highest point in all our history. We have been prosperous and we have had less trouble with budgets than ever before. But the sharp outline of our commitment is no longer observable. The unique witness of Christians seems to have faded into a twilight atmosphere of blurred images. A sickness which could be unto death is the loss of our sense of ultimate loyalties.

John Steinbeck drove leisurely across the nation from east to west and then back again. He wrote about his experiences in a book: *Travels with Charlie*. He tells of a conversation with a New Hampshire farmer by the roadside. He asked what people around there were saying and thinking about the November elections and about the world in general. The farmer said the people didn't say much about any of these things. Steinbeck asked him if it was because they were scared. The farmer said some of them are scared but not all of them and even those who were not scared did not have much to say. Then as the two men wondered why this was, the farmer said, "Well, you take my grandfather and his father. . . . They knew some things they were sure about . . . but now . . . nobody knows. . . . We've got nothing to go on—got no way to think about things."

Surely it is an amazing thing that the more success we have achieved, the less sure we are of the meaning of life. The more wealth we pile up, the more doubt we seem to gather at the same time. Bitterness between races does not disappear with prosperity. Military might has failed to provide us with confidence, with love, or with power.

I despair over young people who are outside the church and have no religious upbringing. To what shall they dedicate themselves if they believe only in atheism and in existential despair? They have seen very few good examples and they have heard very little clear proclamation of faith. How desperately we need someone to stand before us and define anew the propositions to which we are dedicated as American Christians.

A student in a ninth-grade English class in a Texas high school concluded his book report with this appraisal, "I think the author was a pretty good writer not to make the book no duller than it was." Those are often my sentiments when I realize how little opportunity many of our young people have had to be confronted by faith. It is a wonder they are not worse than they are. How little they have been taught about what has brought us on our way and makes us different from other nations. It is a time of darkness and danger because the vision has faded and the darkness of our doubts obscures the path.

The last thing to say is that here is where *Christ helps us.* When we are confronted by God in Christ we see the issues which demand our decisions. Christianity is not a mere coloring of morality with a little emotion but light on our path.

When on Sunday morning in our churches we stand and say, "We believe in God Almighty," we are saying something of such serious importance that I do not know how we say it so easily. For the truth is that the reality of God brings a man's life under a searching judgment. If we believe in God, then we believe that our lives have meaning and we have responsibilities one to another. For if God is, then life has a plot and a purpose.

We believe in brotherhood, which is to say that no man lives unto himself. It is to say that every man is responsible for every other man and that the artificial barriers we place between men are the signs of our sin. No Christian can withdraw unto himself or retreat into his own little circle. He is committed to the belief that since God is the Father of all of us, the withholding of fellowship from any human being is a severing of our relationship with God.

The thing that Christ does for us above all else is to make clear that justice is not a gift we have a right to ration. It is apparent in our Christian faith that justice is something God has decreed for all men. When we talk about civil rights, we are not talking about privileges to be bestowed or withheld at anyone's whim. God demands justice for all of us and we must demand it for one another. The Christian church has no other choice but to dedicate itself to these propositions.

This is painful and it hurts and we will not play down this part of the process. But it seems perfectly clear that every conference, every council, every leader of any Christian church must promise the support of the whole Christian fellowship to any man, black or white, who seeks equal rights for himself and his family. It is too bad that we could not see this for ourselves but must be reminded of it by the sacrifices of our Negro brethren.

Men need God's help to see that evil is evil, nonsense is nonsense, and good is good. The world is in need of men who can make plain the propositions by which we live. This is the task and the responsibility of churchmen. More than that, it is the tremendous privilege that Christians enjoy. In Christ, we know that there is neither male nor female, neither Gentile nor Jew. Indeed, we find in Him the fulfillment of our search for peace and brotherhood.

Many years ago I saw Marc Connelly's *The Green Pastures*. I went to the play unexpectantly, for I thought it would have nothing to say to an American seminary student. But if I went to scoff, I remained to pray. I remember yet the scene where Moses appeared before Pharaoh demanding freedom for his people. The miracles impressed Pharaoh. "I don't say you ain't a good tricker, Moses," the king admitted. "You is one of the best I ever seen." But Moses replied, "It ain't only me dat's goin' to wuk dis trick. It's me an' de Lawd."

It will be neither our cleverness nor our virtue which will bring us through this struggle for human rights, but the power of God. It is for us to remind ourselves of the propositions of our faith. For while there is a little of the black Muslim in every Negro and a little of the Ku Klux Klan in every white man, there is also the cleansing power of God. This struggle belongs to all of us and we can engage in it with the confidence that our victory is the will of God.

In Christ There Is No East or West

ELDER SAKAE KUBO

Sakae Kubo, an Hawaiian by birth, is an associate professor of the New Testament at Andrews University. He received the degrees of Bachelor of Divinity and Master of Arts at the Seventh-day Adventist Seminary in Washington, D.C., and the Doctor of Philosophy from the University of Chicago.

A member of several learned societies, among which are the Society of Biblical Language and Literature and the Chicago Biblical Research Society, Dr. Kubo has published many scholarly articles over the years.

How can we achieve a greater unity within the Christian church among men of all races? This is the question that Dr. Kubo addresses himself to in the sermon, "In Christ There Is No East nor West." The presentation was made at the Pioneer Memorial Seventh-Day Adventist Church in Berrien Springs, Michigan on June 13, 1964.

* * *

Text: I do not pray for these only, but also for those who are to believe in me through their word, that they may all be one; even as thou, Father, art in me, and I in thee, that they also may be in us, so that the world may believe that thou has sent me (John 17:20–21).

We have heard several times, as one comes to expect, at times of commencement, the quotation from Victor Hugo that there is nothing as powerful as an idea whose time has come. The idea whose time has come today is the equality of all races and the oneness of the human race. It is in the light of this prevailing mood throughout the world and in our own country that the words that are spoken today must be assessed. In the light of this prevailing mood, the church can remain silent only at the risk of its becoming impertinent and irrelevant with regard to human problems and conditions. In fact, the situation is changing so rapidly that those who oppose or are mute regarding a positive solution to the race question are not being conservative but radical.

But there are still some of you who may have sincere misgivings about speaking on such a subject in the pulpit. You may say, "We should not get involved in politics." I would agree with you. As Morris Adler says,

> There is a degree of involvement beyond which it [the church] may not venture, since in its entanglement with the immediacies it may become estranged from ultimates. Politics by its very nature is concerned with expediencies, with the possible rather than the ideal.

The church must always stand apart from politics that it may continually serve as a clear, uncompromising, idealistic conscience for society. There is too much compromise and give and take in politics that by its participation in it the church may lose its clear vision. But to speak out on race relations from a Christian perspective is no more political than to speak out against bribery, or gambling, or other social sins. Even the Mennonite Church, which has traditionally stood apart from politics, issued a statement in 1955 on race relations and, of course, with no thought of it as being political.

The church must be the conscience of society, the conscience of the nation. If it is to serve its function, it must be a voice crying in the wilderness and not a mere echo of the secular mores and standards of worldly society.

It is a sad commentary on the church's witness when it cannot speak out boldly on the biblical message of love and brotherhood for fear it might be political. It is considered political only, unfortunately, because the church has not been its true self and the government is helping the church to be the church in implying by its intervention the church's failure not only to affect society but its own members.

You may say that Paul did not concern himself with social problems. He did not speak out against slavery. The analogy to our situation, however, is not what Paul said about slavery in A.D. 50 but what he would have said about it in A.D. 1860 when the conscience of the world was aroused by the very Christian message of Paul that all are one in Christ Jesus. Surely we cannot imagine Paul in favor of slavery or even tolerant of it in the nineteenth century. There is a time, in other words, when an idea is more ripe than at another time.

The point also in regard to Paul is that within his writings were contained the seeds for the overthrow of slavery and superior race attitudes. Should not the Christian help to overthrow the system and attitudes for whose fall the Bible had intended when the conscience of the world has been moved by the Christian ethic and it itself comes to recognize its evil?

Paul while respecting the priority of the Jew preached, nevertheless, the equality of the Gentile in the Christian church. The Gentile did not need to become a Jew, but instead Jew and Gentile became one new man in Christ Jesus. "But now, through the blood of Christ, you who were once outside the pale are with us inside the circle of God's love and purpose." For Christ is our living peace. He has made a unity of the conflicting elements of Jew and Gentile by breaking down the barrier which lay between us. By his sacrifice he removed the hostility of the Law, with all its commandments and rules, and made in Himself out of the two, Jew and Gentile, one new man, thus producing peace. For He reconciled both to God by the sacrifice of one body on the cross, and by this act made utterly irrelevant the antagonism between them. Then He came and told both you who were far from God and us who were near that the war was over. And it is through Him that both of us now can approach the Father in the one spirit.

"So you are no longer outsiders or aliens, but fellow citizens with every other Christian—you belong now to the household of God."

This was the idea whose time had come in Paul's day, but whose time had not yet come in Jesus' day, although the seeds had been sown by Him. Paul did not cater to the Judaizers in regard to the position of the Gentiles, but he heroically championed their cause. It was a thoroughly Christian message and its time had come. So is the matter of racial equality today.

You say Christians should not be troublemakers. It is true "that Christians deny their Prince of Peace," says Haselden, "when they deliberately for any reason incite hostilities between men or between themselves and other men. . . . The Christian is never a deliberate troublemaker, never sows seeds of suspicion, never does the ethical act simply for effect." But the problem is not simply solved by saying he will never cause any kind of trouble. "Consider, first," Haselden continues,

the fact that the silence and inactivity which purchase the white man's peace with his family and his white friends and neighbors offends the Negroes and alienates them. One way or the other, active in racial good will or inactive, he participates in a basic human conflict. If he says and does nothing to aid the oppressed and humiliated Negro, there is a tension between him and the Negro. If he acts in justice and charity, there is tension between him and white people irritated by his action. He cannot, therefore, decide what he should do on a tension-or-no-tension basis. Conflict is inherent in the situation. He must decide his course on the basis of what he concludes is God's will for him in the situation and let tension express itself as it will. What he does will hurt someone, antagonize someone. The Christian in the life-situation does not choose one human conflict over another; he chooses the deed which he believes God wills for him and lets the conflict choose him.

The ethical act . . . does not in fact produce tension. On the contrary the deed is a "scandal" in that it exposes tensions which already exist. The act threatens us because it strips away the formalities, the convivial screens of conversational and fashionable pleasantries, and reveals the ugliness we thought we alone knew hidden in us. . . . The act, in other words, explodes artificial existence by exposing the concealed conflicts which are inherent in all vital social issues. . . . We conclude, then, that the ethical act in the area of racial good will does not create tensions; rather it discloses already existing tensions and by disclosing them makes them potentially creative.[1]

The same situation prevails in our speaking on this subject. We do not decide on it on the basis of tension or no tension but on the basis of its relationship to God's will, and also by disclosing existing tensions it makes it possible for us to do something about them.

You say, "Should we occupy ourselves with social problems when we should be preaching the gospel?"

The validity of the gospel message is seen in its efficacy in social relationships. James 2:10, "For whoever keeps the whole law but fails in one point has become guilty of all of it," is pertinent to social relationships. The law here is primarily "you shall love your neighbor as yourself" (James 2:8), and it deals with the Christian's relationship to the rich and the poor visitors as they come to the Christian churches. The excuse of the recipients of the letter was that they were catering to the rich to fulfill the law that they must love their neighbors as themselves. James's answer is that if you keep the whole law but fail in one point you are guilty of all. If you do not respect your neighbor because he is poor, you are a transgressor of the whole law even though you show respect to the rich. This principle is applicable today in regard to our treatment of people of different races in our churches.

---

[1] Kyle and Elizabeth Haselden, "Racial Tension—Enemy and Ally," *Dialog,* 111 (Spring, 1964), 110–111.

The Decalogue has six commandments that deal with love to our neighbor. Who is our neighbor? The Samaritan considered the wounded Jew his neighbor. Will the modern Jew with his advantages consider the modern Samaritan oppressed and deprived of opportunities his neighbor?

The essence of the gospel is love and it cannot be otherwise for God is love, but love is always social. Love is unthinkable and a contradiction apart from social relationships.

Abraham Heschel's definition of a prophet in the light of the great social prophets who cried out against the oppression of the poor and the widow, who condemned religiosity without morality is this:

A prophet is a person who holds God and men in one thought at one time, at all times. Our tragedy begins with the segregation of God, with the bifurcation of the secular and the sacred. We worry more about the purity of dogmas than the integrity of love.[2]

Dr. William Temple puts it in these words: "It is a great mistake to suppose that God is only or even mainly concerned with religion."[3] The segregation of God! Are we guilty of the segregation of God? Have we taken God out of the practical affairs of life? Have we segregated Him and pushed Him outside our daily life so that we can callously practice racial prejudice without any twinge of conscience?

John in writing his first epistle was troubled about those who claimed the traditional Christian terminology. These Gnostic heretics had a mystic type of religion and were claiming to have the light, claiming to be righteous, claiming to be the children of God, claiming to be born of God, claiming to have the truth, claiming to have the spirit of prophecy.

In meeting this dangerous heresy, whose adherents were destroying the fellowship of the saints by their superior, sophisticated attitude toward those without "knowledge," John lays down some important criteria by which we can test the genuineness of internal claims. Among these criteria, and one which runs throughout the epistle, is love for our brother.

He who says he is in the light and *hates his brother* is in the darkness still. He who loves his brother abides in the light, and in it

[2] "The Segregation of God," *Race: Challenge to Religion,* ed. Matthew Ahmann, p. 64.
[3] Quoted by Morris Adler, "Relation of Church and Synagogue to Other Community Forces." *Race: Challenge to Religion,* ed. Matthew Ahmann, p. 106.

there is no cause for stumbling. But he who *hates his brother* is in the darkness and walks in the darkness, and does not know where he is going, because the darkness has blinded his eyes (I John 2:9–11).

"By this it may be seen who are the children of God, and who are the children of the devil: no one who does not do right is of God, *nor any one who does not love his brother*" (I John 3:10). "We know that we have passed out of death into life, because we love the brethren. He who does not love remains in death. Any one who hates his brother is a murderer, and you know that no murderer has eternal life abiding in him" (I John 3:14–15). In effect he was saying to them, "You may say you have the light, you have been born of God, you are righteous, you are children of God, but if you do not love your neighbor, you are still in darkness. You are children of the devil."

If the gospel does not deal with social relationships, and I speak primarily in a personal sense, then it is an emasculated gospel. As James says, "Faith without works is dead." Many thoughtful people ask why the church is the last institution to integrate. A few years ago, Dean Liston Pope said, "The church has lagged behind the Supreme Court as the conscience of the nation on the question of race and it has fallen far behind trade unions, factories, schools, department stores, athletic gatherings, and most other major human associations, as far as the achievement of integration in its own life is concerned."[4]

"Faith without works is dead." Unless Christianity speaks to the needs and the practical problems of men it will be considered meaningless, impertinent, and irrelevant. John MacMurray spoke these words in an earlier generation but they are just as important today:

Religion stands at the crossroads. Throughout the world the parties of social progress are, in general, either passively or actively antireligious. Organized religion, on the defensive, tends to range itself, actively or passively, with the conservatives and the reactionaries. But the tide of social evolution cannot forever be dammed by the dykes of vested interest. The progressive forces are bound to win; and it looks as though the bursting of the dykes would be quick and catastrophic. If in that hour religion is found still on the side of reaction, as it was in Russia, it must suffer almost total eclipse. Its existing forms will be doomed to destruction.

---

[4] Quoted by Morris Adler, *Ibid.*, p. 109.
[5] Quoted in Luccock and Brentano, *The Questing Spirit*, p. 621.

We have dealt at length with a defense for speaking on this subject for fear that what might be said would prove completely unprofitable. Having said these foregoing words I hope that we will at least get a hearing.

Our concern this morning is directed not on us as human beings with biological identity or as Americans who are witnessing and living within a social revolution, but to ourselves as Christians.

The Christian claim that its gospel is universal and international in scope in contrast to pagan religions must be more than a verbal pronouncement. The church truly is neither American, nor European, nor white, nor Western, but it is made up of peoples of all races and they are all one new man in Christ Jesus. "There is neither Jew nor Greek, there is neither slave nor free, there is neither male nor female, for you are all one in Christ Jesus" (Galatians 2:28). Our faith in Christ must transcend national boundaries and racial backgrounds. Many people from different countries and racial backgrounds feel that we are still very far from this ideal. There are still too many signs which indicate to the colored races that the white man thinks that Christianity is an American or white man's product. As Christians, we need to realize in practice and attitude the international nature of Christianity.

As Christians we need to take more seriously the meaning of creation with regard to the race problem. It means that we have one Father and that all men are created in the image of God. There is no rank or degree in regard to amount of the image of God.

We need to take more seriously the meaning of the word "world" in the verse, "God so loved the world." Each man, we say so frequently, is so valuable that Christ would have died for that man; then this must be true even if he were a Negro. We must come to acknowledge and forever refuse to make a distinction between a Negro and a man. We must come to recognize him as a man. Like Shylock, the Negro can say,

" . . . Hath not a Negro eyes? Hath not a Negro hands, organs, dimensions, senses, affections, passions? Fed with the same food, hurt with the same weapons, subject to the same diseases, healed by the same means, warmed and cooled by the same winter and summer? If you prick us, do we not bleed? If you tickle us, do we not laugh? If you poison us, do we not die?"

It is not enough to recognize him as a man; we must recognize him also as a man who has the need to belong. When Kyle Haselden moved to West Virginia, he found that it was customary for the students in the early grades to kiss their schoolteacher twice a day, noon and afternoon at the dismissal of school. When integration began, his wife happened to be present. At noon one of the first-grade white teachers came out preceded by an attractive Negro boy, the only Negro in her class. She said, "Now you stand there and the other children will join you and you can all march out together." But as he saw the white children file by giving their farewell kisses to their teacher, he made his way into the line but he was gently taken aside again and instructed to wait until all the others had come through. She continued what she was doing before and as she came to the last pupil, it was the Negro boy, a wistful look in his face and his arms outstretched to give her a kiss. This time he was accepted and he went his way happily and contentedly. It was not that the Negro boy had an irrepressible desire to kiss the teacher; but there was in him an impulsive hunger to do what the other children were doing. He wanted to know that he belonged.[6]

As Christians we must come to see what racial prejudice really is. It is an expression of man's self-centeredness and pride. "Prejudice," according to Haselden,

in its ultimate reduction is a specific manifestation of the innate and inevitable self-centeredness of every human being, a self-centeredness which, carried to its logical and final extreme, must exclude God. Racial prejudice is an externalized and objectified form of that self-centeredness, a visible part of that invisible pride which must subdue all rivals and whose last rival is God. We can say, therefore, that prejudice, put theologically, is one of man's several neurotic and perverted expressions of his will to be God.[7]

Prejudice then has its root in man's basic sin of pride, and pride is the characteristic of the anti-Christ. It is in complete opposition and disposition from the mind of Christ which Paul admonishes us to put on.

Do nothing from selfishness or conceit, but in humility count others better than yourselves. Let each of you look not only to his own interests, but also to the interests of others. Have this mind among yourselves, which you have in Christ Jesus, who, though he was in the form of God, did not count equality with God a thing to be grasped, but emptied himself, taking the form of a servant, being born in the likeness of men (Phillipians 2:3–7).

---

[6] Kyle Haselden, *The Racial Problem in Christian Perspective*, p. 130.
[7] *Ibid.*, p. 85.

As Christians we must come to see that racial prejudice is a result of our conformity to the world. Dr. Franklin Littell goes so far as to say that the manifestation of racial prejudice in the Christian church is a "product of indiscipline. Racialism is a kind of heathenism, and its presence among the baptized is above all a sign of lack of religion."[8] He adds, "As Rufus Jones once said, our churches have become so big they are like Robinson Crusoe's goat pasture: the fences are so distant and the fields are so big that the goats inside are as wild as the goats outside!"

The Mennonite Church in its pamphlet on race relations expresses aptly this point:

> We have failed to see that acceptance of the social patterns of segregation and discrimination is a violation of the command to be "not conformed to this world." Often we have been silent when others showed race prejudice and practiced discrimination. Too often our behavior has been determined by our selfish considerations of public and social approval more than by our desire to accept the way of the cross. Some of us have accepted the false propaganda of racism and anti-Semitism which has come into our homes in the guise of Christian literature. Too often we have equated our own culture with Christianity without sensing which elements were genuinely Christian and which were merely cultural accretions from a secular society. Many times we have made it difficult for Christians of national origin different from our own to find fellowship among us because our own cultural pride and attitudes of exclusiveness served as obstacles. For these and our many other sins we repent before our fellow men and our God.

It must never be said of us that expediency as a reason for segregation has become a pretext for racial prejudice. We have said that segregation was necessary for the advancement of the kingdom. We have said that we love the colored brother but that if he worshipped with us our non-Christian white friends would not come to church. Today this motive needs to be scrutinized to see whether it has become only a pretext for racial prejudice. Is it not really because the white Christian is offended?

Christians must recognize that their witness to the power of the Gospel is seen in that oneness that unites them to one another because they each are united to Christ. Christ's prayer was "that they may all be one; even as thou Father, art in me, and I in thee, that they also may be in us, so that the world may believe that thou

---

[8] "Religion and Race," *Race: Challenge to Religion, op. cit.*, p. 39.

hast sent me" (John 17:21). The church must not only claim the truth, but practice it and must actively seek to bring this divine unity and oneness into its midst.

Paul describes the church as the body of Christ. As Christians, therefore, our oneness must transcend the mere oneness of humanity. As Haselden puts it:

> For Paul the ethnological problem within the Christian fellowship was dissolved, not in the awareness of man's biological identity, but in that oneness which men have in Christ, not "after the flesh" but "after the spirit," not in the solid and shared flesh of men but in the broken and shared body of Christ, not in consanguinity but in communion. Christians—Negroes and whites—are not merely members of one flesh, but even more, members of one body.[9]

If such is the fellowship within the church, it transcends mere human oneness. If this is so, how can we claim to be part of the body of Christ and verbalize and practice racial prejudice and superior race attitudes. If the Christian has this awareness of fellowship in Christ and practices it, the church can yet make the biggest contribution to the solution of racial tensions. While laws may grant legal rights, they do not and cannot compel that these rights be granted in such a way as to make the person feel accepted. What we have is "physical proximity without spiritual affinity," which is really a volatile situation. Only the Christian in his relations with peoples of other races can bring the ingredient of love and fellowship which only can make truly effective the mere legal rights granted to them. The laws can bring about desegregation, but only Christians can bring about true *integration*. From this standpoint Christ's words are again meaningful: "You [the church] are the light of the world." So be it.

The Church, The Gospel, and Segregation
ELDER W. S. LEE

Willie S. Lee, an active civil-rights crusader in the Seventh-day Adventist Church, entered the ministry in 1936 in Oklahoma. A native of Dothan, Alabama, he is a graduate of Oakwood College

---

[9] *Op. cit.,* p. 189.

in Huntsville, Alabama. He has served as evangelist and pastor in Arkansas, Louisiana, New York, and California. From 1950 to 1955, he was pastor of one of the denomination's largest churches, Ephesus in New York City. For ten years, he served as the Human Relations Secretary for the Pacific Union Conference of Seventh-day Adventists, which comprises the states of California, Nevada, Utah, and Hawaii. He is now serving as President of the Central States Conference of Seventh-day Adventists in Kansas City, Missouri.

Pastor Lee is a firm believer in a positive, plain approach to the racial problem. He does not believe in generalities and racial evolution. He further believes that it is the duty of the gospel minister to make things happen that will erase the position of the Negro as a second-class citizen within the church and without.

The sermon included here states his position on the church's duties and responsibilities as it relates to practical Christianity. "The Church, The Gospel, and Segregation" was delivered at an inter-racial workshop for religious leaders and church workers in Glendale, California, August 25, 1965.

* * *

The first organized interfaith effort of the institutional church to play an active role as a church in removing the evil of segregation began with the National Conference on Religion and Race in Chicago, January 14–17, 1963. This was the first real racial confrontation by the church. It represents the first formal cooperation of major denominations designed to eliminate segregation in the church and in the nation.

Through the years, the church has taken an apathetic, apologetic, and compromising attitude toward segregation. During these years, it has attempted to justify segregation to the extent that it had practically absolved itself of all responsibility. Thus, this diabolic evil was nourished and permitted to flourish because the church refused to look upon it as evil. The church has shown a slothful attitude in acknowledging its responsibility. Even when it was rightfully and forcefully argued that segregation is a moral issue, which works in direct opposition to the gospel, the voice of the church was heard saying, "Segregation is purely a political issue." When social and political leaders sought the cooperation and support of the church in passing desegregation laws, the voice of the church was heard saying, "You cannot legislate morals."

Color segregation in its American pattern had its beginning after the defeat of the Reconstruction and was born out of the frustration and the hatred brought about by the Reconstruction period. Segregation was a deliberately devised plan to dehumanize the Negro, exercise control over him, keep him available for exploitation. By the enactment of laws, through education, organized intimidation, brutality, segregation became the "way of life" in America.

From the beginning of segregation, the church was not merely apathetic, but defended and practiced segregation. The worship hour became and still is the most segregated period in America. It was mainly the church's attitude that kept the world deceived about the real evil of segregation and its incompatibility with the gospel of Jesus Christ. Even until this day, some are either not informed or ill-informed about the true nature of segregation. Segregation was no accident; it was deliberately planned and made an institutional evil. The church's attitude toward this indescribable evil caused more frustration than help. "Shallow understanding from people of good will is more frustrating than absolute misunderstanding from people of ill will."

The first order of the Christian church when confronted by institutionalized evil such as we find in segregation is to thoroughly investigate, and find an understanding. This has been the church's weakness, perhaps. It is much easier to accept a superficial view of life than to plunge into the depths of its evil. This is where the church is in danger of betraying its faith. We don't let God lead us into any demanding situations.

The racial demonstrations of the past few years have brought segregation, with all of its evil, into the open. These demonstrations have brought before the Christian church its sharpest challenge since the Reformation. In time of racial revolution, the church cannot remain as it was. The soul of the church has been laid bare. It can no longer defend segregation as a Bible plan by distorting the Word of God. In times of revolution, all things are brought to light. Segregation is a challenge of the Sovereignty of God and the church was leading men to take the place of God; to dehumanize the Negro was to break his link with eternity; to destroy his soul; to challenge the Fatherhood of God and the brotherhood of man as established by God Himself and maintained by his limitless love, demonstrated by the death of His Son for all mankind.

The church must do in a short time what it has failed to do over a long period of time. It must undo what it has done. Segregation was established by law, education, deceit, hatred, and cowardice. It can only be removed by education, laws, faith, love, and courage.

What was established by law can only be removed by law. Laws changed deportment, which in turn effected the change of attitude and the change of mind, thus creating an atmosphere where integration can work. Human behavior is influenced more by a situation than by personal attitude. Examples are found in various cities, and in the various churches where there have been the various demonstrations. Education is more effective in practice.

The present racial revolution has brought into focus both the purposes and power of the gospel. The church is unique in that it claims power above that which is inherent in law and education; the power of the gospel, which is the power of the love of God, which the church professes to have. This power does not conform to man, his patterns and way and prejudices, but completely changes the man, both the inherited and the acquired characteristics. The church and gospel is the most potent agency, the only agency that can put things back together where they belong.

This requires a twentieth-century reformation within the church, a reappraisal of the gospel message and its power. The church must look again at James 2:1–10, where James shows that where a person keeps all ten commandments, according to the letter of the law, and yet practices segregation in seating in the church, is guilty of sin and of breaking the whole law. If the Bible takes such a critical attitude of a simple thing as segregation, and partiality in seating, how must the heart of God burn in the treatment of minorities in these tremendous times by the church?

The church must look again at the specific command in Isaiah 1:16–17, "Wash you, make you clean, put away the evil of your doings from before mine eyes. Cease to do evil. Learn to do well, seek judgment, relieve the oppressed, judge the fatherless; plead for the widow." The church must look again at the Sermon on the Mount. They must see in it a sermon on human relations, and explanation of the law founded on love to God and love to man. The church must look again at the gospel of Jesus Christ and His power to change men. The church professes to be motivated by the love of God; not that filial love that responds only to love from the object, but the *agape* love, that is independent of the disposition or attitude of the object; a love that is able to love the unlovable. It must look again at its claim to work miracles in the hearts of men. The acid test of the church's power is in its demonstration of the miracle power of love indicated by Christ when He said, in Matthew 5:43–45, "Ye have heard that it hath been said, thou shalt love thy neighbor and hate thine enemy, but I say unto you, love your enemies, bless them that curse you, do good to them that hate you, pray for them which despitefully use you and persecute you that ye may be the children of your Father which is in heaven, for he maketh his sun to rise on the evil and the good and sendeth rain on the just and the unjust." In verse 46, notice these words, "For if ye love them which love you, what reward have ye? Do not even the publicans the same?" The acid test of divine love is the ability of the church, through this gift of love, to love all men, regardless of race, color, or national origin. The church must show in practice: "for as many as of you as have been baptized into Christ have put on Christ. There is neither Jew nor Greek; there is neither bond nor free; there is neither male nor female, for ye are all one in Christ Jesus" (Galatians 3:27–29).

The church must not adjust to man's attitude and patterns of living, but the gospel must change a man through its power. The power of the Holy Ghost can align men with God's pattern. To compromise human policies at the expense of the divine, is to deny the power of the gospel. Love is not determined by the deportment of the object, but by the quality of the love within the subject.

In this time of racial revolution, the ideal has had to face the real. Theoretical love has had to face love in action. Ministers have preached a limited love, the filial love, the limited fellowship, the limited brotherhood; the love of God is unlimited, unrestricted. It is not determined by color, nationality, or deportment but by the humanity of man and his link with eternity.

The command to love your enemies takes a miracle. Love is that miracle that God bestows upon His children (Romans 5:5). This is the acid test of true conversion. It is the sure way of knowing by what way the church is led. In these tremendous times, the church must again take a firm stand as it did during the time of the Reformation. It must have a renewed courage, a renewed faith in the miracle-working power of love. It must have a renewed faith in its position in this world and its duties and responsibilities. There must be a reappraisal of the power of the gospel of Jesus Christ. And I thank God today that on the horizon, we can see the beginning of a new day. The new day is actually dawning because the church is now coming into its light. The church is beginning to see its responsibilities, its duties, and above all, now has faith in the miracle- working power of love.

The most significant event in the present racial revolution as it pertains to the church was the National Conference on Religion and Race, held in Chicago January 14–17, 1963. In the preface to the report of the conference, entitled "Challenge to Religion," Matthew

Ahman gives an excellent summary of the conference which, if followed as outlined, provides the only solution to racism in America. The church will then be a true witness and prove its uniqueness and its power from on high. It will then be true to its commission. A part of what took place at the conference follows:

> Work groups dealt with concrete matters, racial inclusion in denominations; programs to educate members on moral issues in race relations; use of national and local policy and programs in the desegregation of religious institutions; the responsibility of religious institutions as employers; the responsibility of the church and synagogue as administrators; educational resources of religious institutions; the role of church and synagogue in suburban neighborhoods and in rural areas.

They dwelt on the racial abuses still extant within the life of religion itself. Then they moved on to propose ideas in their programs to correct racial abuses within religious institutions and to quicken the impact of organized religion on United States' racial patterns.

Questions like there were resolved: How do religious values influence and shape our society? How do religious institutions behave if they want their values to produce constructive social change?

In all of the proceedings, the following stands out as the real beginning of the church's work in the right direction:

> Conferees acknowledge the collective guilt of the religious bodies in America; guilt from malpractice, which contributed to the climate which produced the Civil War; guilt for the racial abuses still found in religious bodies; and even more, they acknowledge the massive fear of positive action to open our societies so that every man is accepted by every other man.

The conference further concluded that the conscience of each individual communicant or a religious group must be informed; definitive policies of moral education on racial justice and love must be adopted and administered in all religious bodies. They must affect seminary education; the in-training education of clerical and lay leaders and children and adults from pulpits. This education must be conducted in terms so concrete that the conscience is disturbed so that any man can see that toleration of racial segregation in the neighborhood, his work life, and in the life of his religious body makes his faith irrelevant. Religion is not a creation of man but of God. Christian tradition must fulfill the command of God to draw no artificial line between man and man. In all of the world, if there is any one institution where this is a clear voice giving support to this *command*, it should be the voice of the Christian church.

Religious institutions must correct their own abuses. Again, specific policies eliminating racial segregation in the life of religious and religiously administered institutions must be adopted and administered in all religious bodies. A religious body which preaches a doctrine of the oneness of humanity, the equality of all men created by God, denies its nature if it does not scrupulously rout out those sore spots in its own institutions which divide brother from brother, and conscience from God.

Thank God today for the awakened church, for the power of the gospel is the ultimate answer to all racial problems.

Segregation involves the social, economical, political, and spiritual life of all peoples. Every agency that exercises control in these areas is to be used to eliminate this great evil. The church, the gospel of Jesus Christ, is the greatest influence, the only power in all of these areas because through divine power it affects the inmost life of man. We are thankful for this new day and trust that the institutional church will be true to its declarations and its plans and its purposes as outlined above in the National Conference on Race and religion. It remains now for each denomination, each institution, each local church, each Christian worker, to make religion live in this racial revolution.

How to Live the Life Worth Living
DR. NORMAN VINCENT PEALE

Born in Ohio, Norman Vincent Peale received degrees from Ohio Wesleyan University, Boston University, and Syracuse University. In 1922 Dr. Peale began his great adventure in pulpit preaching when he was ordained for the ministry in the Methodist Episcopal Church. After several pastorates, he became established at the Marble Collegiate Reformed Church in New York City, where he has served since 1932.

Dr. Peale's frank and incisive revelation of how to live "here and now" in this life has emerged from such works of his as *The Art of Living, You Can Win, A Guide to Confident Living, The Power of*

Positive Thinking, The Coming of the King, Stay Alive All Your Life, The Amazing Results of Positive Thinking, and *The Tough-Minded Optimist.* He is the author of the column "Confident Living," appearing in many newspapers. He was technical advisor, representing the Protestant Church, in the motion picture *One Foot in Heaven.*

As a foremost clergyman, Dr. Peale has received numerous honors and awards for his many contributions. He has been recipient of the Freedom Foundation Award, Horatio Alger Award, American Education Award, Government Service Award for Ohio, National Salvation Army Award, and the Dale Carnegie International Human Relations Award.

Active in many phases of civic and social life, Doctor Peale was a member of the Mid-Century White House Conference on Children and Youth, and President of the National Temperance Society. Since 1965 he has been the president of the Protestant Council of the City of New York.

Included here is a part of his sermon, "How to Live the Life Worth Living," delivered in his pulpit at Marble Collegiate Church in New York City, March 21, 1965.

* * *

We have a problem today—this very day. It is a problem affecting millions of our fellow citizens—Negroes and whites alike. It is the problem of civil rights, one of the most serious problems now facing us. But it is not an insoluble one.

The suggestion has been made that we stand apart from this problem. Well, we don't stand apart at all! Recently I had the encouraging experience of accompanying a group of clergymen of all faiths to Washington to meet with the Senators and Congressmen from New York State. We found them in agreement with all of us on the need for new voter legislation, and they shared our conviction that positive action is needed now.

President Johnson, in his message to Congress the other night dealing with voting rights for all citizens, reached heights of authentic greatness as a national leader. The President truly articulated the conscience and moral convictions of the vast majority of the nation. I admire President Johnson for his speech, in which we witnessed one of those rare incidents in which a politician rises to extraordinary greatness. I was impressed. It is interesting to watch a man rise, for a moment at least, to heights of greatness where he can overcome ancient attitudes.

No doubt he had to overcome some prejudices in this field. I never did, myself. It is incredible to me that anybody could have prejudices against a Negro. I wasn't raised that way. I was raised in a home to which Negroes came, not as servants, but as friends, from my earliest boyhood days. I went to school with them. They were my companions. They were my brothers, and even now I receive letters of association from my old friends.

In this church we have had Negro members for years. That is normal and natural in Marble Collegiate Church. We never look at the color of a man's skin; we look only at the color of his commitments. Black or white, Jewish or Gentile, Catholic or Protestant, Puerto Rican, you name him and we receive him as a brother. We look at him as a person, as a man or as a woman, as a child of God. How it could ever be otherwise is beyond my personal comprehension.

Also I'd like to say that we have many, many worshipers from the South in this church. Many of these people are my very dear friends. I respect and honor them. Never once in all the time that I have been pastor of Marble Collegiate Church has a Southerner ever spoken to me about Negro membership in this church. Never once! We would not permit exception to that within the walls of this glorious old sacred edifice that dates back to the first Protestant church in the United States. Here a man is a man for what he is, not for the color of his skin.

Now, I was recently elected president of the Protestant Council of the City of New York. Speaking in that capacity, I want to say that nobody need have any doubts whatsoever about the full weight of the Protestant churches of New York City being thrown behind the effort to get equal justice for every man under the laws of man and of God as well.

The time is long overdue for redress of the wrongs done any citizen of any color or religion through denial of any of the rights of citizenship. This injustice must be fully corrected, and the time is now.

"Once to every man and nation," says Lowell, "comes the moment to decide," and our great moment is now at hand.

We shall not stand silent or apart from the struggle for full civil rights. The churches of New York join those of the nation in throwing the full weight of unqualified Christian support behind the battle to achieve justice for all.

He who gets into these struggles will suffer, but he also will find that he is entering into life in its fullness, now.

Some Spiritual Reflections on the John Kennedy Era
REV. GARDNER C. TAYLOR

Gardner C. Taylor, born in Baton Rouge, Louisiana, was educated at Leland College and Oberlin Graduate School of Theology.

Before beginning his present work as Pastor of the Concord Baptist Church, Brooklyn, New York, in 1948, Reverend Taylor served successively and successfully as Pastor of the Bethany Baptist Church, Ellyria, Ohio; the Beulah Baptist Church, New Orleans, Louisiana; and the Mt. Zion Baptist Church, Baton Rouge, Louisiana. In his present pastorate, he ministers to a membership of more than 11,559 persons. He is a Vice-President, Board of Directors of the Urban League of Greater New York, and is a former member of the General Council of the American Baptist Convention. Reverend Taylor serves presently as Vice-President-at-Large of the Progressive National Baptist Convention, founded in 1961.

In 1947, Reverend Taylor preached in Copenhagen, Denmark, during the session of the World Baptist Alliance. In 1950, Reverend Taylor preached at the 11:00 A.M. worship service of the World Baptist Alliance in the Municipal Auditorium in Cleveland. He has spoken at many universities, both in this country and abroad. In 1953, Oberlin College conferred upon him one of its first Alumni Citations for his influence as a preacher. In 1955, he addressed the Golden Jubilee of the World Baptist Alliance in Westminster Hall, London, England.

Dr. Taylor recently completed his tenure as President of the Protestant Council of the City of New York. He was the first Negro and the first Baptist ever to hold this position. He is a former member of the Board of Education of the City of New York.

In the summer of 1963, Reverend Taylor led the clergy of Brooklyn in protests against discrimination against Negroes in the building trades in New York. At the site of a public project, the Downstate Medical Center, he was arrested twice along with 700 citizens of Brooklyn, including many clergymen.

The sermon following, "Some Spiritual Reflections on the John Kennedy Era," was delivered by Reverend Taylor at the Concord Baptist Church of Christ in Brooklyn, New York, on December 1, 1964.

* * *

Greater love hath no man than this that a man lay down his life
for his friends, (John 15:13).

The nation has passed through a profoundly moving experience in
the tragic and incredible assassination of the thirty-fifth President
of the United States, John F. Kennedy. The immeasurable sadness of
the event has been compounded by the fact that, for the first time in
the history of our country, so many people participated as eyewitnesses
via television to the events leading up to, including, and following the
President's sad and terrible death. Unbelief was the nation's first
reaction to the news that its youthful and vigorous leader had fallen
victim to the assassin's bullet. Shock followed close on behind unbelief, only to be joined by an indescribable grief, as if someone of
each American's household had passed.

It is the preacher's province, and solemn responsibility, to take every
event and seek to let the truth of God shine through it. It is the
preacher's duty to attempt "Some Spiritual Reflections on the John
Kennedy Era." Such a word must at some points be personal and, at
any time other than when pardoned by the nation's desire to recall
every detail about its martyred Captain, presumptuous and inappropriate.

I remember how I first met President Kennedy. It was during his
1960 campaign for the Presidency. I was deeply troubled by what I
interpreted as Senator Kennedy's sparse commitment to the civil-rights
aspirations of Negroes. Frank Reeves, the Washington lawyer, called
me about meeting the Senator. Having misgivings about the Senator's
views on Negro aspirations, I felt less than enthusiastic about a conference. Finally a meeting was arranged. I was arriving from preaching responsibilities in Houston and Mr. Kennedy was coming to New
York for campaign speeches. We met at the East River Drive as his
motorcade turned into 116th Street. There was something about his
earnestness which touched the heart. One gathered that here was a
man deeply conscious of the nation's history and reverently hopeful
about its future. The feeling grew from that first meeting that John
F. Kennedy considered himself called of God to prod the nation
toward a high destiny which God had ordained for this republic.

Sadly enough God has brought the nation, more than once, to a
destiny-filled moment when it could forever declare its firm intention
to be what God meant it to be. Each time it has somehow fallen
cravenly back from that high moment. Bruce Catton, the historian,
has characterized such a moment in the nation's life as being the

meeting between Grant and Lee at McLean's farmhouse at Appomattox on Palm Sunday, 1865. Catton says Appomattox had been an unknown name, but after this meeting, it would be a name to haunt the national memory. Describing the scene, he said that on that Palm Sunday the last mile had been paced off and "Sunset and Sunrise came together in a streaked glow that was half twilight and half dawn." If the nation, North and South, both guilty, had followed the high principles given opportunity of incarnation in the fearful birth pangs of the Civil War, what a different land we would have? If the nation had gone to its knees in true repentance and and dedication to God following Appomattox and to its own brave claim of freedom, how different might have been our history? Now we might have a spirit to match our science, a moral strength to match our technological eminence, citizens who value human dignity and human worth so highly that they would not think of wanton slaughter of either the highest or the lowest citizen in the nation. North and South we failed at that junction point, that moment of truth. Instead the nation turned to political bargaining and profiteering. Ugly trades were made, with the pawns and stakes being men's souls. The result was that the old sickness, the old plague of bitterness and hatred continued to haunt the land.

Ralph McGill, brave, gifted, articulate son of the Southland, has made the same comment about our generation. May 17, 1954, marked a crucial moment. The highest refuge of American justice and jurisprudence took a leap of courage away from the stagnant shores of judicial conservatism. The federal judiciary until May 17, 1954, had not found the vision or the vigor to make a forthright and clean-cut break from the shadowed past of America's life. The Supreme Court had chipped away at the Dred Scott decision, but the heart of that decision which established a difference in Americans on the basis of color had never been repudiated. The May 17th decision did break with the past. It let a fresh and draughty and, for some, a chilly breath of air into the household of the republic.

Ralph McGill says that a hush crossed the nation and particularly the Southland. It was a God-given chance for the entire nation to make a choice. It was the hour of decision for our country. It was another moment streaked with the mixed light of dawn and dusk. It was another chance, a new birth pang, a fresh opportunity. A hush crossed the country. It was a chance for decent people of all creeds and colors to speak up and speak out. The nation might have been set upon a high road. Something chilled good people and frightened them. Our faith was not equal to the hour! The sad result has been the long season of division and hatred and American set against American which followed. The unhappy exposure of violence and repression which has followed all too often and all over the country has not only damaged the nation abroad, but has given birth to a terrifying uncertainty at home as to which way ahead.

The ascension of John F. Kennedy to the Presidency of The United States sent a ray of light and a sense of hope through millions. I believe God gave him to the nation. Here was a young man, vigorous, charming, profoundly reverent toward the nation's high ordination in history, supremely confident about the nation's future. At his inaugural he spoke the words of youthful buoyancy and hopefulness. He spoke of the torch of leadership passing to the hands of those born in this century, tempered by war, disciplined by a hard peace, and proud of the past. He spoke with a fresh urgency about the right of the nation to ask of its people loyalty and sacrifice. "Ask not what your country can do for you, but ask what you can do for your country."

The republic had a new chance. And to its credit, at least in one sense, it rose to meet its bright, illumined destiny as a nation which has no distinctions of creed or color. Too long the test of religion had surrounded the nation's highest secular office with the shame of bias. A sigh of relief passed through decent men with the knowledge that a worthy American, Catholic though he was, could live at 1600 Pennsylvania Avenue, Washington, could direct the affairs of men. In life, John Kennedy delivered the nation from the hypocrisy and shame of drawing distinctions as to creed and religion. God grant that we shall never again move back into that darkness. We must, under God, if this nation is to come to its full flower, neither fail to elect a man because of his religion, nor, on the other hand, elect him because he is of a certain religious creed. This is what God has willed for our nation.

Mr. Kennedy did not live to see the passing of the test of color for true American chitizenship. He was, himself, sometimes uncertain about the details and specific direction this pre-eminent issue in our national life should take. When I met him first on a chill autumn day at a curbstone on 116th Street, the question arose. I said to him, "Senator, there is question among Negroes about your position as to the future of civil rights in this country." Bareheaded in the wind we stood there. He a child and heir of the culture of Massachusetts and New England, I a child of Louisiana and heir of all the problems of an unhappy South whose mood has affected the nation. Said he in reply, "I asked for time to formulate my thinking in the matter of specific direction about the problem of race in this country. I have now spoken and intend to honor my responsibility. However this election turns out, let us all work together on this matter." There was something about his earnestness which convinced me. After a few more minutes of conversation while his motorcade waited, we shook hands and I said, "I will do what I can in your support."

He kept his commitment. He seemed slow and uncertain sometimes and some of us criticized his hesitancy, but there was never any doubt, as Roy Wilkins said after his death, as to where his heart was. I never felt so much an American as the night I sat and head him speak after the unhappy occurrence at Oxford, Mississippi. He said that America does not say "white only" when it asks its sons to defend the nation. Any American, then, ought to be free to find shelter in a hotel anywhere in America, vote freely, attend the best schools, and work where his talents and training qualify him. Thus he spoke and thus he believed.

In life, President Kennedy increasingly addressed himself to the unhappy divisions of race in our nation life. I sat in the White House last June with religious leaders from over America and heard him plead for the cooperation of the religious leaders of our country in bringing to bear the great traditions of the nation's spiritual heritage, rooting in the Hebrew prophets, on this vexing and haunting and bedeviling problem of color which has scarred and marred our nation and brought it more than once to the brink of civil conflict. Many heard and some sensed the vision he saw, but many did not heed.

There occurred the historic and awesomely orderly March on Washington, with the late President's blessing so clear and unmistakable that some said he sponsored it. He wanted the nation to see and listen and learn and act. I do not know how much import the March made as the Congress took up his Civil Rights Bill, balked, sparred, delayed, temporized. Ten or twelve persons, representing the three great faiths, called on the Attorney General and members of the Congress three or four weeks ago in the interest of the Civil Rights Bill. Senator Hubert Humphrey said to us, "Gentlemen, I hope you can stimulate some commitment here. There are many gentlemen on the hill, not all from the South, who have, to put it mildly, no great interest in this question of Civil Rights." The nation had not quite heard John Kennedy's summons nor had it seen his vision. The nation had two years and ten months of John F. Kennedy's eloquent, urgent prodding. Sadly enough, the message did not seem to get through.

Now he is dead. The quick smile is vanished, the persuasive voice is silenced. Will the nation take his death as what may be its last cue, its final overture from God after a bloody sequence of murders by sniping and bombings and evasions? Will the nation hear God's voice speaking through the mute corpse of John Kennedy? This is no time for bitter differences and shrill accusations. Our nation is on the brink of ruin, spiritual ruin. Yes, our image abroad is damaged, but worse our soul at home is imperiled. Hatred, be it white for black or black for white, is destructive and irrational. It cannot make distinctions as to where and when it will vent its venom and spew its destructive poison. The most critical peril before us now is the loss of confidence in our institutions, as witness our wanton attacks on the Supreme Court and the murder of the Chief of State. We need now a great coming together of soul in this nation. We need a reconsecration to the principles of rights and responsibilities. We need to settle our differences between the races and join hands and hearts to serve the national goals as the republic moves toward its awesome role in history and among the sons of men everywhere. If we cannot, North and South, black and white, immediately settle our differences, we need to create a climate of good will and trust in every city, village, and hamlet of the land in which our differences can be discussed and dealt with. We are Americans and all must be dedicated to the propositions of liberty which underlie our government. Is America equal to this? If not, the nation is lost, tragically, pathetically, everlastingly lost. We stand at the junction between life and death. We stand now at the crossroads between a bright future and an awful doom.

There is a personal word called forth by this tragic and untimely death. Each of us ought to examine himself. The words of warning we often hear are called morbid or the expected, and are not heeded. The message of the murder of the President is that life is not for always. He arose that fateful morning a laughing, youthful leader; that evening the bright eyes were sightless, the nimble tongue was mute, the brave heart was stilled, the quick intellect was no more. Let every man take notice. If death and destruction can do this in a green tree, what can they do in a dry? Let us be reminded. One day the summons will come and the task must be dropped, the report made, the judgment rendered. Let us then be about our Father's business, ready when he calls.

We might all pray today for the nation and for ourselves. God give us strength to stand the stress. God give us courage to fight the good faith. God give us a light by which to walk, a high road upon which to walk, a home toward which we walk.

A Memorial Tribute for Mrs. Viola Liuzzo
DR. HOWARD THURMAN

Howard Thurman, born in Daytona Beach, Florida, graduated from Morehouse College and Colgate-Rochester Theological Seminary. He was Professor of Systematic Theology and Dean of Chapel at Howard University from 1932 to 1944. In 1944 he organized the Church for One Fellowship of All Peoples in San Francisco, California. Under Dr. Thurman's leadership (1944 to 1953), this was the first church completely integrated in leadership and membership in American life. He has served as Dean of Marsh Chapel and Professor of Spiritual Resources and Disciplines in the School of Theology at Boston University since 1953.

A fellow in The American Academy of Arts and Sciences and the National Council of Religion in Higher Education, he has served on the boards of Hampton Institute, Institute on Religion in an Age of Science, Massachusetts Advisory Board against Discrimination, Meals for Millions Foundation, The American Committee on Africa, and the Urban League of Greater Boston.

Dr. Thurman has addressed faculty and students in some five hundred institutions around the globe. This number would include more than four hundred in the United States and Canada alone. Among them are the University of Chicago, the State Universities of Pennsylvania, Ohio, Iowa, Arizona, Oregon, and Washington; Harvard, Yale, Princeton, Vassar, Wellseley; the University Center in Atlanta, Fisk, and Howard; the Universities of Toronto, Manitoba, Dalhousie, and McGill. He has been a guest lecturer in Tokyo, Hong Kong, Silliman College, the Phillipines, Cairo, Beirut, and preacher at the church of St. Martin's in the Field, London, on an American British Pulpit Exchange.

As a gifted, literate, and human author, he has contributed to the knowledge and inspiration of people all over the world in such works as *The Greatest of These, Deep River, The Negro Spiritual Speaks of Life and Death, Meditation for Apostles of Sensitiveness, Jesus and the Disinherited, Deep Is the Hunger, Meditations of the Heart, The Growing Edge, Footprints of a Dream, Mysticism and the Experience of Love, The Inward Journey, Temptations of Jesus,* and *Disciplines of the Spirit.*

In response to the murder of Mrs. Viola Liuzzo, who was shot and killed following her participation in a Freedom March between Selma and Montgomery, Alabama, Dr. Thurman delivered the following memorial tribute at Christ Church in Cincinnati, Ohio, on March 30, 1965.

* * *

THE INNOCENT ONES

One of the characters in Margaret Kennedy's novel *The Feast* suggests that the entire human race is tolerated for its innocent minority. There is a strange and aweful vitality in the suffering of the innocent. It does not fall within any category. The mind moves very easily in the balance of the swinging pendulum. We are accustomed to equating things in terms of the order of equilibrium. Our values are defined most easily as merit and demerit, reward and punishment. There is great sustenance for the spirit in the assurance that reverses can somehow be balanced by the deeds which brought them about. Many men find the depths of contentment in their suffering when they remember that their pain is deserved, their payment is for a just and honest debt. Of course there may be a full measure, pressed down and overflowing, but the hard core of the pain is for acknowledged wrong done, the essence of the hardship is atonement for evil done. All of this falls into a simple pattern of checks and balances, of sowing and reaping, of planting and harvesting.

But where the pain is without apparent merit, where innocence abounds and no case can be made that will give a sound basis for the *experience of the agony*, then the mind spins in a crazy circle. Always there must be an answer, there must be found some clue to the mystery of the suffering of the innocent. It is not enough to say that the fathers have eaten sour grapes and their children's teeth are set on edge. This is not enough. It is not enough to say that the individual sufferer is a victim of circumstances over which he is unable to exercise any controls. There is apt ever to be an element of truth in such assertions. But the heart of the issue remains untouched. The innocent do suffer; this is the experience of man.

Margaret Kennedy's idea is an arresting one. It is that mankind is protected and sustained by undeserved suffering—that swinging out beyond the logic of antecedent and consequence, of sowing and reaping, there is another power, another force, supplementing and restoring the ravages wrought in human life by punishment and reward. The innocent ones are always present when the payment falls due—they may not be heroes or saints, they are not those who are the conscious burden-bearers of the sins and transgressions of men. They are the innocent ones—they are always there. Their presence in the world is the stabilizing factor, the precious ingredient that maintains the delicate balance preventing humanity from plunging into the abyss. It is not to be wondered at that in all the religions of mankind there is ever at work the movement to have the word *made* flesh, without being *of* the flesh. It is humanity's way of *affirming* that the innocent ones *hold* while all that evil men do exacts its due.

> Their shoulders hold the sky suspended
> They stand, and earth's foundations stay.

THE TRAGIC FACTS

The facts are as simple as they are tragic. A young mother from Detroit, Italian in background and national origin—an isolated stretch of highway between Selma and Montgomery, Alabama—a young Negro man, a Freedom Marcher being ferried by her to join others who had participated in an historic fifty-mile Freedom Trek between the two cities—four Alabama white men, alleged members of the Ku Klux Klan—two cars that meet and pass in the night—two shots that splinter the silence—the young mother, bleeding to death, slumped over the steering wheel of the car out of control—a frightened young man hitchhiking in the darkness to tell the story—a heartbroken husband—five hurt, weeping, bereft children—a citizenry feeling itself under siege—an enraged American conscience puzzled and frightened by the stirring of a deep and violent guilt—of such materials is the drama created which brings us here today sharing together across all lines of creed and race in an act of memorial for Mrs. Viola Liuzzo.

THE TRAGIC REASON

The men who murdered Mrs. Liuzzo did not know her. They knew only one thing—she was a white woman from outside the region, but a white woman even as their mothers and sisters were white women and that her presence in their midst on such a mission as hers was a bitter judgment upon them and the angry world of hate and fear in which they were born and nurtured. To strike her down in the nighttime was their irrational way to try to purge themselves of their own agony and to seek to confirm in their fear-ridden spirits the vanishing myth upon which their own emotional security rested that they were superior to the Negro, who to them was a thing, a body, but not a man, a person even as they.

In one tragic act, premeditated or spontaneous, they tore away the veil from before the deserted altar which had been for generations their dedication and their glory—namely, to respect, honor, and defend white womanhood against all who would threaten or do her harm. Stripped of this pretension, they stand naked before the world and henceforth men of good will in their region can move creatively away from the contamination of the ancient hypocrisy.

AND WHAT OF US?

The rest of us who were not present on that fateful night—what of us? But were we present? *No!* We were there, you and I. But who represented us? The men who delivered the fatal shots and in whose twisted brains and frightened hearts hate ran riot? Did they represent us, you and me? Or were we represented by Mrs. Liuzzo and her colleagues? Who spoke for us on that stretch of deserted highway? And in which voice—the sound of the shot or the cry of the wounded and dying? Now that Mrs. Liuzzo is dead, joining the ranks of those others who have gone before, and the stark drama unfolds before our startled conscience, how may we make atonement? You must find your answer even as I find mine. We are all of us involved—the Book says we are members one of another—even as Eugene Debs wrote long ago.

> While there is a lower class I am in it
> While there is a criminal element, I am of it
> While there is a man in jail, I am not free

How may our country atone? What can we say to our soldiers in Vietnam? For whose freedom do they fight, suffer and die? What can we say to them?

> Her shoulders hold the sky suspended,
> She stands and earth's foundations stay!

THANK GOD, THERE IS A SPIRIT ABROAD . . .

But we do have an abiding assurance. There is a spirit abroad in life of which the Judeo-Christian ethic is but one expression. It is a spirit, that makes for wholeness and for community; it finds its way into the quiet solitude of a Supreme Court Justice when he ponders the constitutionality of an Act of Congress which guarantees civil rights to all its citizens; it settles in the pools of light in the face of a little girl as with her frailty she challenges the hard frightened heart

of a police chief; it walks along the lonely road with the solitary protest marcher and settles over him with a benediction as he falls by
the assassin's bullet fired from ambush; it kindles the fires of unity
in the heart of Jewish rabbi, Catholic priest, and Protestant minister
as they join arms together, giving witness to their God in behalf of a
brotherhood that transcends creed, race, sex, and religion; it makes
a path to Walden Pond and ignites a flame of nonviolence in the mind
of a Thoreau and burns through his liquid words from the Atlantic
to the Pacific; it broods over the demonstrators for justice and brings
comfort to the desolate and forgotten who bear no memory of what
it is to feel the rhythm of belonging to the race of men; it knows no
country, and its allies are to be found wherever the heart is kind and
the collective will and the private endeavor seek to make justice where
injustice abounds, to make peace where chaos is rampant, and to make
the voice heard on behalf of the helpless and the weak. It is the Voice
of God and the Voice of Man; it is the meaning of all the stirrings of
the whole human race toward a world of friendly men underneath
a friendly sky.

> She died.
> But we who live must do a harder thing
> Than dying is. For we must think!
> And ghosts shall drive us on.

The Church, Nonviolence, and Revolutions
REV. WYATT T. WALKER

Wyatt Tee Walker, a graduate of Virginia Union University, is now
waging war on "cultural blackout," a term he has used to describe
the intentional exclusion from the history texts of our public schools
of the Negro's significant contribution to the American experience.

Before joining Educational Heritage, Wyatt Tee Walker's name had
become synonomous with SCLC—the Southern Christian Leadership
Conference. For a period of time administratively, the youthful clergyman functioned as chief of staff for Dr. Martin Luther King, Jr.

Mr. Walker's tenure with the Southern Christian Leadership Con-
ference began during its infancy. Prior to his joining Dr. King in
Atlanta, the Reverend Mr. Walker was the minister of the historic
Gillfield Baptist Church in Petersburg, Virginia.

As Executive Assistant to Dr. King, Mr. Walker had the major responsibility for coordinating the activities of strategic thrusts across the Deep South wherever SCLC was a principal participant.

Despite the fact that Mr. Walker's work was "behind the scenes," his contribution to the freedom struggle has not gone unnoticed. Commonly referred to as the "alter ego" of Martin Luther King, Jr., the IBPOE of the world (Elks) honored him with their civil-rights award in 1961. He has appeared in several network television documentaries, notably the award-winning Bell and Howell "Walk in My Shoes" and the CBS "Eyewitness to History," a special report on the struggle in Albany, Georgia. More recently, he has appeared on "Open End," Walter Cronkite's "CBS Reports on Atlanta," and several other network programs. During the summer of 1964, Mr. Walker was honored by the Shriners and the Alpha Phi Alpha fraternity for his outstanding work in civil rights.

On July 15, 1964, Mr. Walker was appointed Vice-President in Charge of Marketing and Services by Noel N. Marder, President of Educational Heritage, Inc. The library is aimed at diminishing the "cultural blackout" within the Negro community in America. Recently, he was appointed pastor of the Canaan Baptist Church in New York City.

"The Church, Nonviolence, and Revolutions" was delivered by Mr. Walker at the State Conference on Religion and Race, held at the University of Nebraska, Lincoln, Nebraska, March 2, 1964. The audience was made up of a cross section of church officials from the Protestant, Catholic, and Jewish communities of the state.

*   *   *

INTRODUCTION

Our Christian tradition patently condemns racism again and again, and this company is much too religiously oriented and theologically erudite to presumptuously list all of the arguments. It goes without saying.

The subject of concern here is not so much to academically decide what our posture is going to be on one of the great issues of our nation and of our world, but rather, honestly and boldly to find ways to do something about that which we know is sinful in the sight of Almighty God.

What am I saying? Simply put, the question of segregation versus integration seems moot legally, morally, psychologically, spiritually, sociologically—any kind of way you want to measure it. The central focus of the energies and resources of the Church and the Temple needs now to be the healing process for the wounds the system has produced in our midst.

To be sure, the wound-producing system has not yet been decimated, but we might optimistically hazard a guess that the end is in sight. I give here my sincere witness that the task that is most formidable now is the day-by-day, flesh-and blood consideration of the transition to the *beloved community*, and somehow, finding the *modus operandi* by which the terrible results of segregation and discrimination can be ultimately resolved.

Close scrutiny will reveal that the results of man's sinfulness quite appropriately were the object of the burning zeal of the eighth-century prophets *and* the Galilean Prince. And when we look about us, what has racism produced other than the things that they sought to eliminate from their society: exploitation of the poor, oppression of the weak, debasement of human personality, crippling of the human spirit, slaying of the innocents, violence to the defenseless—the entire spectrum of man's inhumanity to man. We who are the forces of religion in America must come shamefaced before the altar of God, if we do not hasten to heal the stripes that have been laid on the Negro and his compatriots in poverty.

There is something more than the biblical mandate that requires our hand to be busied with our Father's work. It might be described as the empiricism of history that relates to the Church. In reality, when one considers the plight of the Negro particularly, and the poor generally, over the last one hundred years, nobody has ever really given a Continental.[1] And here, at the height of the twentieth century, in just a few years the Negro has become the dominant figure on the American scene. The goals we seek and the healing of our wounds are nothing short of revolutionary. I submit to you that we, the church forces, by the very nature of our beginnings, must be involved, for the basic tenets by which we were structured, were and remain *revolutionary*.

Whatever we are to do with this critical moment of our nation's history, we could do and move in no more appropriate context than that of the nonviolent social revolution taking place at this very moment all over America. If we of the church fail now after so long an accommodating silence, we will have failed our nation, ourselves, and our God.

For the purposes of these moments that have been given to me, let us make some analysis of whence we have come and where we

---

[1] A nearly worthless coin of Revolutionary War days. (Editor.)

must go, if we are to be meaningful in making the nation and our problems feel the impress of the church's influence.

I. SOME OF THE DIMENSIONS OF THE NONVIOLENT REVOLUTION

Consider, first, some of the dimensions of this nonviolent revolution. What is the frame of reference in which we move? Where is the battle being waged?

One of the things to which the Governor [Gov. Frank B. Morrison] alluded in general terms was that in our American heritage there are some things which are a basic, inherent part of citizenship. There is no single thing which is more basic than the right to vote. And yet, I suppose, it seems inconceivable that this one exercise of constitutional privilege in some of the areas where we work is a matter of life and death to people who are black.

Take Clarendon County, South Carolina, where I visited last October, I believe. I was talking with a tall, strapping undertaker named Billy Fleming who, for all of his stature, was yet a whipped man. Standing in his bedroom, needing very badly a listening post, he was telling Dr. King and me about the problems he was having because he and some of the men who worked with him were trying to get the simple and plain people of the land to register and to vote. He said that at planting time they were unable to buy gasoline for their tractors so that they might plant; and when their grain stood ripe in the fields, they couldn't rent the commercial combines to harvest them. And not because they were bad or evil men, but because they wanted to function as citizens in our American tradition! This is where the battle is waged for many of us in the Deep South.

In Greenwood, Mississippi, where this past summer the NAACP, CORE, the Student Nonviolent Coordinating Committee, and ourselves (SCLC) cooperated in a coordinated registration campaign, Negroes had hardly ever attempted to register during the last 100 years. I think there were about 105 who registered since Reconstruction. Last summer, over a protracted period, we managed to train them laboriously, take them through the twenty-five-item questionnaire, teach them how to read and write and overcome the inertia and fear of going down to the court house in the presence of white people. Under the threat of arrest and facing dogs, 2,000 went down to try. And, when the tally was totaled, we had fifty who were accepted by the Board of Registrars! This is where the battle is waged —on the right to vote.

Then we are concerned about public accommodation. It would be interesting, I suppose, for you to know really the background of how this nonviolent business got started in the very beginning. Dr. King and Ralph Abernathy sound amused when they tell it. We talk about bus segregation and we have in mind something anomalous and vague —Negroes sit in the back, whites in front—but it was a little deeper than that in Montgomery, Alabama. Dr. King and Ralph Abernathy say that when they first went to the bus company they never really had integration in mind. In negotiating with the bus company, they were trying to get them to serve on a "first-come, first-served" basis. If you were a Negro, you would pay your fare at the front end of the bus and then go to the back door to get on; and in the rush hours, you could easily, after having paid your fare, be left standing at the back door when the bus pulled off. Or, you had ten or twelve seats assigned, no matter how tired you were at the end of your day's labor, and no matter how many vacant seats beyond the twelve were empty, you still had to stand when those twelve were filled. Vice versa, if there were more white people than Negro, you would have to give up your "colored" seat for white people to sit down. This was the humiliation and embarrassment that the Negro people faced when they first started talking about the bus troubles in Montgomery, Alabama. Then it occurred to them that the whole system of bus transportation for Negroes was bad and needed to be corrected.

The matter of public accommodations is more than inconvenience. In many instances, it can be a matter of life and death. Oliver Holmes, who is one of the staff members of the Atlanta Council on Human Relations, was driving from Savannah to Atlanta. He happens to be a diabetic. That trip is a five and one-half hour drive, and he had taken an injection of insulin as diabetics are required; and I believe you have to have a certain amount of food within a certain time to burn up the insulin. But there isn't a single place on the U.S. Highway from Savannah to Atlanta where a Negro can get anything to eat. He went into insulin shock and went off the road at eighty miles per hour. Fortunately, it was in a wide-open field where there was nothing much to hit. His automobile was torn to pieces and he barely survived. And yet this is just one of the countless instances where the business of lodging and food can be a matter of life and death to the Negro. This is why the public accommodations section in the present civil-rights legislation that is now pending before the Senate is so absolutely critical to the fortunes of the Negro community in the South. This, again, is where the battle is waged.

And then there is the business of citizenship training. So many times when we encourage communities to register and vote, it is like telling them to run when they can't walk. Beyond the poll tax, there is still the literacy test. So many Negroes are functionally illiterate. Oh, we brag about Atlanta as being the flower of the South, and one of the garden spots of culture where race relations are so progressive. And, yet, in Atlanta, Georgia, there are 50,000 people who are functionally illiterate, 30,000 of them Negroes. I guess a lot of this has been produced by the agrarian economy of the South shifting to a semi-industrial economy, so that people are flocking to cities with inadequate opportunities and are ill-trained to cope with our present system of automation and the like. But, yet, are we to write off these people? They are still human beings with aspirations, and hopes, and feelings, and desires. So we in the South are trying to take some time to train some of these people to make their letters and to learn about government at the fourth-grade level, so that they can somehow edge their way into the mainstream of American life. It is true that we do possess a "cultural lag." We have had inferior schooling, and we *will* drag some of the standards down. But, it is a crying shame to cripple us and then blame us for limping. Even with all of the external obstacles with which we are grappling and trying to resolve, we have to be concerned with trying to bring along some of these people who got a rabbit punch so long ago that it crippled their opportunity to function as American citizens.

Up in Bolivar County, Mississippi, there is a 2,000-acre tract of land owned by some British syndicate, I understand. On it are about two hundred Negro families, 90 percent of whom can neither read nor write! I felt slavery was over, until 1960 when I visited Clarksdale, Mississippi. I went to south Alabama, and even in parts of my home state, Virginia, I didn't know what was going on. But right this moment in 1964, there are what we call the "landed people" of the South who are sharecroppers whose existence is so inextricably tied up with the land, that they work the field from seed time to harvest and back again, without any real compensation. They get a streak of lean meat, ground meal, and two pairs of overalls, and start the vicious cycle all over again. Some of them are third-generation sharecroppers who in this day and time have never really handled money. In the Delta of Mississippi, there is now a reprisal against voter registration efforts and many of these sharecroppers are starving. Oh, there is plenty of federal surplus food—consumer goods—but it must be administered by the state. The Eastlands and the Barnetts see to it that it doesn't happen, in order to "let you niggers know that we goin' keep you in your place." This is where the battle is waged.

And then there is the problem of employment. I don't think many of us in this room really foresee the tremendous crisis that's coming in the next six to eighteen months. We're going to have our troubles down South against the inflexible laws and traditions of the so-called Southern way of life. But the real trouble spots are going to be in Chicago, in Detroit, in Cleveland, and New York, and Omaha, Nebraska. You see, there is another factor in the equation now, called automation. We are not doing enough as a nation to cope with the dislocation of the semiskilled and unskilled laborer, not to speak of the Negro who makes up the largest part of this labor force. With the undercurrent discontent that is already alive in the Negro community, with 100 years' painful journey from the auction block that he has suffered, coupled with the compounded burden of economic dislocation the Negro now suffers, thus there is the prospect of hundreds and thousands of Negroes being on the streets of our large urban cities cold, hungry, and mad, desperately trying to survive, not knowing where they will sleep or what they will eat. And *nobody* is doing anything about it. This, importantly, is where the battle is being waged. This is why the dimensions of the nonviolent revolution must be the concern of the church.

II. NONVIOLENT REVOLUTION BORN AND DEVELOPED IN THE LOINS OF CHURCH

Now there is no need for me to make any broad indictments or to browbeat the white church about what hasn't been done; that is a matter of history, and no one can change that. Our concern is how to find a handle to do something with the problem as it stands. Paradoxically, it is interesting to note that in the Negro community, it has been the church, almost exclusively, which has produced and developed the nonviolent revolution. Even with our stereotyped, other-worldly religion—with its handclapping and ecstatic expression—and despite the fact that we have "cracking" verbs and splitting infinitives, talking about "long white robes" and "golden streets," at least there has been some transfer that has made the bread-and-butter considerations of daily life relevant to faith and religion. That which has produced the dynamic of the Negro movement has been ninety-nine and forty-four hundredths percent the honor and glory of the Negro church.

You see, the Negro church in a very real sense is the Negro community. Whatever it is you want done, if it's organizing a picket line against unfair employment practices, or recruiting for the Red Cross blood program, or selling Wilkie buttons—whatever it is you want done—you had better do it through the Negro church, or you're like a lost ball in high grass.

This is a sociological phenomenon, I suppose; it is unique to the Negro church, particularly in the South. The church has been the one forum of the Negro. He owns it, he operates it, and Mr. Charlie can't say anything about how he handles it. And the Negro preacher is as free as any Negro can be in the Negro community. It has provided the broadest opportunity for social intercourse. The churches are the seat of our protest meetings, and the Negro minister had traditionally been the leader of the movement. If you take any city in the South where there has been any dynamic and virile movement, you would find that nine times out of ten, some Negro preacher has been the leader who has been giving it the arms and the legs and the direction.

I think a large part of this is due to the fact that as limited as was our religious expression, at least the church was a citadel of hope that we would go to week after week. Somehow the faith that was crystallized as it dropped from the white man's table in the days following slavery during the Reconstruction developed into a pristine and pure faith that convinced the simple and plain Negro people that "there's a better day coming." And this is the thing that held us together; that give our spirit the capacity and the resiliency to absorb all that has happend to us.

I suppose this faith-filled religion, as emotional as it may be at times, produced the other side of the coin. Without this kind of faith, we wouldn't have been able to keep our balance, and we might have turned to something far more enervating to the Negro community and to the nation. All through our movement, there are humorous stories which reflect how we manage to look back and laugh at what we've been through. I heard one recently that concerned an old gent from Mississippi who died and went to heaven. When he knocked on the door, St. Peter met him and observed that he was a "member of the club" (that's the way we refer to ourselves); and then proceeded to direct him to the side entrance. The Negro straightened up and said, "What the hell do you mean, the side entrance? Don't you know what is going on down in the United States of America? Why, the Supreme Court passed a unanimous decision outlawing segregation in public education; those students in 1960 started sitting in at lunch counters in more than 100 cities and we've got that just about worked out; Freedom Riders went through Alabama and Mississippi, and you can ride on the bus anywhere you want all over the South without any trouble; and President Kennedy, before he died, issued an executive order outlawing discrimination in federally financed houses. Take me, I'm from Mississippi, I just moved into a white neighborhood. I joined a white church. Got a white pastor. Why he took me down to the river the other day to baptize me—that's funny—that's the last thing I remember."

Now, what I am getting at is this. If you can visit Mississippi and see the bizarre circumstances under which a Negro lives daily, moving about with his emotions at tiptoe stand, not ever knowing what to expect, and then see that this kind of humorous story could grow out of it, then this gives to you some kind of idea of the resiliency that a Negro's faith and religion have given him.

This has produced, in these later years for him, a new sense of worth and self-respect, even for his own person. You know we always used to have this stereotype of a Negro down South, around the court house. Whenever in the presence of a white person he would be scratching where he wasn't itching, and grinning when he wasn't tickled—you see the whole system had produced what we call a *plantation psychology*. It wasn't something that we really wanted to do; it was a means of survival. We had to be accommodating to exist. We had to say what the white man wanted us to say, in order that we could have come to this present day. Even in our pastimes, in our music, the brainwashing was applied. I remember when I was a kid in school, they taught me a plantation song—"I'm coming, I'm coming, and my head is bending low, I hear the gentle voices calling Old Black Joe." That's a degrading song when you think seriously about it. Langston Hughes, somehow catching the spirit of this new day, has paraphrased the words which now depict this new sense of worth and dignity:

> I'm comin', I'm comin'
> And my head ain't bending low;
> I'm walking hard, and talking strong,
> I'm America's *new Black Joe!*

That's the new self-respect and dignity that the Negro now possesses.

And I submit to you that, were it not for the real *ecclesia* spirit in the Negro church, we would not have come as far as we have. I can never forget James Weldon Johnson's two words in the second verse of the "National Hymn" of the Negro. It says:

> Stormy the road we trod,
> Bitter the chastening rod,

Felt in the day when hope unborn had died!
That's how bad it really was.

Yet somehow, the Negro found a faith-filled, substantive religion.
To a large degree, I guess, it came from those simple and unlettered
Negro preachers, who would say to their congregations—"You ain't
no slave, you ain't no nigger, you God's child." And out of that, and
the prayers of the elders, we have *come* to perhaps Pisgah's heights
to view the Promised Land.

III. THE LOVE ETHIC IS CENTRAL

In this revolution, you must be concerned—I must be concerned—
as churchmen and religionists, because all that is happening keeps
the love ethic central. All the cardinal rules of our nonviolent movement are consistent with the Hebraic-Christian tradition. Though we
do speak a great deal of Gandhi and give notice of our debt to
Thoreau, there was a man named Jesus before either of them. And
before him a man named Hosea. And these two men, more than
any other two, as interpreted today in our own theology, give us the
principle and the dynamic by which we move. For what we seek
is not a victory over white men, only a victory for justice. What we
seek with our brothers is reconciliation. Because we recognize that
when the struggle is over, somehow we've got to sit down and hold
hands and live together in the "beloved community."

Over against this, we have to absorb so very many things. I try
as I travel the South (that is, in the years' experiences that have been
mine) to decide for myself what has been the worst experience that
I have had. I remember being trapped in a church in Montgomery,
Alabama, by a mob of two or three thousand that night during the
Freedom Ride; the tear-gas bombs sailing in through the windows,
trying to flush us out into the streets where they could stone us with
cinder blocks that had been carted in and broken up with sledge
hammers. I remember some of the dark days of Birmingham when
the rioting broke out, and it looked as if the city would be burned;
I remember Mother's Day during Freedom Rides . . . so many. But
I think the worst spectacle that has ever come to my vision and my
own personal experience was the morning of August 15, 1962, when
I had to attend the funeral of a church. Not the funeral of a *person*,
but the funeral of a *church*. We got a call at daybreak and went up
to Lee County from Albany. When we got there, Shadygrove Baptist
Church—what was left of it with a gaping wound in its side—was

blown out by dynamite or something. As we came near, you could still feel the heat two or three hours after the flames had burned themselves out. The blue smoke reached way up into the sky, and you could look inside and see the open pews and floors just ashes. As I stood there, tears came to my eyes. I got sick deep down in my soul and wondered what kind of world is this we live in. Have men's minds become so degenerate that they would destroy the very house of the Lord? And I thought I should never see anything quite as bad again in my life. But I was wrong.

Three weeks later, I happened to be going to Albany, Georgia, for a voter registration rally with Jackie Robinson, formerly of the Brooklyn Dodgers. When we got off the plane, they told us that two more churches had been burned. We went to Terrell County and, within three miles of each other, I had to see the same thing all over again; two churches completely leveled. In one, an old bell tower standing and, at the other, only a chimney.

I know that so many times that I talk to college people principally, they want to know intellectually how it is you can say, commit yourselves to loving your enemies when they do everything possible to thwart your progress, your own fulfillment. I really do not know how we do it, except by the grace of God. But I suppose it is a commitment to a continuing principle. I once heard Richard Gregg say nonviolent commitment is like the winter solstice. When it comes on December 21 of each year, two minutes of daylight are added to each day's round of twenty-four hours each, which doesn't seem like very much. But as those two minutes are added in the day, the weeks, and the months that pass, successively and persistently, after a while what happens? The earth's crust begins to thaw, the grass begins to push its way up through the sod, the trees and flowers begin to take on green verdure, and "the voice of the turtle is heard throughout the land." Scarcely without our perception someone tells us that spring has come. And all because of two minutes of daylight added to the day's round of twenty-four hours.

And it is our faith that God is trying to say to us at this moment of history, that we must let two minutes of *love* become operative in our lives. Wherever we go and whatever we say, we must persistently and successively and continuously let these two minutes of love become operative. It is our hope that after a while, little blades of freedom will begin to sprout; the trees and flowers will begin to take on the green verdure of the American ideal of democracy, and one day we hope to see the springtime of the fatherhood of God and the brotherhood of man; and the fulfillment of the prophecy that promises, "Every valley shall be exalted, every hill and mountain shall be brought low, the rough places shall be made plain and the crooked shall be made straight. And every man shall sit down under his own vine and fig tree, and none shall be afraid because the mouth of the Lord has said it."

And all because of two minutes of love in your life and in mine. At the very center of our revolution is the business of the love ethic.

IV. PRESENT CHALLENGE OF REVOLUTION TO THE CHURCH

Now I hope this, in some capsule form, describes to you what we face, what we are about, and how we cope with it. You must know, as well as I, that the American Negro, the Southern Negro, the poor —we cannot do it by ourselves; we need your help. We need allies, resources. That is why I say again and again that the National Conference on Religion and Race in Chicago last year will be epoch-making, if the kind of continuing follow-up is done as it is being done in this kind of conference. To recognize not only that we have a problem, but to somehow search honestly and boldly to find a handle by which we can do something about it.

This brings us to, I suppose, the crux of the matter—the present challenge of the nonviolent revolution to the church.

What is it that you in Nebraska can do? What is it that you can do in your local Lutheran congregation, or your local Catholic parish? Or in your temple? Where can you put your hands on some of the ills and heal the wounds and provide the balm?

Well, one of the challenges is the political challenge. It is not only fashionable for the church to be concerned with the morality of legislation; it is your duty to be concerned. This present civil-rights legislation is a case in point. When I consider Nebraska's role, I think of all the elite of the church who surround me, close to my left and to my right and before me. I am persuaded that there really is something you can do about so creating a crisis in the constituency of Senators Hruska and Curtis that you can *make* them support the public-accommodations section.

I am not sure but I would guess that Nebraska does not have an open-occupancy law. You may say that you do not need it because it isn't much of a problem here. That may or may not be true, because most white people are insulated from Negroes. You never come in contact with us. But if you did have one, it would reflect to this nation and to the people who live within your environs that *this is where Nebraska stands on this issue,* and that is important in itself.

Then there is the economic challenge which is inevitably coming. All across our nation, in Omaha and Lincoln (we in the movement have no alternative because it is a matter of our survival), you will hear more and more about selective patronage. The prophets of doom will say, "You're hurting businessmen; you're trying to put them out of business." That's not true at all. Or, "You are violating property rights." Well, property rights in our American, or even in our English tradition, are superseded by human rights.

You will be hearing more about preferential treatment for Negroes. The hue and cry has already begun that this is discrimination in reverse, and I would grant you that technically this is true. But you see, if I had time to catalogue what you have done to me for the last 100 years, you would be the first to agree that I need a little edge to catch up.

And you need to look around in Nebraska. I am really at a terrible disadvantage here as I run in and I run out. I am so busy trying to get the monkey off my back down in Georgia, Mississippi, and Alabama, that I can't stay here with you to find out what is really going on. But I would submit to you that you ought to look into your banking institutions and see how many black faces you find other than those pushing a broom. Where are the bank tellers and the clerks? Or take your other industries, or your city government, or your state government? We really have to let the chips fall where they may. It may take some doing, and it's going to be awkward, and if you have two applicants of equal ability who come before you, there may be some morality in giving the Negro a chance that he never had, and his father before him, and his mother and his grandfather and grandmother never had; there is such a thing as compensatory discrimination for all of the shortchanging that has gone on for the last 100 years.

There will be no other way to avert this terrible economic crisis that is coming to us. And Nebraska must be concerned with bringing to the federal government its awareness that the Manpower Retraining Act to offset the onslaught of automation is totally inadequate. What we're going to need is a massive retraining program, not only for Negroes but for poor whites all over the South who have been dislocated by automation. President Johnson talks about a war on poverty. And it is commendable that he is concerned about it. But 1 billion dollars isn't a drop in the bucket to what must be done. And it is up to the forces of the church and temple to keep on prodding and insisting that there are flesh-and-blood people here who are going to be starving and who have no place to go, no place to sleep. Somehow, I can hear the voice of the Nazarene saying, "Verily, verily, I say unto you, inasmuch as you did it not unto the least of these my brethren, you did it not unto Me." I hear Micah and Hosea and Amos chastising the rich and the affluent and even the marginal livers for "selling the poor for a pair of shoes." This is the economic challenge of the revolution to the church.

There is finally a religious challenge. We have about run out of classic, well-worded, balanced, pontifical speeches about the problem. It really doesn't matter what you say you believe about race and prejudice and discrimination and unfair hiring practices. It really matters what you do about it.

And for us who are committed to the Ark of the Covenant and to the holy way of the Galilean Prince, it is not enough to throw up our arms and say, "Well, I don't know what to do, I am just one person." And, yet, across the board, it is very largely determined as to what we are going to do insofar as we are personally committed through our religious heritage. It matters about our denomination; it matters about our individual church and the congregation; it matters about you as an individual member.

I cannot leave the rostrum without saying that we must honestly face that fact that if you agree in giving the Negro his right to vote, and the right to public accommodation for lodging and eating, even if you go so far as to endorse preferential treatment, and if you respond to all of the other challenges that are his, you also must say with all candor and honesty, that, if I believe in God, then I also believe in intermarriage. This has always been the red herring, you know. And we have been fooled by the opposition. We in the movement haven't said much about intermarriage. We say, "Oh no, that's not really what we want," and it really isn't. And we are asked, "If there is more integration, won't there be more intermarriage?" And we say, "Oh, not necessarily so." But it is true that, as people come together, and ethnic cultures make exchange, there will be intermarriage. And if you have reservations about intermarriage, then you must honestly confess before the God you serve that prejudice still reigns in the throne room of your heart. Because until you honestly face the right of the individual to choose whom he may marry and have children grow out of the loins of his life, then you deny the basic humanity of the Negro, and are saying that God, somewhere in His creation, made a mistake. (*Applause.*)

I do not know if our paths will ever cross again. I hope they will. But as we leave this conference to go to our several responsibilities, we lose somehow the pressure of what those of common commitment are doing, and it resolves itself ultimately to what we as individuals are going to do. I am convinced—call me a mystic if you will—that a day is coming, a day somewhere at the end of our personal histories when we will have to stand before the judgment bar of God and answer for that to which we have given our lives. I ask you sincerely and genuinely, what kind of accounting will your life give?

Be under no illusion, you will gather to yourself the images of the things you prefer; they will come to you, inveterately, inevitably, as bees to their hives. And in your mind and spirit, they will leave their distilled essence, as sweet as honey, or as bitter as gall. As men see the color in the wave, so shall men see in you the images of the things you prefer: out of your eyes will look the spirit of the thing you have chosen. And in your smile or frown the years will speak! You will not sit, nor stand, nor walk nor will your hand move, but you betray the one you serve. And the image thereof is written on your brow as by a revealing pen. Cleverness may invent skillful words to cast a veil about you, and circumspection may ever sleep, but you will not be hid. That face of yours, which once like an unwritten page lay smooth in its baby crib, will take on lines and more lines like the parchment of an old historian who jealously sets down all of the story. And in it will grow the inscribed narrative of your mental habits, the emotion of your heart, your sense of conscience, your response to duty, what you think of yourself, your fellow man, and your God! Yes, it will all be there, for men become like that which they love. And the image thereof is written on their brow.

PART SIX

Civil Rights Activists

In every age men have arisen, and, by the force of character, conviction, genius, and a lofty aspiration, have come to stand as heralds in the forefront of national progress. The purpose of this final section is to set forth speeches presented by some of the most eminent and eloquent defenders of human freedom in our times.

These speeches will serve, at least, as a contribution to the history of the black man's struggle, and especially of the method and spirit of that movement which brings the perspective of the black revolt into sharper focus.

The missions of these black leaders have been both evangelistic and prophetic. They have identified the flagrant way in which America has betrayed her own principles of liberty, fraternity, and equality among men. In addition, they have pointed with a prophetic finger to the terrifying results that this nation will reap unless she is willing to awaken some fresh aspirations and, in fact, provide absolute freedom for all of her citizens.

The dauntless courage of men like A. Phillip Randolph, Roy Wilkins, James Farmer, Malcolm X, Whitney Young, and Ralph Abernathy cannot be minimized. Each, in his way, helped to sway and elevate with commanding eloquence the public mind. Each pursued his own elected course, and in his own style, an unfaltering steadiness of purpose. Their contributions will go down in history as worthy memorials to the triumph of the principles which they espoused.

In this tremendous struggle for human freedom, however, it was Martin Luther King who stood forth pre-eminent as a prophet, as a preacher, as a scholar, as an unflinching friend of the oppressed; and to his brave outlook over the whole civil-rights conflict, to his extensive knowledge of political and social history, must be ascribed the ardor which aroused the nation. Others grandly spoke and fought for freedom; but none more eloquently, more learnedly, more effectively, enunciated its principles than he; nor more profoundly and persistently instilled into the public mind its justice, grandeur, and necessity.

AS I GREW OLDER
—Langston Hughes

It was a long time ago.
I have almost forgotten my dream.
But it was there then,
In front of me,
Bright like a sun—
My dream.

And then the wall rose,
Rose slowly,
Slowly,
Between me and my dream.
Rose slowly, slowly,
Dimming,
Hiding,
The light of my dream.
Rose until it touched the sky—
The wall.

Shadow.
I am black.

I lie down in the shadow.
No longer the light of my dream before me,
Above me.
Only the thick wall.
Only the shadow.

My hands!
My dark hands!
Break through the wall!
Find my dream!
Help me to shatter this darkness,
To smash this night,
To break this shadow
Into a thousand lights of sun,
Into a thousand whirling dreams
Of sun!

They Didn't Know Who He Was
DR. RALPH DAVID ABERNATHY

The man who succeeded Martin Luther King, Jr., as President of the Southern Christian Leadership Conference was a well-known voice to Americans long before the assassination of Dr. King.

Ralph David Abernathy was described by Dr. King in his last speech, April 3, 1968, as "the best friend that I have in the world." Often called "the civil rights twins," the two men were inseparable as they made the grand strategy for every major nonviolent movement, from Montgomery to Memphis, from 1955 to 1968.

Ralph David Abernathy was born March 11, 1926, in Linden (Marenge County), Alabama. The young Ralph began his education in the public elementary school system of Marenge County and was graduated from Linden Academy, a Baptist high school. In 1950 he was graduated with a Bachelor of Arts degree at Alabama State College in Montgomery, and later he received a Master's in Sociology at Atlanta University and an honorary doctorate from the same institution.

On the night Mrs. Rosa Parks was arrested for refusing to give up her bus seat to a white man in Montgomery, December 1, 1955, Ralph David Abernathy, Martin Luther King, Jr., and their wives decided to risk all. Dr. Abernathy publicly issued the call for a meeting the next day which started the nonviolent civil rights movement.

Upon the founding of SCLC, Dr. Abernathy was elected Financial Secretary-Treasurer. In 1965, in addition to that position, he assumed the newly created position of Vice President At-Large of SCLC, from which he succeeded to the Presidency on April 9, 1968. The SCLC Board of Directors unanimously voted him to that post the night of Dr. King's funeral.

Through the years, Dr. Abernathy's leadership closely paralleled that of Dr. King in his involvements with the Montgomery Bus Boycott, voter registration, nonviolent education, school desegregation, sit-ins, Freedom Rides, Citizenship Education schools, SCLC Operation Breadbasket, Birmingham, the March on Washington, the Civil Rights Act of 1964, St. Augustine, Selma, the Voting Rights Act of 1965, Chicago, the Mississippi March Against Fear, Cleveland, the peace movement . . . and Memphis.

Since Memphis and April 4, Ralph David Abernathy has carried the honor and the burden of a position he never wanted. His first victory for his fallen brother was a just settlement of the garbage strike which had brought Dr. King and Dr. Abernathy to Memphis in behalf of poor workers.

And Dr. Abernathy carried out another mission for his friend—the Poor People's Campaign, the most massive nonviolent movement in history. From every corner of the nation, the new SCLC President led the poor—black, white, red, and brown—to the Nation's Capital in May, 1968. There, on the Great Mall, they built Resurrection City, USA, a community of America's poor that lives in history as a stunning, unforgettable rebuke to racism, poverty, and injustice in America.

The address given below was given at the Commemoration Services for Dr. Martin Luther King, Jr., at the Ebenezer Baptist Church in Atlanta, Georgia, January 15, 1969. It reflects the content of his social gospel, his political and economic thinking, and his philosophy of nonviolence as developed over the years through his friendship with Dr. King and their closest associates.

* * *

There is a traditional spiritual that is sung with as much familiarity and fervor at Christmas time as are the carols. The title of this spiritual is "Sweet Little Jesus Boy," and the words that follow are these: "Sweet Little Jesus Boy." They made Him be born in a manger. Sweet Little Jesus Boy. *They didn't know who He was."*

You have heard it from the choir lofts of Baptist and Protestant Churches and Catholic cathedrals across the land. For me, and for many of you, it is a favorite. It is as familiar as "Silent Night" or "Joy to the World."

The question that comes to my mind at this hour is whether we really understand the meaning, significance and profundity of the story in this spiritual. The story is plain and simple. They made Jesus—the Prince of Peace, the Saviour of the world, the most moving and dynamic figure in history—be born in a manger, simply because *they did not know who He was.*

Just as Jesus came as the Saviour, on this day, January the 15th,

40 years ago, Martin Luther King, Jr. came a few doors down the street as the saviour, the deliverer, the emancipator, the Moses to his people. *But we didn't know who he was.*

Unlike Jesus, his birth did not take place in a manger, but he was born in a ghetto. But like Jesus, he was permitted to live on the earth only for a brief period, and like Jesus he was cut down while still in his thirties. Like Jesus, he was misunderstood, castigated, rebuked and even despised and rejected by his own because *we didn't know who he was.*

Like Jesus, he opposed the system of injustice and inequality, and stood in the courts of the Pharaohs and cried, "Let my people go." Like Jesus, he unstopped the ears of the deaf, he opened the eyes of the blind as he challenged the most powerful and unjust system in the world. Like Jesus, he fed the hungry, he worked to clothe the naked, he lived an unselfish life and he was concerned about "the least of these"—*but we didn't know who he was.*

Who did we think he was?

We thought he might be an ordinary Baptist preacher, well trained in theology and philosophy. We thought his days were to end at an old age when his eloquent and melodious baritone voice would still be lifting thousands to lofty peaks of inspiration.

Many people thought he was out of his mind when he led an army, not armed with guns or bricks or stones, 50,000 strong in Montgomery, Alabama, in 1955, and said to his followers: "Love your enemies, pray for them that curse and despitefully use you." Some of us may have wondered about him when he led us without physical weapons in the battles of Albany, Georgia; St. Augustine, Florida; and Danville, Virginia. And we knew something must have been wrong with him when defenseless we stood before Bull Connor in Birmingham, facing vicious and hungry dogs, fire hoses and brutal policemen. Or when he journeyed into the Black Belt of Alabama—the worst area of oppression in the nation—and confronted the very embodiment of racism, Jim Clark, in Selma.

Some felt that he was merely a seeker of publicity, a preacher of that which he was unwilling to suffer for. Much of the nation felt, as expressed by a high and powerful government official, that he was the world's most notorious liar.

But *in fact—we didn't know who he was.*

And nine months and eleven days ago, on April 4, 1968, a man representing what I believe a conspiracy fired a bullet and stilled his heartbeat and silenced his physical voice, because *he didn't know who he was.*

In truth, who was Martin Luther King, Jr.?

He was, first of all, an emancipator. He was sent by God to fulfill the dreams expressed by the founding fathers of this nation in 1776. The founding document had said that this was a nation under God, a nation "dedicated to the proposition that all men are created equal, and that they are endowed by their Creator with certain inalienable rights, and among these are life, liberty and the pursuit of happiness." It was an inspired and glorious document, but in reality, America was not such a nation, and America had written a lie.

The black man had been enslaved for 244 years in this nation, and when Martin Luther King, Jr. came, 100 years later, the black man was still oppressed and had lost all hope for fulfilling the dream of America.

But Dr. King came to declare that the nation must live by those beautiful words and pronouncements in the Declaration of Independence, and he became the emancipator of his people.

He was, secondly, the redeemer of the soul of America. As the redeemer he taught his people in Montgomery that their "feet may be tired, but their souls could be rested." He taught the nation that "an eye for an eye, and a tooth for a tooth," if followed to its ultimate conclusion, would only end in a totally blind and toothless society. He discovered that the most potent force for revolution and reform in America is nonviolence. He knew, as the eminent historian Arnold Toynbee has written, that if America is saved, it will be through the black man who can inject new dimensions of nonviolence into the veins of our civilization. Therefore, Dr. King both practiced and preached nonviolence, in his home, in his family, in our SCLC family and in all of our movements. On April 4, 1967, exactly one year before his assassination, he was striving to redeem the soul of America when he spoke to the Riverside Church in New York City and warned the nation that it must end the unjust and vicious war in Vietnam.

Martin Luther King, Jr. was, finally, a "drum major for justice." He talked about this right here in Ebenezer Baptist Church last February 4th. He said, "I have tried to love and serve humanity," and that was the way he wanted to be remembered—as a man loving and serving all people in the cause of justice. His last act was a mission in this cause. He went to Memphis, Tennessee, to lead a movement for poor garbage workers. They are the men who pick up the filth and clean the city—but they are scorned and abused and impoverished. They sent out the Macedonian call for help to a man who had earned the highest academic degree and had been awarded dozens of honorary degrees. They sent out the trumpet call to a man who had been entertained by kings and queens and been awarded the Nobel Prize for Peace. He did not ignore that call because it came from garbage workers. Rather, Dr. King went there to serve his brothers. He was in the front ranks in a campaign for equality. And he was not content with freedom for black people alone. He worked for freedom of all people. He worked for the Baptist and other Protestants, the Catholics, the Jews; yes, he worked for all believers as well as the unbelievers. He followed his "drum major instinct" to be out in front as the leader of a mighty parade with a mighty band, on the way to freedom's land.

It was my privilege and my honor to stand by the side of this great, beautiful and sensitive man. Like Gibran, I learned my lesson well: "to be close, but not too close, for the cyprus tree does not flourish in the shadow of the oak." I had to be near when needed, but never so near that I would be in the way and impede the progress of this 20th-century prophet. I would gladly have given my life in exchange for his, and I would *even* give it today if I could bring him back. I would turn my eyes into a fountain of tears, I would mourn and grieve every day and night if this would do any good.

To the best of my ability, I worked with him. We went to jail together 19 times in 13 years. I prayed with him during the dark and lonely hours of the night. I was with him when he went atop Mount Pisgah's lofty heights, and like Elijah, he flung his mantle upon me and spoke with the authority of Moses and said: "Joshua, take the children of Israel on across the Jordan into the land of Canaan."

So today I stand on January the 15th, his birthday, and I want to send him this birthday greeting:

To Martin Luther King, in the city called Heaven, in care of Jesus Christ the Saviour: Greetings and felicitations. Many years we celebrated your birthday with you in person. But today we must celebrate it with you physically removed. Even so, I know that you are here. I can feel your spirit in the air. During this period, many streets are being named for you, many scholarship funds are being established in your name, and monuments, statues, hospitals, schools and buildings are being erected in your honor.

Martin, I know that all of these are significant and important, and I praise those courageous persons who take steps in this direction. But, Martin, I know you. You were never interested in mortar, brick or stone. You always were interested in freeing the captives and setting at liberty them that are bruised, exalting the valleys, making low the hills and mountains, straightening the crooked, and creating a society with no gulf between the haves and have-nots.

Therefore, we in the Southern Christian Leadership Conference are determined to make January 15th, your birthday, a legal and national holiday so that the wheels of industry and commerce will stop, banks and schools will close, and on this day each year the nation can pay tribute to you, our hero and the hero of black people and all men and women of good will throughout the world.

Martin, this is not an adequate gift for you on your birthday, for we admit that we are selfish in our gifts and we are so limited in what we can give you today for you gave all, even your life. The making of your birthday a legal and national holiday will be a gift to black and white America which enrich our heritage and strengthen our faith in the democratic process.

Also, Martin, you should know about the New Thrust in SCLC, for we feel that the greatest tribute we can pay you will be the continuation of your feeble and humble efforts to redeem the soul of America. So in our staff retreat in Frogmore, South Carolina, last week, we decided that we would make the following gifts to America, in keeping with your wishes:

Number One, we will help poor people get decent homes for their families. Incidentally, Martin, this will be done under the housing act that was passed because of our Poor People Campaign.

Number Two, we will organize the poor workers of America—the garbage men, the hospital workers, the domestic workers and the millions of other hard-working poor people—so that they can gain their rightful incomes and security.

Number Three, we will work for economic development and freedom in the black community, not seeking riches for the few businessmen, but seeking a rich community for all.

Number Four, we will demand that America will provide the best modern education for all children, equipping them with the wondrous skills of technology and the beautiful wisdom of humanity and brotherhood.

Number Five, we will continue your quest for peace in the world, to save not only America but all mankind from destruction.

Number Six, we will mobilize and work with students and young people in all these endeavors. Martin, you always did love to be with young people, because you were young yourself. You saw in them the hope for America's salvation, and so do we, for we are going out among the young to enlist their support and participation at the high school, college and university levels.

Number Seven, we will work for political gains for poor people so that they will have true and honest representation in the councils of their governments. . . .

Everywhere, Martin, we will battle for the rights of all people, using the armor of nonviolence which you molded for us. And we know that you will be with us wherever we go—into the homes and churches of the poor, into the offices of the rich and powerful, into the streets and highways whenever it is necessary.

Finally, we have another gift. In remaining true to the principles of non-violence, I call upon the forces of good will throughout this land, to exert their total influence in seeing to it that life of James Earl Ray or whoever is proven to have pulled the trigger that felled our Sainted and beloved leader, is spared.

I say, unto you today, it is needless to kill one man for the sins of millions. . . . For us to kill of those that are truly guilty of taking Dr. King's life, we would *but* be guilty of mass murder perpetuating an atrocity no less than that of Adolf Hitler.

We must understand that the elimination of Earl Ray or whoever killed Dr. King, does not deal with our major problem. This would only be dealing with the symptom of our major problem. Our job is to deal with the cause of our problem. Our problem is that our society is sick, our nation is a sick nation, concentrated with violence, saturated with hate. This sick system of ours is constantly conceiving, giving birth, nurturing and producing millions of Rays.

And, I say to the American system today, the true killer of Martin Luther King, Jr., a man who tried to teach everybody to love, one who gave his life in an effort to redeem your soul, one who tried to make the American dream a living reality: Don't go deeper into degration by participating in the philosophy of genocide but change this system, get your soul right with God. Stop the hunger and the illiteracy perpetrated upon the poor. Stop these unjust wars, raise up no more assassins; instead, as God said Let Justice raise up a nation that will obey. Yes, my friends, this evil system killed Dr. King and will kill many more of us unless we rid ourselves of a system that produces assassins, and instead redeem the soul of America.

These are gifts which we can not send to you, Martin, so we shall give them to the people you love.

I thought of sending you a flashlight, but where you are today there is no need of a light, for the sun never goes down. I thought of sending you a birthday cake today, but you are in a place where food never gives out for your Saviour and mine is the bread of life. I thought of sending you a color television set, but the stars and the moon now give you a sweeping telescopic view of the universe and there is nothing more colorful and beautiful than the sunset. I thought of other gifts, but the angels now await your command for any need imaginable.

And so we are giving our gifts to the people you love, the people to whom you gave the ultimate gift of your earthly life.

I must close now, Martin. But honesty impels me to admit that, "nights are long since you went away, I think of you, Martin, both night and day, my buddy, my buddy," your buddy misses you. . . . But you may be assured that I am going to tell the world who you were.

If Not Now, When?
JAMES FARMER

An organization that has gained enthusiastic support by young Negroes in their struggle for civil rights, especially in the South, is the Congress of Racial Equality. Under the leadership of its National Director, James Farmer, CORE has pioneered successfully in such tactics as Freedom Rides, sit-ins, stand-ins, and jail-ins.

Farmer was one of the group that founded CORE in 1942. He was its first National Chairman and became its National Director in 1961. In the spring of 1961, he led CORE's first Freedom Ride; as a result, he was held in Mississippi jails for more than a month. Farmer has also worked for the Fellowship of Reconciliation, the NAACP, and several labor unions.

James Farmer earned his B.S. degree in chemistry from Wiley College when he was only eighteen years old. He enrolled in the School of Religion of Howard University, Washington, D.C., to prepare for the Methodist ministry. Farmer received the degree of Bachelor of Divinity in 1941, but declined ordination. Recalling that the Methodist Church in the South was then segregated, he says, "I didn't see how I could honestly preach the Gospel of Christ in a church that practiced discrimination. . . . But I never abandoned His teaching. It is still very much part of my thinking."

Instead of entering the ministry, Farmer turned his energies toward social action. From 1941 to 1945 he served as race-relations secretary of the Fellowship of Reconciliation. From 1946 to 1948 he took part in the organizing drive in the South of the Upholsterers' International Union. Later he served as international representative of the State, County, and Municipal Employees Union, and in 1958 he was designated one of a five-man delegation from the International Confederation of Free Trade Unions to fifteen African countries. Farmer also served as a Program Director for the NAACP and was a commentator on radio and television programs sponsored by the United Auto Workers in Detroit.

In 1942, with a group of students at the University of Chicago, Farmer organized the first chapter of CORE. The group intended, in his words, "to substitute bodies for exhortations," and to apply to the struggle for racial equality in the United States the techniques of nonviolence and passive resistance that Gandhi used so successfully in India's struggle for independence.

As National Director of CORE, Farmer not only plans projects but also participates in carrying many of them out. He was one of the original Freedom Riders, and like most of the group, he spent forty days in jail in 1961. Since that time he has been imprisoned on numerous occasions for his participation in civil-rights demonstrations.

President of the Center for Community Action Education since 1965, Farmer served as professor of social welfare at Lincoln University (Pa.) 1966–1967. He has been sponsor of the American Negro Leadership Conference on Africa since 1962. Active as a lecturer, he became an author in 1965 when he completed *Freedom—When?* Recently, Mr. Farmer was appointed an assistant secretary in the Department of Health, Education and Welfare.

The speech included here, "If Not Now, When?", was delivered on October 26, 1964, at Central State College in Wilberforce, Ohio, in a special convocation for students and faculty alike. It is a body of personal information on the civil-rights revolution that is taking place in the South.

* * *

President Wesley, Mr. Chairman, Reverend Karsten, Dr. Hale, ladies and gentlemen:

I note that I have a very broad subject assigned—that of civil rights —which gives me a great deal of leeway. I can say just about anything I want and still be talking on that subject.

I remember speaking on that subject several years ago; then it was almost disastrous and I must share it with you. This also was on a college campus. I can never forget it. The following day I walked across the campus and a middle-aged lady stopped me and said, "Now let me see, you are James Farmer, aren't you?" I said, "Why yes, madam." She said, "I am awfully sorry I didn't get to hear you yesterday when you spoke. I had been planning for a long time to be there but at the last minute something turned up and I couldn't possibly make it." I smiled and said very modestly, "Why madam, you didn't miss much." She said, "Yes, that's what they tell me, but I wish I had heard you just the same."

Whenever I speak on a subject that broad, I am forced to recall that incident. I do recall, however, that on that trip another incident occurred in Pittsburgh. It was in the latter days of the war. I was fortunate in getting the last Pullman berth that was available from New York to Pittsburgh for an overnight trip. However, before the train left the station, I discovered that there was an elderly lady who had not been so lucky, so I turned my berth over to her and went into the day coach. I tried unsuccessfully, of course, to rest as the train was rocking back and forth. At the very first stop of the train, I left it, went into the station and telephoned a wire to my wife, telling her what a horrible time I was having trying to sleep on the rocking train. When I arrived in Pittsburgh there was a reply from her which completely baffled me. I could not figure it out. The reply said simply, "Congratulations. Hope you are both doing well." Well, I didn't know the solution to this problem—what interpretation could be formed. I pondered it from every conceivable angle. I finally decided that she must have sent two telegrams at the same time and undoubtedly got the addresses mixed up; no doubt I had received one intended for someone else. It sounded like a satisfactory answer. When I got back home, I asked her, "Now, honey, you did send two telegrams at the time you sent the one to me, didn't you?" She said, "No, I only sent one." "Well then, what did you mean by this: 'Congratulations. Hope you both are doing well.'" She said, "Well, what in the world did you mean by this: 'Having terrible night, can't sleep. Just gave berth to old lady.'"?

But seriously, I am pleased to have the opportunity to address this group of students at Central State College tonight. I am pleased because I feel that I am not bringing the civil-rights revolution to you; I am coming to you to share with you the civil-rights revolution which you have already found and participated in. I am honored that in introducing me, Dr. Hale indicated that I am among those who have spent some time in jail. I am not alone. Many of you have done the same. There are roughly about 250,000 of us all over the country now who have on occasions been in and out of jails in the struggle for civil rights, and it happens that we are wearing those jail sentences as literal badges of honor.

This is the nature of the fight—the nature of the civil-rights revolution in which we find ourselves, and in which you are sharing. It is in reality part two of another revolution—the American Revolution. Part one of that revolution was fought for a very simple reason—to establish the principle of liberty in our land. Tht revolution—that phase of it—was essentially successful. The principle was established but that principle did not include all Americans. For many people it did not mean liberty. It did not, for example, apply to women in the early days of America. Women did not have the rights which were guaranteed to other Americans. They did not have even the right of suffrage, and they had to struggle to achieve that right. They struggled under the banner of the suffragettes and significantly, my friends, they used techniques which are quite similar to those which for the past several years have dominated the civil-rights movement. They demonstrated, they picketed, they marched; on occasions they —if not in this country, then in some other country—chained themselves across sidewalks. Here in our country they picketed the White House and they won. Their struggle is not ended, but they established the principle of their own inclusion in the compact of liberty.

This principle established in the eighteenth century in the first stage of the American Revolution did not include workers. Working men and women of our country got half the freedoms which had been proclaimed. Their hours spent at work were one-half to one-third of their lives; and one-half of their waking hours were spent not under democracy but under autocracy. They had no voice concerning their wages or hours or establishing their working conditions. That was not freedom. They then had to struggle for their freedom, for their own inclusion in the American compact of liberty. They fought hard with the same weapons—the demonstration, the march, the picket line, the boycott; and in Flint, Michigan, in the mid 30's they got in and they won. They established the principle of their inclusion; they won the right to collective bargaining and the right for union recognition. They won the Wagner Act which was their Magna Carta. I would suggest to you this evening that the civil-rights revolution is now in the 60's at the same stage that the trade-unions revolution was in the 30's.

We have now established basically the constitutional issue of what our rights are. The Civil Rights Act of 1964 did that. That does not mean the problem is solved any more than the problem of the trade

unions was solved in the 30's. It insisted that at least we have a
useful tool with which we can work. And now the next stage of the
civil-rights revolution itself will be a stage of planning, a predetermi-
nation of where we are going, what the targets are, what methods
are going to be used to aim at each target, and what the relationship
is between the method and the target. We have to broaden our base.
We have become more active in politics than we have ever been
before. We will seek to develop political power commensurate with
our numerical strength, and we will seek also to develop an economic
power likewise commensurate. We will seek to improve the educational level to achieve equality as we have fought so hard to achieve
freedom.

But that's the upcoming stage of the civil-rights revolution. What
is *this* revolution about? What happened? For so many years like
a great slumbering giant, Negroes accepted the status quo. I remember asking Thomas Mboya of Kenya on one of his numerous trips over
here what he thought of the American Negro. Tom, being a philosophical sort, was silent for a long time. Then he shot his sharp eyes
at me and said, "Brother Farmer, what does the American Negro
think of himself?"

That was the question, and that was the answer. For a long time,
we thought so little of ourselves that we accepted segregation and
discrimination, with all of its degradation. Oh, perhaps we talked
against it. When I was in college down in Texas twenty-five years or
twenty-eight years ago, I didn't like segregation any more than you
do. But I didn't do anything about it. You have been doing something about it. We talked against it, yes; we had bull sessions in the
men's dormitory every night and we ranted and raved and railed
against segregation. If words could destroy, it would have died a
thousand deaths, but it went on. We walked right out of those bull
sessions and the next morning went downtown and climbed the back
stairs of the Paramount Theatre and sat up in the buzzard's roof and
watched the movie and suffered no qualms of conscience whatever.
We did it and I did it every week like all the others, so I am not
attacking anybody else. I didn't realize then that my deeds were giving the lie to my words. Well, I couldn't do it any more. I couldn't
climb those stairs because I know that each time I did I was by that
very act perpetuating the system of segregation which verbally I
sought to destroy. With my lips I was against it; but with my deeds
I took part in it, participated in it, cooperated with it, paid my parents' hard-earned money for the privilege of keeping segregation going. And there are thousands, tens of thousands of people—largely

young, but not only young—in the South now who have joined the revolution too who can no longer do it. And that is the revolution essentially—the change in the thinking and the mood of the people.

People who heretofore were bowing and scraping and scratching where they didn't itch are now standing up and facing the society. This is the point. My heart got a lift in Atlantic City where there were sixty-eight persons from the Freedom Democratic Party of Mississippi. Some of them were just ordinary folk—from small towns and rural areas, the counties of Mississippi, sharecroppers, and tenant farmers. Do you think they were bowing and scraping in Atlantic City? Quite to the contrary. They were standing and facing representatives of the political power structure of that state. They were talking to "Mr. Charlie" and they were saying, "We want your seat; we want to vote!" This gave my heart a lift. Here were people who had lost their fear. Ten years ago, that would have been incredible and unthinkable. But now it seemed the most natural thing in the world. That's the nature of the revolution.

Like the old lady in her eighties in Greenwood, Mississippi, who attended a mass rally for voter registration. All her life she had spent working in somebody else's kitchen. I am sure she never dreamed about freedom, never thought about it, never before thought about registering. But she came up in the middle of that meeting and took the microphone and said, "Children, I want to talk to you about freedom. All of my life I have been scared and I have been running. Well, I am tired of being scared, and I ain't running no more." The next morning that old lady was in the line of march—marching nonviolently into the teeth of the police dogs and billy clubs for whatever the day might hold in an attempt to register to vote.

There could be no turning back for the people who had found that kind of courage and motivation. But what brought it about? Why the change? I said to my father who was at that time in Freedman's Hospital on his deathbed the day before the Freedom Riders left Washington, D.C., on May 3, 1961, that tomorrow I was going on a Freedom Ride. He asked, what's a Freedom Ride? I described it to him and told him that we were trying to demonstrate the great gap that existed between the law on one hand and its implementation on the other. And, therefore, we were going to ride unsegregated through the South in the buses stopping at all the bus terminals, demanding the use of all the facilities and accepting the consequences of our action. Well, the old man thought and said, "Where you going, what states?" I told him and he said, "Alabama and Mississippi too?" I said yes. He said, "Well, I tell you what: I am glad you are going, and I hope you survive it. I realize that this may be the last trip you will ever take. But I'm glad you're going and I'll tell you why. When I was a boy in South Carolina and Georgia, we didn't like segregation either. We hated it. It burned us up inside. But we thought that was the way things always had been and the way they had to be and there was nothing we could do about it. So we put up with it, accepted it, even as we burned up. But I am glad," he continued, "that there are lots of people today who know better, and who know that these things can be changed and are willing to risk a great deal, even their lives, in the attempt to change them." He was right. That transformation has come about. What brought it about? I am sure you can answer it as well as I.

One thing was the war, World War II, which you can't remember, most of you. But the lads who were in uniform fighting the masquerade theory of Nazism tell me that almost every second day they wondered which way they ought to point their guns. They said, what about the masquerade theory back home? Shouldn't we fight against that just as hard? They tell a tale about a possible story, that could well be true, about the young man in uniform during the war on a train heading South. As he crossed the Mason-Dixon Line the conductor said to him, "Boy, get up out of that seat and go up to the front coach where you belong, the Jim Crow coach." The young man ignored him. The order was repeated and ignored again, repeated. Finally the youngster looked up at the conductor and said, "You see this uniform?" He said, "Yes, I see it." The soldier said, "I didn't ask them for it, they put it on me. They are going to send me to Timbuctoo or some other place to fight and die for democracy. But if I've got to fight and die for democracy over there, I'd just as soon start here." And the conductor walked away. Well, that feeling was very strong then and I would suggest to you that it has not grown weaker; it has instead grown deeper and stronger throughout the country. And it is one of the reasons for the change in mood.

Another reason, of course, is the increasing education of the young people. How are you going to teach any man or woman about the Constitution or the Declaration of Independence without realizing that at some point he's going to stop and think and ask himself, well, what about me? Don't these things mean me too? When, if not now? That really is the question that those four freshman kids from Greensboro A & T College, North Carolina, asked themselves and their country when they walked into Woolworth and sat at the lunch counter; it wasn't coffee they wanted. It was dignity; and if not now, when? And they began a movement in the South that didn't stop until something that was symbolic like lunch counters set in motion a revolution. That's what happened within the past few years.

A third reason for this change is Africa. How many of you, I wonder, are interested in Africa today? Don't hold up your hands. Ten or twelve years ago the hands would be practically none. Now I would venture to suggest that more than half would be interested in what is happening in Africa. Prior to Ghana—before the Gold Coast became Ghana—Negroes had no more interest in Africa than anybody else. As a matter of fact, we have the same stereotyped image of Africa that most Americans have—you know a dark continent with a few half-naked people riding on the backs of elephants and throwing spears around. A common saying in the pre-Ghana days was, "Man, I ain't lost nothing in Africa." We wanted to forget Africa then. We wanted to blot it out. And this fear emits a terrible situation as far as Negro Americans are concerned. We alone among American people were a people without umbilical cords, without roots, without a tradition, without a heritage. Our ties with Africa had been snuffed out without a single link since the slavery period, and we had even lost the emotional ties because we wanted to forget our Africa. We also wanted to forget slavery because that was a dark and unhappy page out of history. We were then like a people suddenly sprung alive in the Reconstruction period full blown. No roots. A man cannot have a sense of destiny for the future unless he also has a consciousness or awareness of roots into the past. There was no dignity.

I see a different Negro when I walk the streets of our country now among the young and old. Heretofore there was the shuffling, head-bowed man who was going no place because he had come from nowhere. Now there is more pride; their heads are held high as Negro Americans have been emerging nations in Africa—a proud people—meeting the emergence and in many cases fighting against terrible odds and making themselves known and struggling to solve the problems of building new nations. There has been more pride, more self-esteem than ever before. This has helped produce the new mood that was lacked heretofore and what Baldwin has called identity. Others have put it less elegantly in an assorted jest of being somebody, being something which Negroes have lacked and now are beginning to find.

We have not completely found it yet because the concept of superiority and inferiority is so deeply rooted in our relations and culture that it is extremely difficult for any individual—black or white—to completely escape its clutches. The tendency is for the child to breathe it in the air, to suckle it from the breast of his mother. Only through a conscious effort or through luck or chance along the way can he completely rid himself of it. I had the occasion in the past couple of years of looking through some preschool books, wanting to see what kind of image my little girl who is now five would get from the stack of books friends had given here. I went through them and found in most cases—I can put a few aside that I think are pretty good—she doesn't see herself in the books at all, unless she is carrying somebody's bag or in some absurd or impossible position with a string tied around her toes. This is the kind of image she gets of herself. How will she stand in the world? What will be her importance to society and in society? That's what I mean by the cultural miasma that makes it so difficult for man woman or child to develop his self-esteem and self-respect. But we are developing more of it now and that is another reason for the revolution that is taking place.

Motivation has been found such as never before. You know what motivation is: if a person has motivation all things become possible. I have seen bad students become excellent students when they become involved in a movement that is greater, bigger, more important than they. I have seen students in colleges whose professors swore to me had no leadership ability at all, no talent, no promise, less than average intelligence, suddenly spring alive and become leaders and find qualities of leadership which they did not know existed and no one ever dreamed that they had. And they could think on their feet; they could plan because all of a sudden they had something worth living for. I remember down in Atlanta talking with one youngster who became involved in the sit-ins in the early stages—1960. His professors told me that he was a "C" student. He was not a big man on campus, not a frat leader; hardly anybody knew him, just an ordinary Joe. But when he became involved in the movement he suddenly came alive and became somebody. I was talking to the lad. He said to me, "Jim, do you realize that I myself desegregated that lunch counter on Peachtree Street?" He said, "Nobody else—I did it—little me. I did it by sitting there; I did it by picketing; I did it by marching." Then he grinned and looked at me shyly and said, "I didn't have the weight of a Martin Luther King, or Roy Wilkins or you. I did it myself." And they couldn't take it away from him. Or take the prize fighter wo went on the Freedom Ride. He was a young, up-and-coming middleweight who joined the Freedom Ride. When I heard this prize fighter was going on the Freedom Ride, I was quite concerned. I called him over and said, "Look, are you sure you want to go?" He said, "Yes." "Now what's going to happen if somebody takes a punch at you?" Well, he hesitated for a moment and said, "Well, Mr. Farmer, it's all right if they take a punch at me; just tell them don't ring a bell." It seems nobody rang a bell; it worked out all right. I saw him later after the Freedom Ride and asked him how his career in the ring was coming along. He said not very well. What happened, I asked? "Well," he said, "I had a fight last month and I lost it." "What went wrong?" "Well, to tell you the truth, I suddenly didn't want to hit the fellow. I've lost what they call the killer instinct. I've lost interest in the whole proceedings." He looked suddenly very sad but very wise. He said "I've come to the conclusion the only fight I want now is the freedom fight." And he was right. This happens to practically everyone who becomes involved in it. They get the motivation. Some get it from one thing and some get it from another. And when you have the motivation, no matter how great the difficulty, all things are possible.

I heard a story illustrating that—the power of motivation. There were two friends who, if you pardon the reference, used to take a daily trip to the bar in town. They would take a shortcut through the graveyard. Well, one night these two buddies decided that they wanted to go to their favorite rendezvous, but one of them said, "No, not taking the short cut, not tonight. In the day, yes; but tonight I'm going to take the long way around by the railroad tracks." The other one said, "Nope, I am going to take the shortcut, right through the graveyard; all by myself. Nothing there but dead people; they don't hurt you. I am only afraid of the living." So he struck out alone through the graveyard whistling loudly. He saw no ghosts; nothing grabbed him. He got halfway through the graveyard, still whistling, and stepped off into an open grave. Now, I don't need to tell you that he pressed the panic button. He tried to jump out; he tried to climb out; he tried to grab the top and pull himself out. Then he tried to scramble his way out—one foot on one side and one foot on the other. And he got halfway up almost made it but then slipped back down. He got a grip on himself, and said I had better think. Surely they won't put a body on top of me, not in the middle of the night; so I might as well rest and relax and wait until morning. Then I can call for help and somebody will pull me out of here. He crawled up in one corner of the grave and fell asleep. He was awakened a bit later by a thud at the other end of the grave. He opened his eyes to find that another poor unfortunate fellow had fallen in. So he watched this fellow go through the same panic routine. He tried to climb out, he tried to jump out, he tried to scramble out; finally, the first man spoke out and said, "You can't get out." But he did!!! He had motivation. He was thoroughly motivated.

I have seen something else happen through this revolution and the stage of the revolution through which we have just come. I have seen people—Negro people in community after community in the South— uniting. I wish to God we had that same unity in the Northern community that I have found in the Southern community. But the unity in the Southern community has been welded under fire. I have been in Placquemines where a community was under siege and it came together. It was the roughest period for Uncle Tom you ever saw. He found out that in spite of "Tomming," he was still a Negro when the chips were down, and he joined the movement. Even the "nervous Nellies" joined the movement and became part and parcel of it. The whole community was part of it together. But what did it take to do it? It didn't start out that way—last summer, summer of '63—no.

I had been in jail for ten and one-half days there for taking part in the demonstration. You may recall that unfortunately I had to miss the memorable March on Washington because I was otherwise occupied at the time in Placquemines, Louisiana. Well, after getting out, some of the youngsters demonstrated; they marched protesting segregation and they had specific demands. They got halfway to town; the chief of police stopped them, arrested the leaders, and held the youngsters there until state troopers arrived on horseback; then they charged right into the group of the youngsters. One girl was stepped on by a horse. Others were trampled. They came running, screaming back to the church. A few were hysterical; some had been knocked down, stuck with electric cattle prods and told, "Get up; run, Nigger, run." They came back to the church and we met. The adults came together for the first time. The ministers had been divided up until that time. There was only one minister with the movement up to that point—a brave man named Rev. Jenson W. Davis. His church was called the Plymouth Rock Baptist Church; we renamed it the Freedom Rock Baptist Church. But he stood alone. Now all of the ministers got together. They said that if they do this to our kids, we are going to take up the punishment. Tomorrow morning, Sunday, all of us are going to preach about freedom. We are bringing all of our congregations after the service to the Freedom Rock Baptist Church and from there we, the ministers of the community, will lead the demonstration.

Well, I was overjoyed. That morning, after the services, the congregations converged on Freedom Rock. The line started, the ministers got up front; some of them began to get cold feet. One of them about halfway up the front stopped and said, "Where's my wife? I think I'll go home." Well his wife was standing right behind him. She said, "Man, if you don't get up there in front of that line and march, you ain't got no wife." He marched. When they got about halfway to town the police stopped them, arrested the ministers, kept the others there until federal vans loaded with horses arrived; a large number of squad cars loaded with state troopers arrived; the troopers got out and mounted the horses and then charged into the adults swinging clubs, sticking them with cattle prods, screaming, "Get up; run, Nigger, run," and beating down again. The adults came back to the church; there we had a couple of nurses bandaging people up, taking care of those who were hysterical and those who had fainted; they were singing, "We Shall Overcome." The troopers rolled right up to the door of the church and began throwing tear-gas bombs into the crowd of people packed into the church. The place was so thick with tear gas you couldn't breathe. The people then ran out of the back door into the parsonage. The troopers then turned high-pressure fire hoses into the inside of the church, ripping over benches and pews, and as the New Orleans *Times Picayune* put it the next morning, "Bibles and hymnals were floating in the aisles."

There was no respite in the parsonage. There were about three hundred of us packed in there. We heard a glass—a window—break; then came a tear-gas bomb. Another window, another bomb, another window, another bomb, another, another . . . until every window in the house was broken. The place was so full of tear gas that you could feel it even as you could smell it. One girl apparently stopped breathing but one of the four field secretaries, Ronnie Moore, administered mouth-to-mouth resuscitation, successfully. Others had dropped to the floor, hoping to climb out, unsuccessfully. We could hear the troopers screaming outside as they roved through the streets yelling like cowboys. If they saw a Negro on the street, he was run down, beaten to the ground, struck with a cattle prod, told to get and run, Nigger, run. We could hear them screaming, "We'll let you go, Nigger, if you tell us where Farmer is."

That night there was a search for me. I had done nothing: I wasn't even in the demonstration march. We learned that there was a house-to-house search going on in the community. Troopers were kicking open doors in a house-to-house search, ransacking houses, looking under beds and in closets, screaming, "Come on out Farmer; we know you're in there." Not finding me, they would throw in a tear-gas bomb and break down doors. Then they would go on to the next house. Two girls who were hiding under the church reported to us that they heard one trooper say to another, "When we catch that blankety-blank, so-and-so Farmer, we going to lynch him." We tried to get phone calls out. They weren't putting through any long-

distance calls from the Negro community that night. We would get
the operator, give the number, and lose connections. Three of my
four lawyers from New Orleans were in town and reported to me that
at this time they tried to escape by crawling through high grass to
get to a graveyard. When they reached the graveyard, the place came
alive. There was a Negro behind every tombstone. That explodes
another myth. We're not even afraid of graveyards anymore.

So it went. The parsonage was full of tear gas so we rushed out
through the backyard. Troopers came around back and began throwing tear-gas bombs in the backyard, forcing us back into the parsonage. Then more into the parsonage to force us back into the yard
and back and forth and back and forth. By this time, of course, night
had fallen and we sent a couple of people crawling through grass
to get to a funeral home a half block away to find out if we could
come there for refuge. The lady who owned the place said yes. So
we all managed—in twos, threes, and fours—to get to the mortuary
before the troopers figured out where we were going. No more than
ten minutes later, however, after the last of us got in there, they
kicked open the back door of that place. I was standing in the front
part of the funeral home looking overhead down the hall into the
back room where the trooper had entered. There he was, his name
plate taped over, his badge number covered, his face dripping with
sweat, his hair hanging over his eyes, his face twisted in a contor-
tionist hate and frenzy. He yelled, "Come on out, Farmer; we know
you're in there. We're coming in to get you." I said to myself, if they
are looking for me, I have no right, of course, to jeopardize the lives
of these other people. The thing for me to do is to go out, confront
them, ask them what the charges are, and if they had a warrant for
my arrest—the usual questions.

I then actually started making my way down the hall toward the
trooper. The Negroes who were with me, fortunately, had much better sense than I had. They stopped me, put their hands over my
mouth, pulled me to the front part of the home and said, "You are
not ready to go out there tonight. If you go out there, you won't be
alive tomorrow morning; that's a lynch mob."

The woman who owned the funeral home—and incidentally she had
been one of the "nervous Nellies" I was referring to earlier—arose to
the occasion. She made her way out to the back and faced the
trooper, shook her finger in his face, and said, "Do you have a search
warrant to come into my place of business?" This confused him,
baffled him. He blinked and backed up and said, "No." She continued to advance, still shaking her finger at him. You know, a Negro

woman can get away with an awful lot at times. She said, "Well, you're not coming into my place of business without a search warrant. I am a taxpayer and a law-abiding citizen." And he said, "Well, well, well." She said, "I'm having a wake here." Answering that these people gathered had not come to a wake, he stepped to the door and consulted with the other troopers. He put his head back in and said, "All right; we've got all the tear gas and all the guns; you ain't got nothing. We give you just five minutes to get Farmer out of here. Five minutes. That's all," and slammed the door.

Well, I don't need to try to tell you what people think about at a time like that. I thought of many things. My whole life came before my eyes. Some people dropped to their knees and said the Lord's Prayer. Rev. Jenson Davis, whom I mentioned earlier, led the group in prayer. Others were softly singing "We Shall Overcome." One husky fellow standing next to me reached in his pocket and pulled out a pistol—I think it was a .38. He said, "Mr. Farmer, if a trooper comes through that door, he'll be dead." Well, I took the gun away from him. He gave it up, but reluctantly. I told him that he could shoot the trooper—the trooper probably would come through the door —but he would jeopardize the lives of all the other people packed in there and he would jeopardize the lives of people throughout the Negro community in this town and in neighboring counties. He gave up the gun and I gave it to the lady who owned the place and told her to put it away. She did. Five minutes passed and the troopers did not come in.

About ten minutes later two friends of mine from a neighboring town who had heard what was happening had driven into town. They knocked on the front door. I opened the door. They came in and reported that the troopers were still kicking open doors in the Negro community in the house-to-house search. They had set up roadblocks at every road leading out of town and that there was a real, honest-to-goodness manhunt. We still could not get any phone calls out of town at that time. They told me that the troopers who had been in back of the funeral home had now gotten into a car and were speeding toward the house of one of the officials, presumably to get a search warrant. They would get it and return; then my life wouldn't be worth a wooden nickel.

We had to plot an escape, and obviously it worked. I got out of town in a hearse. We used two hearses. We used one as a decoy to cruise by the roadblocks to try to pull the troopers away so that they would pursue that hearse. It worked. As soon as they spotted the hearse, suspecting that I had been in that funeral home, they pursued it in a frenzy. They finally surrounded the hearse, closed in on it, stopped it, and searched it. By that time, I was in back of the second hearse, going at high speed down country roads to New Orleans. It took us four and one-half hours to make a trip which by highway would take us one and one-half hours. But we were taking the back way.

In New Orleans we called a press conference to describe what had happened, and announced that the next morning I was returning to Placquemines, and if they had a warrant for my arrest I would be there to be served with it. I got back there the next morning and, of course, the FBI was all over town and there was no warrant for my arrest. The state troopers had no warrant at all and no charges. The Negro community had galvanized as a unit.

A voter-registration drive that was a costly voter-registration drive got underway immediately. The sheriff of the parish came up for re-election. The Negro vote stumped him, defeated him. They did a little fancy footwork there. Reverend Davis announced that he was a candidate for sheriff too. There was another white man who had entered. They knew where the incumbent stood. He was the one who had called in the cattle prods, the troopers, and the billy clubs and tear gas; but we didn't know where this other white man stood. So the Negro leaders of the town called him one day and asked him to come over to a certain place one night. He came. They said, "Where do you stand, what's your platform?" He said, "Well, I am not for integration." They explained that that was not what they were asking. "We know you are not going to come out for integration; but we want to know where you stand on billy clubs, tear gas, cattle prods?" And he said, "I am opposed to the use of those, and my platform is going to be 'Get these billy clubs off these Negroes' heads.'" They agreed then to help him in their own way on the basis of that platform.

He did campaign on it, and a few days before the election, Reverend Davis withdrew from the race and threw his votes to this man, too late for the incumbent to use it to his own advantage. And it was the Negro vote that Reverend Davis threw to him that defeated the sheriff. One of the other persons who was riding one of the horses that night was a state representative and a friend, I'm told, of Leander Perez. He was up for re-election and was stopped at the polls, defeated. This is what voter registration can do. The Negro community is a solid unit there. It will become that all over the country if we know what we are doing in this day.

Mississippi is becoming unified now. The Mississippi Freedom

Democratic Party was the first really significant political move by Negroes since the Reconstruction period. When I was back in Mississippi two weeks ago, I saw that they are not resting on their laurels; instead, they are planning to get out the vote for Johnson on November 3 and they are going to be the only ones. The regular Democrats there are going to vote for Goldwater; but the Negro vote is going for Johnson. They are preparing for other elections too. They told me about an election I hadn't heard of. They said there's another election in December that we are already working for. This it seems is the election of a committee in each county that will determine the cotton allocation for the next year, under the Agricultural Output Stabilization Board. They explained that in this election you don't have to be registered to vote. The only qualification is that you received a cotton allocation last year, no matter how small or how large. More Negroes received cotton allocations than whites because there are more Negroes than whites, three times as many in Madison County, in fact. They are already going from farmhouse to farmhouse, shack to shack, telling people on such and such a date that they are to go to such and such a place and vote. It will be a five-man committee that will determine the allocation. They say, of course, that they have them three to one and that they're all going to vote; they know more about it than they do now. "We can elect all five, but we're not going to do that. We're going to give them one, free!"

I must bring this to a close now; but I do want to say that the battle has moved north, and the struggle is much harder in the North than in the South—much more difficult, much more complex. Progress has been made in the South and some battles are won; but in the North progress is not nearly as obvious because the complexities are much greater indeed.

I think, for example, that we are not really making progress in housing. Residential segregation has increased in the past ten to fifteen years in our Northern cities. Are we making progress in employment? Not when one considers the facts of automation, the fact that we are being thrown out of jobs because of automation, because we are unskilled and semi-skilled and are stunted and dismayed over the so-called gray area in one large city. It was found that of all of our youth between the ages of 16 and 21, 70 percent were out of school and out of work. 70 percent! Absolutely incredible!

You ask me why there was rioting in Harlem; anyone knows the answer. The rioting was because the youth have nothing to do; society has locked its doors on them. We had a talk with Mayor Wagner last April and said that the long hot summer can be prevented if we will begin now setting up work brigades for the unemployed youth of the ghetto so that as soon as school is over, our youth, whether they are black or white or Puerto Rican, can be put to work cleaning up the vacant lots, rehabilitating slum property under skilled supervision. Or if necessary, if they cannot be rehabilitated, ripping them down at city pay rates after they have been taken over by the city into receivership. They would be off the streets then. The kids will be off the streets because they will be doing something and they will be earning money. They took it under advisement. They started it after the riot, but not before. It was too little and too late.

We must now gain the political power so that we will not have to be petitioning the decision-makers politically. We will be a part of the decision-making complex. Have you ever wondered why in city after city now in the North we hear about urban renewal, plans about new schools going to be built and where they are going to be located after the decision has been made, not before? Then it's too late: we can protest, we can scream, and we can picket them, but the decision has been made. With the use of political power—that means not only registering, it means voting, it means getting active in the ward politics and the precinct politics, and it means getting good people on the city planning commission, black or white, on the boards of education to help make the decisions—then we can participate in the decision-making proper, and then we will have achieved a power that is commensurate with our numerical strength.

Economic power too, economic power in the form of co-ops—the building of co-ops in the ghetto communities throughout city after city; credit unions—pooling resources to start banks; building businesses—not black business to compete against white business at the national core, but businesses which will be competitive in the whole picture of American history so that white people can patronize them as well as black and thusly develop their economic base for the community so that the community can have political, economic, and educational strength.

Our youth are being hurt and crippled. I have seen seventeen-year-old youngsters in high school who could not read. My sister teaches in Washington, D.C. She says that in one high school class she pointed to a youngster who was seventeen and asked him to read a paragraph from the textbook. He didn't open his mouth. She thought he was being insolent. She pursued it and found out that the young man could not read. She asked him to read any words that he could identify. She was almost crying. The only word he could identify was the word "a." He had been pushed along and moved from class to class because they had to make room for somebody else in those seats with the double-shift and triple-shift classes. They couldn't keep him around. She said he was not dumb; he was not stupid; he could learn. In New York in Bank Street last summer they took the youth whom teachers had said were uneducable, who were a waste of time, who couldn't learn. In two months they found these youth—who were not reading, who did not know how to read—actually reading. One young man was not only reading, but he was writing poetry at the end of the summer. One youngster wrote a one-act play when he could not read at the beginning of the summer, and his play was produced by a little theater group. Yes, we need a massive remedial and compensatory educational program.

The fight for freedom is combined with the fight for equality, and we must realize that this is the fight for America—not just black America but all America. It is the fight to make America America again for all of our people, North and South, black and white. In the words of the great rabbi who wrote, 2,000 years ago, "Hither, if I am not for myself, who will be for me; if I am for myself alone, what am I? If not now, when?"

Letter from a Birmingham Jail
I Have a Dream
Nobel Peace Prize Acceptance Speech
DR. MARTIN LUTHER KING, JR.

The magnificence with which Dr. Martin Luther King, Jr., lived a full life in such a short span is a testimony to the dazzling contribution that he made to this nation and to the world.

As a scholar, Mr. King displayed ambition and genius at an early age. He is a graduate of Morehouse College, Crozer Theological Seminary, and Boston University, where he received the Doctor of Philosophy in Systematic Theology in 1955. In addition, he received more than twenty honorary degrees from colleges and universities. As a preacher he pursued a quiet and peaceful career at Dexter Avenue Baptist Church in Montgomery, Alabama, until Rosa Parks challenged the Southern status quo and refused to give up her seat to a white man. As a fighter for freedom he shocked his contemporaries with his realistic forthrightness, touching off a Black Revolution that has been great, stormy, and triumphant.

In 1957 The Gallup Poll revealed that he was one of the most admired religious leaders in the world. In 1957 *Time Magazine* selected him as one of the ten most outstanding personalities of the year. He received more than one hundred and twenty-five citations and awards for his work in civil rights. In a poll conducted by *Link Magazine* of New Delhi, India, he ranked as one of the sixteen world leaders who had contributed most of the advancement of freedom during 1959. In 1963 *Time Magazine* selected him as its Man of the Year, stating that he had become "The unchallenged voice of the Negro people and the disquieting conscience of the white." In 1964 Dr. King was awarded the Nobel Peace Prize. He became the youngest person ever to receive this international honor.

Dr. King is the author of *Stride toward Freedom, The Measure of a Man, Strength of Love, Why We Can't Wait, Where Do We Go from Here: Chaos or Community?*, and *The Trumpet of Conscience.*

In addition, he traveled and lectured extensively in Europe, Asia, South America, and Africa. In the United States alone, he delivered addresses in more than two hundred colleges and universities.

Prior to his assassination in Memphis, Tennessee on April 4, 1968, he served as President of the Southern Christian Leadership Conference. He was active as a titan in spearheading the crusade for the rights of man. Fearless and forgiving, he combined nonviolent fervor with inexhaustible power. His wife and four children provided him with the quiet strength and serenity to meet the stresses which responsibility and involvement pressed upon him. Then, too, he was buttressed by the inner support which the Christian ethic and the Gandhian doctrine of nonviolence nurtured in his soul.

From the Birmingham Jail where he was imprisoned, Dr. King wrote the letter on April 16, 1963, which follows. It is a most cogent and stirring expression of his philosophy of nonviolence. One of his most celebrated addresses at the March on Washington in 1963 was his brilliant inspirational message, "I Have a Dream." It is included here along with his Acceptance Statement at the Nobel Peace Prize Ceremony in Oslo, Norway, on December 10, 1964.

* * *

Martin Luther King, Jr.
Birmingham City Jail
April 16, 1963

Bishop C. C. J. Carpenter
Bishop Joseph A. Durick
Rabbi Milton L. Grafman
Bishop Paul Hardin

Bishop Nolan B. Harmon
The Rev. George M. Murray
The Rev. Edward V. Ramage
The Rev. Earl Stallings

My dear Fellow Clergymen,

While confined here in the Birmingham City Jail, I came across your recent statement calling our present activities "unwise and untimely." Seldom, if ever, do I pause to answer criticism of my work and ideas. If I sought to answer all of the criticisms that cross my desk, my secretaries would be engaged in little else in the course of the day and I would have no time for constructive work. But since I feel that you are men of genuine good will and your criticisms are sincerely set forth, I would like to answer your statement in what I hope will be patient and reasonable terms.

I think I should give the reason for my being in Birmingham, since you have been influenced by the argument of "outsiders coming in." I have the honor of serving as president of the Southern Christian Leadership Conference, an organization operating in every Southern state with headquarters in Atlanta, Georgia. We have some eighty-five affiliate organizations all across the South—one being the Alabama Christian Movement for Human Rights. Whenever necessary and possible we share staff, educational, and financial resources with our affiliates. Several months ago our local affiliate here in Birmingham invited us to be on call to engage in a nonviolent direct-action program if such were deemed necessary. We readily consented and when the hour came we lived up to our promises. So I am here, along with several members of my staff, because we were invited here. I am here because I have basic organizational ties here. Beyond this, I am in Birmingham because injustice is here. Just as the eighth-century prophets left their little villages and carried their "thus saith the Lord" far beyond the boundaries of their home town, and just as the Apostle Paul left his little village of Tarsus and carried the gospel of Jesus Christ to practically every hamlet and city of the Graeco-Roman world, I too am compelled to carry the gospel of freedom beyond my particular home town. Like Paul, I must constantly respond to the Macedonian call for aid.

Moreover, I am cognizant of the interrelatedness of all communities and states. I cannot sit idly by in Atlanta and not be concerned about what happens in Birmingham. Injustice anywhere is a threat to justice everywhere. We are caught in an inescapable network of mutuality tied in a single garment of destiny. Whatever affects one directly affects all indirectly. Never again can we afford to live with the narrow, provincial "outside agitator" idea. Anyone who lives inside the United States can never be considered an outsider anywhere in this country.

You deplore the demonstrations that are presently taking place in Birmingham. But I am sorry that your statement did not express a similar concern for the conditions that brought the demonstrations into being. I am sure that each of you would want to go beyond the superficial social analyst who looks merely at effects, and does not grapple with underlying causes. I would not hesitate to say that it is unfortunate that so-called demonstrations are taking place in Birmingham at this time, but I would say in more emphatic terms that it is even more unfortunate that the white power structure of this city left the Negro community with no other alternative.

In any nonviolent campaign there are four basic steps: (1) collection of the facts to determine whether injustices are alive; (2) negotiation; (3) self-purification; and (4) direct action. We have gone through all of these steps in Birmingham. There can be no gainsaying of the fact that racial injustice engulfs this community. Birmingham is probably the most thoroughly segregated city in the United States. Its ugly record of police brutality is known in every section of this country. Its unjust treatment of Negroes in the courts is a notorious reality. There have been more unsolved bombings of Negro homes and churches in Birmingham than any city in this nation. These are the hard, brutal, and unbelievable facts. On the basis of these conditions Negro leaders sought to negotiate with the city fathers. But the political leaders consistently refused to engage in good-faith negotiation.

Then came the opportunity last September to talk with some of the leaders of the economic community. In these negotiating sessions certain promises were made by the merchants—such as the promise to remove the humiliating racial signs from the stores. On the basis of these promises. Reverend Shuttlesworth and the leaders of the Alabama Christian Movement for Human Rights agreed to call a moratorium on any type of demonstrations. As the weeks and months unfolded we realized that we were the victims of a broken promise. The signs remained. As in so many experiences of the past we were confronted with blasted hopes, and the dark shadow of a deep disappointment settled upon us. So we had no alternative except that of preparing for direct action, whereby we would present our very bodies as a means of laying our case before the conscience of the local and national community. We were not unmindful of the difficulties involved. So we decided to go through a process of self-purification. We started having workshops on nonviolence and repeatedly asked ourselves the questions, "Are you able to accept blows without retaliating?" "Are you able to endure the ordeals of jail?"

We decided to set our direct action program around the Easter season, realizing that with the exception of Christmas, this was the largest shopping period of the year. Knowing that a strong economic withdrawal program would be the by-product of direct action, we felt that this was the best time to bring pressure on the merchants for the needed changes. Then it occurred to us that the March election was ahead, and so we speedily decided to postpone action until after election day. When we discovered that Mr. Connor was in the run-off, we decided again to postpone action so that the demonstrations could not be used to cloud the issues. At this time we agreed to begin our nonviolent witness the day after the runoff.

This reveals that we did not move irresponsibly into direct action. We too wanted to see Mr. Connor defeated; so we went through postponement after postponement to aid in this community need. After this we felt that direct action could be delayed no longer.

You may well ask, "Why direct action? Why sit-ins, marches, etc.? Isn't negotiation a better path?" You are exactly right in your call for negotiation. Indeed, this is the purpose of direct action. Nonviolent direct action seeks to create such a crisis and establish such creative tension that a community that has constantly refused to negotiate is forced to confront the issue. It seeks so to dramatize the issue that it can no longer be ignored. I just referred to the creation of tension as a part of the work of the nonviolent resister. This may sound rather shocking. But I must confess that I am not afraid of the word tension. I have earnestly worked and preached against violent tension, but there is a type of constructive nonviolent tension that is necessary for growth. Just as Socrates felt that it was necessary to create a tension in the mind so that individuals could rise from the bondage of myths and half-truths to the unfettered realm of creative analysis and objective appraisal, we must see the need of having non-violent gadflies to create the kind of tension in society that will help men rise from the dark depths of prejudice and racism to the majestic heights of understanding and brotherhood. So the purpose of the direct action is to create a situation so crisis-packed that it will inevitably open the door to negotiation. We, therefore, concur with you in your call for negotiation. Too long has our beloved Southland been bogged down in the tragic attempt to live in monologue rather than dialogue.

One of the basic points in your statement is that our acts are untimely. Some have asked, "Why didn't you give the new administration time to act?" The only answer that I can give to this inquiry is that the new administration must be prodded about as much as the outgoing one before it acts. We will be sadly mistaken if we feel that the election of Mr. Boutwell will bring the millennium to Birmingham. While Mr. Boutwell is much more articulate and gentle than Mr. Connor, they are both segregationists dedicated to the task of maintaining the status quo. The hope I see in Mr. Boutwell is that he will be reasonable enough to see the futility of massive resistance to desegregation. But he will not see this without pressure from the devotees of civil rights. My friends, I must say to you that we have not made a single gain in civil rights without determined legal and nonviolent pressure. History is the long and tragic story of the fact that privileged groups seldom give up their privileges voluntarily. Individuals may see the moral light and voluntarily give up their unjust posture; but as Reinhold Niebuhr has reminded us, groups are more immoral than individuals.

We know through painful experience that freedom is never voluntarily given by the oppressor; it must be demanded by the oppressed. Frankly I have never yet engaged in a direct-action movement that was "well timed," according to the timetable of those who have not suffered unduly from the disease of segregation. For years now I have heard the word "Wait!" It rings in the ear of every Negro with a piercing familiarity. This "wait" has almost always meant "never." It has been a tanquilizing thalidomide, relieving the emotional stress for a moment, only to give birth to an ill-formed infant of frustration. We must come to see with the distinguished jurist of yesterday that "justice too long delayed is justice denied." We have waited for more than three hundred and forty years for our constitutional and God-given rights. The nations of Asia and Africa are moving with jetlike speed toward the goal of political independence, and we still creep at horse-and-buggy pace toward the gaining of a cup of coffee at a lunch counter.

I guess it is easy for those who have never felt the stinging darts of segregation to say wait. But when you have seen vicious mobs lynch your mothers and fathers at will and drown your sisters and brothers at whim; when you have seen hate-filled policemen curse, kick, brutalize, and even kill your black brothers and sisters with impunity; when you see the vast majority of your 20 million Negro brothers smothering in an airtight cage of poverty in the midst of an affluent society; when you suddenly find your tongue twisted and your speech stammering as you seek to explain to your six-year-old daughter why she can't go to the public amusement park that has just been advertised on television, and see tears welling up in her little eyes when she is told that Funtown is closed to colored children, and see the depressing clouds of inferiority begin to form in her little mental sky, and see her begin to distort her little personality by unconsciously developing a bitterness toward white people; when you have to concoct an answer for a five-year-old son asking in agonizing pathos: "Daddy, why do white people treat colored people so mean?"; when you take a cross-country drive and find it necessary to sleep night after night in the uncomfortable corners of your automobile because no motel will accept you; when you are humiliated day in and day out by nagging signs reading "white" men and "colored"; when your first name becomes "nigger" and your middle name becomes "boy" (however old you are) and your last name becomes "John," and when your wife and mother are never given the respected title "Mrs."; when you are harried by day and haunted by night by the fact that you are a Negro, living constantly at tiptoe stance never quite knowing what to expect next, and plagued with inner fears and outer resentments; when you are forever fighting a degenerating sense of "nobodiness"— then you will understand why we find it difficult to wait. There comes a time when the cup of endurance runs over, and men are no longer willing to be plunged into an abyss of injustice where they experience the bleakness of corroding despair. I hope, sirs, you can understand our legitimate and unavoidable impatience.

You express a great deal of anxiety over our willingness to break laws. This is certainly a legitimate concern. Since we so diligently urge people to obey the Supreme Court's decision of 1954 outlawing segregation in the public schools, it is rather strange and paradoxical to find us consciously breaking laws. One may well ask, "How can you advocate breaking some laws and obeying others?" The answer is found in the fact that there are two types of laws: There are *just* laws and there are *unjust* laws. I would be the first to advocate obeying just laws. One has not only a legal but moral responsibility to obey just laws. Conversely, one has a moral responsibility to disobey unjust laws. I would agree with Saint Augustine that "An unjust law is no law at all."

Now what is the difference between the two? How does one determine when a law is just or unjust? A just law is a manmade code that squares with the moral law or the law of God. An unjust law is a code that is out of harmony with the moral law. To put it in the terms of Saint Thomas Aquinas, an unjust law is a human law that is not rooted in eternal and natural law. Any law that uplifts human personality is just. Any law that degrades human personality is unjust. All segregation statutes are unjust because segregation distorts the soul and damages the personality. It gives the segregator a false sense of superiority and the segregated a false sense of inferiority. To use the words of Martin Buber, the great Jewish philosopher, segregation substitutes an "I-it" relationship for the "I-thou" relationship, and ends up relegating persons to the status of things. So segregation is not only politically, economically, and sociologically unsound, but it is morally wrong and sinful. Paul Tillich has said that sin is separation. Isn't segregation an existential expression of man's tragic separation, an expression of his awful estrangement, his terrible sinfulness? So I can urge men to obey the 1954 decision of the Supreme Court because it is morally right, and I can urge them to disobey segregation ordinances because they are morally wrong.

Let us turn to a more concrete example of just and unjust laws. An unjust law is a code that a majority inflicts on a minority that is not binding on itself. This is *difference* made legal. On the other hand a just law is a code that a majority compels a minority to follow that it is willing to follow itself. This is *sameness* made legal.

Let me give another explanation. An unjust law is a code inflicted upon a minority which that minority had no part in enacting or creating because they did not have the unhampered right to vote. Who can say the legislature of Alabama which set up the segregation laws was democratically elected? Throughout the state of Alabama all types of conniving methods are used to prevent Negroes from becoming registered voters and there are some counties without a single Negro registered to vote despite the fact that the Negro constitutes a majority of the population. Can any law set up in such a state be considered democratically structured?

These are just a few examples of unjust and just laws. There are some instances when a law is just on its face but unjust in its application. For instance, I was arrested Friday on a charge of parading without a permit. Now there is nothing wrong with an ordinance which requires a permit for a parade, but when the ordinance is used to preserve segregation and to deny citizens the First Amendment privilege of peaceful assembly and peaceful protest, then it becomes unjust.

I hope you can see the distinction I am trying to point out. In no sense do I advocate evading or defying the law as the rabid segregationist would do. This would lead to anarchy. One who breaks an unjust law must do it *openly, lovingly* (not hatefully as the white mothers did in New Orleans when they were seen on television screaming "nigger, nigger, nigger"), and with a willingness to accept the penalty. I submit that an individual who breaks a law that conscience tells him is unjust, and willingly accepts the penalty by staying in jail to arouse the conscience of the community over its injustice, is in reality expressing the very highest respect for law.

Of course there is nothing new about this kind of civil disobedience. It was seen sublimely in the refusal of Shadrach, Meshach, and Abednego to obey the laws of Nebuchadnezzar because a higher moral law was involved. It was practiced superbly by the early Christians who were willing to face hungry lions and the excruciating pain of chopping blocks, before submitting to certain unjust laws of the Roman Empire. To a degree academic freedom is a reality today because Socrates practiced civil disobedience.

We can never forget that everything Hitler did in Germany was "legal" and everything the Hungarian freedom fighters did in Hungary was "illegal." It was "illegal" to aid and comfort a Jew in Hitler's Germany. But I am sure that, if I had lived in Germany during that time, I would have aided and comforted my Jewish brothers even though it was illegal. If I lived in a Communist country today where certain principles dear to the Christian faith are suppressed, I believe I would openly advocate disobeying these antireligious laws.

I must make two honest confessions to you, my Christian and Jewish brothers. First I must confess that over the last few years I have been gravely disappointed with the white moderate. I have almost reached the regrettable conclusion that the Negroes' great stumbling block in the stride toward freedom is not the White Citizens' "Counciler" or the Ku Klux Klanner, but the white moderate who is more devoted to "order" than to justice; who prefers a negative peace which is the absence of tension to a positive peace which is the presence of justice; who constantly says "I agree with you in the goal you seek, but I can't agree with your methods of direct action"; who paternalistically feels that he can set the timetable for another man's freedom; who lives by the myth of time and who constantly advises the Negro to wait until a "more convenient season." Shallow understanding from people of good will is more frustrating than absolute misunderstanding from people of ill will. Lukewarm acceptance is much more bewildering than outright rejection.

I had hoped that the white moderate would understand that law and order exist for the purpose of establishing justice, and that when they fail to do this they become the dangerously structured dams that block the flow of social progress. I had hoped that the white moderate would understand that the present tension in the South is merely a necessary phase of the transition from an obnoxious negative peace, where the Negro passively accepted his unjust plight, to a substance-filled positive peace, where all men will respect the dignity and worth of human personality. Actually, we who engage in nonviolent direct action are not the creators of tension. We merely bring to the surface the hidden tension that is already alive. We bring it out in the open where it can be seen and dealt with. Like a boil that can never be cured as long as it is covered up but must be opened with all its pus-flowing ugliness to the natural medicines of air and light, injustice must likewise be exposed, with all of the tension its exposing creates, to the light of human conscience and the air of national opinion before it can be cured.

In your statement you asserted that our actions, even though peaceful, must be condemned because they precipitate violence. But can this assertion be logically made? Isn't this like condemning the robbed man because his possession of money precipitated the evil act of robbery? Isn't this like condemning Socrates because his unswerving commitment to truth and his philosophical delvings precipitated the misguided popular mind to make him drink the hemlock? Isn't this like condemning Jesus because His unique God consciousness and never-ceasing devotion to His will precipitated the evil act of crucifixion? We must come to see, as federal courts have consistently affirmed, that it is immoral to urge an individual to withdraw his efforts to gain his basic constitutional rights because the quest precipitates violence. Society must protect the robbed and punish the robber.

I had also hoped that the white moderate would reject the myth of time. I received a letter this morning from a white brother in Texas which said: "All Christians know that the colored people will receive equal rights eventually, but is it possible that you are in too great of a religious hurry? It has taken Christianity almost 2000 years to accomplish what it has. The teachings of Christ take time to come to earth." All that is said here grows out of a tragic misconception of time. It is the strangely irrational notion that there is something in the very flow of time that will inevitably cure all ills. Actually time is neutral. It can be used either destructively or constructively. I am coming to feel that the people of ill will have used time much more effectively than the people of good will. We will have to repent in this generation not merely for the vitriolic words and actions of the bad people, but for the appalling silence of the good people. We must come to see that human progress never rolls in on wheels of inevitability. It comes through the tireless efforts and persistent work of men willing to be co-workers with God, and without this hard work time itself becomes an ally of the forces of social stagnation.

We must use time creatively, and forever realize that the time is always ripe to do right. Now is the time to make real the promise of democracy, and transform our pending national elegy into a creative psalm of brotherhood. Now is the time to lift our national policy from the quicksand of racial injustice to the solid rock of human dignity.

You spoke of our activity in Birmingham as extreme. At first I was rather disappointed that fellow clergymen would see my nonviolent efforts as those of the extremist. I started thinking about the fact that I stand in the middle of two opposing forces in the Negro community. One is a force of complacency made up of Negroes who, as a result of long years of oppression, have been so completely drained of self-respect and a sense of "somebodiness" that they have adjusted to segregation, and of a few Negroes in the middle class who, because of a degree of academic and economic security, and because at points they profit by segregation, have unconsciously become insensitive to the problems of the masses. The other force is one of bitterness and hatred and comes perilously close to advocating violence. It is expressed in the various black nationalist groups that are springing up over the nation, the largest and best known being Elijah Muhammad's Muslim movement. This movement is nourished by the contemporary frustration over the continued existence of racial discrimination. It is made up of people who have lost faith in America, who have absolutely repudiated Christianity, and who have concluded that the white man is an incurable "devil." I have tried to stand between these two forces saying that we need not follow the "do-nothingism" of the complacent or the hatred and despair of the black nationalist. There is the more excellent way of love and nonviolent protest. I'm grateful to God that, through the Negro church, the dimension of nonviolence entered our struggle. If this philosophy had not emerged I am convinced that by now many streets of the South would be flowing with floods of blood. And I am further convinced that if our white brothers dismiss us as "rabble rousers" and "outside agitators"—those of us who are working through the channels of nonviolent direct action—and refuse to support our nonviolent efforts, millions of Negroes, out of frustration and despair, will seek solace and security in black nationalist ideologies, a development that will lead inevitably to a frightening racial nightmare.

Oppressed people cannot remain oppressed forever. The urge for freedom will eventually come. This is what has happened to the American Negro. Something within has reminded him of his birthright of freedom; something without has reminded him that he can gain it. Consciously and unconsciously, he has been swept in by what the Germans call the *Zeitgeist*, and with his black brothers of Africa, and his brown and yellow brothers of Asia, South America, and the Caribbean, he is moving with a sense of cosmic urgency toward the promised land of racial justice. Recognizing this vital urge that has engulfed the Negro community, one should readily understand public demonstrations. The Negro has many pent-up resentments and latent frustrations. He has to get them out. So let him march sometime; let him have his prayer pilgrimages to the city hall; understand why he must have sit-ins and freedom rides. If his repressed emotions do not come out in these nonviolent ways, they will come out in ominous expressions of violence. This is not a threat; it is a fact of history. So I have not said to my people, "Get rid of your discontent." But I have tried to say that this normal and healthy discontent can be channeled through the creative outlet of nonviolent direct action. Now this approach is being dismissed as extremist. I must admit that I was initially disappointed in being so categorized.

But as I continued to think about the matter I gradually gained a bit of satisfaction from being considered an extremist. Was not Jesus an extremist in love? "Love your enemies, bless them that curse you, pray for them that despitefully use you." Was not Amos an extremist for justice—"Let justice roll down like waters and righteousness like a mighty stream." Was not Paul an extremist for the gospel of Jesus Christ—"I bear in my body the marks of the Lord Jesus." Was not Martin Luther an extremist—"Here I stand; I can do none other so help me God." Was not John Bunyan an extremist—"I will stay in jail to the end of my days before I make a butchery of my conscience." Was not Abraham Lincoln an extremist—"This nation cannot survive half slave and half free." Was not Thomas Jefferson an extremist—"We hold these truths to be self evident that all men are created equal." So the question is not whether we will be extremist but what kind of extremist will we be. Will we be extremists for hate or will we be extremists for love? Will we be extremists for the preservation of injustice—or will we be extremists for the cause of justice? In that dramatic scene on Calvary's hill three men were crucified. We must never forget that all three were crucified for the same crime—the crime of extremism. Two were extremists for immorality, and thus fell below their environment. The other, Jesus Christ, was an extremist for love, truth, and goodness, and thereby rose above His environment. So, after all, maybe the South, the nation, and the world are in dire need of creative extremists.

I had hoped that the white moderate would see this. Maybe I was too optimistic. Maybe I expected too much. I guess I should have realized that few members of a race that has oppressed another race can understand or appreciate the deep groans and passionate yearnings of those that have been oppressed, and still fewer have the vision to see that injustice must be rooted out by strong, persistent, and determined action. I am thankful, however, that some of our white brothers have grasped the meaning of this social revolution and committed themselves to it. They are still all too small in quantity, but they are big in quality. Some like Ralph McGill, Lillian Smith, Harry Golden, and James Dabbs have written about our struggle in eloquent, prophetic, and understanding terms. Others have marched with us down nameless streets of the South. They have languished in filthy, roach-infested jails, suffering the abuse and brutality of angry policemen who see them as "dirty nigger lovers." They, unlike so many of their moderate brothers and sisters, have recognized the urgency of the moment and sensed the need for powerful "action" antidotes to combat the disease of segregation.

Let me rush on to mention my other disappointment. I have been so greatly disappointed with the white church and its leadership. Of course there are some notable exceptions. I am not unmindful of the fact that each of you has taken some significant stands on this issue. I commend you, Reverend Stallings, for your Christian stand on this past Sunday, in welcoming Negroes to your worship service on a nonsegregated basis. I commend the Catholic leaders of this state for integrating Springhill College several years ago.

But despite these notable exceptions I must honestly reiterate that I have been disappointed with the church. I do not say that as one of those negative critics who can always find something wrong with the church. I say it as a minister of the gospel, who loves the church; who was nurtured in its bosom; who has been sustained by its spiritual blessings and who will remain true to it as long as the cord of life shall lengthen.

I had the strange feeling when I was suddenly catapulted into the leadership of the bus protest in Montgomery several years ago that we would have the support of the white church. I felt that the white ministers, priests, and rabbis of the South would be some of our strongest allies. Instead, some have been outright opponents, refusing to understand the freedom movement and misrepresenting its leaders; all too many others have been more cautious than courageous and have remained silent behind the anesthetizing security of stained-glass windows.

In spite of my shattered dreams of the past, I came to Birmingham with the hope that the white religious leadership of this community would see the justice of our cause and, with deep moral concern, serve as the channel through which our just grievances could get to the power structure. I had hoped that each of you would understand. But again I have been disappointed.

I have heard numerous religious leaders of the South call upon their worshipers to comply with a desegregation decision because it is the law, but I have longed to hear white ministers say follow this decree because integration is morally right and the Negro is your brother. In the midst of blatant injustices inflicted upon the Negro, I have watched white churches stand on the sideline and merely mouth pious irrelevancies and sanctimonious trivialities. In the midst of a mighty struggle to rid our nation of racial and economic injustice, I have heard so many ministers say, "Those are social issues with which the gospel has no real concern," and I have watched so many churches commit themselves to a completely otherworldly religion which made a strange distinction between body and soul, the sacred and the secular.

So here we are moving toward the exit of the twentieth century with a religious community largely adjusted to the status quo, standing as a tail light behind other community agencies rather than a headlight leading men to higher levels of justice.

I have traveled the length and breadth of Alabama, Mississippi, and all the other Southern states. On sweltering summer days and crisp autumn mornings I have looked at her beautiful churches with their spires pointing heavenward. I have beheld the impressive outlay of her massive religious education buildings. Over and over again I have found myself asking: "Who worships here? Who is their God? Where were their voices when the lips of Governor Barnett dripped with words of interposition and nullification? Where were they when Governor Wallace gave the clarion call for defiance and hatred? Where were their voices of support when tired, bruised, and weary Negro men and women decided to rise from the dark dungeons of complacency to the bright hills of creative protest?"

Yes, these questions are still in my mind. In deep disappointment, I have wept over the laxity of the church. But be assured that my tears have been tears of love. There can be no deep disappointment where there is not deep love. Yes, I love the church; I love her sacred walls. How could I do otherwise? I am in the rather unique position of being the son, the grandson, and the great-grandson of preachers. Yes, I see the church as the body of Christ. But, oh! How we have blemished and scarred that body through social neglect and fear of being nonconformist.

There was a time when the church was very powerful. It was during that period when the early Christians rejoiced when they were deemed worthy to suffer for what they believed. In those days the church was not merely a thermometer that recorded the ideas and principles of popular opinion; it was a thermostat that transformed the mores of society. Wherever the early Christians entered a town the power structure got disturbed and immediately sought to convict them for being "disturbers of the peace" and "outside agitators." But they went on with the conviction that they were a "colony of heaven" and had to obey God rather than man. They were small in number but big in commitment. They were too God-intoxicated to be "astronomically intimidated." They brought an end to such ancient evils as infanticide and gladiatorial contest.

Things are different now. The contemporary church is so often a weak, ineffectual voice with an uncertain sound. It is so often the arch-supporter of the status quo. Far from being disturbed by the presence of the church, the power structure of the average community is consoled by the church's silent and often vocal sanction of things as they are.

But the judgment of God is upon the church as never before. If the church of today does not recapture the sacrificial spirit of the early church, it will lose its authentic ring, forfeit the loyalty of millions, and be dismissed as an irrelevant social club with no meaning for the twentieth century. I am meeting young people every day whose disappointment with the church has risen to outright disgust.

Maybe again I have been too optimistic. Is organized religion too inextricably bound to the status quo to save our nation and the world? Maybe I must turn my faith to the inner spiritual church, the church within the church, as the true *ecclesia* and the hope of the world. But again I am thankful to God that some noble souls from the ranks of organized religion have broken loose from the paralyzing chains of conformity and joined us as active partners in the struggle for freedom. They have left their secure congregations and walked the streets of Albany, Georgia, with us. They have gone through the highways of the South on tortuous rides for freedom. Yes, they have gone to jail with us. Some have been kicked out of their churches and lost the support of their bishops and fellow ministers. But they have gone with the faith that right defeated is stronger than evil triumphant. These men have been the leaven in the lump of the race. Their witness has been the spiritual salt that has preserved the true meaning of the gospel in these troubled times. They have carved a tunnel of hope through the dark mountain of disappointment.

I hope the church as a whole will meet the challenge of this decisive hour. But even if the church does not come to the aid of justice, I have no despair about the future. I have no fear about the outcome of our struggle in Birmingham, even if our motives are presently misunderstood. We will reach the goal of freedom in Birmingham and all over the nation, because the goal of America is freedom. Abused and scorned though we may be, our destiny is tied up with the destiny of America. Before the pilgrims landed at Plymouth, we were here. Before the pen of Jefferson etched across the pages of history the majestic words of the Declaration of Independence, we were here. For more than two centuries our foreparents labored in this country without wages; they made cotton "king"; and they built the homes of their masters in the midst of brutal injustice and shameful humiliation—and yet out of a bottomless vitality they continued to thrive and develop. If the inexpressible cruelties of slavery could not stop us, the opposition we now face will surely fail. We will win our freedom because the sacred heritage of our nation and the eternal will of God are embodied in our echoing demands.

I must close now. But before closing I am impelled to mention one other point in your statement that troubled me profoundly. You warmly commended the Birmingham police force for keeping "order" and "preventing violence." I don't believe you would have so warmly commended the police force if you had seen its angry violent dogs literally biting six unarmed, nonviolent Negroes. I don't believe you would so quickly commend the policemen if you would observe their ugly and inhuman treatment of Negroes here in the city jail; if you would watch them push and curse old Negro women and young Negro girls; if you would see them slap and kick old Negro men and young Negro boys; if you will observe them, as they did on two occasions, refuse to give us food because we wanted to sing our grace together. I'm sorry that I can't join you in your praise for the police department.

It is true that they have been rather disciplined in their public handling of the demonstrators. In this sense they have been rather publicly "nonviolent." But for what purpose? To preserve the evil system of segregation. Over the last few years I have consistently preached that nonviolence demands that the means we use must be as pure as the ends we seek. So I have tried to make it clear that it is wrong to use immoral means to attain moral ends. But now I must affirm that it is just as wrong, or even more so, to use moral means to preserve immoral ends. Maybe Mr. Connor and his policemen have been rather publicly nonviolent, as Chief Prichett was in Albany, Georgia, but they have used the moral means of nonviolence to maintain the immoral end of flagrant racial injustice. T. S. Eliot has said that there is no greater treason than to do the right deed for the wrong reason.

I wish you had commended the Negro sit-inners and demonstrators of Birmingham for their sublime courage, their willingness to suffer, and their amazing discipline in the midst of the most inhuman provocation. One day the South will recognize its real heroes. They will be the James Merediths, courageously and with a majestic sense of purpose, facing jeering and hostile mobs and the agonizing loneliness that characterizes the life of the pioneer. They will be old, oppressed, battered Negro women, symbolized in a seventy-two-year-old woman of Montgomery, Alabama, who rose up with a sense of dignity and with her people decided not to ride the segregated buses, and responded to one who inquired about her tiredness with ungrammatical profundity: "My feets is tired, but my soul is rested." They will be young high school and college students, young ministers of the gospel and a host of the elders, courageously and nonviolently sitting in at lunch counters and willingly going to jail for conscience' sake. One day the South will know that when these disinherited children of God sat down at lunch counters they were in reality standing up for the best in the American dream and the most sacred values in our Judeo-Christian heritage, and thus carrying our whole nation back to great wells of democracy which were dug deep by the founding fathers in the formulation of the Constitution and the Declaration of Independence.

Never before have I written a letter this long (or should I say a book?). I'm afraid that it is much too long to take your precious time. I can assure you that it would have been much shorter if I had been writing from a comfortable desk, but what else is there to do when you are alone for days in the dull monotony of a narrow jail cell other than write long letters, think strange thoughts, and pray long prayers?

If I have said anything in this letter that is an overstatement of the truth and is indicative of an unreasonable impatience, I beg you to forgive me. If I have said anything in this letter that is an understatement of the truth and is indicative of my having a patience that makes me patient with anything less than brotherhood, I beg God to forgive me.

I hope this letter finds you strong in the faith. I also hope that circumstances will soon make it possible for me to meet each of you, not as an integrationist or a civil-rights leader, but as a fellow clergyman and a Christian brother. Let us all hope that the dark clouds of racial prejudice will soon pass away and the deep fog of misunderstanding will be lifted from our fear-drenched communities and in

some not too distant tomorrow the radiant stars of love and brotherhood will shine over our great nation with all of their scintillating
beauty.

Yours for the cause of
Peace and Brotherhood,
MARTIN LUTHER KING, JR.

* * *

I am happy to join with you today in what will go down in history
as the greatest demonstration for freedom in the history of our nation.

Five score years ago, a Great American, in whose symbolic shadow
we stand today, signed the Emancipation Proclamation. This momentous decree came as the great beacon light of hope for millions of
Negro slaves who had been seared in the flames of withering injustice.
It came as the joyous daybreak to end the long night of their
captivity.

But 100 years later the Negro still is not free. One hundred years
later, the life of the Negro is still badly crippled by the manacles of
segregation and the chains of discrimination. One hundred years
later, the Negro lives on a lonely island of poverty in the midst of a
vast ocean of material prosperity. One hundred years later, the Negro
is still languished in the corners of American society and finds himself
an exile in his own land. So we have come here today to dramatize
the shameful condition.

In a sense we've come to our nation's capital to cash a check. When
the architects of our republic wrote the magnificent words of the
Constitution and the Declaration of Independence, they were signing
a promissory note to which every American was to fall heir. This
note was a promise that all men, yes, black men as well as white men,
should be guaranteed the unalienable rights of life, liberty, and the
pursuit of happiness.

It is obvious today that America has defaulted on this promissory
note insofar as her citizens of color are concerned. Instead of honor-
ing this sacred obligation, America has given the Negro people a
bad check, a check which has come back marked "Insufficient Funds."
But we refuse to believe the bank of justice is bankrupt. We refuse
to believe that there are insufficient funds in the great vaults of opportunity of this nation. So we have come to cash this check, a check
that will give us, upon demand, the riches of freedom and the security
of justice. We have also come to this hallowed spot to remind America
of the fierce urgency of now.

This is no time to engage in the luxury of cooling off or to take
the tranquilizing drug of gradualism. Now is the time to make real

the promises of democracy. Now is the time to rise from the dark and desolate valley of segregation to the sunlit path of racial justice. Now is the time to lift our nation from the quicksands of racial injustice to the solid rock of brotherhood. Now is the time to make justice a reality for all of God's children.

It would be fatal for the nation to overlook the urgency of the moment. This sweltering summer of the Negro's legitimate discontent will not pass until there is an invigorating autumn of freedom and equality. Nineteen sixty-three is not an end but a beginning. Those who hoped that the Negro needed to blow off steam and will not be content will have a rude awakening if the nation returns to business as usual. There will be neither rest nor tranquility in America until the Negro is guaranteed his citizenship rights. The whirlwinds of revolt will continue to shake the foundations of our nation until the bright day of justice emerges.

But there is something I must say to my people who stand on the warm threshold which leads them to the palace of justice. In the process of gaining our rightful place we must not be guilty of wrongful deeds. Let us not seek to satisfy our thirst for freedom by drinking from the cup of bitterness and hatred. We must forever conduct our struggle on the high plane of dignity and discipline. We must not allow our creative protest to degenerate into physical violence. Again and again we must rise to the majestic heights of meeting physical force with soul force.

The marvelous new militancy which has engulfed the Negro community must not lead us to a distrust of all white people, for many of our white brothers, as evidenced by their presence here today, have come to realize that their destiny is tied up with our destiny. They have come to realize that their freedom is inextricably bound to our freedom. We cannot walk alone.

And as we walk we must make the pledge that we shall always march ahead. We cannot turn back. There are those who are asking the devotees of civil rights: "When will you be satisfied?" We can never be satisfied as long as the Negro is the victim of the unspeakable horrors of police brutality. We can never be satisfied as long as our bodies, heavy with fatigue of travel, cannot gain lodging in the motels of the highways and the hotels of the cities. We cannot be satisfied as long as the Negro's basic mobility is from a smaller ghetto to a larger one. We can never be satisfied as long as our children are stripped of their selfhood and robbed of their dignity by signs stating: "For Whites Only." We cannot be satisfied as long the Negro in Mississippi cannot vote and the Negro in New York believes he has nothing for which to vote. No, no, we are not satisfied and we will not be satisfied until justice rolls down like waters and righteousness like a mighty stream.

I am not unmindful that some of you have come here out of great trials and tribulations, some of you have come fresh from narrow jail cells, some of you have come from areas where your quest for freedom left you battered by the storms of persecution and staggered by the winds of police brutality. You have been the veterans of creative suffering. Continue to work with the faith that unearned suffering is redemptive.

Go back to Mississippi, go back to Alabama, go back to South Carolina, go back to Georgia, go back to Louisiana, go back to the slums and ghettos of our Northern cities, knowing that somehow this situation can and will be changed. Let us not wallow in the valley of despair.

I say to you today, my friends, even though we face the difficulties of today and tomorrow, I still have a dream. It is a dream deeply rooted in the American dream. I have a dream that one day this nation will rise up and live out the true meaning of its creed: "We hold these truths to be self-evident that all men are created equal." I have a dream that one day on the red hills of Georgia the sons of former slaves and the sons of former slaveowners will be able to sit down together at the table of brotherhood.

I have a dream that one day even the state of Mississippi, a state sweltering with the heat of injustice, sweltering with the heat of oppression, will be transformed into an oasis of freedom and justice. I have a dream that my four little children will one day live in a nation where they will not be judged by the color of their skin but by the content of their character. I have a dream today.

I have a dream that one day down in Alabama with its vicious racists, with its governor having his lips dripping with the words of interposition and nullification—one day right there in Alabama, little black boys and black girls will be able to join hands with little white boys and white girls as sisters and brothers.

I have a dream today.

I have a dream that one day every valley shall be exalted, every hill and mountain shall be made low, the rough places will be made plain and the crooked places will be made straight, and the glory of the Lord shall be revealed, and all flesh shall see it together.

This is our hope. This is the faith that I go back to the South with. With this faith we will be able to hew out of the mountain of despair a stone of hope. With this faith we will be able to transform the jangling discords of our nation into a beautiful symphony of brother-hood. With this faith we will be able to work together, to pray to-gether, to struggle together, to go to jail together, to stand up for freedom together, knowing that we will be free one day.

This will be the day when all of God's children will be able to sing with new meaning:

"My country 'tis of thee,
Sweet land of liberty,
Of thee I sing:
Land where my fathers died,
Land of the pilgrims' pride,
From every mountainside
Let Freedom ring."

And if America is to be a great nation, this must become true. So, let freedom ring from the prodigious hilltops of New Hampshire. Let freedom ring from the mighty mountains of New York. Let free-dom ring from the heightening Alleghenies of Pennsylvania. Let freedom ring from the snowcapped Rockies of Colorado. Let free-dom ring from the curvaceous slopes of California. But not only that, let freedom ring from Stone Mountain of Georgia.

Let freedom ring from Lookout Mountain of Tennessee.

Let freedom ring from every hill and molehill of Mississippi. From every mountainside, let freedom ring. And when we allow freedom to ring, when we let it ring from every village, from every hamlet, from every state and every city, we will be able to speed up that day when all of God's children, black men and white men, Jews and Gentiles, Protestants and Catholics, will be able to join hands and sing in the words of the old Negro spiritual: "Free at last! Free at last! Thank God almighty, we are free at last!"

NOBEL PEACE PRIZE ACCEPTANCE STATEMENT

Your Majesty, Your Royal Highness, Mr. President, Excellencies, ladies and gentlemen:

I accept the Nobel Prize for Peace at a moment when twenty-two million Negroes of the United States of America are engaged in a creative battle to end the long night of racial injustice. I accept this award in behalf of a civil-rights movement which is moving with determination and a majestic scorn for risk and danger to establish a reign of freedom and a rule of justice. I am mindful that only yesterday in Birmingham, Alabama, our children, crying out for brotherhood, were answered with fire hoses, snarling dogs, and even death. I am mindful that only yesterday in Philadelphia, Mississippi, young people seeking to secure the right to vote were brutalized and murdered. And only yesterday more than forty houses of worship in the state of Mississippi alone were bombed or burned because they offered a sanctuary to those who would not accept segregation. I am mindful that debilitating and grinding poverty afflicts my people and chains them to the lowest rung of the economic ladder.

Therefore, I must ask why this prize is awarded to a movement which is beleaguered and committed to unrelenting struggle; to a movement which has not won the very peace and brotherhood which is the essence of the Nobel Prize.

After contemplation, I conclude that this award which I receive on behalf of that movement is a profound recognition that nonviolence is the answer to the crucial political and moral question of our time—the need for man to overcome oppression and violence without resorting to violence and oppression. Civilization and violence are antithetical concepts. Negroes of the United States, following the people of India, have demonstrated that nonviolence is not sterile passivity, but a powerful moral force which makes for social transformation. Sooner or later, all the people of the world will have to discover a way to live together in peace, and thereby transform this pending cosmic elegy into a creative psalm of brotherhood. If this is to be achieved, man must evolve for all human conflict a method which rejects revenge, aggression, and retaliation. The foundation of such a method is love.

The tortuous road which has led from Montgomery, Alabama, to Oslo bears witness of this truth. This is a road which millions of Negroes are traveling to find a new sense of dignity. This same road has opened for all Americans a new era of progress and hope. It has led to a new Civil Rights Bill, and it will, I am convinced, be widened and lengthened into a superhighway of justice as Negro and white men in increasing numbers create alliances to overcome their common problem.

I accept this award today with an abiding faith in America and an audacious faith in the future of mankind. I refuse to accept the idea that the "isness" of man's present nature makes him morally incapable of reaching up for the eternal "oughtness" that forever confronts him. I refuse to accept the idea that man is mere flotsam and jetsam in a river of life, unable to influence the unfolding events which surround him. I refuse to accept the view that mankind is so tragically bound to the starless midnight of racism and war that the bright daybreak of peace and brotherhood can never become a reality.

I refuse to accept the cynical notion that nation after nation must spiral down a militaristic stairway into the hall of thermonuclear destruction. I believe that unarmed truth and unconditional love will have the final word in reality. This is why right temporarily defeated is stronger than evil triumphant. I believe that even amid today's motor bursts and whining bullets, there is still hope for a brighter tomorrow. I believe that wounded justice, lying prostrate on the blood-flowing streets of our nations, can be lifted from this dust of shame to reign supreme among the children of men. I have the audacity to believe that peoples everywhere can have three meals a day for their bodies, education and culture for their minds, and dignity, equality, and freedom for their spirits. I believe that what self-centered men have torn down, men other-centered can build up. I still believe that one day mankind will bow before the altars of God and be crowned triumphant over war and bloodshed, and non-violent redemptive good will proclaimed the rule of the land. "And the lion and the lamb shall lie down together and every man shall sit under his own vine and fig tree and none shall be afraid." I still believe that we *shall* overcome!

This faith can give us courage to face the uncertainties of the future. It will give our tired feet new strength as we continue our forward stride toward the city of freedom. When our days become dreary with low-hovering clouds and our nights become darker than a thousand midnights, we will know that we are living in the creative turmoil of a genuine civilization struggling to be born.

Today I come to Oslo as a trustee, inspired with renewed dedication to humanity. I accept this prize on behalf of all men who love peace and brotherhood. I say I come as a trustee, for in the depths of my heart I am aware that this prize is much more than an honor to me personally.

Every time I take a flight, I am always mindful of the many people who make a successful journey possible—the known pilots and the unknown ground crew.

So you honor the dedicated pilots of our struggle who have sat at the controls as the freedom movement soared into orbit. You honor, once again, Chief Luthuli of South Africa, whose struggles with and for his people are still met with the most brutal expression of man's inhumanity to man. You honor the ground crew without whose labor and sacrifices the jet flights to freedom could never have left the earth. Most of these people will never make the headlines and their names will not appear in *Who's Who.* Yet when years have rolled past and when the blazing light of truth is focused on this marvelous age in which we live—men and women will know and children will be taught that we have a finer land, a better people, a more noble civilization—because these humble children of God were willing to suffer for righteousness' sake.

I think Alfred Nobel would know what I mean when I say that I accept this award in the spirit of a curator of some precious heirloom which he holds in trust for its true owners—all those to whom beauty is truth and truth beauty—and in whose eyes the beauty of genuine brotherhood and peace is more precious than diamonds or silver or gold.

The Black Revolution
MALCOLM X

When Malcolm Little was four years old, the house where he and his family lived was burned down by members of the Ku Klux Klan. He was only six when his father met a violent death that his family always believed was a lynching. It would be difficult to understand the man without understanding the extent to which these early incidents in his life helped to shape his opinion about matters of race as they affect the black man in American society.

Malcolm's mother was born as a result of her mother being raped by a white man in the West Indies. His father was a disciple of Marcus Garvey, the black nationalist. His life is the story of the black man in search of himself. An early school dropout, Malcolm entered the "world." He was a shoeshine boy, waiter, bus boy, dining-car crewman, gambler, and "junkie."

It took prison (after his arrest for burglary) to transform his life. While in this state of involuntary exile, he was introduced to the Black Muslim movement. After his release from prison, he joined the Nation of Islam under Elijah Muhammad; after being named Malcolm X he immediately became a leader within the organization and drew notice to the movement.

It was inevitable that one so magnetic and so completely accepted as the spokesman for the Black Muslim movement could, in overshadowing his leader, Elijah Muhammad, create trouble with the organization. The separation came in November, 1963, and the rest, of course, is history. The final chapter was written on the day of his assassination, February 21, 1965.

As a speaker, he had a dynamism that at times surpassed that of King or Farmer. His speeches abounded with invective. Fearless and uncompromising, he befuddled, berated, and battered his opponents with such a catalogue of facts and colorful figures of speech that the audience sat spellbound and stunned.

The speech which follows offers the reader the full range of Malcolm's versatility as an orator.

* * *

Friends and enemies, tonight I hope that we can have a little fireside chat with as few sparks as possible being tossed around. Especially because of the very explosive condition that the world is in today. Sometimes, when a person's house is on fire and someone comes in yelling fire, instead of the person who is awakened by the yell being thankful, he makes the mistake of charging the one who awakened him with having set the fire. I hope that this little conversation tonight about the Black Revolution won't cause any of you to accuse us of igniting it when you find it at your doorstep.

I'm still a Muslim, that is, my religion is still Islam. I still believe that there is no god but Allah and that Mohammed is the apostle of Allah. That just happens to be my personal religion. But in the capacity which I am functioning in today, I have no intention of mixing my religion with the problems of 22 million black people in this country. Just as it's possible for a great man whom I greatly respect, Ben Bella, to be a Muslim and still be a nationalist, and another one whom I greatly respect, Gamal Nasser, to be a Muslim and still be a nationalist, and Sukarno of Indonesia to be a Muslim and still be a nationalist, it was nationalism which enabled them to gain freedom for their people.

I'm still a Muslim but I'm also a nationalist, meaning that my political philosophy is black nationalism, my economic philosophy is black nationalism, my social philosophy is black nationalism. And when I say that this philosophy is black nationalism, to me this means that the political philosophy of black nationalism is that which is designed to encourage our people, the black people, to gain complete control over the politics and the politicians of our own community.

Our economic philosophy is that we should gain economic control over the economy of our own community, the businesses and the other things which create employment so that we can provide jobs for our own people instead of having to picket and boycott and beg someone else for a job.

And, in short, our social philosophy means that we feel that it is time to get together among our own kind and eliminate the evils that are destroying the moral fiber of our society, like drug addiction, drunkenness, adultery that leads to an abundance of bastard children, welfare problems. We believe that we should lift the level or the standard of our own society to a higher level wherein we will be satisfied and then not inclined toward pushing ourselves into other societies where we are not wanted.

All of that aside, tonight we are dealing with the Black Revolution. During recent years there has been much talk about a population explosion, and whenever they are speaking of the population explosion, in my opinion they are referring primarily to the people in Asia or in Africa—the black, brown, red, and yellow people. It is seen by people of the West that as soon as the standard of living is raised in Africa and Asia, automatically the people begin to reproduce abundantly. And there has been a great deal of fear engendered by this in the minds of the people of the West, who happen to be, on this earth, a very small minority.

In fact, in most of the thinking and planning of whites in the West today it's easy to see the fear in their minds—conscious minds and subconscious minds—that the masses of dark people in the West, in the East rather, who already outnumber them, will continue to increase and multiply and grow until they eventually overrun the people of the West like a human sea, a human tide, a human flood. And the fear of this can be seen in the minds, in the actions, of most of the people here in the West in practically everything that they do. It governs political views and it governs their economic views and it governs most of their attitudes toward the present society.

REASON FOR FILIBUSTER

I was listening to Dirksen, the Senator from Illinois, in Washington, D.C., filibustering the civil-rights bill and one thing that he kept stressing over and over and over was that if this bill is passed it will change the social structure of America. Well, I know what he's getting at, and I think that most other people today, and especially our people, know what is meant when these whites who filibuster these bills, and express fears of changes in the social structure, our people are beginning to realize what they mean.

Just as we can see that all over the world one of the main problems facing the West is race, likewise here in America today, most of your Negro leaders as well as the whites agree that 1964 itself appears to be one of the most explosive years yet in the history of America on the racial front, on the racial scene. Not only is this racial explosion probably to take place in America, but all of the ingredients for this racial explosion in America to blossom into a worldwide racial explosion present themselves right here in front of us. America's racial powder keg, in short, can actually fuse or ignite a worldwide powder keg.

And whites in this country who are still complacent when they see the possibilities of racial strife getting out of hand and you are complacent simply because you think you outnumber the racial minority in this country, what you have to bear in mind is wherein you might outnumber us in this country, you don't outnumber us all over the earth.

And any kind of racial explosion that takes place in this country today, in 1964, is not a racial explosion that can be confined to the shores of America. It is a racial explosion that can ignite the racial powder keg that exists all over the planet that we call Earth. Now I think that nobody would disagree that the dark masses of Africa and Asia and Latin America are already seething with bitterness, animosity, hostility, unrest, and impatience with the racial intolerance that they themselves have experienced at the hands of the white West.

And just as they themselves have the ingredients of hostility toward the West in general, here we also have 22 million African-Americans, black, brown, red, and yellow people in this country who are also seething with bitterness and impatience and hostility and animosity at the racial intolerance not only of the white West but of white America in particular.

BLACK NATIONALIST PARTY

And by the hundreds of thousands today we find our own people have become impatient, turning away from your white nationalism, which you call democracy, toward the militant uncompromising policy of black nationalism. I point out right here that as soon as we announced we were going to start a black nationalist party in this country, we received mail from coast to coast, especially from young people at the college level, the university level, who expressed complete sympathy and support and a desire to take an active part in any kind of political action based on black nationalism, designed to correct or eliminate immediately evils that our people have suffered here for 400 years.

The black nationalists to many of you may represent only a minority in the community. And therefore you might have a tendency to classify them as something insignificant. But just as the fuse is the smallest part or the smallest piece in the powder keg it is yet that little fuse that ignites the entire powder keg. The black nationalists to you may represent a small minority in the so-called Negro community. But they just happen to be composed of the type of ingredient necessary to fuse or ignite the entire black community. And this is one thing that whites—whether you call yourselves liberals or conservatives or racists or whatever else you might choose to be—one thing that you have to realize is, where the black community is concerned, although there the large majority you come in contact with may impress you as being moderate and patient and loving and long-suffering and all that kind of stuff, the minority who you consider to be Muslims or nationalists happen to be made of the type of ingredient that can easily spark the black community. This should be understood. Because to me a powder keg is nothing without a fuse.

Nineteen sixty-four will be America's hottest year; her hottest year yet; a year of much racial violence and much racial bloodshed. But it won't be blood that's going to flow only on one side. The new generation of black people that have grown up in this country during recent years are already forming the opinion, and it's a just opinion, that if there is to be bleeding, it should be reciprocal—bleeding on both sides.

It should also be understood that the racial sparks that are ignited here in America today could easily turn into a flaming fire abroad, which only means it could engulf all the people of this earth into a giant race war. You cannot confine it to one little neighborhood, or one little community, or one little country. What happens to a black man in America today happens to the black man in Africa. What happens to a black man in America and Africa happens to the black man in Asia and to the man down in Latin America. What happens to one of us today happens to all of us. And when this is realized I think that the whites—who are intelligent even if they aren't moral or aren't just or aren't impressed by legalities—those who are intelligent will realize that when they touch this one, they are touching all of them, and this in itself will have a tendency to be a checking factor.

The seriousness of this situation must be faced up to. I was in Cleveland last night, Cleveland, Ohio. In fact I was there Friday, Saturday, and yesterday. Last Friday the warning was given that this is a year of bloodshed, that the black man has ceased to turn the other cheek, that he has ceased to be nonviolent, that he has ceased to feel that he must be confined to all these restraints that are put upon him by white society in struggling for what white society says he was supposed to have had a hundred years ago.

So today, when the black man starts reaching out for what America says are his rights, the black man feels that he is within his rights—when he becomes the victim of brutality by those who are depriving him of his rights—to do whatever is necessary to protect himself. And an example of this was taking place last night at this same time in Cleveland, where the police were putting water hoses on our people there and also throwing tear gas at them and they met a hail of stones, a hail of rocks, a hail of bricks. Couple weeks ago in Jacksonville, Florida, a young teen-age Negro was throwing Molotov cocktails.

Well Negroes didn't do this ten years ago. But what you should learn from this is that they are waking up. It was stones yesterday, Molotov cocktails today; it will be hand grenades tomorrow, and whatever else is available the next day. The seriousness of this situation must be faced up to. You should not feel that I am inciting someone to violence. I'm only warning of a powder-keg situation. You can take it or leave it. If you take the warning perhaps you can still save yourself. But if you ignore it or ridicule it, well, death is already at your doorstep. There are 22 million African-Americans who are ready to fight for independence right here. When I say fight for independence right here, I don't mean any nonviolent fight, or turn-the-other-cheek fight. Those days are gone. Those days are over.

If George Washington didn't get independence for this country nonviolently, and if Patrick Henry didn't come up with a nonviolent statement, and you taught me to look upon them as patriots and heroes, then its time for you to realize that I have studied your books well.

POWER OF MINORITY

Our people, 22 million African-Americans, are fed up with America's hypocritical democracy and today we care nothing about the odds that are against us. Every time a black man gets ready to defend himself some Uncle Tom tries to tell us, how can you win? That's Tom talking. Don't listen to him. This is the first thing we hear: the odds are against you. You're dealing with black people who don't care anything about odds. We care nothing about odds.

Again I go right back to the people who founded and secured the independence of this country from the colonial power of England. When George Washington and the others got ready to declare or come up with the Declaration of Independence, they didn't care anything about the odds of the British Empire. They were fed up with taxation without representation. And you've got 22 million black people in this country today, 1964, who are fed up with taxation without representation, and will do the same thing. Who are ready, willing, and justified to do the same thing today to bring about independence for our people that your forefathers did to bring about independence for your people.

And I say your people because I certainly couldn't include myself among those for whom independence was fought in 1776. How in the world can a Negro talk about the Declaration of Independence when he is still singing "We Shall Overcome"? Our people are increasingly developing the opinion that we just have nothing to lose but the chains of segregation and the chains of second-class citizenship.

STRUGGLES WILL MERGE

So 1964 will see the Negro revolt evolve and merge into the world-wide Black Revolution that has been taking place on this earth since 1945. The so-called revolt will become a real Black Revolution. Now the Black Revolution has been taking place in Africa and Asia and in Latin America. Now when I say black, I mean nonwhite. Black, brown, red, or yellow. Our brothers and sisters in Asia, who were colonized by the Europeans, our brothers and sisters in Africa, who were colonized by the Europeans, and in Latin America, the peasants, who were colonized by the Europeans, have been involved in a struggle since 1945 to get the colonialists, or the colonizing powers, the Europeans, off their land, out of their country.

This is a real revolution. Revolution is always based on land. Revolution is never based on begging somebody for an integrated cup of coffee. Revolutions are never fought by turning the other cheek. Revolutions are never based upon love your enemy, and pray for those who spitefully use you. And revolutions are never waged singing "We Shall Overcome." Revolutions are based on bloodshed. Revolutions are never compromising. Revolutions are never based upon negotiations. Revolutions are never based upon any kind of tokenism whatsoever. Revolutions are never even based upon that which is begging a corrupt society or a corrupt system to accept us into it. Revolutions overturn systems, and there is no system on this earth which has proven itself more corrupt, more criminal than this system, that in 1964 still colonizes 22 million African-Americans, still enslaves 22 million Afro-Americans.

There is no system more corrupt than a system that represents itself as the example of freedom, the example of democracy, and can go all over this earth telling other people how to straighten out their house, and you have citizens of this country who have to use bullets if they want to cast a ballot. The greatest weapon the colonial powers have used in the past against our people has always been divide and conquer.

America is a colonial power. She has colonized 22 million Afro-Americans by depriving us of first-class citizenship, by depriving us of civil rights, actually by depriving us of human rights. She has not only deprived us of the right to be a citizen, she has deprived us of the right to be human beings, the right to be recognized and respected as men and women. And in this country the black can be fifty years old and he is still a "boy."

I grew up with white people. I was integrated before they even invented the word and I have never met white people yet—if you are around them long enough—who won't refer to you as a "boy" or a "gal," no matter how old you are or what school you came out of, no matter what your intellectual or professional level is. In this society we remain "boys."

AMERICA'S STRATEGY

So America's strategy is the same strategy as that which was used in the past by the colonial powers: divide and conquer. She plays one Negro leader against the other. She plays one Negro organization against the other. She makes us think we have different goals, different objectives. As soon as one Negro says something, she runs to this Negro and asks him what do you think about what he said. Why anybody can see through that today—except some of the Negro leaders.

All of our people have the same goals. The same objective. That objective is freedom, justice, equality. All of us want recognition and respect as human beings. We don't want to be integrationists. Nor do we want to be separationists. We want to be human beings. Integration is only a method that is used by some groups to obtain freedom, justice, equality, and respect as human beings. Separation is only a method that is used by other groups to obtain freedom, justice, equality, or human dignity.

So our people have made the mistake of confusing the methods with the objectives. As long as we agree on objectives, we should never fall out with each other just because we believe in different methods or tactics or strategy to reach a common objective.

We have to keep in mind at all times that we are not fighting for integration, nor are we fighting for separation. We are fighting for recognition as human beings. We are fighting for the right to live as free humans in this society. In fact, we are actually fighting for rights that are even greater than civil rights and that is human rights.

We are fighting for human rights in 1964. This is a shame. The civil-rights struggle has failed to produce concrete results because it has kept us barking up the wrong tree. It has made us put the cart ahead of the horse. We must have human rights before we can secure civil rights. We must be respected as humans before we can be recognized as citizens.

Among the so-called Negroes in this country, as a rule the civil-rights groups, those who believe in civil rights, they spend most of their time trying to prove they are Americans. Their thinking is usually domestic, confined to the boundaries of America, and they always look upon themselves as a minority. When they look upon themselves upon the American stage, the American stage is a white stage. So a black man standing on that stage in America automatically is in the minority. He is the underdog, and in his struggle he always uses an approach that is a begging, hat in hand, compromising approach.

Whereas the other segment or section in America, known as the nationalist, black nationalists, are more interested in human rights than they are in civil rights. And they place more stress on human rights than they do on civil rights. The difference between the thinking and the scope of the Negroes who are involved in the human-rights struggle and those who are involved in the civil-rights struggle —those so-called Negroes involved in the human-rights struggle don't look upon themselves as Americans.

They look upon themselves as a part of dark mankind. They see the whole struggle not within the confines of the American stage, but they look upon the struggle on the world stage. And, in the world context, they see that the dark man outnumbers the white man. On the world stage the white man is just a microscopic minority.

So in this country you find two different types of Afro-Americans, the type who looks upon himself as a minority and you as the majority, because his scope is limited to the American scene; and then you have the type who looks upon himself as part of the majority and you as part of a microscopic minority. And this one uses a different approach in trying to struggle for his rights. He doesn't beg.

He doesn't thank you for what you give him, because you are only giving him what he should have had a hundred years ago. He doesn't think you are doing him any favors.

NO PROGRESS

He doesn't see any progress that he has made since the Civil War. He sees not one iota of progress because, number one, if the Civil War had freed him, he wouldn't need civil-rights legislation today. If the Emancipation Proclamation, issued by that great shining liberal called Lincoln, had freed him, he wouldn't be singing "We Shall Overcome" today. If the amendments to the Constitution had solved his problem, his problem, still his problem wouldn't be here today. And even if the Supreme Court desegregation decision of 1954 was genuinely and sincerely designed to solve his problem, his problem wouldn't be with us today.

So this kind of black man is thinking, he can see where every maneuver that America has made—supposedly to solve this problem—has been nothing but political trickery and treachery of the worst order. So today he doesn't have any confidence in these so-called liberals. Now I know that you—all that have come in here tonight don't call yourselves liberals. Because that's a nasty name today. It represents hypocrisy. So these two different types of black people exist in the so-called Negro community and they are beginning to wake up and their awakening is producing a very dangerous situation.

So you have whites in the community who express sincerity when they say they want to help. Well, how can they help? How can a white person help the black man solve his problem? Number one: you can't solve it for him. You can help him solve it, but you can't solve it for him today. One of the best ways that you can solve it—or help him solve it—is to let the so-called Negro, who has been involved in the civil-rights struggle, see that the civil-rights struggle must be expanded beyond the level of civil rights to the level of human rights, it opens the door for all of our brothers and sisters in Africa and Asia, who have their independence, to come to our rescue.

CRIMINAL SITUATION

Why, when you go to Washington, D.C., expecting those crooks down there to pass some kind—and that's what they are—to pass some kind of civil-rights legislation to correct a very criminal situation, what you are doing is encouraging the black man, who is the victim, to take his case into the court that's controlled by the criminal that made him the victim. It will never be solved in that way. Just like running from the wolf to the fox. The civil-rights struggle involves the black man taking his case to the white man's court. But when he fights it at the human-rights level, it is a different situation. It opens the door to take Uncle Sam to the world court. The black man doesn't have to go to court to be free. Uncle Sam should be taken to court and made to tell why the black man is not free in a so-called free society. Uncle Sam should be taken into the United Nations and charged with violating the UN Charter on human rights.

You can forget civil rights. How are you going to get civil rights with men like Eastland and men like Dirksen and men like Johnson? It has to be taken out of their hands and taken into the hands of those whose power and authority exceed theirs. Washington has become too corrupt. Uncle Sam's conscience—Uncle Sam has become bankrupt when it comes to conscience—it is impossible for Uncle Sam to solve the problem of 22 million black people in this country. It is absolutely impossible to do it in Uncle Sam's courts—whether it is the Supreme Court or any other kind of court that comes under Uncle Sam's jurisdiction.

The only alternative that the black man has in America today is to take it out of Senator Dirksen's and Senator Eastland's and President Johnson's jurisdiction and take it downtown on the East River and place it before that body of men who represent international law and let them know that the human rights of black people are being violated in a country that professes to be the moral leader of the free world.

Any time you have a filibuster in America, in the Senate, in 1964 over the rights of 22 million black people, over the citizenship of 22 million black people or that will effect the freedom and justice and equality of 22 million black people, it's time for that government itself to be taken before a world court. How can you condemn South Africa? There are only 11 million of our people in South Africa, there are 22 million of them here. And we are receiving an injustice which is just as criminal as that which is being done to the black people of South Africa.

So today those whites who profess to be liberals—and so far as I am concerned it's just lip profession—you understand why our people don't have civil rights. You're white. You can go and hang out with another white liberal and see how hypocritical they are. While a lot of you sitting right here, know that you've seen whites up in a Negro's face with flowery words and as soon as that Negro walks away you listen to how your white friend talks. We have black people who can pass as white. We know how you talk.

We can see that it is nothing but a governmental conspiracy to continue to deprive the black people in this country of their rights. And the only way we will get these rights restored is by taking it out of Uncle Sam's hands. Take him to court and charge him with genocide, the mass murder of millions of black people in this country —political murder, economic murder, social murder, mental murder. This is the crime that this government has committed and, if you yourself don't do something about it in time, you are going to open the doors for something to be done about it from outside forces.

I read in the paper yesterday where one of the Supreme Court Justices, Goldberg, was crying about the violation of human rights of 3 million Jews in the Soviet Union. Imagine this. I haven't got anything against Jews, but that's their problem. How in the world are you going to cry about problems on the other side of the world when you haven't got the problems straightened out here? How can the plight of 3 million Jews in Russia be qualified to be taken to the United Nations by a man who is a Justice in this Supreme Court, and is supposed to be a liberal, supposed to be a friend of black people, and hasn't opened up his mouth one time about taking the plight of black people down here to the United Nations?

POLITICALLY MATURE

Our people are becoming more politically mature. Their eyes are coming open. They are beginning to see the trend in all of the American politics today. They notice that every time there is an election it is so close among whites that they have to count the votes over again. This happened in Massachusetts when they were running for governor, this happened in Rhode Island, it happened in Minnesota, and many other places, and it happened in the election between Kennedy and Nixon. Things are so close that any minority that has a bloc vote can swing it either way.

And I think that most students of political science agree that it was the 80 percent support that Kennedy got from the black man in this country that enabled him to sit in the White House. Sat down there four years and the Negro was still in the doghouse. The same ones that we put in the White House have continued to keep us in the doghouse. The Negro can see that he holds the balance of power in this country politically.

It is he who puts in office the one who gets in office. Yet when the Negro helps that person get in office the Negro gets nothing in return. All he gets is a few appointments. A few hand-picked Uncle Tom handkerchief-head Negroes are given big jobs in Washington, D.C. And those Negroes come back and try and make us think that that administration is going to lead us to the promised land of integration. And the only ones whose problems have been solved have been those hand-picked Negroes. A few big Negroes got jobs who didn't even need the jobs. They already were working. But the masses of black people are still unemployed.

The present administration, the Democratic administration, has been down there for four years. Yet no meaningful legislation has been passed by them that proposes to benefit black people in this country, despite the fact that in the House they have 257 Democrats and only 177 are Republicans. They control two-thirds of the House. In the Senate there are 67 Democrats and only 33 Republicans. The Democrats control two-thirds of the government and it is the Negroes who put them in a position to control the government. Yet they give the Negroes nothing in return but a few handouts in the form of appointments that are only used as window dressing to make it appear that the problem is being solved.

TRICKERY AND TREACHERY

No, something is wrong. And when these black people wake up and find out for real the trickery and the treachery that has been heaped upon us you are going to have revolution. And when I say revolution I don't mean that stuff they were talking about last year about "We Shall Overcome." The Democrats get Negro support, yet the Negroes get nothing in return. The Negroes put the Democrats first, yet the Democrats put the Negroes last. And the alibi that the Democrats use—they blame the Dixiecrats.

A Dixiecrat is nothing but a Democrat in disguise. You show me a Dixiecrat and I'll show you a Democrat. And chances are, you show me a Democrat and I'll show you a Dixiecrat. Because Dixie in reality means all that territory south of the Canadian border. There are sixteen Senatorial committees that run this government. Of the sixteen Senatorial committees that run the government, ten of them are controlled by chairmen that are from the South. Of the twenty Congressional committees that help run the government, twelve of them are controlled by Southern segregationists.

Think of this: ten of the Senatorial committees are in the hands of the Dixiecrats, twelve of the twenty Congressional committees are in the hands of the Dixiecrats. These committees control the government. And you're going to tell us that the South lost the Civil War? The South controls the government. And they control it because they have seniority. And they have seniority because in the states that they come from, they deny Negroes the right to vote.

If Negroes could vote south of the—yes, if Negroes could vote south of the Canadian border—south South, if Negroes could vote in the southern part of the South, Ellender wouldn't be the head of the Agricultural and Forestry Committee, Richard Russell wouldn't be head of the Armed Services Committee, Robertson of Virginia wouldn't be head of the Banking and Currency Committee. Imagine that, all of the banking and currency of the government is in the hands of a Cracker.

In fact, when you see how many of these committee men are from the South you can see that we have nothing but a cracker government in Washington, D.C. And their head is a Cracker President. I said a Cracker President. Texas is just as much a Cracker state as Mississippi—and even more so. In Texas they lynch you with a Texas accent and in Mississippi they lynch you with a Mississippi accent.

And the first thing this man did when he came in office was invite all the big Negroes down for coffee. James Farmer was one of the first ones—the head of CORE. I have nothing against him. He's all right—Farmer, that is. But could that same President have invited James Farmer to Texas for coffee? And if James Farmer went to Texas, could he have taken his white wife with him to have coffee with the President? Any time you have a man who can't straighten out Texas, how can he straighten out the country? No, you're barking up the wrong tree.

If Negroes in the South could vote, the Dixiecrats would lose power. When the Dixiecrats lost power, the Democrats would lose power. A Dixiecrat lost is a Democrat lost. Therefore the two of them have to conspire with each other to stay in power. The Northern Dixiecrat puts all the blame on the Southern Dixiecrat. It's a con game. The job of the Northern Democrat is to make the Negro think that he is our friend. He is always smiling and wagging his tail and telling us how much he can do for us if we vote for him. But, at the same time he's out in front telling us what he's going to do, behind the door he's in cahoots with the Southern Democrat setting up the machinery to make sure he'll never have to keep his promise.

This is the conspiracy that our people have faced in this country for the past 100 years. And today you have a new generation of black people who have come on the scene who have become disenchanted with the entire system, who have become disillusioned over the system and who are ready now and willing to do something about it. So in my conclusion in speaking about the black revolution, America today is at a time or in a day or at an hour where she is the first country on this earth that can actually have a bloodless revolution. In the past revolutions have been bloody. Historically you just don't have a peaceful revolution. Revolutions are bloody, revolutions are violent, revolutions cause bloodshed, and death follows in their paths. America is the only country in history in a position to bring about a revolution without violence and bloodshed. But America is not morally equipped to do so.

Why is America in a position to bring about a bloodless revolution? Because the Negro in this country holds the balance of power and if the Negro in this country were given what the Constitution says he is supposed to have, the added power of the Negro in this country would sweep all of the racists and the segregationists out of office. It would change the entire political structure of the country. I would wipe out the Southern segregationism that now controls America's foreign policy, as well as America's domestic policy.

And the only way without bloodshed that this can be brought about is that the black man has to be given full use of the ballot in every one of the fifty states. But if the black man doesn't get the ballot, then you are going to be faced with another man who forgets the ballot and starts using the bullet.

Revolutions are fought to get control of land, to remove the absentee landlord and gain control of the land and the institutions that flow from that land. The black man has been in a very low condition because he has had no control whatsoever over any land. He has been a beggar, economically, a beggar politically, a beggar socially, a beggar even when it comes to trying to get some education. So that in the past the type of mentality that was developed in this colonial system among our people, today is being overcome. And as the young ones come up they know what they want. And as they listen to your beautiful preaching about democracy and all those flowery words, they know what they're supposed to have.

So you have a people today who not only know what they want, but also know what they are supposed to have. And they themselves are creating another generation that is coming up that not only will know what it wants and know what it should have, but also will be ready and willing to do whatever is necessary to see that what they should have materializes immediately.

Thank you.

The Advance Guard

A. PHILIP RANDOLPH

For nearly fifty years the name of Asa Philip Randolph has been associated with the American labor movement. A labor organizer accustomed to facilitating the peaceable settlement of railroad disputes in those areas affecting the Brotherhood of Sleeping Car Porters, which he organized in 1925 and of which became President in 1934, this son of Crescent City, Florida, has proceeded from crisis to crisis with phenomenal success in gaining benefits for his organization.

Again and again Randolph has been called in to advise Presidents, Cabinet members, Congressmen, and party leaders. He was the Director of the March on Washington Movement which led President Roosevelt to start the Committee on Fair Employment Practices in 1941. Appointed Vice-President of the AFL-CIO in 1957, he has served on the Executive Council of that organization since that time.

Mr. Randolph has been a consistent crusader for civil rights, and he was one of the organizers of the August, 1963, March on Washington, where he delivered the address that follows.

* * *

Fellow Americans, we are gathered here in the largest demonstration in the history of this nation. Let the nation and the world know the meaning of our numbers. We are not a pressure group. We are not an organization or a group of organizations. We are not a mob. We are the advance guard of a massive moral revolution for jobs and freedom.

This revolution reverberates throughout the land touching every city, every town, every village where black men are segregated, oppressed, and exploited. But this civil-rights revolution is not confined to the Negro nor is it confined to civil rights, for our white allies know that they cannot be free while we are not and we know that we have no future in a society in which 6 million black and white people are unemployed and millions more live in poverty. Nor is the goal of our civil-rights revolution merely the passage of civil-rights legislation.

Yes, we want all public accommodations open to all citizens, but those accommodations will mean little to those who cannot afford to use them. Yes, we want a Fair Employment Practices Act, but what good will it do if profit-geared automation destroys the jobs of millions of workers, black and white? We want integrated public schools but that means we also want federal aid to education—all forms of education. We want a free democratic society dedicated to the political, economic, and social advancement of man along moral lines.

Now we know that real freedom will require many changes in the nation's political and social philosophies and institutions. For one thing we must destroy the notion that Mrs. Murphy's property rights include the right to humiliate me because of the color of my skin. The sanctity of private property takes second place to the sanctity of the human personality.

It falls to the Negro to reassert this profit priority of values because our ancestors were transformed from human personalities into private property. It falls to us to demand new forms of social planning, to create full employment, and to put automation at the service of human needs, not at the service of profits—for we are the worse victims of unemployment. Negroes are in the forefront of today's movement for social and racial justice because we know we cannot expect the realization of our aspirations through the same old antidemocratic social institutions and philosophies that have all along frustrated our aspirations.

And so we have taken our struggle into the streets as the labor movement took its struggle into the streets, as Jesus Christ led the multitudes through the streets of Judea. The plain and simple fact is that until we went into the streets the federal government was indifferent to our demands. It was not until the streets and jails of Birmingham were filled that Congress began to think about civil-rights legislation. It was not until thousands demonstrated in the South that lunch counters and other public accommodations were integrated. It was not until the Freedom Riders were brutalized in Alabama that the 1946 Supreme Court decision banning discrimination in interstate travel was enforced, and it was not until construction sites were picketed in the North that Negro workers were hired.

Those who deplore our militancy, who exhort patience in the name of a false peace, are in fact supporting segregation and exploitation. They would have social peace at the expense of social and racial justice. They are more concerned with easing racial tension than enforcing racial democracy. The months and years ahead will bring new evidence of masses in motion for freedom. The March on Washington is not the climax of our struggle but a new beginning, not only for the Negro but for all Americans who thirst for freedom and a better life.

Look for the enemies of Medicare, of higher minimum wages, of Social Security, of federal aid to education, and there you will find the enemy of the Negro—the coalition of Dixiecrats and reactionary Republicans that seeks to dominate the Congress. We must develop strength in order that we may be able to back and support the civil-rights program of President Kennedy. In the struggle against these forces all of us should be prepared to take to the streets. The spirit and technique that built the labor movement, founded churches, and now guide the civil-rights revolution must be a massive crusade, must be launched against the unholy coalition of Dixiecrats and the racists that seek to strangle Congress. We here today are only the first wave. When we leave it will be to carry the civil-rights revolution home with us into every nook and cranny of the land and we shall return again and again to Washington in ever-growing numbers until total freedom is ours. We shall settle for nothing less and may God grant that we may have the courage, the strength, and faith in this hour of trial by fire never to falter.

High-Octane Hypocrisy
WALTER REUTHER

Walter Philip Reuther is probably the most widely known labor leader in the world. Born in Wheeling, West Virginia, September 1, 1907, he began his career as an apprentice tool-and-die maker in the Wheeling Steel Corporation in 1924. He then worked for the Briggs Manufacturing Company, General Motors, and the Ford Motor Company, after which he traveled by bicycle through Europe and the Orient, observing auto plants and machine shops, and returned to the United States to organize auto workers in 1935.

He became successively organizer and President of Local 174, United Auto Workers; Honorary President of the West Side Local; Vice-President of the International Union, United Automobile, Air-craft, and Agricultural Workers of America, CIO; and has been its President since 1946; President of the CIO from 1952; President of the CIO in the combined American Federation of Labor–Congress of Industrial Organizations, since 1955. During World War II, he proposed a plan which made it possible to produce defense aircraft by mass-production methods in automobile plants. It was his leadership in the 113-day strike of General Motors Workers, November 21, 1945 to March 13, 1946, winning a wage increase and improved working conditions, that focused national attention on the union demand for "wage increases without price increases."

A long-time champion of justice and human dignity, he has been a foremost leader in the civil-rights cause. The oration given at the time of the March on Washington is a good example of the protest against those reactionary elements that would deny the Negro his rights as an American citizen.

* * *

Brother Randolph, fellow Americans and friends. I am here today with you because with you I share the view that the struggle for civil rights and the struggle for equal opportunity is not the struggle of Negro Americans but the struggle for every American to join in.

For 100 years the Negro people have searched for first-class citizenship and I believe that they cannot and should not wait until some distant tomorrow. They should demand freedom now. Here and now.

It is the responsibility of every American to share the impatience of the Negro American. And we need to join together, to march together, and to work together until we have bridged the moral gap between American democracy's noble promises and its ugly practices in the field of civil rights. American democracy has been too long on pious platitudes and too short on practical performance in this important area.

Now one of the problems is that there is too much high-octane hypocrisy in America. There is a lot of noble talk about brotherhood, and some Americans drop the brother and keep the hood. To me the civil-rights question is a moral question. It transcends partisan politics. And this rally today is the first step in a total effort to mobilize the moral conscience of America and to ask the people in Congress of both parties to rise above their partisan differences and enact civil-rights legislation now.

Now the President, President Kennedy, has offered a comprehensive but moderate bill. That bill is the first meaningful step. It needs to be strengthened. It needs FEPC and other strong provisions and the job question is crucial because we will not solve education or housing or public accommodations as long as millions of Americans, Negroes, are treated as second-class economic citizens and denied jobs. And as one American I take the position, if we can have full employment and full production for the negative end of war, then why can't we have a job for every American in the pursuit of peace? And so our slogan has got to be fair employment but fair employment within the framework of full employment so that every American can have a job.

I am for civil rights as a matter of human decency, as a matter of common morality, but I am also for civil rights because I believe that freedom is an indivisible value, that no one can be free unto himself. And when Bull Connor, with his police dogs and fire hoses, destroys freedom in Birmingham, he destroys my freedom in Detroit. And let us keep in mind, since we are the strongest of the free nations of the world, since you cannot make your freedom secure except as we make freedom universal so that all may enjoy its blessings, let us understand that we cannot defend freedom in Berlin as long as we deny freedom in Birmingham.

This rally is not the end, it is the beginning. It is the beginning of a great moral crusade to arouse Americans to the unfinished work of American democracy. The Congress has to act and after they act we have much work to do in the vineyards of American democracy in every community. Men of good will must join together, men of all races and creeds and colors and political persuasion and motivated by the spirit of human brotherhood. We must search for the answer in the light of reason through rational and responsible action because if we fail, the vacuum of our failure will be filled by the apostles of hatred who will search in the darkened night, and reason will yield to riot and brotherhood will yield to bitterness and bloodshed and we will tear asunder the fabric of American democracy.

So, let this be the beginning of that great crusade to mobilize the moral conscience of America so that we can win freedom and justice and equality and first-class citizenship for every American, not just for certain Americans, not only in certain parts of America, but in every part of America, from Boston to Birmingham, from New York to New Orleans, and from Michigan to Mississippi.

Thank you.

From Protest to Politics
BAYARD RUSTIN

Bayard Rustin was born on March 17, 1910, in West Chester, Pennsylvania. After graduating from West Chester High School, where he was on the championship football and track teams, he traveled extensively, doing odd jobs to earn money for college. In 1931 he entered Wilberforce University and later attended Cheyney State Teachers College, Pennsylvania, and the City College of New York, where he earned his tuition by singing with Josh White and Leadbelly, the folksingers.

From 1941 to 1953, Mr. Rustin served as Race-relations Secretary of the Fellowship of Reconciliation. During that period he was also a youth organizer for A. Philip Randolph's March on Washington (1941), and became the first field secretary of the newly formed Congress of Racial Equality (1941). In 1942, he went to California to help protect the property of Japanese-Americans who had been placed in work camps. The following year, Mr. Rustin was imprisoned in Lewisburg Penitentiary as a conscientious objector.

Upon his release in 1945, Mr. Rustin became chairman of the Free India Committee and was frequently arrested for sitting in at the British Embassy. Three years later, at the invitation of the Congress Party, he made his first of several trips to India, working there for six months.

In 1947, Mr. Rustin participated in the first Freedom Ride, the Journey of Reconciliation designed to test enforcement of the 1946 Irene Morgan case outlawing discrimination in interstate travel. Arrested in North Carolina, he served thirty days on a chain gang. His report of this experience appeared in the *New York Post* and prompted an investigation which led to the abolition of the chain gang in North Carolina.

In 1951, Mr. Rustin went to West Africa, where he worked with Azikewe and Nkrumah. With George Hauser he had organized the Committee to Support South African Resistance, which in 1953 became the American Committee on Africa. Also, during this time, he became Director of Mr. Randolph's Committee against Discrimination in the Armed Forces, which secured President Truman's executive order eliminating segregation in the armed forces.

In 1953, Mr. Rustin became executive secretary of the War Resisters' League, a pacifist organization. Two years later he went to Montgomery, Alabama, at the invitation of Dr. Martin Luther King, Jr., to assist in the organization of the bus boycott. The following year, he drew up, at Dr. King's request, the first plans for the founding of the Southern Christian Leadership Conference. For seven years Mr. Rustin served as special assistant to Dr. King.

Mr. Rustin went to England in 1957, where he helped mobilize the first of the massive Aldermaston peace marches, and in the same year coordinated the 35,000 strong Prayer Pilgrimage to Washington for civil rights. The Youth Marches for Integrated Schools, which he directed, followed in 1958 and 1959.

When in 1960 Dr. King was indicted on false charges of perjury in connection with his income-tax returns, Mr. Rustin was appointed director of his defense committee, which succeeded in winning Dr. King's case. The same election year saw him organize marches on the Democratic and Republican party conventions, and participate in the Sahara protest against nuclear testing by the French government. He returned to Africa again in 1962 for the All-African People's Conference in Addis Ababa.

Mr. Rustin was Deputy Director of the March on Washington of August 28, 1963. He directed the New York school boycott of February 3, 1964—the largest civil-rights demonstration up to that time.

Mr. Rustin has been arrested some twenty-four times in the struggle for civil rights. He is currently Executive Director of the A. Philip Randolph Institute.

The article included here is the first in a series of Occasional Papers printed in *Commentary*, February, 1965.

* * *

The decade spanned by the 1954 Supreme Court decision on school desegregation and the Civil Rights Act of 1964 will undoubtedly be recorded as the period in which the legal foundations of racism in America were destroyed. To be sure, pockets of resistance remain; but it would be hard to quarrel with the assertion that the elaborate legal structure of segregation and discrimination, particularly in relation to public accommodations, has virtually collapsed. On the other hand, without making light of the human sacrifices involved in the direct-action tactics (sit-ins, freedom rides, and the rest) that were so instrumental to this achievement, we must recognize that in desegregating public accommodations, we affected institutions which are relatively peripheral both to the American socioeconomic order and to the fundamental conditions of life of the Negro people. In a highly industrialized, twentieth-century civilization, we hit Jim Crow precisely where it was most anachronistic, dispensable, and vulnerable—in hotels lunch counters, terminals, libraries, swimming pools, and the like. For in these forms, Jim Crow does impede the flow of commerce in the broadest sense: it is a nuisance in a society on the move (and on the make). Not surprisingly, therefore, it was the most mobility-conscious and relatively liberated groups in the Negro community—lower-middle-class college students—who launched the attack that brought down this imposing but hollow structure.

The term "classical" appears especially apt for this phase of the civil-rights movement. But in the few years that have passed since the first flush of sit-ins, several developments have taken place that have complicated matters enormously. One is the shifting focus of the movement in the South, symbolized by Birmingham; another is the spread of the revolution to the North; and the third, common to the other two, is the expansion of the movement's base in the Negro community. To attempt to disentangle these three strands is to do violence to reality. David Danzig's perceptive article, "The Meaning of Negro Strategy," correctly saw in the Birmingham events the victory of the concept of collective struggle over individual achievement as the road to Negro freedom. And Birmingham remains the unmatched symbol of grass-roots protest involving all strata of the black community. It was also in this most industrialized of Southern cities that the single-issue demands of the movement's classical stage gave way to the "package deal." No longer were Negroes satisfied with integrating lunch counters. They now sought advances in employment, housing, school integration, police protection, and so forth.

Thus, the movement in the South began to attack areas of discrimination which were not so remote from the Northern experience as were Jim Crow lunch counters. At the same time, the interrelationship of these apparently distinct areas became increasingly evident. What is the value of winning access to public accommodations for those who lack money to use them? The minute the movement faced this question, it was compelled to expand its vision beyond race relations to economic relations, including the role of education in modern society. And what also became clear is that all these interrelated problems, by their very nature, are not soluble by private, voluntary efforts but require government action—or politics. Already Southern demonstrators had recognized that the most effective way to strike at the police brutality they suffered from was by getting rid of the local sheriff—and that meant political action, which in turn meant, and still means, political action within the Democratic party where the only meaningful primary contests in the South are fought.

And so in Mississippi, thanks largely to the leadership of Bob Moses, a turn toward political action has been taken. More than voter registration is involved here. A conscious bid for *political power* is being made, and in the course of that effort a tactical shift is being effected: direct-action techniques are being subordinated to a strategy calling for the building of community institutions or power bases. Clearly, the implications of this shift reach far beyond Mississippi. What began as a protest movement is being challenged to translate itself into a political movement. Is this the right course? And if it is, can the transformation be accomplished?

II

The very decade which has witnessed the decline of legal Jim Crow has also seen the rise of *de facto* segregation in our most fundamental socioeconomic institutions. More Negroes are unemployed today than in 1954, and the unemployment gap between the races is wider. The median income of Negroes has dropped from 57 percent to 54 percent of that of whites. A higher percentage of Negro workers is now concentrated in jobs vulnerable to automation than was the case ten years ago. More Negroes attend *de facto* segregated schools today than when the Supreme Court handed down its famous decision; while school integration proceeds at a snail's pace in the South, the number of Northern schools with an excessive proportion of minority youth proliferates. And behind this is the continuing growth of racial slums, spreading over our central cities and trapping Negro youth in a milieu which, whatever its legal definition, sows an unimaginable demoralization. Again, legal niceties aside, a resident of a racial ghetto lives in segregated housing, and more Negroes fall into this category than ever before.

These are the facts of life which generate frustration in the Negro community and challenge the civil-rights movement. At issue, after all, is not *civil rights*, strictly speaking, but social and economic conditions. Last summer's riots were not race riots; they were outbursts of class aggression in a society where class and color definitions are converging disastrously. How can the (perhaps misnamed) civil-rights movement deal with this problem?

Before trying to answer, let me first insist that the task of the movement is vastly complicated by the failure of many whites of good will to understand the nature of our problem. There is a widespread assumption that the removal of artificial barriers should result in the automatic integration of the Negro into all aspects of American life. This myth is fostered by facile analogies with the experience of various ethnic immigrant groups, particularly the Jews. But the analogies with the Jews do not hold for three simple but profound reasons. First, Jews have a long history as a literate people, a resource which has afforded them opportunities to advance in the academic and professional worlds, to achieve intellectual status even in the midst of economic hardship, and to evolve sustaining value systems in the context of ghetto life. Negroes, for the greater part of their presence in this country, were forbidden by law to read or write. Second, Jews have a long history of family stability, the importance of which in terms of aspiration and self-image is obvious. The Negro family structure was totally destroyed by slavery and with it the possibility of cultural transmission (the right of Negroes to marry and rear children is barely a century old). Third, Jews are white and have the *option* of relinquishing their cultural-religious identity, intermarrying, passing, etc. Negroes, or at least the overwhelming majority of them, do not have this option. There is also a fourth, vulgar reason. If the Jewish and Negro communities are not comparable in terms of education, family structure, and color, it is also true that their respective economic roles bear little resemblance.

This matter of economic role brings us to the greater problem—the fact that we are moving into an era in which the natural functioning of the market does not by itself ensure every man with will and ambition a place in the productive process. The immigrant who came to this country during the late nineteenth and twentieth centuries entered a society which was expanding territorially and/or economically. It was then possible to start at the bottom, as an unskilled or semiskilled worker, and move up the ladder, acquiring new skills along the way. Especially was this true when industrial unionism was burgeoning, giving new dignity and higher wages to organized workers. Today the situation has changed. We are not expanding territorially, the Western frontier is settled, labor organizing has leveled off, our rate of economic growth has been stagnant for a decade. And we are in the midst of a technological revolution which is altering the fundamental structure of the labor force, destroying unskilled and semiskilled jobs —jobs in which Negroes are disproportionately concentrated.

Whatever the pace of this technological revolution may be, the *direction* is clear: the lower rungs of the economic ladder are being lopped off. This means that an individual will no longer be able to start at the bottom and work his way up; he will have to start in the middle or on top, and hold on tight. It will not even be enough to have certain specific skills, for many skilled jobs are also vulnerable to automation. A broad educational background, permitting vocational adaptability and flexibility, seems more imperative than ever. We live in a society where, as Secretary of Labor Willard Wirtz puts it, machines are the equivalent of a high school diploma. Yet the average educational attainment of American Negroes is 8.2 years.

Negroes, of course, are not the only people being affected by these developments. It is reported that there are now 50 percent fewer unskilled and semiskilled jobs than there are high school dropouts. Almost one-third of the 26 million young people entering the labor market in the 1960's will be dropouts. But the percentage of Negro dropouts nationally is 57 percent, and in New York City, among Negroes twenty-five years of age or over, it is 68 percent. They are without a future.

To what extent can the kind of self-help campaign recently prescribed by Eric Hoffer in *The New York Times Magazine* cope with such a situation? I would advise those who think that self-help is the answer to familiarize themselves with the long history of such efforts in the Negro community, and to consider why so many foundered on the shoals of ghetto life. It goes without saying that any effort to combat demoralization and apathy is desirable, but we must understand that demoralization in the Negro community is largely a common-sense response to an objective reality. Negro youths have no need of statistics to perceive, fairly accurately, what their odds are in American society. Indeed, from the point of view of motivation, some of the healthiest Negro youngsters I know are juvenile delinquents: vigorously pursuing the American dream of material acquisition and status, yet finding the conventional means of attaining it blocked off, they do not yield to defeatism but resort to illegal (and often ingenious) methods. They are not alien to American culture. They are, in Gunnar Myrdal's phrase, "exaggerated Americans." To want a Cadillac is not un-American; to push a cart in the garment center is. If Negroes are to be persuaded that the conventional path (school, work, etc.) is superior, we had better provide evidence which is now sorely lacking. It is a double cruelty to harangue Negro youth about education and training when we do not know what jobs will be available for them. When a Negro youth can reasonably foresee a future free of slums, when the prospect of gainful employment is realistic, we will see motivation and self-help in abundant enough quantities.

Meanwhile, there is an ironic similarity between the self-help advocated by many liberals and the doctrines of the Black Muslims. Professional sociologists, psychiatrists, and social workers have expressed amazement at the Muslims' success in transforming prostitutes and dope addicts into respectable citizens. But every prostitute the Muslims convert to a model of Calvinist virtue is replaced by the ghetto with two more. Dedicated as they are to maintenance of the ghetto, the Muslims are powerless to effect substantial moral reform. So too with every other group or program which is not aimed at the destruction of slums, their causes and effects. Self-help efforts, directly or indirectly, must be geared to mobilizing people into power units capable of effecting social change. That is, their goal must be genuine self-help, not merely self-improvement. Obviously, where self-improvement activities succeed in imparting to their participants a feeling of some control over their environment, those involved may find their appetites for change whetted; they may move into the political arena.

III

Let me sum up what I have thus far been trying to say: the civil-rights movement is evolving from a protest movement into a full-fledged *social movement*—an evolution calling its very name into question. It is now concerned not merely with removing the barriers to full *opportunity* but with achieving the fact of *equality*. From sit-ins and freedom rides we have gone into rent strikes, boycotts, community organization, and political action. As a consequence of this natural evolution, the Negro finds himself today stymied by obstacles of far greater magnitude than the legal barriers he was attacking before: automation, urban decay, *de facto* school segregation. These are problems which, while conditioned by Jim Crow, do not vanish upon its demise. They are more deeply rooted in our socioeconomic order; they are the result of the total society's failure to meet not only the Negro's needs, but human needs generally.

These propositions have won increasing recognition and acceptance, but with a curious twist. They have formed the common premise of two apparently contradictory lines of thought which simultaneously nourish and antagonize each other. On the one hand, there is the reasoning of *The New York Times* moderate who says that the problems are so enormous and complicated that Negro militancy is a futile irritation, and that the need is for "intelligent moderation." Thus, during the first New York school boycott, *The Times* editorialized that Negro demands, while abstractly just, would necessitate massive reforms, the funds for which could not realistically be anticipated; therefore the just demands were also foolish demands and would only antagonize white people. Moderates of this stripe are often correct in perceiving the difficulty or impossibility of racial progress in the context of present social and economic policies. But they accept the context as fixed. They ignore (or perhaps see all too well) the potentialities inherent in linking Negro demands to broader pressures for radical revision of existing policies. They apparently see nothing strange in the fact that in the last twenty-five years we have spent nearly a trillion dollars fighting or preparing for wars, yet throw up our hands before the need for overhauling our schools, clearing the slums, and really abolishing poverty. My quarrel with these moderates is that they do not even envision radical changes; their admonitions of moderation are, for all practical purposes, admonitions to the Negro to adjust to the status quo, and are therefore immoral.

The more effectively the moderates argue their case, the more they convince Negroes that American society will not or cannot be reorganized for full racial equality. Michael Harrington has said that a successful war on poverty might well require the expenditure of 100 billion dollars. Where, the Negro wonders, are the forces now in motion to compel such a commitment? If the voices of the moderates were raised in an insistence upon a reallocation of national resources at levels that could not be confused with tokenism (that is, if the moderates stopped being moderates), Negroes would have greater grounds for hope. Meanwhile, the Negro movement cannot escape a sense of isolation.

It is precisely this sense of isolation that gives rise to the second line of thought I want to examine—the tendency within the civil-rights movement which, despite its militancy, pursues what I call a "no-win" policy. Sharing with many moderates a recognition of the magnitude of the obstacles to freedom, spokesmen for this tendency survey the American scene and find no forces prepared to move toward radical solutions. From this they conclude that the only visible strategy is shock; above all, the hypocrisy of white liberals must be exposed. These spokesmen are often described as the radicals of the movement, but they are really its moralists. They seek to change white hearts—by traumatizing them. Frequently abetted by white self-flagellants, they may gleefully applaud (though not really agreeing with) Malcolm X because, while they admit he has no program, they think he can frighten white people into doing the right thing. To believe this, of course, you must be convinced, even if unconsciously, that at the core of the white man's heart lies a buried affection for Negroes—a proposition one may be permitted to doubt. But in any case, hearts are not relevant to the issue; neither racial affinities nor racial hostilities are rooted there. It is institutions—social, political, and economic institutions—which are the ultimate molders of collective sentiments. Let these institutions be reconstructed *today,* and let the ineluctable gradualism of history govern the formation of a new psychology.

My quarrel with the "no-win" tendency in the civil-rights movement (and the reason I have so designated it) parallel my quarrel with the moderates outside the movement. As the latter lack the vision or will for fundamental change, the former lack a realistic strategy for achieving it. For such a strategy they substitute militancy. But militancy is a matter of posture and volume and not of effect.

I believe that the Negro's struggle for equality in America is essentially revolutionary. While most Negroes—in their hearts—unquestionably seek only to enjoy the fruits of American society as it now exists, their quest cannot *objectively* be satisfied within the framework of existing political and economic relations. The young Negro who would demonstrate his way into the labor market may be motivated by a thoroughly bourgeois ambition and thoroughly "capitalist" considerations, but he will end up having to favor a great expansion of the public sector of the economy. At any rate, that is the position the movement will be forced to take as it looks at the number of jobs being generated by the private economy, and if it is to remain true to the masses of Negroes.

The revolutionary character of the Negro's struggle is manifest in the fact that this struggle may have done more to democratize life for whites than for Negroes. Clearly, it was the sit-in movement of young Southern Negroes which, as it galvanized white students, banished the ugliest features of McCarthyism from the American campus and resurrected political debate. It was not until Negroes assaulted *de facto* school segregation in the urban centers that the issue of quality education for *all* children stirred into motion. Finally, it seems reasonably clear that the civil-rights movement, directly and through the resurgence of social conscience it kindled, did more to initiate the war on poverty than any other single force.

It will be—it has been—argued that these by-products of the Negro struggle are not revolutionary. But the term "revolutionary," as I am using it, does not connote violence; it refers to the qualitative transformation of fundamental institutions, more or less rapidly, to the point where the social and economic structure which they comprised can no longer be said to be the same. The Negro struggle has hardly run is course; and it will not stop moving until it has been utterly defeated or won substantial equality. But I fail to see how the movement can be victorious in the absence of radical programs for full employment, abolition of slums, the reconstruction of our educational system, new definitions of work and leisure. Adding up the cost of such programs, we can only conclude that we are talking about a refashioning of our political economy. It has been estimated, for example, that the price of replacing New York City's slums with public housing would be 17 billion dollars. Again, a multibillion-dollar federal public-works program, dwarfing the currently proposed 2-billion-dollar program, is required to reabsorb unskilled and semi-skilled workers into the labor market—and this must be done if Negro workers in these categories are to be employed. "Preferential treatment" cannot help them.

I am not trying here to delineate a total program, only to suggest the scope of economic reforms which are most immediately related to the plight of the Negro community. One could speculate on their political implications—whether, for example, they do not indicate the obsolescence of state government and the superiority of regional structures as viable units of planning. Such speculations aside, it is clear that Negro needs cannot be satisfied unless we go beyond what has so far been placed on the agenda. How are these radical objectives to be achieved? The answer is simple, deceptively so: *through political power.*

There is a strong moralistic strain in the civil-rights movement which would remind us that power corrupts, forgetting that the absence of power also corrupts. But this is not the view I want to debate here, for it is waning. Our problem is posed by those who accept the need for political power but do not understand the nature of the object and therefore lack sound strategies for achieving it; they tend to confuse political institutions with lunch counters.

A handful of Negroes, acting alone, could integrate a lunch counter by strategically locating their bodies so as *directly* to interrupt the operation of the proprietor's will; their numbers were relatively unimportant. In politics, however, such a confrontation is difficult because the interests involved are merely *represented.* In the execution of a political decision a direct confrontation may ensue (as when federal marshals escorted James Meredith into the University of Mississippi—to turn from an example of nonviolent coercion to one of force backed up with the threat of violence). But in arriving at a political decision, numbers and organizations are crucial, especially for the economically disenfranchised. (Needless to say, I am assuming that the forms of political democracy exist in America, however, imperfectly, that they are valued, and that elitist or putchist conceptions of exercising power are beyond the pale of discussion for the civil rights movement.)

Neither that movement nor the country's 20 million black people can win political power alone. We need allies. The future of the Negro struggle depends on whether the contradictions of this society can be resolved by a coalition of progressive forces which becomes the *effective* political majority in the United States. I speak of the coalition which staged the March on Washington, passed the Civil Rights Act, and laid the basis for the Johnson landslide—Negroes, trade unionists, liberals, and religious groups.

There are those who argue that a coalition strategy would force the Negro to surrender his political independence to white liberals, that he would be neutralized, deprived of his cutting edge, absorbed into the Establishment. Some who take this position urged last year that votes be withheld from the Johnson-Humphrey ticket as a demonstration of the Negro's political power. Curiously enough, these people who sought to demonstrate power through the nonexercise of it, also point to the Negro "swing vote" in crucial urban areas as the source of the Negro's independent political power. But here they are closer to being right: the urban Negro vote will grow in importance in the coming years. If there is anything positive in the spread of the ghetto, it is the potential political power base thus created, and to realize this potential is one of the most challenging and urgent tasks before the civil-rights movement. If the movement can wrest leadership of the ghetto vote from the machines, it will have acquired an organized constituency such as other major groups in our society now have.

But we must also remember that the effectiveness of a swing vote depends solely on "other" votes. It derives its power from them. In that sense, it can never be "independent," but must opt for one candidate or the other, even if by default. Thus coalitions are inescapable, however tentative they may be. And this is the case in all but those few situations in which Negroes running on an independent ticket might conceivably win. "Independence," in other words, is not a value in itself. The issue is which coalition to join and how to make it responsive to your program. Necessarily there will be compromise. But the difference between expediency and morality in politics is the difference between selling out a principle and making smaller concessions to win larger ones. The leader who shrinks from this task reveals not his purity but his lack of political sense.

The task of molding a political movement out of the March on Washington coalition is not simple, but no alternatives have been advanced. We need to choose our allies on the basis of common political objectives. It has become fashionable in some no-win Negro circles to decry the white liberal as the main enemy (his hypocrisy is what sustains racism); by virtue of this reverse recitation of the reactionary's litany (liberalism leads to socialism, which leads to communism) the Negro is left in majestic isolation, except for a tiny band of fervent white initiates. But the objective fact is that *Eastland and Goldwater* are the main enemies—they and the opponents of civil rights, of the war on poverty, of medicare, of Social Security, of federal aid to education, of unions, and so forth. The labor movement, despite its obvious faults, has been the largest single organized force in this country pushing for progressive social legislation. And where the Negro-labor-liberal axis is weak, as in the farm belt, it was the religious groups that were most influential in rallying support for the Civil Rights Bill.

The durability of the coalition was interestingly tested during the election. I do not believe that the Johnson landslide proved the "white backlash" to be a myth. It proved, rather, that economic interests are more fundamental than prejudice: the backlashers decided that loss of Social Security was, after all, too high a price to pay for a slap at the Negro. This lesson was a valuable first step in re-educating such people, and it must be kept alive, for the civil-rights movement will be advanced only to the degree that social and economic welfare gets to be inextricably entangled with civil rights.

The 1964 elections marked a turning point in American politics. The Democratic landslide was not merely the result of a negative reaction to Goldwaterism; it was also the expression of a majority liberal consensus. The near unanimity with which Negro voters joined in that expression was, I am convinced, a vindication of the July 25th statement by Negro leaders calling for a strategic turn toward political action and a temporary curtailment of mass demonstrations. Despite the controversy surrounding the statement, the instinctive response it met with in the community is suggested by the fact that demonstrations were down 75 per cent as compared with the same period in 1963. But should so high a percentage of Negro voters have gone to Johnson, or should they have held back to narrow his margin of victory and thus give greater visibility to our swing vote? How has our loyalty changed things? Certainly the Negro vote had higher visibility in 1960, when a switch of only 7 percent from the Republican column of 1956 elected President Kennedy. But the slimness of Kennedy's victory—of his "mandate"—dictated a go-slow approach on civil rights, at least until the Birmingham unheaval.

Although Johnson's popular majority was so large that he could have won without such overwhelming Negro support, that support was important from several angles. Beyond adding to Johnson's total national margin, it was specifically responsible for his victories in Virginia, Florida, Tennessee, and Arkansas. Goldwater took only those states where fewer than 45 percent of the eligible Negroes were registered. That Johnson would have won those states had Negro voting rights been enforced is a lesson not likely to be lost on a man who would have been happy with a unanimous electoral college. In any case, the 1.6 million Southern Negroes who voted have had a shattering impact on the Southern political party structure, as illustrated in the changed composition of the Southern Congressional delegation. The "backlash" gave the Republicans five House seats in Alabama, one in Georgia, and one in Mississippi. But on the Democratic side, seven segregationists were defeated while all nine Southerners who voted for the Civil Rights Act were re-elected. It may be premature to predict a Southern Democratic party of Negroes and white moderates and a Republican Party of refugee racists and economic conservatives, but there certainly is a strong tendency toward such a realignment; and an additional 3.6 million Negroes of voting age in the eleven Southern states are still to be heard from. Even the *tendency* toward disintegration of the Democratic party's racist wing defines a new context for Presidential and liberal strategy in the Congressional battles ahead. Thus the Negro vote (North as well as South), while not decisive in the Presidential race, was enormously effective. It was a dramatic element of a historic mandate which contains vast possibilities and dangers that will fundamentally affect the future course of the civil-rights movement.

The liberal Congressional sweep raises hope for an assault on the seniority system, Rule Twenty-two, and other citadels of Dixiecrat-Republican power. The overwhelming of this conservative coalition should also mean progress on much bottlenecked legislation of profound interest to the movement (e.g., bills by Senators Clark and Nelson on planning, manpower, and employment). Moreover, the irrelevance of the South to Johnson's victory gives the President more freedom to act than his predecessor had and more leverage to the movement to pressure for executive action in Mississippi and other racist strongholds.

None of this *guarantees* vigorous executive or legislative action, for the other side of the Johnson landslide is that it has a Gaullist quality. Goldwater's capture of the Republican party forced into the Democratic camp many disparate elements which do not belong there, Big Business being the major example. Johnson, who wants to be President "of all people," may try to keep his new coalition together by sticking close to the political center. But if he decides to do this, it is unlikely that even his political genius will be able to hold together a coalition so inherently unstable and rife with contradictions. It must come apart. Should it do so while Johnson is pursuing a centrist course, then the mandate will have been wastefully dissipated. However, if the mandate is seized upon to set fundamental changes in motion, then the basis can be laid for a new mandate, a new coalition including hitherto inert and dispossessed strata of the population.

Here is where the cutting edge of the civil-rights movement can be applied. We must see to it that the reorganization of the "consensus party" proceeds along lines which will make it an effective vehicle for social reconstruction, a role it cannot play so long as it furnishes Southern racism with its national political power. (One of Barry Goldwater's few attractive ideas was that the Dixiecrats belong with him in the same party.) And nowhere has the civil-rights movement's political cutting edge been more magnificently demonstrated than at Atlantic City, where the Mississippi Freedom Democratic Party not only secured recognition as a bona fide component of the national party, but in the process routed the representatives of the most rabid racists —the white Mississippi and Alabama delegations. While I still believe that the FDP made a tactical error in spurning the compromise, there is no question that they launched a political revolution whose logic is the displacement of Dixiecrat power. They launched that revolution within a major political institution and as part of a coalitional effort.

The role of the civil-rights movement in the reorganization of American political life is programmatic as well as strategic. We are challenged now to broaden our social vision, to develop functional programs with concrete objectives. We need to propose alternatives to technological unemployment, urban decay, and the rest. We need to be calling for public works and training, for national economic planning, for federal aid to education, for attractive public housing—all this on a sufficiently massive scale to make a difference. We need to protest the notion that our integration into American life, so long delayed, must now proceed in an atmosphere of competitive scarcity instead of in the security of abundance which technology makes possible. We cannot claim to have answers to all the complex problems of modern society. That is too much to ask of a movement still battling barbarism in Mississippi. But we can agitate the right questions by probing at the contradictions which still stand in the way of the "Great Society." The questions having been asked, motion must begin in the larger society, for there is a limit to what Negroes can do alone.

Deep-South Crisis

ROY WILKINS

Roy Wilkins is Executive Director of the National Association for the Advancement of Colored People, having been unanimously named by the Board of Directors on April 11, 1955, to succeed Walter White, who died on March 21. He lives in New York City, where the Association has its national headquarters at 20 West 40th Street.

He joined the staff of the NAACP in 1931 as Assistant Executive

Secretary and while filling that position was also editor of *The Crisis,* the monthly magazine that is the official organ of the NAACP. He served in the capacity of editor from 1934 to 1949. Mr. Wilkins was Acting Secretary of the NAACP from June 1, 1949 to May 31, 1950, during Walter White's leave of absence. From 1950 to his election as Executive Secretary, Mr. Wilkins served as Administrator.

He was born in St. Louis, Missouri, but grew up in St. Paul, Minnesota, where he went to public school and was graduated from the University of Minnesota. For eight years he worked on the staff of the *Kansas City Call,* a weekly newspaper in Kansas City, Missouri.

The NAACP has had an interracial membership and corps of directors and officers since its founding in 1909.

The speech included was delivered in Washington, D. C., at the time of the March on Washington. In it, he gives his demand for "Freedom Now" for the Negro.

* * *

First of all, I want to thank all of you for coming here today because you saved me from being a liar. I told them you would be here. They didn't believe me because you always make up your mind at the last minute, and you had me scared. But isn't it a great day? I want some of you to help me win a bet. I want everybody out here in the open to keep quiet and I want to hear a yell and a thunder from all those people out there under the trees. Let's hear you. There is one of them in the tree! I just want to let you know those of you who are sitting down front here that there are a whole lot of people out there under the trees.

My friends, we are here today because we want the Congress of the United States to hear from us in person what many of us have been telling our public officials back home and, that is, *we want freedom now!* We came here to petition our lawmakers to be as brave as our sit-ins and our marchers, to be as daring as James Meredith, to be as unafraid as the nine children of Little Rock, and to be as forthright as the Governor of North Carolina, and to be as dedicated as the Archbishop of St. Louis. We came to speak to our Congress, to those men and women who speak here for us in that marble forum over yonder on the Hill. They know from their vantage point here of the greatness of this whole nation, of its reservoirs of strength and of the sicknesses which threaten always to sap the strength and to erode in one or another selfish and stealthy and specious fashion the precious liberty of the individual which is the hallmark of our country among the nations of the earth.

We have come asking the enactment of legislation that will affirm the rights of life, liberty, and the pursuit of happiness and that will place the resources and the honor of the government of all the people behind the pledge of equality of the Declaration of Independence. We want employment and with it we want the pride and responsibility and self-respect that goes with equal access to jobs—therefore, we want an FEPC bill as a part of the legislative package.

Now for nine years our parents and their children have been met with either a flat refusal or a token action in school desegregation. Every added year of such treatment is a leg iron upon our men and women of 1980. The Civil Rights Bill now under consideration in the Congress must give new powers to the Justice Department to enable it to speed the end of Jim Crow schools, South and North. We are sick of those jokes about public accommodations. We think, for example, that if Mrs. Murphy, rugged individualist as she must be, has taken her chances with the public thus far, she can get along without the solicitous protection of the august Senate of the United States. It is true, of course, that Mrs. Murphy might get a Negro traveler here and there in her boarding house, or in her tourist home, but then we must remember this, she might get a white procurer, or a white embezzler too. So the Congress must require nondiscriminatory accommodations.

Now, my friends, all over this land and especially in parts of the Deep South, we are beaten and kicked and maltreated and shot and killed by local and state law-enforcement officers. It is simply incomprehensible to us here today and to millions of others far from this spot that the U.S. government, which can regulate the contents of a pill, apparently is powerless to prevent the physical abuse of citizens within its own borders. The Attorney General must be empowered to act on his own initiative in the denial of any civil rights, not just one or two, but any civil rights in order to wipe out this shameful situation.

Now the President's proposal represents so moderate an approach that if it is weakened or eliminated the remainder will be little more than sugar water. Indeed, as it stands today, the package needs strengthening and the President should join us in fighting to be sure that we get something more than pap.

And finally, we hear talk of protocol and procedures and rules, including the Senate filibuster rule. Well, we have a thought on that. We declare that rules are made to enable the Congress to legislate and not to keep it from legislating and we are tired of hearing rules cited as a reason why they can't act. Now we expect the passage of an effective civil-rights bill. We commend those Republicans in both

Houses who are working for it. We salute those Democrats in both Houses who are working for it. In fact, we even salute those from the South who want to vote for it but don't dare do so and we say to those people, just give us a little time and one of these days we will emancipate you! It will get to the place where they can come to a civil-rights rally too. If those who support the bill will fight for it as hard and as skillfully as the Southern opposition fights against it, victory will be ours.

Just by your presence here today we have spoken loudly and eloquently to our legislature. When we return home, keep up the speaking by letters and telegrams and telephone and, wherever possible, by personal visit. Remember that this has been a long fight. We were reminded of it by the news of the death yesterday in Africa of Dr. W. E. B. DuBois. Now, regardless of the fact that in his later years Dr. DuBois chose another path, it is incontrovertible that at the dawn of the twentieth century his was the voice that was calling to you to gather here today in this cause. If you want to read something that applies to 1963 go back and get a volume of *The Souls of Black Folk* by DuBois published in 1903.

Well, my friends, you got religion here today. Don't backslide tomorrow. Remember Luke's account of the warning that was given to us all: "No man," he wrote, "having put his hand to the plow and looking back is fit for the Kingdom of God."

Thank you.

Revolution of Participation

WHITNEY M. YOUNG, JR.

Whitney M. Young, Jr., became executive director of the National Urban League on October 1, 1961. At the time of his appointment he was dean of the Atlanta University School of Social Work, a post he had held since 1954.

He joined the Urban League in 1948 as industrial-relations secretary of the St. Paul affiliate, and rose rapidly. In 1950 he was named executive director of the Omaha Urban League, a post he held until he went to Atlanta.

Mr. Young was born on July 31, 1921, in Lincoln Ridge, Kentucky,

the son of the president of Lincoln Institute. During the Second World
War he rose from the ranks to sergeant and saw service in the European theater.

He completed his undergraduate work at Kentucky State College in
1941 and did his graduate work at MIT and the University of Minnesota in 1947.

During his tenure at the St. Paul Urban League, he taught at St.
Catherine's College. While in Omaha, he taught at the School of
Social Work of the University of Nebraska and Creighton University,
which conferred an Honorary Doctor of Laws degree on him on
June 1, 1964.

During the academic year 1960–1961, he was a visiting scholar at
Harvard University. He has also received honorary doctorates (L.L.D.)
from North Carolina A & T College, Tuskegee Institute, and George
Williams College in Chicago.

Since becoming the executive director of the National Urban League,
he has worked to expand the interracial social-work agency, which
seeks to aid Negro and other disadvantaged citizens obtain equal
opportunities in all phases of urban life.

Mr. Young is one of the leaders in the struggle of Negro citizens
for equal rights. He helped plan the March on Washington, August
28, 1963, and is one of the members of the Council for United Civil
Rights Leadership.

He is one of the leading architects of the current War on Poverty,
and conferred frequently on this and related subjects with the late
President John F. Kennedy and with President Lyndon B. Johnson.

He serves on a number of Presidential committees including Youth
Employment; Equal Opportunity in the Armed Forces; the National
Commission on Technology, Automation, and Economic Progress; and
the National Advisory Council on Economic Opportunity.

He is vice-president of the National Association of Social Workers;
a member of the Board of Trustees of the Eleanor Roosevelt Me-
morial Foundation and the John F. Kennedy Memorial Library; the
Advisory Council of the New York School of Social Work, Columbia
University; the National Committee on Youth Employment; and the
Unitarian Universalist Service Committee.

His articles have appeared in a wide number of professional journals
and national magazines and he is the author of *To Be Equal* (1964).
His weekly column, "To Be Equal," appears in forty-three newspapers
across the nation.

The address, "Revolution of Participation," was delivered at the

National Conference of the Urban League in Louisville, Kentucky,
August 2, 1964.

* * *

I am delighted to welcome you to this National Conference of the
Urban League—the largest in our history. In fact, the more than five
hundred advance registrations so startled our Conference Committee
that they made a hasty survey of all the entertainment scheduled for
Louisville to see if *you* knew something they didn't! They found the
explanation for your turning out in unprecedented numbers: the new
intensity of interest, the new degree of dedication, the new determination to participate in the central events of our time. These, I am sure,
are the real reasons for our being here—and in such great number.

Tonight I want to talk with you about the Urban League in relation to three specific things: One, the theme of our Conference:
Poverty Re-Examined: Old Problems—New Challenges; two, the 1964
Civil Rights Law; and three, the direct action to meet the challenge
of both.

Three years ago, when I first had the honor to address you as
executive director, I spoke of the challenge we would face and the
program emphases the League required to meet these challenges. I
referred to that talk as "The Threshold of Tomorrow."

In 1962, as the tempo of the civil-rights crusade increased, the conference keynote dealt with the swiftly changing nature of race relations in the nation—what we termed "The Revolution of Expectation."
At that time I reviewed the continued migration and urbanization of
the Negro, the impact of industrialization and automation, the dis-
ruption and dislocation caused by urban renewal, slum clearance, and
highway construction. We noted that Negro expectations would increase as challenges to overt discrimination continued, and that impatience and disillusionment with ineffective methods, leaders, and
institutions would accelerate. And we made a self-analysis of our
program, our goals, and our methods.

Last year, plumbing the changing mood of the American people,
our emphasis was on "The Revolution of Witnessing." In this we
viewed the increasing willingness of Americans of every imaginable
background to stand up and be counted for freedom. The March on
Washington a month later was a magnificent demonstration of this and
proved to the nation and the world that the demands of the Negro
were no longer parochial and self-seeking. They were—and are—
obviously the will of the American people. In that setting the League

was challenged, we said, to look beyond—to see that when yesterday's barriers finally crumble new barriers of apathy, undeveloped skills and lack of training do not replace them.

It was with this new tide of civil-rights concern that the Urban League exercised its leadership just over a year ago in issuing its mobilization call for direct action in the form of a domestic Marshall Plan—a massive effort, we said—to make it truly possible for Negro citizens to take advantage of the opportunity to be equal. We spelled out the kinds of special effort needed to close the "discrimination gap" and we presented unimpeachable evidence that 300 years of deprivation and denial have inflicted both visible and invisible handicaps—handicaps that make a travesty of equality of opportunity.

No runner, we noted, can enter a race barefoot when it is half over and hope to finish among the well-shod, well-trained winners. Our Negro citizens, we said, after surviving precariously on the barest minimums in health, education, welfare, housing, job and cultural opportunities, cannot compete equally for nor share in the full rewards and responsibilities of our society simply by an announcement, with impressive flourishes, that *now* a state of equal opportunity exists.

This is why I would like for you to consider with me this year another revolution—a *revolution of participation*, participation *by* and *with* America's Negro citizens that will transform equal opportunity from a challenging slogan into a meaningful reality.

Our theme—Poverty Re-examined—takes on extraordinary significance this year. For never before has the nation been so aroused to this problem; never before have so many men of good will joined together in common cause to do something about poverty in America; and never before has a major nation committed such significant resources to a sustained attack on poverty.

As the agency which has historically dealt with the living needs of Negro Americans for more than a half century, the Urban League has long been aware of what the rest of the nation is only now beginning to focus on: that one of every four poverty-stricken families are Negro families; that nearly one of every two Negro families has an income of less than $3,000 a year; and that three out of every five of these eke out an existence on $1,500 or less per year.

The National Urban League is proud of the part it has played in suggesting—in helping to frame—and in supporting the antipoverty legislation now pending before the Congress. At best it is a bare beginning, but even so it represents an important symbol of this country's awakened concern. In the face of overwhelming evidence to the contrary there are those who would contend that existing programs slightly expanded would meet the needs of the poor. To them I would say that even assuming this misrepresentation to be true, let this country for once err, if it must, on the side of trying to do too much, and on time—rather than too little too late.

In the final analysis, all of the proposed antipoverty measures together will scarcely make a dent in the problem, and the fact that the proposed allocation of $250 million out of a total federal expenditure of $123 billion is only about two-tenths of 1 percent hardly reflects this country's professed humanitarianism. We *can* afford more for the sake of those who cannot afford to wait longer. We *must* do more.

At this conference our examination of poverty and the Urban League direct-action program will take place in a new arena, an arena which passage of the new Civil Rights Act is even now shaping. Will it be an arena in which the affluence or the apathy of America is applied? What will be the dimensions and perimeters of this new law? How deeply will it affect the lives and the fortunes of all Americans?

These are questions with which we, as concerned citizens, must deal. That America stands today at the crossroads in the midst of her greatest crisis in race relations since 1864 is no longer a cliché. We find ourselves confronted with two of the most volatile emotions known to human beings—anger and fear. Anger—born out of frustration—which gave rise to stepped-up boycotts, sit-ins, lie-ins, and other actions which reflected the Negro's desperate plight and his doubts that the dreams expressed at that magnificent March on Washington would ever be revealed.

We find, also, a counterforce, ofttimes in the guise of patriotism—a superanger that became hate, such as was evidenced in the assassination of a beloved President, one who had championed the cause of Negro citizens; a superanger that displayed itself in the firing of bullets into the homes of Negroes in Jacksonville, in the burning of churches and the killing of youngsters in Alabama, in the brutal beatings and mysterious disappearance of three young freedom fighters in Mississippi. That two of these were white and one Negro should alert every American to the fact that the enemies of freedom make no distinction when protected by a state government which predicts, if not encourages, such actions.

Fear—unprecedented fear and anxiety in their rawest form—are evident in what has come to be called the "white backlash." What this so-called backlash says in effect is that the Negro citizen who has been condemned and stereotyped for years as being "lazy," "indifferent," and "apathetic" must now be condemned for being "aggressive," "pushy," and "ambitious." He is being told that the price of securing the good will and support of whites is passive acceptance of injustice and second-class citizenship. The Negro citizen is being told to forget the glorious part of other Americans' struggles for political and economic rights. He is being told to forget the women's suffrage movement, to forget the rise of labor unions, to forget the American Revolution itself. It is ironic that many of the "backlashers" have conveniently forgotten their past. For, without exception, they or their ancestors too fled from oppression abroad, seeking freedom and equality of opportunity here.

These exaggerated fears have become so widespread that there are those who feel that they can run for public office and win national majorities through exploitation of the insecure and encouragement of the racists. The voters of this country will make a mistake from which the nation may never recover if out of fear and misunderstanding of the race problem they permit the election of those who would encourage extremists and racists—those who ignore the problems of poverty, ill-health, and inadequate education, and those who see bigness an evil—whether it be big government, big labor, or big business—but who are indifferent to big social problems.

The world watches today with amazement—and even fright—to see whether America has truly come of age, and whether it is capable of the moral world leadership which hopefully would parallel its economic development. Urban League leadership has been left with no other choice but to continue to set before the country its position on the issues. The Urban League believes in the need for a poverty program—for Medicare for the aged—federal support to equalize educational opportunities—and expanded federal support of housing. This realistic concern for the hopeless and the helpless is our heritage and our reason for being. Let, therefore, those who will seek public office, from the highest to the lowest, Democrat or Republican, make their decision whether to seek our support by endorsing these humane measures or reject our support by callously opposing or ignoring them.

The Urban League is more concerned with states' *responsibilities* than with states' *rights*. The Urban League is more concerned with building strong, independent, intelligent citizens than with building bigger and better bombs. The Urban League believes that extremism, whether in the form of black nationalism or white Ku Kluxism, is not a virtue but a vice. The Urban League believes that moderation as exemplified by positive, responsible action on the part of enlightened businessmen, labor leaders, government officials, and all decent Americans is a virtue.

To meet these forces the Urban League challenges all Americans to participate as never before, not only in bringing to fruition the American dream for all our citizens, but also in the forthright repudiation of those who would divide our country and deliberately exploit the fears and insecurities of any of our citizens.

The theme of our conference is also very much related to the recent riots in several of our urban areas. We deplore violence, looting, vandalism, and criminal action of any type, and strongly urge the cooperation of all local leaders with intelligent police enforcement officials toward the eradication of such activity.

But peace is more than an absence of conflict. It is the presence of justice. Obsession with law and order, while ignoring poverty and suffering, is unrealistic. Responsible Negro leadership needs responsive white leadership. America cannot afford a police state.

Today we stand on the threshold of what I would call the Great Beyond. We are stepping into an age that generations of Negroes viewed as the millennium—that great time beyond equality of opportunity—a Great Beyond in which the rules work *for*, instead of against; a Great Beyond in which the power and aid of private free enterprise and of the federal establishment are committed to ensure equality of opportunity. But, beyond equality of opportunity, life will be great only if laws are implemented; if citizen participation is extensive and intensive to prepare Negroes for opportunities and responsibilities.

Discrimination and segregation, because of the Civil Rights Act, no longer have the sanction or the respectability of law anywhere in the United States. Thus, in its intent, this law is a landmark visible not only nationally, but as a beacon to the oppressed and non-whites of the world. It is a delayed articulation of the fact that the Negro is a true citizen of this nation. The Act removes the stigma of inferiority, restores dignity and heightens morale. It creates a launching pad that can help rocket Negroes into full participation in this society. This Civil Rights Act is the end of an era of fighting for recognition of a man's rights; it is the beginning of an era of fighting for a man's place in the sun.

The issue for all of us, North and South, is no longer whether there shall be or shall not be civil rights for the Negro. This has at long last been decided. And this time it has been decided not by the Supreme Court, with which so many are inclined to disagree, but by the elected representatives of all the people, after deliberate and due process. The issue now, as many of its sons have said recently, is that the South can not keep the Negro a third-class citizen without keeping whites second-class citizens. The South must move on industrially and compete. As Senator Hubert Humphrey has said, the South must get out of the shadow of states' rights and walk in the bright sunlight of human rights.

Yet there are realities of history and impersonal forces of the present and immediate future that can render completely meaningless this significant legislation. We look over the threshold of this Great Beyond and, with our conference theme in mind, we wonder.

Can the future be great if half of the school dropouts in one city, for example, are juvenile delinquents and if, nationally about half of all dropouts are Negro youngsters?

Can the future be great if those who earn less than $2,000 per year are ill twice as many days annually as those who earn $4,000; and if one out of four Negro Americans earn less than $2,000?

Can the future be great if one out of five American families are poverty-stricken and nearly half of all Negro families are below the poverty line?

Can the future be great if less than 2 percent of the nation's apprentices are Negroes?

Can the future be great if the unemployed American with less than a high school education is doomed to dependency and only one out of four Negroes has a high school diploma; and for those who *do* graduate the unemployment rate is twice that of white high school graduates? Can it be great if the Negro high school graduate earns only as much as whites who complete the eighth grade?

It is to give direction and to participate in removing these handicaps that the League is so uniquely qualified and so deeply committed. In moving forward to stamp out poverty, the League machinery can be used effectively in cooperation with government and private voluntary programs. Our interracial boards, committees, and staffs can and must be more aggressive in tackling these central problems.

The new law calls for a Revolution of Participation; it places equal opportunity almost within grasp. Now the law moves from legislative chambers to our homes, our neighborhoods, our communities, cities, and states. The real challenge to individual citizens is just beginning. The danger here is that many will believe that with passage of the law the job is done. We know differently. We know that it can succeed only through a Revolution of Participation.

A century ago many thought the Emancipation Proclamation was the beginning of the millennium. Well, it has been and still is a long, hard road from there to equality. Similarly, the Civil Rights Act does not magically create a millennium; we—white and Negro— by our determined, enthusiastic participation must *bring about* the millennium.

How does one participate in the translation of legal rights to actual experiences as a first-class citizen? None are better qualified than Urban Leaguers for such translation. For decades the Urban League approach was one of the few avenues by which advances were made, by which victories were achieved over prevailing discrimination. Through unstinting effort the League succeeded in bringing about a change in the moral climate which made possible the recent advances on the civil-rights front. In recent months the situation has called for people skilled in community services, law, in legislation, people with the courage and opportunity to demonstrate in the streets and to go to jail. Now we are at a point where those skills must be supplemented by another kind of participation.

The Negro citizen and the Urban League are challenged today as never before—to help citizens help themselves in the use of the tools and resources of existing institutions—to take direct action and to participate fully in the life of their communities. As I said at the March on Washington a year ago, it is not enough to march on picket lines; our citizens must also march beyond protest to *participate*. We must march to PTA meetings, to libraries, to voting booths. We must march to party caucuses, to adult education classes, to vocational and apprentice training courses. We must march to decision-making meetings on town zoning, urban renewal, health, welfare, and education. These are the sensitive points in which our participation will determine how our children and grandchildren will live.

Specifically, therefore, I am calling upon local Urban Leagues to mobilize and organize the Negro community into effective, disciplined social action, bring about change in conditions through intelligent use of existing social, economic, and political institutions, nationally and locally.

Today the American Negro knows, just as labor learned, that he needs skilled, knowledgeable spokesmen not only for protest and mediation, but for implementation—to put meaning into civil-rights victories. The Negro citizen knows that he needs spokesmen such as Urban Leaguers who know his living needs to help him get vocational education, secure retraining, and enter apprenticeship programs. Otherwise, he cannot get the skills to get the jobs to pay his way in the restaurants, movies, beaches, and theaters. He cannot buy the decent housing that he needs, nor the wholesome food and clothing that his family needs.

The challenge of positive change must also be met by our public institutions at all government levels; by our voluntary institutions—the private schools, hospitals, health, welfare, community-service agencies—as well as our business, labor, and philanthropic institutions. Surely the challenge to participate need not be spelled out in detail for each and every institution. The ingenuity which for so long has segregated with such sophistication can surely integrate with inventiveness.

In implementing the new law the federal government must set an example for the rest of the nation's institutions. We will expect leadership which will place properly qualified Negro citizens in strategic spots where their abilities and experiences can be brought to bear. One major test of our government's sincerity will be willingness to staff Negroes at key spots at decision-making levels. And a crucial indication of the government's true intentions will be its willingness to allocate financial resources for implementation of the antipoverty campaign to already well-established Negro organizations or new agencies which are directed by Negro specialists.

Already specific, pace-setting government-sponsored projects are being administered by local Urban Leagues in Washington, in New York City, and in Milwaukee. In each of these cities new ground has been broken:

In Milwaukee, $103,000 of taxpayers' money has been allocated to help low-income families find, build, maintain, and improve homes. In Washington, the League's "Future for Jimmy" program reaches 36,000 troubled youngsters and their parents, in a coordinated tutoring, counseling effort. In New York City, the League, with $120,000 in federal funds and with the cooperation of Yeshiva University, is helping Southern-educated school teachers qualify for the New York teaching license. Another League project in New York includes federal government and private industry in an on-the-job training program. When the men are trained, after six months, the IBM Corporation expects to employ them in its operations.

From its beginning the Urban League has been a direct-action agency. Its techniques have not purposely sought headlines in the press. Its successes speak for themselves:

Direct Action has found jobs—and increasingly better jobs—for hundreds of thousands of American citizens—and a job translates directly into meat on the table.

Direct Action put thousands of Negro families into clean, ratfree living quarters for the first time, through League successes in fighting for public housing, through helping thousands become home owners, and through victories in breaking through the white nooses around the ghettos when Negroes have been aided to move into suburbia.

Direct Action has changed the lives of literally millions of Negro youngsters—through more than thirty years of back-to-school campaigns, by motivating high school and college youths with our annual Vocational Opportunity Campaigns and the TST programs. Furthermore, we pioneered career conferences in which corporation executives met and talked with Negro college students on the campuses, thereby encouraging career effort and leading to corporate recruitment.

Direct Action has caused welfare departments to change their policies on training and retraining of educationally disadvantaged Negroes.

Direct Action broke through in industry after industry with the Pilot Placement Project. Thousands of qualified Negroes smashed the doors of discrimination in upper-echelon jobs and lifted the horizons of hundreds of thousands of Negro youngsters by their success.

Direct Action established the first nationwide placement bureau last year. In its first six months the Urban League's National Skills Bank placed more than 1,700 skilled and professional Negroes in top jobs.

Direct Action has developed church-centered tutoring projects.

Direct Action by working with business, labor, voluntary agency and government officials ceaselessly over the years has given them indispensable understanding of the needs and problems of American Negroes.

This is only a sampling. I cite these because the League is ofttimes excluded in discussions of direct-action agencies, for people tend to think of boycotts, demonstrations, sit-ins, and picketing first. Often people are confused by the smoke of headlines, overlooking the steady, burning flame of continuing action which also accomplishes positive results.

But we would caution Negro citizens and the mass media as well of the dangers of labeling a Negro leader anyone who is vocal and loud or who may be a significant personality in some other field. Leadership must have a followership. Leaders must establish organizations or constituents. Leaders are not self-appointed or pressdesignated. It is not a question of whether a leadership is accommodating, moderate, or militant. The leadership which *counts* is the leadership which get results.

We are gratified that in the past two years there has been increasing support and recognition of the Urban League within the Negro community. This reflects a kind of maturity which understands the necessity of a diversified approach to the problems of civil rights in America. The Negro community understands that today it has no monolithic structure by which one spokesman can represent it adequately in all things. It recognizes that we have developed specialists qualified to represent us *all* more effectively in specific areas of concern.

The Urban League has the know-how, the machinery, the proven effectiveness to lead and participate in this drive. Our experienced professional staff, our volunteers—board and committee members—in sixty-six strategic American cities, know intimately the structures and means, priorities and problems of the metropolitan centers where 77 percent of America's population lives. This Urban League mastery is available to the Negro and to the nation's institutions—to government at all levels, to business, labor, philanthropy, welfare, and education.

To meet the new responsibilities of the Great Beyond, of the Civil Rights Law and the antipoverty program, the Urban League must and will expand. I foresee a network of 100 local Leagues in the next five years—the need for ten times that number is as clear as the daily newspaper headlines. I foresee local League budgets tripled by contributions and support from United Funds and Community Chests, from other institutions—public and private—which recognize our unique capabilities. In our sessions at this conference we will consider expansion plans, programs of action, means of greater community involvement.

As the Civil Rights Act unfurls it is the responsibility of every Urban Leaguer to seek out ways and means of increased participation. Each of us must go back to our homes inspired, determined, and committed to carry our programs to the total community. We must deliberately reach out and bring into our orbit not only the safe and sympathetic, but we must spark the indifferent and apathetic and convert the bigoted and antagonistic. Here I urge League board and staff members to meet these responsibilities with missionary enthusiasm and special effort.

The National Office of the Urban League has already reassessed its obligations and its leadership role. As a result, it has retooled its operations to meet the increased tempo and intensity of current demands. We have done so by reorganizing and enlarging our regional structure, in order to decentralize responsibility, speed up services, and provide greater flexibility and aid in backstopping local

League operations. Furthermore, we have vastly increased our national staff counseling and service functions to local Leagues.

We face the era of the Great Beyond with confidence stemming from accomplishment: the overall Urban League budget in 1964, for example, will be more than $4 million, an increase of more than 33 percent in just three short years.

Clearly, on this threshold of the Great Beyond we are poised not with smugness, not with a renewed self-congratulation or pious proclamations, but with a renewed commitment to participate and to promote participation.

We must help citizens, Negro and white, understand that it is in their own self-interest that the transition from technical and legal release from oppression to full citizenship for Negroes be a quick, cooperative one. The white citizen is challenged to participate and help this change. He must not suddenly get amnesia about 300 years of deprivation. And he must not seek to evade his responsibility by calling for the impossible—like the businessman who stopped me last week and said, "Send me five Negro engineers who have five years experience each; I'm ready to hire them." We may properly term this kind of employment order a request for "instant Negroes." This man can't get engineers of any color with such experience unless he raids his competitors. This spurious or unrealistic bid for Negro professional workers does not relieve the employer from responsibility. He has *not* done his part by sending in an employment order impossible to fill. He is challenged, though, to seek ways of upgrading his present Negro employees of pioneering new on-the-job training methods for qualified Negroes, and so on.

Negroes are challenged to participate in community service programs of every kind—to tutor and help their fellow men, to join in Big Brother and Sister, Boys and Girls Clubs, YMCA and YWCA and similar activities, and programs such as the Urban League's Friends and Neighbors project, in which an established family "adopts" a newcomer family and helps it cope with the hurdles of city life. We are at a point in time where we cannot afford the luxury of the frivolous diversions found among our white brethren. In closing the discrimination gap we need skills more than luck— counseling more than gossip—books more than bop—tutoring more than TV—and participation more than criticism.

The League is challenged to participate at all levels in efforts to make the new law bear fruit. We will exercise vigilance and press for fulfillment of the law's provisions.

We must act now—positively and forcefully. We must begin our

Revolution of Participation immediately. In our sessions at this conference let us move with resolution toward a new democracy. Having taken the soundings in our home communities, here set the course for the campaign against poverty, the participation which will take America triumphantly into a new era.

And in the war against poverty and the implementation of the Civil Rights Law we of the Urban League shall participate to the fullest. Let us go from this hall to the business of the conference with determination to make this the meeting of which the future will say, "That was the point at which the Urban League really took off in unprecedented service and effectiveness." For we have come of age; we *are* skilled, we *are* strong, we *are* influential. From this moment, let *all* Urban Leaguers join in dedicating themselves to that participation which will harness our maturity, our power, and our influence to move America into that Great Beyond of true opportunity for all.

In this hour of trial, we have no time to lose. We must act now, positively and forcefully.

If we are successful, *we* will not benefit alone—America will benefit, and I mean *all* the people of America.

If we are successful, we will take idle youth off the streets, and give them a new chance and a new hope—and we will make our streets safer, too, and not merely by adding more policemen.

If we are successful, we will improve our schools and see to it that every American child receives a first-class quality education.

If we are successful, we will train more professional and skilled workers, obtain better jobs, expand our national purchasing power, and create new employment.

If we are successful, not a single worker will be displaced—but millions of new jobs will be added.

If we are successful, property values will continue to rise, neighborhoods will become better, and our cities will become greater, finer, safer places in which to work and raise our children.

Our current revolution does not seek to detract, but to add; not to destroy, but to create; not to sanction disorder, but to increase respect for law.

It is not a protest to weaken America but to strengthen it; not to divide America but to unify it; not to decry America but to purify it; not to separate America but to become a part of it.

This is our land. Here we have risen from slavery to freedom and here we will rise from poverty to prosperity.

This is our land.

Here we shall overcome.